Linear Programming

MTE-12

For

B.Sc., B.Com., B.A., and BSW

Useful For

IGNOU, KSOU (Karnataka), Bihar University (Muzaffarpur), Nalanda University, Jamia Millia Islamia, Vardhman Mahaveer Open University (Kota), Uttarakhand Open University, Kurukshetra University, Seva Sadan's College of Education (Maharashtra), Lalit Narayan Mithila University, Andhra University, Pt. Sunderlal Sharma (Open) University (Bilaspur), Annamalai University, Bangalore University, Bharathiar University, Bharathidasan University, HP University, Centre for distance and open learning, Kakatiya University (Andhra Pradesh), KOU (Rajasthan), MPBOU (MP), MDU (Haryana), Punjab University, Tamilnadu Open University, Sri Padmavati Mahila Visvavidyalayam (Andhra Pradesh), Sri Venkateswara University (Andhra Pradesh), UCSDE (Kerala), University of Jammu, YCMOU, Rajasthan University, UPRTOU, Kalyani University, Banaras Hindu University (BHU) and all other Indian Universities.

Closer to Nature  We use Recycled Paper

GULLYBABA PUBLISHING HOUSE PVT. LTD.

ISO 9001 & ISO 14001 CERTIFIED CO.

Published by:

GullyBaba Publishing House Pvt. Ltd.

Regd. Office:
2525/193, 1st Floor, Onkar Nagar-A,
Tri Nagar, Delhi-110035
(From Kanhaiya Nagar Metro Station Towards Old Bus Stand)
Call: 9991112299, 9312235086
WhatsApp: 9350849407

Branch Office:
1A/2A, 20, Hari Sadan,
Ansari Road, Daryaganj,
New Delhi-110002
Ph.011-45794768
Call & WhatsApp:
8130521616,8130511234

E-mail: hello@gullybaba.com, **Website**:GullyBaba.com

New Edition

ISBN: 978-93-85533-70-9

Author: Gullybaba.com Panel

Preface

The technique of linear programming was formulated by a Russian mathematician L.V. Kantorovich. But the present version of simplex method was developed by Geoge B. Dentzig in 1947. Linear programming (LP) is an important technique of operations research developed for optimum utilization of resources. Linear Programming is a system of procedures for the optimization of linear functions subject to certain given linear constraints which consist of linear equalities or inequalities.

Linear programming is used daily in the real world to optimize the allocation of resources or activities to generate the most benefit or profit. Linear programming can take multiple factors into account into the thousands and is used extensively by business managers, economists and public planners.

In this GPH book ***"Linear Programming (MTE-12)"*** we are going to learn the techniques used by the mathematicians in solving problem of real life. In the book, we will study simplex method and duality, games theory etc.

In the book, various practical problems have been solved in every chapter which will give confidence to the students to solve the questions themselves. We have tried to solve all possible questions from the exams' point of view. Solutions of previous years' question papers have also been included to help students to understand the unique examination structure.

We hope that this book would not only be a favourite study material for the students but also can be a nice resource for teaching.

An attempt has been carefully made to present this book more useful and meet the requirement and challenges of the course prescribed by Indian Universities.

We wish you a successful and rewarding career ahead. Feedback in this regard is solicited.

– GPH Panel of Experts

Acknowledgement

Our compliments go to the **GullyBaba Publishing House (P) Ltd.,** and its meticulous team who have been enthusiastically working towards the perfection of the book.

Their teamwork, initiative and research have been very encouraging. Had it not been for their unflagging support, this work wouldn't have been possible. The creative freedom provided by them along with their aim of presenting the best to the reader has been a major source of inspiration in this work. Hope that this book would be successful.

– GPH Panel of Experts

Publisher's Note

The present book MTE-12 is targeted for examination purpose as well as enrichment. With the advent of technology and the Internet, there has been no dearth of information available to all; however, finding the relevant and qualitative information, which is focused, is an uphill task.

We at **GullyBaba Publishing House (P) Ltd.,** have taken this step to provide quality material which can accentuate in-depth knowledge about the subject. GPH books are a pioneer in the effort of providing unique and quality material to its readers. With our books, you are sure to attain success by making use of this powerful study material. Provided book is just a reference book based on the syllabus of particular University/Board. For a profound information, see the textbooks recommended by the University/Board.

Our site **gullybaba.com** is a vital resource for your examination. The publisher wishes to acknowledge the significant contribution of the Team Members and our experts in bringing out this publication and highly thankful to Almighty God, without His blessings, this endeavor wouldn't have been successful.

– Publisher

Topics Covered

Content

Question Papers

1 Basic Algebra

An Overview

Matrices, determinants, vectors, etc. are included in basic algebra. A matrix is a rectangular array of numbers or other mathematical objects for which operations such as addition and multiplication are defined. Most commonly, a matrix over a field F is a rectangular array of scalars each of which is a member of F.

Determinants occur throughout mathematics. For example, a matrix is often used to represent the coefficients in a system of linear equations, and the determinant can be used to solve those equations, although more efficient techniques are actually used, some of which are determinant-revealing and consist of computationally effective ways of computing the determinant itself.

1.1 MATRICES

Definition of Matrix

A matrix is a rectangular array of numbers. In other words, a set of mn numbers arranged in the form of rectangular array of m rows and n column is called m × n matrix (to be read as 'm' by 'n' matrix). The general form of a matrix of order m × n is usually written as

$$A = \begin{bmatrix} a_{11} & a_{12} & a_{13} \cdots & a_{1j} \cdots & a_{1n} \\ a_{21} & a_{22} & a_{23} \cdots & a_{2j} \cdots & a_{2n} \\ \vdots & \vdots & \vdots & \vdots & \vdots \\ a_{i1} & a_{i2} & a_{i3} \cdots & a_{ij} \cdots & a_{in} \\ \vdots & \vdots & \vdots & \vdots & \vdots \\ a_{m1} & a_{m2} & a_{m3} \cdots & a_{mj} \cdots & a_{mn} \end{bmatrix}_{m \times n}$$

The numbers $a_{11}, a_{12}, a_{13}, \ldots\ldots\ldots\ldots, a_{ij}$, etc. are called the elements of the matrix. m is the number of rows and n is the number of columns.

Notations of Matrices

Matrices are denoted by capital letters A, B, C or X, Y, Z, etc. and its elements by small letters a, b, c,... . The elements of the matrix are enclosed by any of the brackets, i.e. [ ], ( ), { }. The position of the elements of matrix is indicated by the subscripts attached to the element. For example, a_{12} indicates that the element lies in the first row and second column, i.e. first subscript denotes row and second denotes column.

Order of A Matrix

The number of rows and columns of a matrix determines the order of the matrix. Thus, a matrix, having m rows and n column is said to be of the order m × n (read as 'm' by 'n'). In particular, a matrix having 3 rows and 4 columns is of the order 3 × 4 and it is called a 3 × 4 matrix.

For example, $A = \begin{pmatrix} 3 & 5 & 6 \\ 2 & 4 & 8 \end{pmatrix}_{2 \times 3}$ is a matrix of order 2 × 3 since there are two rows and three columns.

Types of Matrices

(1) Rectangular Matrix: A matrix in which the number of rows and columns are not equal is called a square matrix. For example,

$A = \begin{bmatrix} 2 & 5 & 1 \\ 3 & 4 & 1 \end{bmatrix}$ is a rectangular matrix of order 2 × 3.

(2) Square Matrix: A matrix in which the number of rows is equal to the number of columns is called a square matrix. For example,

$$A = \begin{pmatrix} 2 & 1 & 5 \\ 3 & 2 & 4 \\ 3 & 3 & 6 \end{pmatrix}$$ is a square matrix of order 3 × 3, i.e., of order 3.

Note: the elements 2, 2, 6 in this matrix are called **diagonal elements** and the line along which they lie is called the **principal diagonal**.

(3) Diagonal Matrix: A square matrix whose all elements except those on the principal diagonal are zero is called a diagonal matrix. For example,

$$A = \begin{bmatrix} 1 & 0 & 0 \\ 0 & 3 & 0 \\ 0 & 0 & 5 \end{bmatrix}$$ is a diagonal matrix of order 3 × 3.

(4) Scalar Matrix: A square matrix whose all elements except those on the principal diagonal are zero and all principal diagonal elements are equal, is called a scalar matrix. For example,

$$A = \begin{pmatrix} 2 & 0 & 0 \\ 0 & 2 & 0 \\ 0 & 0 & 2 \end{pmatrix}$$ is a scalar matrix of order 3 × 3.

(5) Identity (or Unit) Matrix: A square matrix whose principal diagonal elements are all unity and the other elements are all zero is called an identity (or unit) matrix. An identity matrix of order 3 is denoted by I_3. For example,

$$I_3 = \begin{pmatrix} 1 & 0 & 0 \\ 0 & 1 & 0 \\ 0 & 0 & 1 \end{pmatrix}$$ is an identity matrix of order 3.

(6) Null or Zero Matrix: A matrix of any order (rectangular or square) whose all elements are zero is called a null matrix (or a zero matrix) and is denoted by O. For example,

$$O = \begin{pmatrix} 0 & 0 \\ 0 & 0 \end{pmatrix} \text{ and } O = \begin{pmatrix} 0 & 0 & 0 \\ 0 & 0 & 0 \end{pmatrix}$$ are null matrices of order 2 × 2 and 2 × 3 respectively.

(7) Row Matrix: A matrix having only one row and any number of columns is called a row matrix (or a row vector). For example,

A = [1, 2, 3] is a row matrix or order 1 × 3.

(8) Column Matrix: A matrix having only one column and any number of rows is called a column matrix (or a column vector). For example,

$$A = \begin{pmatrix} 1 \\ 2 \\ 3 \end{pmatrix}$$ is a column matrix of order 3 × 1.

(9) Upper Triangular and Lower triangular Matrix: A square matrix is called an upper triangular matrix if all the elements below the principal diagonal are zero and it is said to be lower triangular matrix if all the elements above the principal diagonal are zero. For example,

$$A = \begin{pmatrix} 2 & 3 & 3 \\ 0 & 5 & 4 \\ 0 & 0 & 8 \end{pmatrix}$$ is an upper triangular matrix and

$$A = \begin{pmatrix} 2 & 0 & 0 \\ 4 & 5 & 0 \\ 3 & 3 & 8 \end{pmatrix}$$ is an lower triangular matrix.

(10) Sub Matrix: A matrix obtained by deleting some rows or column or both of a given matrix is called its sub matrix. For example,

$$\begin{pmatrix} 4 & 5 \\ 5 & 2 \end{pmatrix}_{2\times 2} \text{ is a sub matrix of } A = \begin{pmatrix} 4 & 5 & 6 \\ 3 & 3 & 6 \\ 5 & 2 & 1 \end{pmatrix}_{3\times 3}$$

The sub matrix of the order 2×2 is obtained by deleting 2nd row and 3rd column of matrix A.

(11) Trace of a Matrix: The sum of all the elements on the principal diagonal of a square matrix is called the trace of the matrix. It is denoted by tr. A. For example,

$$\text{If } A = \begin{pmatrix} 2 & 3 & 1 \\ 4 & 1 & 2 \\ 5 & 2 & 3 \end{pmatrix}_{3\times 3}, \text{ then}$$

trace of A = tr. A = sum of its diagonal elements = 2 + 1 + 3 = 6

(12) Equality of Two Matrices: Two matrices A and B are said to be equal if and only if they are of the same order and each element of A is equal to the corresponding element of B. For example,

$$\text{If } A = \begin{pmatrix} 3 & 4 \\ 0 & -1 \end{pmatrix} \text{ and } B = \begin{pmatrix} 3 & 4 \\ 0 & -1 \end{pmatrix}, \text{ then } A = B$$

since the matrix A is of the order 2×2 and the matrix B is of the order 2×2 and also the corresponding elements of A and B are equal.

Operations on Matrices (Or Matrix Operations)

(1) Addition (or Subtractions) of Matrices

The addition (or subtraction) of two or more matrices is possible only if these matrices have the same dimension, i.e., the matrices must have the same number of rows and same number of columns. For example,

If $A = \begin{bmatrix} 1 & 3 & 4 \\ -2 & 4 & 8 \\ 3 & -2 & -1 \end{bmatrix}$ and $B = \begin{bmatrix} 4 & 1 & 0 \\ 1 & 3 & 5 \\ 0 & 1 & 6 \end{bmatrix}$

Then, we have

$$A + B = \begin{bmatrix} 1 & 3 & 4 \\ -2 & 4 & 8 \\ 3 & -2 & -1 \end{bmatrix} + \begin{bmatrix} 4 & 1 & 0 \\ 1 & 3 & 5 \\ 0 & 1 & 6 \end{bmatrix}$$

$$= \begin{bmatrix} 1+4 & 3+1 & 4+0 \\ -2+1 & 4+3 & 8+5 \\ 3+0 & -2+1 & -1+6 \end{bmatrix} = \begin{bmatrix} 5 & 4 & 4 \\ -1 & 7 & 13 \\ 3 & -1 & 5 \end{bmatrix}$$

$$A - B = \begin{bmatrix} 1 & 3 & 4 \\ -2 & 4 & 8 \\ 3 & -2 & -1 \end{bmatrix} - \begin{bmatrix} 4 & 1 & 0 \\ 1 & 3 & 5 \\ 0 & 1 & 6 \end{bmatrix}$$

$$= \begin{bmatrix} 1-4 & 3-1 & 4-0 \\ -2-1 & 4-3 & 8-5 \\ 3-0 & -2-1 & -1-6 \end{bmatrix} = \begin{bmatrix} -3 & 2 & 4 \\ -3 & 1 & 3 \\ 3 & -3 & -7 \end{bmatrix}$$

(2) Multiplication of Matrix by a Scalar

The multiplication of a matrix by a scalar K implies multiplication of every element of the matrix A by K.

If $A = \left[a_{ij}\right]$ is any matrix of dimension $m \times n$ and K is any scalar, then the multiplication of the matrix A by the scalar K is denoted by KA and is obtained by multiplying each element of A by the scalar K, i.e.,

$$KA = K\left[a_{ij}\right]_{m \times n} = \left[Ka_{ij}\right]_{m \times n}$$

For example, if $A = \begin{pmatrix} 2 & 3 & 1 \\ 0 & -1 & 5 \end{pmatrix}$ and K = 3, then we have

$$KA = 3A = 3\begin{pmatrix} 2 & 3 & 1 \\ 0 & -1 & 5 \end{pmatrix} = \begin{pmatrix} 2\times 3 & 3\times 3 & 1\times 3 \\ 0\times 3 & -1\times 3 & 5\times 3 \end{pmatrix} = \begin{pmatrix} 6 & 9 & 3 \\ 0 & -3 & 15 \end{pmatrix}$$

(3) Properties of Matrix Addition

If A, B and C are any three matrices of same dimension, then

(i) **Matrix addition is commutative, i.e.,**
$A + B = B + A$

(ii) **Matrix addition is associative, i.e.,**
$(A + B) + C = A + (B + C)$

(iii) **Matrix addition is distributive with respect to scalar K, i.e.,**
$K(A + B) = KA + KB$

(4) Product of Matrices

Two matrices A and B are conformable for the product AB **if the number of columns in A (pre-multiplier) is same as the number of rows in B (post-multiplier)**. Thus, if $A = \left[a_{ij}\right]_{m \times n}$ and $B = \left[b_{ij}\right]_{n \times p}$ are two matrices of order m × n and n × p respectively, then their product AB is of order m × p and is defined as

$$(AB)_{ij} = \sum_{r=1}^{n} a_{ir} b_{rj} = a_{i1} b_{1j} + a_{i2} b_{2j} + \ldots + a_{in} b_{nj}$$

$$\Rightarrow (AB)_{ij} = \begin{bmatrix} a_{i1} & a_{i2} & \cdots & a_{in} \end{bmatrix} \begin{bmatrix} b_{1j} \\ b_{2j} \\ \vdots \\ b_{nj} \end{bmatrix} = \left(i^{th} \text{row of A}\right)\left(j^{th} \text{ column of B}\right) \qquad \ldots(i)$$

$i = 1, 2, \ldots, m$ and $j = 1, 2, \ldots, p$.

Now we define the product of a row matrix and a column matrix.

Let $A = \begin{bmatrix} a_1 & a_2 \ldots a_n \end{bmatrix}$ be a row matrix and $B = \begin{bmatrix} b_1 \\ b_2 \\ \vdots \\ b_n \end{bmatrix}$ be a column matrix. Then,

$$AB = a_1 b_1 + a_2 b_2 + \ldots + a_n b_n \qquad \ldots(ii)$$

Thus, from (i), we have

$(AB)_{ij}$ = Sum of the product of elements of ith row of A with the corresponding elements of jth column of B

Note: If A and B are two matrices such that AB exists, then BA may or may not exist.

For example,

If $A = \begin{bmatrix} 2 & 1 & 3 \\ 3 & -2 & 1 \\ -1 & 0 & 1 \end{bmatrix}$ and $B = \begin{bmatrix} 1 & -2 \\ 2 & 1 \\ 4 & -3 \end{bmatrix}$, then A is a 3 × 3 matrix and B is a 3 × 2 matrix, therefore, A and B are conformable for the product AB and it is of order 3 × 2 such that

$(AB)_{11}$ = (First row of A) (First column of B)

$$\Rightarrow \quad (AB)_{11} = \begin{bmatrix} 2 & 1 & 3 \end{bmatrix} \begin{bmatrix} 1 \\ 2 \\ 4 \end{bmatrix} = 2 \times 1 + 1 \times 2 + 3 \times 4 = 16$$

$(AB)_{12}$ = (First row of A) (Second column of B)

$$\Rightarrow \quad (AB)_{12} = \begin{bmatrix} 2 & 1 & 3 \end{bmatrix} \begin{bmatrix} -2 \\ 1 \\ -3 \end{bmatrix} = 2\times-2+1\times1+3\times-3=-12$$

$(AB)_{21}$ = (Second row of A) (First column of B)

$$\Rightarrow \quad (AB)_{21} = \begin{bmatrix} 3 & -2 & 1 \end{bmatrix} \begin{bmatrix} 1 \\ 2 \\ 4 \end{bmatrix} = 3\times1+(-2)\times2+1\times4=3$$

Similarly, we have

$(AB)_{22} = -11$, $(AB)_{31} = 3$ and $(AB)_{32} = -1$

$$\therefore \quad AB = \begin{bmatrix} 16 & -12 \\ 3 & -11 \\ 3 & -1 \end{bmatrix}$$

(5) Properties of Matrix Multiplication

(i) Matrix multiplication, in general, is not commutative, i.e.

$AB \neq BA$

(ii) Matrix multiplication is associative, i.e.

A (BC) = (AB) C

where A, B, C are any three matrices of dimension $m \times n$, $n \times p$, $p \times q$ respectively.

(iii) Matrix multiplication is distributive, i.e.

A (B + C) = AB + AC

where A, B, C are any three matrices of dimension $m \times n$, $n \times p$ and $n \times p$ respectively.

Transpose of a Matrix

Let $A = [a_{ij}]$ be a matrix of order $m \times n$. Then the matrix $B = [b_{ji}]$ of order $n \times m$ is called transpose of the matrix A if $b_{ji} = a_{ij}$ for all values of i and j, i.e., the $(j, i)^{th}$ element of B is equal to the $(i, j)^{th}$ element of A.

In other words, the transpose of a matrix A is obtained by interchanging its rows and columns.

For example, $A = \begin{bmatrix} 1 & 5 & 2 \\ 0 & 1 & 3 \end{bmatrix}$

Then its transpose is the matrix $\begin{bmatrix} 1 & 0 \\ 5 & 1 \\ 2 & 3 \end{bmatrix}$ and is denoted by $\mathbf{A}^t$ or $\mathbf{A}'$.

Hence, we have

$$A^t = \begin{bmatrix} 1 & 0 \\ 5 & 1 \\ 2 & 3 \end{bmatrix}$$

Taking the transpose of A^t.

$$\left(A^t\right)^t = \begin{bmatrix} 1 & 5 & 2 \\ 0 & 1 & 3 \end{bmatrix}$$

which is the matrix A. This shows that

$$\left(A^t\right)^t = A$$

Similarly, we can prove that if A and B are two matrices, then

$$(A+B)^t = A^t + B^t$$

$$(AB)^t = B^t A^t \text{ (Reversal law of transposes)}$$

Symmetric Matrix

A square matrix A is said to be symmetric matrix if the transpose of A is equal to A, i.e., $A' = A$. For example,

$\begin{bmatrix} 1 & 5 & 4 \\ 5 & 2 & 7 \\ 4 & 7 & 3 \end{bmatrix}$ is a symmetric matrix of order 3 as in this case $A = A'$.

Note: In a symmetric matrix, $a_{ij} = a_{ji}$ for all values of i and j.

Skew Symmetric Matrix

A square matrix A is said to be skew-symmetric if the transpose of A is equal to –A, i.e., $A' = -A$. For example,

$\begin{bmatrix} 0 & 3 & 5 \\ -3 & 0 & 4 \\ -5 & -4 & 0 \end{bmatrix}$ is a skew-symmetric matrix of order 3 as in the case $A = -A'$.

Note: In a skew-symmetric matrix, the main diagonal elements are zero and $a_{ij} = -a_{ji}$.

1.2 DETERMINANT OF A MATRIX

Definition of Determinant

The determinant is a number associated to a square matrix. Determinants are possible only for square matrices. If A is a square matrix, then the determinant of A is denoted by $|\mathbf{A}|$ or **det A** or $\mathbf{\Delta}$.

Determinant of Different Orders

Determinants of different order are as follows:

(1) Determinant of Order One: Let $A = \left[a_{11}\right]$ be a matrix of order 1, then its determinant is defined as: $|A| = |a_{11}| = a_{11}$

(2) Determinant of Order Two: Let $A = \begin{bmatrix} a_{11} & a_{12} \\ a_{21} & a_{22} \end{bmatrix}$ be a square matrix of order 2, then its determinant is defined as:

$$|A| = \begin{vmatrix} a_{11} & a_{12} \\ a_{21} & a_{22} \end{vmatrix} = a_{11}\,a_{22} - a_{21}\,a_{12}$$

For example, if $A = \begin{bmatrix} 3 & 4 \\ 5 & 6 \end{bmatrix}$, then $|A| = \begin{vmatrix} 3 & 4 \\ 5 & 6 \end{vmatrix} = 3\times6-5\times4 = 18-20 = -2$

Rule: The value of the determinant of order 2 is obtained by multiplying the two elements on the principal diagonal and subtracting the product of the elements on the cross diagonal.

(3) Determinant of Order Three: Let $A = \begin{bmatrix} a_{11} & a_{12} & a_{13} \\ a_{21} & a_{22} & a_{23} \\ a_{31} & a_{32} & a_{33} \end{bmatrix}$ be a square matrix of order 3, then its determinant is defined as:

$$|A| = \begin{vmatrix} a_{11} & a_{12} & a_{13} \\ a_{21} & a_{22} & a_{23} \\ a_{31} & a_{32} & a_{33} \end{vmatrix}$$

Expanding it along the first row, we have

$$|A| = (-1)^{1+1} a_{11} \begin{vmatrix} a_{22} & a_{23} \\ a_{32} & a_{33} \end{vmatrix} + (-1)^{1+2} a_{12} \begin{vmatrix} a_{21} & a_{23} \\ a_{31} & a_{33} \end{vmatrix} + (\ 1)^{1+3} a_{13} \begin{vmatrix} a_{21} & a_{22} \\ a_{31} & a_{32} \end{vmatrix} \quad \ldots\text{(i)}$$

$$= a_{11}(a_{22}a_{33} - a_{32}a_{23}) - a_{12}(a_{21}a_{33} - a_{31}a_{23}) + a_{13}(a_{21}a_{32} - a_{31}a_{22})$$

Rule: The value of the determinant is obtained by multiplying each element of the first row by a determinant obtained by deleting from the given determinant, the row and the column to which element belongs, the signs being taken positive and negative alternatively.

Note: We have expanded the above determinant by first row. In fact, we can expand the given determinant with respect to the IInd row, IIIrd row, Ist column, IInd column or IIIrd column. In case of 3 × 3 determinant, we can expand in 3 + 3 = 6 ways. However, care should be taken to attach appropriate sign to various terms of the expansion. Generally, it should be remembered that the sign of a_{ij} element appearing before any sub-determinant in expansion (i) is given by $(-1)^{i+j}$.

Minors and Cofactors

(1) Minors: Let A be a square matrix of order 3, then minor of an element a_{11} is the determinant of the sub matrix obtained from A by deleting first row and first column containing the elements a_{11}.

Consider determinant of order 3:

$$\begin{vmatrix} a_{11} & a_{12} & a_{13} \\ a_{21} & a_{22} & a_{23} \\ a_{31} & a_{32} & a_{33} \end{vmatrix}$$

The minor of the element a_{11} is obtained by deleting first row and first column containing the element a_{11}. It is denoted by M_{11} and is given by:

$$M_{11} = \begin{vmatrix} a_{22} & a_{23} \\ a_{32} & a_{33} \end{vmatrix}$$

Similarly, minor of a_{12} is obtained as:

$$M_{12} = \begin{vmatrix} a_{21} & a_{23} \\ a_{31} & a_{33} \end{vmatrix}$$

(2) Cofactors: The cofactor C_{ij} of an element a_{ij} is defined as:

$$C_{ij} = (-1)^{i+j} M_{ij}$$

where M_{ij} is the minor of an element a_{ij}.

Thus, the minor of an element with a proper sign is called the cofactor to the element. Consider the determinant of order 3:

$$\begin{vmatrix} a_{11} & a_{12} & a_{13} \\ a_{21} & a_{22} & a_{23} \\ a_{31} & a_{32} & a_{33} \end{vmatrix}$$

Cofactor of a_{11} is

$$C_{11} = (-1)^{1+1} M_{11} = (-1)^{1+1} \begin{vmatrix} a_{22} & a_{23} \\ a_{32} & a_{33} \end{vmatrix} = \begin{vmatrix} a_{22} & a_{23} \\ a_{32} & a_{33} \end{vmatrix}$$

Similarly, cofactor of a_{12} is

$$C_{12} = (-1)^{1+2} M_{12} = (-1)^{1+2} \begin{vmatrix} a_{21} & a_{23} \\ a_{31} & a_{33} \end{vmatrix} = -\begin{vmatrix} a_{21} & a_{23} \\ a_{31} & a_{33} \end{vmatrix}$$

1.3 ADJOINT OF A MATRIX

Definition

If A is any square matrix, then adjoint of A is defined as the transpose of the matrix obtained by the replacing the element of A by their corresponding co-factors. In other words, the adjoint of a matrix A is the transpose of the cofactor matrix. It is denoted by **Adj. A** or **adj. A**.

Thus if $A = \begin{pmatrix} a_{11} & a_{12} & a_{13} \\ a_{21} & a_{22} & a_{23} \\ a_{31} & a_{32} & a_{33} \end{pmatrix}$

$$C(A) = \begin{pmatrix} C_{11} & C_{12} & C_{13} \\ C_{21} & C_{22} & C_{23} \\ C_{31} & C_{32} & C_{33} \end{pmatrix}$$

Thus, adj. A = Transpose of the cofactor matrix $\begin{pmatrix} C_{11} & C_{12} & C_{13} \\ C_{21} & C_{22} & C_{23} \\ C_{31} & C_{32} & C_{33} \end{pmatrix}$

$$= \begin{pmatrix} C_{11} & C_{21} & C_{31} \\ C_{12} & C_{22} & C_{32} \\ C_{13} & C_{23} & C_{33} \end{pmatrix}$$

Steps to Compute Adjoint of a Matrix

(1) Check that the given matrix A is a square.

(2) Compute Cofactor Matrix C(A). It is obtained by replacing each element in the matrix by its corresponding cofactor.

(3) Take the transpose of the Cofactor Matrix. The result would give the adjoint of the matrix.

1.4 INVERSE OF A MATRIX

Let A be any square matrix of order n. Then, a square matrix B of the same order is called the inverse of A if AB = BA = I.

The inverse of the matrix A is denoted by A^{-1}, therefore, $B = A^{-1}$.

Note: For the inverse of the matrix, the matrix must be **non-singular**. A matrix (let A) is said to be **non-singular** if its determinant is not equal to zero, i.e., $|A| \neq 0$. Whereas a matrix (let A) is said to be **singular** if its determinant is equal to zero, i.e., $|A| = 0$.

The inverse of A is calculated by the following formula:

$$A^{-1} = \frac{\text{adj. A}}{|A|}, \quad |A| \neq 0$$

Steps to find the inverse of a matrix

(1) Find the value of $|A|$. If $|A| \neq 0$, i.e., matrix is non-singular, go to next step. If $|A| = 0$, i.e., matrix is singular, we cannot find the inverse of the matrix.

(2) We shall then find the adjoint of the matrix.

(3) Apply the following formula to calculate the inverse of A

$$A^{-1} = \frac{\text{adj. A}}{|A|}, \qquad |A| \neq 0$$

Note: The necessary condition for finding the inverse of a matrix A is that (i) the given matrix is a square matrix and (ii) the determinant of the matrix is not equal to zero, i.e., $|A| \neq 0$.

1.5 RANK OF A MATRIX

A number r is said to be the rank of a matrix A of order m × n if

(1) at least one minor of order r is not zero and

(2) every minor of order (r + 1) is zero.

It is generally denoted by $\rho(A)$ where $\rho(A) = r$.

For example,

$$A = \begin{bmatrix} 2 & 0 & 7 \\ 3 & 3 & 6 \\ 2 & 2 & 4 \end{bmatrix}$$

Its minor of order 3 is

$$\begin{vmatrix} 2 & 0 & 7 \\ 3 & 3 & 6 \\ 2 & 2 & 4 \end{vmatrix}$$

Its value is 2 (12 – 12) + 7 (6 – 6) = 0.

There are nine minors of order 2 × 2. Consider the minor

$$\begin{vmatrix} 2 & 0 \\ 3 & 3 \end{vmatrix},$$

Its value is 6, i.e., it is not zero. Hence, rank of A is 2.

1.6 VECTORS

Vector Quantity

Quantities, which are specified by a magnitude and a direction in space, are called vector quantities.

Representation of Vectors

In two-dimensional space, each vector can be represented by a point or by a line from the origin to the point. For example,

$$\vec{a} = \begin{bmatrix} 4 \\ 7 \end{bmatrix}, \ \vec{b} = \begin{bmatrix} 2 \\ 3 \end{bmatrix}, \ \vec{c} = \begin{bmatrix} -1 \\ 5 \end{bmatrix} \qquad \text{...(i)}$$

are vectors. The numbers 4, 7 are the components of the vector $\vec{a}$, numbers 2, 3 are the components of the vector $\vec{b}$ and the numbers –1, 5 are the components of vector $\vec{c}$. Vectors $\vec{a}$, $\vec{b}$ and $\vec{c}$ are **two-component vectors.** In

Eq. (i), these vectors are denoted in column matrix form of order 2×1. These vectors can also be denoted in the form of row matrix of order 1×2, i.e.,

$$\vec{a}=[4,7],\ \vec{b}=[2,3],\ \vec{c}=[-1,5] \qquad ...(ii)$$

Similarly, a three-component vector is given by

$$\begin{bmatrix} a_1 \\ a_2 \\ a_3 \end{bmatrix} \text{ or } [a_1, a_2, a_3]$$

having three components a_1, a_2, a_3. An n-component vector $\vec{a}$ is given by

$$\vec{a}=\begin{bmatrix} a_1 \\ a_2 \\ \vdots \\ a_n \end{bmatrix} \text{ or } \vec{a}=[a_1, a_2, ..., a_n]$$

Geometric Representation of Vectors

Let $\vec{a}=\begin{bmatrix} 3 \\ 5 \end{bmatrix}=[3, 5]$

Vector $\vec{a}$ can be represented as a directed line segment as shown in Fig 1.1.

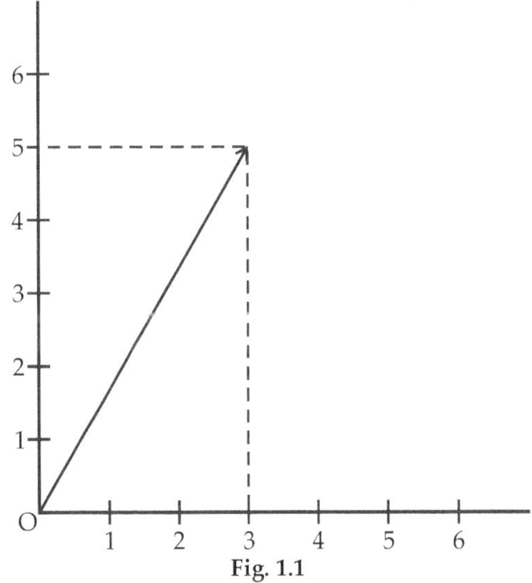

Fig. 1.1

Types of Vectors

Following are the different types of vectors:

(1) Zero Vector: A vector with all its component equal to zero is called a **Zero Vector** or a **Null Vector.** It is denoted by $\vec{0}$ and is referred to as the origin.

(2) Unit Vector: A vector, having all its components zero except the ith component, which is 1, is called **Unit Vector** and is denoted by $\hat{e}_i$. For example, $\hat{e}_1 = (1, 0, 0, 0, ..., 0)$, $\hat{e}_2 = (0, 1, 0, 0, ..., 0), ..., \hat{e}_n = (0, 0, ..., 0, 1)$ are unit vectors.

(3) Sum Vector $\vec{1}$: A vector having unity as a value for each component is called **Sum Vector** and is denoted by $\vec{1}$. i.e.,

$$\vec{1} = (1, 1, 1, ..., 1)$$

(4) Equal Vectors: Two vectors $\vec{a}$ and $\vec{b}$ are said to be **equal** if their corresponding components are equal. i.e.,

$$x_i = y_i, \quad i = 1, 2, ..., n$$

For example, if $\vec{a} = (5, 4, 2)$ and $\vec{b} = (5, 4, 2)$, then $\vec{a} = \vec{b}$ and if $\vec{c} = (1, 4, 2)$ then $\vec{a} \neq \vec{c}$

Algebra of Vectors

Algebra of vectors is as follows:

(1) Addition and subtraction of Two Vectors: Two vectors of the same size can be added or subtracted component wise. For example,

If $\vec{a} = (1, 4, 2)$ and $\vec{b} = (2, 1, 5)$

Then, $\vec{a} + \vec{b} = (1, 4, 2) + (2, 1, 5) = (1+2, 4+1, 2+5) = (3, 5, 7)$

and $\vec{a} - \vec{b} = (1, 4, 2) - (2, 1, 5) = (1-2, 4-1, 2-5) = (-1, 3, -3)$

Note: Here we can see that **sum vector** and **the sum of the vectors** are not same.

(2) Multiplication of a Vector by a Scalar: A vector can be multiplied by a scalar by multiplying each component of vector by scalar. If $\vec{a} = (a_1, a_2, ..., a_n)$ is any vector and k is a scalar then,

$$k\vec{a} = (ka_1, ka_2, ..., ka_n)$$

For example, $\vec{a} = (1, 3, 5)$ and $k = 5$ then

$$5\vec{a} = 5(1, 3, 5) = (5, 15, 25)$$

(3) Scalar Product of Vectors: The scalar product of two n-component vectors $\vec{a}$ and $\vec{b}$ given as

$\vec{a} = (a_1, a_2, ..., a_n)$, $\vec{b} = (b_1, b_2, ..., b_n)$ is defined to be the scalar $a_1b_1 + a_2b_2 + ... + a_nb_n = \sum_{i=1}^{n} a_ib_i$ and is denoted by $\vec{a}.\vec{b}$ spoken as $\vec{a}$ dot $\vec{b}$.

For example, if $\vec{a} = (2, 3)$ and $\vec{b} = (-1, 2)$

Then, $\vec{a}.\vec{b} = 2 \times -1 + 3 \times 2 = -2 + 6 = 4$

(4) Magnitude of a Vector: If a vector $\vec{a} = (a_1, a_2, ..., a_n)$, then the magnitude of vector $\vec{a}$ is $|\vec{a}| = \sqrt{a_1^2 + a_2^2 + ...a_n^2}$

For example, if $\vec{a} = (2, 4, 6)$ then

$$|\vec{a}| = \sqrt{(2)^2 + (4)^2 + (6)^2} = \sqrt{4+16+36} = \sqrt{56}$$

(5) Angle between Two Vectors: If two vectors are given as $\vec{a} = (a_1, a_2, ... a_n)$ and $\vec{b} = (b_1, b_2, ..., b_n)$ then the angle θ between these two vectors $\vec{a}$ and $\vec{b}$ is defined as

$$\cos\theta = \frac{\vec{a}.\vec{b}}{|\vec{a}||\vec{b}|} = \frac{\sum_{i=1}^{n} a_i b_i}{\sqrt{\sum_{i=1}^{n} a_i^2}\sqrt{\sum_{i=1}^{n} b_i^2}}$$

(6) Vector Product of Two Vectors: The vector or cross product of vectors $\vec{a}$ and $\vec{b}$, written as $\vec{a} \times \vec{b}$, is defined to be the vector as

$$\vec{c} = \vec{a} \times \vec{b} = |\vec{a}||\vec{b}| \sin\theta \ \hat{n}$$

where θ is the angle between vectors $\vec{a}$ and $\vec{b}$ $(0 \leq \theta \leq \pi)$. $\hat{n}$ is a unit vector and it is perpendicular to $\vec{a}$ and $\vec{b}$.

(7) Distance between Two Vectors: The distance from the vector (point) $\vec{a} = (a_1, a_2, ..., a_n)$ to the vector point $\vec{b} = (b_1, b_2, ..., b_n)$, written $|\vec{a} - \vec{b}|$, is defined as

$$|\vec{a} - \vec{b}| = \sqrt{(a_1 - b_1)^2 + (a_2 - b_2)^2 + ... + (a_n - b_n)^2}$$

1.7 EUCLIDEAN SPACE

The notion of distance in R^2 imposes upon it a special characteristic because of which, we call R^2 as a Euclidean space of dimension 2. It is generally denoted by E^2. Thus, a Euclidean space E^2 is defined as the set of all vector points $a = (x_1, x_2)$. In general, the set of all vectors each of dimension n, i.e., $a = (x_1, x_2, ..., x_n)$ is called a Euclidean Space denoted by E^n in which the addition and multiplication by a scalar are defined and there exists a non-negative number associated with any two vectors in this set called the distance between the two vectors.

(1) Linear Combination

Assume that E^n has k vectors given by $\vec{v}_1, \vec{v}_2, ..., \vec{v}_k$. Any vector $\vec{u}$ in E^n is said to be a linear combination of $\vec{v}_1, \vec{v}_2, ..., \vec{v}_k$, if $\vec{u}$ can be written as

$$\vec{u} = \sum_{i=1}^{k} \alpha_i v_k = \alpha_1 v_1 + \alpha_2 v_2 + ... + \alpha_k v_k$$

where $\alpha_1, \alpha_2, ..., \alpha_k$ are real numbers.

For example, if in E^3, we have

$$\vec{v}_1 = \begin{bmatrix} 3 \\ 2 \\ -1 \end{bmatrix}, \quad \vec{v}_2 \begin{bmatrix} 2 \\ 1 \\ 3 \end{bmatrix}$$

then, $\vec{u} = \begin{bmatrix} 18 \\ 11 \\ 5 \end{bmatrix}$ can be written as $4\vec{v}_1 + 3\vec{v}_2$, which is a linear combination of the vectors $\vec{v}_1$ and $\vec{v}_2$.

(2) Linear Dependence

A set of vectors $a_1, a_2, ..., a_n$ in E^n is said to be **linearly dependent** if there exist scalars $\lambda_1, \lambda_2, \lambda_3, ..., \lambda_m$ not all zero such that

$$\lambda_1 a_1 + \lambda_2 a_2 + ... + \lambda_m a_m = 0$$

If the only set of λ_1 for which this relation holds is such that $\lambda_1 = \lambda_2 = ... = \lambda_m = 0$, then the vectors $a_1, a_2, ..., a_m$ are said to be **linearly independent**.

Spanning Set and Basis: A collection of vectors $a_1, a_2, ..., a_k$ in E^n is said to span E^n if every vector in E^n can be expressed as a linear combination of $a_1, a_2, ..., a_k$.

For example, if we consider E^3 and suppose

$a_1 = \begin{bmatrix} 1 \\ 0 \\ 0 \end{bmatrix}$, $a_2 = \begin{bmatrix} 0 \\ 1 \\ 0 \end{bmatrix}$, $a_3 = \begin{bmatrix} 0 \\ 0 \\ 1 \end{bmatrix}$, are any three vectors in E^3.

Then any vectors in E^3 can be expressed as a linear combination of a_1, a_2, a_3.

Indeed, take any vector in E^3. For example, $b = \begin{bmatrix} 3 \\ 4 \\ 5 \end{bmatrix}$, or $c = \begin{bmatrix} 2 \\ 0 \\ 3 \end{bmatrix}$

Then we have $b = \begin{bmatrix} 3 \\ 4 \\ 5 \end{bmatrix} = 3a_1 + 4a_2 + 5a_3$

and we have $c = \begin{bmatrix} -2 \\ 0 \\ 3 \end{bmatrix} = -2a_1 + 0.a_2 + 3a_3$

Thus, a_1, a_2, a_3 span E^3. However, if we consider only a_1 and a_2, then vector b in E^3 cannot be written as a linear combination of a_1 and a_2.

Hence, a_1 and a_2 do not span E^3. The set of vectors a_1, a_2, a_3 satisfy the additional property that these are linearly independent. Therefore, the set of vectors a_1, a_2, a_3 is called a basis of E^n. In general, we can define the basis as follows:

A set of vectors $a_1, a_2, ..., a_k$ form a basis of E^n if the following conditions hold:

(i) The vectors $a_1, a_2, ..., a_k$ span E^n.

(ii) The set of vectors $a_1, a_2, ..., a_k$ is linearly independent.

Vector Space: A set V is called a vector space over R, the field of real numbers, if it has two operations, namely addition (denoted by +) and multiplication of elements of V by elements of R (denoted by .) such that the following hold:

VS1) + is a binary operation, i.e.

$u + v \in V \;\; \forall\, u, v \in V$

VS2) + is associative, i.e. $(u + v) + w = u + (v + w)$

VS3) V has an identity element with respect to +,

i.e., $\exists 0 \in V$ such that $0 + v = v + 0 \;\; \forall\, v \in V$

VS4) Every element of V has an inverse with respect to +: For every

$u \in V, \exists\, v \in V$ such that $u + v = 0$

VS5) + is commutative, i.e. $u + v = v + u \;\; \forall\, u, v \in V$

VS6) $\cdot : F \times V \to V : (\alpha \cdot v) = \alpha \cdot V$ is a well defined operation, i.e.

$\forall \alpha \in F$ and $v \in V$, $\alpha \cdot v \in V$

VS7) $\forall \alpha \in F$ and $u, v \in V$, $\alpha \cdot (u + v) = \alpha \cdot u + \alpha \cdot v$

VS8) $\forall \alpha, \beta \in F$ and $v \in V$, $(\alpha + \beta) \cdot v = \alpha \cdot v + \beta \cdot v$

VS9) $\forall \alpha, \beta \in F$ and $v \in V$, $(\alpha \beta) \cdot v = \alpha \cdot (\beta v)$

VS10) $1 . v = v$ for all $v \in V$

Subspace: A subset $W \subset V$ is a subspace of (V, + , .) if it forms a vector space under the operations (+, .).

However, to check that W is subspace of V, it is enough to check that:

(i) $u + v \in W$, for all $u, v \in W$

(ii) $\alpha \cdot v \in W$ for all $u \in W$

Solved Practical Problems

Q1. Calculate 2 × 2 matrix whose elements a_{ij} are given by $a_{ij} = 2i - j$.

Ans. Let 2 × 2 matrix is given by

$$A = \begin{bmatrix} a_{11} & a_{12} \\ a_{21} & a_{22} \end{bmatrix}$$

It is given that

$$a_{ij} = 2i - j$$

Putting i = 1, 2 and j = 1, 2, we have

$$a_{11} = 2(1) - 1 = 1$$

$$a_{12} = 2(1) - 2 = 0$$

$$a_{21} = 2(2) - 1 = 3$$

and $a_{22} = 2(2) - 2 = 2$

Thus, we have $A = \begin{bmatrix} 1 & 0 \\ 3 & 2 \end{bmatrix}$

Q2. If $A = \begin{bmatrix} -2 & 5 & 0 \\ -1 & 0 & 3 \end{bmatrix}$, $B = \begin{bmatrix} 1 & -3 & 5 \\ 2 & 4 & -6 \end{bmatrix}$, find 7A – 5B.

Ans. $7A - 5B = 7\begin{bmatrix} -2 & 5 & 0 \\ -1 & 0 & 3 \end{bmatrix} - 5\begin{bmatrix} 1 & -3 & 5 \\ 2 & 4 & -6 \end{bmatrix}$

$$= \begin{bmatrix} -14 & 35 & 0 \\ -7 & 0 & 21 \end{bmatrix} - \begin{bmatrix} 5 & -15 & 25 \\ 10 & 20 & -30 \end{bmatrix} = \begin{bmatrix} -14 & -5 & 35+15 & 0-25 \\ -7 & -10 & 0-20 & 21+30 \end{bmatrix}$$

$$= \begin{bmatrix} -19 & 50 & -25 \\ -17 & -20 & 51 \end{bmatrix}$$

Q3. Suppose two matrices A and B are given as

$$A = \begin{bmatrix} 3 & 4 & 7 \\ 5 & 6 & 9 \end{bmatrix} \text{ and } B = \begin{bmatrix} 3 & 6 \\ 4 & 7 \\ 5 & 8 \\ 9 & 10 \end{bmatrix}$$

can you define AB? What can you say about product BA?

Ans. Number of Columns of A = 3

Number of rows of A = 2

Number of Columns of B = 2

Number of rows of B = 4

We cannot define AB because the number of columns of A is not equal to the number of rows of B.

However, we can define the product BA because the number of columns of B is equal to the number of rows of A.

Q4. If $A=\begin{bmatrix}1 & -2 & 3\\ -4 & 2 & 5\end{bmatrix}$ **and** $B=\begin{bmatrix}2 & 3\\ 4 & 5\\ 2 & 1\end{bmatrix}$**, compute AB and BA and show that AB ≠ BA.**

Ans. Since the order of A is 2 × 3 and the order of B is 3 × 2, i.e., the number of column of A is equal to the number of rows of B. Hence, AB is defined. Now,

$$AB=\begin{bmatrix}1 & -2 & 3\\ -4 & 2 & 5\end{bmatrix}\begin{bmatrix}2 & 3\\ 4 & 5\\ 2 & 1\end{bmatrix}=\begin{bmatrix}1\times2+(-2)\times4+3\times2 & 1\times3+(-2)\times5+3\times1\\ -4\times2+2\times4+5\times2 & -4\times3+2\times5+5\times1\end{bmatrix}$$

$$=\begin{bmatrix}2-8+6 & 3-10+3\\ -8+8+10 & -12+10+5\end{bmatrix}=\begin{bmatrix}0 & -4\\ 10 & 3\end{bmatrix}$$

Since B is 3 × 2 and A is 2 × 3, then BA is also defined.

$$\therefore BA=\begin{bmatrix}2 & 3\\ 4 & 5\\ 2 & 1\end{bmatrix}\begin{bmatrix}1 & -2 & 3\\ -4 & 2 & 5\end{bmatrix}=\begin{bmatrix}2\times1+3\times(-4) & 2\times(-2)+(3\times2) & 2\times3+3\times5\\ 4\times1+5\times(-4) & 4\times(-2)+5\times2 & 4\times3+5\times5\\ 2\times1+1\times(-4) & 2\times(-2)+1\times2 & 2\times3+1\times5\end{bmatrix}$$

$$=\begin{bmatrix}2-12 & -4+6 & 6+15\\ 4-20 & -8+10 & 12+25\\ 2-4 & -4+2 & 6+5\end{bmatrix}=\begin{bmatrix}-10 & 2 & 21\\ -16 & 2 & 37\\ -2 & -2 & 11\end{bmatrix}$$

Hence, it has been proved that AB ≠ BA.

Q5. If $A=\begin{bmatrix}1 & 1 & 2\\ 2 & 1 & 0\end{bmatrix}$, $B=\begin{bmatrix}1 & 2\\ 2 & 0\\ -1 & 1\end{bmatrix}$**, show that** $(AB)^t=B^t A^t$.

Ans. $A=\begin{bmatrix}1 & 1 & 2\\ 2 & 1 & 0\end{bmatrix}$

$$\Rightarrow \quad A^t=\begin{bmatrix}1 & 2\\ 1 & 1\\ 2 & 0\end{bmatrix}$$

and $B=\begin{bmatrix}1 & 2\\ 2 & 0\\ -1 & 1\end{bmatrix}$

$\Rightarrow \quad B^t = \begin{bmatrix} 1 & 2 & -1 \\ 2 & 0 & 1 \end{bmatrix}$

$$\text{Now } AB = \begin{bmatrix} 1 & 1 & 2 \\ 2 & 1 & 0 \end{bmatrix} \begin{bmatrix} 1 & 2 \\ 2 & 0 \\ -1 & 1 \end{bmatrix} = \begin{bmatrix} 1+2-2 & 2+0+2 \\ 2+2+0 & 4+0+0 \end{bmatrix}$$

$\therefore \quad AB = \begin{bmatrix} 1 & 4 \\ 4 & 4 \end{bmatrix}$

$\Rightarrow \quad (AB)^t = \begin{bmatrix} 1 & 4 \\ 4 & 4 \end{bmatrix}$ ...(i)

$$\text{Now } B^tA^t = \begin{bmatrix} 1 & 2 & -1 \\ 2 & 0 & 1 \end{bmatrix} \begin{bmatrix} 1 & 2 \\ 1 & 1 \\ 2 & 0 \end{bmatrix}$$

$$= \begin{bmatrix} 1+2-2 & 2+2-0 \\ 2+0+2 & 4+0+0 \end{bmatrix}$$

$\therefore \quad B^tA^t = \begin{bmatrix} 1 & 4 \\ 4 & 4 \end{bmatrix}$ ...(ii)

From Eqs. (i) and (ii), we have

$$\boxed{(AB)^t = B^t A^t}$$

Q6. Test whether or not the following matrices are symmetric or skew-symmetric.

$$\mathbf{A} = \begin{bmatrix} 2 & -1 & 6 \\ -1 & 3 & 7 \\ 6 & 7 & 8 \end{bmatrix}, \mathbf{B} = \begin{bmatrix} 0 & -1 & 6 \\ 1 & 0 & -7 \\ -6 & 7 & 0 \end{bmatrix}$$

Ans. Given, $A = \begin{bmatrix} 2 & -1 & 6 \\ -1 & 3 & 7 \\ 6 & 7 & 8 \end{bmatrix}$

$\Rightarrow$ Transpose of A

$$A^t = \begin{bmatrix} 2 & -1 & 6 \\ -1 & 3 & 7 \\ 6 & 7 & 8 \end{bmatrix}$$

Thus, $A^t = A$. Hence, matrix A is symmetric.

Now, $B = \begin{bmatrix} 0 & -1 & 6 \\ 1 & 0 & -7 \\ -6 & 7 & 0 \end{bmatrix}$

$\Rightarrow$ Transpose of B

$$B^t = \begin{bmatrix} 0 & 1 & -6 \\ -1 & 0 & 7 \\ 6 & -7 & 0 \end{bmatrix}$$

$$\Rightarrow \quad B^t = -\begin{bmatrix} 0 & -1 & 6 \\ 1 & 0 & -7 \\ -6 & 7 & 0 \end{bmatrix}$$

$\Rightarrow \quad B^t = -B$

Hence, matrix B is skew-symmetric.

Q7. Determine the value of the determinant $\begin{vmatrix} 3 & 4 & 2 \\ 1 & 5 & 3 \\ 2 & 6 & 7 \end{vmatrix}$.

Ans. Expanding the given determinant according to the first row, we have

$$\begin{vmatrix} 3 & 4 & 2 \\ 1 & 5 & 3 \\ 2 & 6 & 7 \end{vmatrix}$$

$$= (-1)^{1+1} 3(5\times7-3\times6)+(-1)^{1+2} 4(1\times7-2\times3)+(-1)^{1+3} 2(1\times6-2\times5)$$

$$= 3\,(35-18) - 4\,(7-6) + 2\,(6-10) = 3\,(17) - 4\,(1) + 2\,(-4) = 51-4-8 = 39$$

Q8. If the determinant A = $\begin{vmatrix} 4 & 2 & 5 \\ 3 & 1 & 0 \\ 8 & 7 & 6 \end{vmatrix}$, find the minors with respect to the elements 4, 5 and 6.

Ans. We can see that element 4 is in first row and first column in determinant A. Therefore, for the minor with respect to the element 4, we delete the first row and first column, i.e.

$\begin{vmatrix} 1 & 0 \\ 7 & 6 \end{vmatrix} = 6\times1-0\times7 = 6$ is the minor with respect to the element 4.

Similarly, the minor with respect to the element 5 is $\begin{vmatrix} 3 & 1 \\ 8 & 7 \end{vmatrix} = 7\times3-8\times1 = 13$ and the minor with respect to the element 6 is $\begin{vmatrix} 4 & 2 \\ 3 & 1 \end{vmatrix} = 1\times4-3\times2 = -2.$

Q9. If the determinant $A = \begin{vmatrix} 0 & -1 & 2 \\ -2 & 1 & 0 \\ 3 & -3 & -1 \end{vmatrix}$, **find the co-factors with respect to the elements –2, 3 and 2.**

Ans. –2 is in first column and second row. Hence, co-factor

$$C_{21} = (-1)^{2+1} \begin{vmatrix} -1 & 2 \\ -3 & -1 \end{vmatrix} = -(1+6) = -7$$

3 is in third row and first column. Hence, co-factor

$$C_{31} = (-1)^{3+1} \begin{vmatrix} -1 & 2 \\ 1 & 0 \end{vmatrix} = +(0-2) = -2$$

2 is in first row and third column. Hence, co-factor

$$C_{13} = (-1)^{1+3} \begin{vmatrix} -2 & 1 \\ 3 & -3 \end{vmatrix} = +(6-3) = 3$$

Q10. Evaluate the following determinant with respect to second column:

$$\begin{vmatrix} 0 & -2 & 3 \\ -1 & 1 & -3 \\ 2 & 0 & -1 \end{vmatrix}$$

Ans.

$$\begin{vmatrix} 0 & -2 & 3 \\ -1 & 1 & -3 \\ 2 & 0 & -1 \end{vmatrix} = (-1)^{1+2}(-2)\begin{vmatrix} -1 & -3 \\ 2 & -1 \end{vmatrix} + (-1)^{2+2}(1)\begin{vmatrix} 0 & 3 \\ 2 & -1 \end{vmatrix} + (-1)^{3+2}(0)\begin{vmatrix} 0 & 3 \\ -1 & -3 \end{vmatrix}$$

$$= 2(1+6) + (0-6) - 0 = 2(7) - 6 = 8$$

Q11. Find the adjoint of the matrix $A = \begin{bmatrix} 2 & 0 & 1 \\ 2 & 1 & -1 \\ 3 & 1 & -1 \end{bmatrix}$. **Also find the inverse of A if it exists.**

Ans. Given matrix $A = \begin{bmatrix} 2 & 0 & 1 \\ 2 & 1 & -1 \\ 3 & 1 & -1 \end{bmatrix}$

$$\Rightarrow |A| = \text{det. } A = \begin{vmatrix} 2 & 0 & 1 \\ 2 & 1 & -1 \\ 3 & 1 & -1 \end{vmatrix}$$

Now, cofactors of all elements of A,

$$C_{11} = (-1)^{1+1} \begin{vmatrix} 1 & -1 \\ 1 & -1 \end{vmatrix} = (-1) - (-1) = 0$$

$$C_{12} = (-1)^{1+2}\begin{vmatrix} 2 & -1 \\ 3 & -1 \end{vmatrix} = -(-2+3) = -1$$

$$C_{13} = (-1)^{1+3}\begin{vmatrix} 2 & 1 \\ 3 & 1 \end{vmatrix} = (2-3) = -1$$

$$C_{21} = (-1)^{2+1}\begin{vmatrix} 0 & 1 \\ 1 & -1 \end{vmatrix} = -(0-1) = 1$$

$$C_{22} = (-1)^{2+2}\begin{vmatrix} 2 & 1 \\ 3 & -1 \end{vmatrix} = (-2-3) = -5$$

$$C_{23} = (-1)^{2+3}\begin{vmatrix} 2 & 0 \\ 3 & 1 \end{vmatrix} = -(2-0) = -2$$

$$C_{31} = (-1)^{3+1}\begin{vmatrix} 0 & 1 \\ 1 & -1 \end{vmatrix} = (0-1) = -1$$

$$C_{32} = (-1)^{3+2}\begin{vmatrix} 2 & 1 \\ 2 & -1 \end{vmatrix} = -(-2-2) = 4$$

$$C_{33} = (-1)^{3+3}\begin{vmatrix} 2 & 0 \\ 2 & 1 \end{vmatrix} = (2-0) = 2$$

Hence,

$$\text{adj A} = \begin{bmatrix} 0 & 1 & -1 \\ -1 & -5 & 4 \\ -1 & -2 & 2 \end{bmatrix}$$

Now $|A| = \begin{vmatrix} 2 & 0 & 1 \\ 2 & 1 & -1 \\ 3 & 1 & -1 \end{vmatrix}$ = 2 [–1 + 1] –0 [–2 + 3] + 1 (2 – 3) = 0 – 0 – 1

$= -1 \neq 0$

Hence, inverse of A exists.

$$\Rightarrow A^{-1} = \frac{\text{adj A}}{|A|} = \frac{1}{-1}\begin{bmatrix} 0 & 1 & -1 \\ -1 & -5 & 4 \\ -1 & -2 & 2 \end{bmatrix}$$

$$\therefore\ A^{-1} = \begin{bmatrix} 0 & -1 & 1 \\ 1 & 5 & -4 \\ 1 & 2 & -2 \end{bmatrix}$$

Q12. If $A = \begin{bmatrix} 2 & 0 & 1 \\ 3 & 1 & -1 \\ -2 & -2 & 4 \end{bmatrix}$. Does the inverse of A exist? If yes, find it.

Ans. Given that

$$A = \begin{bmatrix} 2 & 0 & 1 \\ 3 & 1 & -1 \\ -2 & -2 & 4 \end{bmatrix}$$

$$\Rightarrow \quad |A| = \begin{vmatrix} 2 & 0 & 1 \\ 3 & 1 & -1 \\ -2 & -2 & 4 \end{vmatrix} = 2\,(4-2) - 0 + 1\,(-6+2) = 4 - 4 = 0$$

Thus, $|A| = 0$, hence the inverse of A does not exist.

Q13. Find the rank of the matrix:

$$A = \begin{bmatrix} 1 & 2 & 3 & 2 \\ 2 & 3 & 5 & 1 \\ 1 & 3 & 4 & 5 \end{bmatrix}$$

Ans. Given matrix is not a square matrix, so we can delete any one column to obtain a square matrix and then find the minor of order 3.

Case I: Deleting IVth column we get,

$$|A| = \begin{vmatrix} 1 & 2 & 3 \\ 2 & 3 & 5 \\ 1 & 3 & 4 \end{vmatrix} = 1\begin{vmatrix} 3 & 5 \\ 3 & 4 \end{vmatrix} - 2\begin{vmatrix} 2 & 5 \\ 1 & 4 \end{vmatrix} + 3\begin{vmatrix} 2 & 3 \\ 1 & 3 \end{vmatrix}$$

$$= 1\,(12-15) - 2\,(8-5) + 3\,(6-3) = -3 - 6 + 9 = 0$$

Case II: Deleting IIIrd column we get,

$$|A| = \begin{vmatrix} 1 & 2 & 2 \\ 2 & 3 & 1 \\ 1 & 3 & 5 \end{vmatrix} = 1\begin{vmatrix} 3 & 1 \\ 3 & 5 \end{vmatrix} - 2\begin{vmatrix} 2 & 1 \\ 1 & 5 \end{vmatrix} + 2\begin{vmatrix} 2 & 3 \\ 1 & 3 \end{vmatrix}$$

$$= 1\,(15-3) - 2\,(10-1) + 2\,(6-3) = 12 - 18 + 6 = 0$$

Case III: Deleting IInd column we get,

$$|A| = \begin{vmatrix} 1 & 3 & 2 \\ 2 & 5 & 1 \\ 1 & 4 & 5 \end{vmatrix} = 1\begin{vmatrix} 5 & 1 \\ 4 & 5 \end{vmatrix} - 3\begin{vmatrix} 2 & 1 \\ 1 & 5 \end{vmatrix} + 2\begin{vmatrix} 2 & 5 \\ 1 & 4 \end{vmatrix}$$

$$= 1\,(25-4) - 3\,(10-1) + 2\,(8-5) = 21 - 27 + 6 = 0$$

Case IV: Deleting Ist column we get,

$$|A| = \begin{vmatrix} 2 & 3 & 2 \\ 3 & 5 & 1 \\ 3 & 4 & 5 \end{vmatrix} = 2\begin{vmatrix} 5 & 1 \\ 4 & 5 \end{vmatrix} - 3\begin{vmatrix} 3 & 1 \\ 3 & 5 \end{vmatrix} + 2\begin{vmatrix} 3 & 5 \\ 3 & 4 \end{vmatrix}$$

$= 2\,(25-4) - 3\,(15-3) + 2\,(12-15) = 42 - 36 - 6 = 0$

As all minors of order 3 are zero, the rank of the matrix cannot be 3. Now we shall take any minor of order 2

$\begin{vmatrix} 1 & 2 \\ 2 & 3 \end{vmatrix} = 3 - 4 = -1 \neq 0.$ Here, we see that at least one minor of order 2 is non-zero and every minor of order 3 is zero. Therefore, the rank of the matrix is 2, i.e., $\rho(A) = 2$.

Q14. If $\vec{a} = (1, 3, 5)$ and $\vec{b} = (2, 5, 3)$, then find the angle θ between $\vec{a}$ and $\vec{b}$.

Ans. We know that

$$\cos\theta = \frac{\vec{a}.\vec{b}}{|\vec{a}||\vec{b}|} = \frac{(1\times2+3\times5+5\times3)}{\sqrt{(1)^2+(3)^2+(5)^2}\sqrt{(2)^2+(5)^2+(3)^2}}$$

$$= \frac{2+15+15}{\sqrt{1+9+25}\sqrt{4+25+9}} = \frac{32}{\sqrt{35}\sqrt{38}} = \frac{32}{\sqrt{1330}} = \frac{32}{36.469}$$

$\Rightarrow \quad \cos\theta = 0.88 \quad \Rightarrow \quad \boxed{\theta = \cos^{-1}(0.88)}$

Q15. If $\vec{a} = (0,1,2)$ and $\vec{b} = (2,3,5)$, find the distance between these two vectors.

Ans. Distance between $\vec{a}$ and $\vec{b}$ is

$$d = |\vec{a} - \vec{b}| = \sqrt{(0-2)^2 + (1-3)^2 + (2-5)^2} = \sqrt{4+4+9} = \sqrt{17} \text{ units}$$

Q16. Show that the vectors $\vec{a}_1 = \begin{bmatrix} 1 \\ -1 \\ 1 \end{bmatrix}, \vec{a}_2 = \begin{bmatrix} -1 \\ 1 \\ 1 \end{bmatrix}, \vec{a}_3 = \begin{bmatrix} 1 \\ 1 \\ -2 \end{bmatrix}$ are linearly independent.

Ans. The relation $\lambda_1\vec{a}_1 + \lambda_2\vec{a}_2 + \lambda_3\vec{a}_3 = 0$ gives rise to the following three equations

$$\lambda_1 - \lambda_2 + \lambda_3 = 0 \qquad \text{...(i)}$$

$$-\lambda_1 + \lambda_2 + \lambda_3 = 0 \qquad \text{...(ii)}$$

$$\lambda_1 + \lambda_2 - 2\lambda_3 = 0 \qquad \text{...(iii)}$$

Adding Eq (i) and Eq (ii), we get

$2\lambda_3 = 0$

$\Rightarrow \quad \lambda_3 = 0$

Putting the value of λ_3 in Eq. (ii) and (iii) we get

$$-\lambda_1 + \lambda_2 = 0 \qquad ...(iv)$$

and

$$\lambda_1 + \lambda_2 = 0 \qquad ...(v)$$

Adding Eqs. (iv) and (v), we get

$$2\lambda_2 = 0 \Rightarrow \lambda_2 = 0$$

Now putting the values of λ_2 and λ_3 in Eq. (i), we get

$$\lambda_1 = 0$$

Hence, $\lambda_1 = \lambda_2 = \lambda_3 = 0$

Hence, the given vectors $\vec{a}_1$, $\vec{a}_2$ and $\vec{a}_3$ are linearly independent.

Q17. Show that the set of vectors $\vec{a}_1 = \begin{vmatrix} 1 \\ 2 \\ 0 \end{vmatrix}, \vec{a}_2 = \begin{vmatrix} 2 \\ 0 \\ 2 \end{vmatrix}, \vec{a}_3 = \begin{vmatrix} 0 \\ 2 \\ 3 \end{vmatrix}$ form a basis for E^3. **[Dec-2015, Q.No.-6(b)]**

Ans. Let $\vec{b} = \begin{bmatrix} b_1 \\ b_2 \\ b_3 \end{bmatrix}$ be any given vector in E^3.

From $\vec{b} = \lambda_1 \vec{a}_1 + \lambda_2 \vec{a}_2 + \lambda_3 \vec{a}_3$, we get the following equations

$$b_1 = \lambda_1 + 2\lambda_2 \qquad ...(i)$$

$$b_2 = 2\lambda_1 + 2\lambda_3 \qquad ...(ii)$$

$$b_3 = 2\lambda_2 + 3\lambda_3 \qquad ...(iii)$$

Eq. (i) × 2 – Eq. (ii), we get

$$\begin{array}{r} 2\lambda_1 + 4\lambda_2 = 2b_1 \\ \underline{_{-}2\lambda_1 \,{}_{\pm}\, 2\lambda_3 = {}_{-}b_2} \\ 4\lambda_2 - 2\lambda_3 = 2b_1 - b_2 \end{array} \qquad ...(iv)$$

Eq. (iii) × 2 – Eq. (iv), we get

$$\begin{array}{r} 4\lambda_2 + 6\lambda_3 = 2b_3 \\ \underline{{}_{-}4\lambda_2 \,{}_{+}^{-}\, 2\lambda_3 = {}_{-}2b_1 \,{}_{+}^{-}\, b_2} \\ 8\lambda_3 = 2b_3 - 2b_1 + b_2 \end{array}$$

$$\Rightarrow \lambda_3 = \frac{1}{8}\left[2b_3 - 2b_1 + b_2\right]$$

Putting the value of λ_3 in Eq. (ii), we get

$$\lambda_1 = \frac{1}{8}\left[2b_1 + 3b_2 - 2b_3\right]$$

Now putting the value of λ_1 in Eq. (i), we get

$$\lambda_2 = \frac{1}{16}[6b_1 - 3b_2 + 2b_3]$$

Hence, we have

$$\lambda_1 = \frac{1}{8}[2b_1 + 3b_2 - 2b_3]$$

$$\lambda_2 = \frac{1}{16}[6b_1 - 3b_2 + 2b_3]$$

and $\lambda_3 = \frac{1}{8}[2b_3 - 2b_1 + b_2]$

This shows that the set of vectors $\vec{a}_1, \vec{a}_2, \vec{a}_3$ span E^3 since any vector $\vec{b}$ is expressible as a linear combination of $\vec{a}_1, \vec{a}_2$, and $\vec{a}_3$.

Now the relation $\lambda_1 \vec{a}_1 + \lambda_2 \vec{a}_2 + \lambda_3 \vec{a}_3 = 0$ gives rise to the following three equations

$$\lambda_1 + 2\lambda_2 = 0 \quad \text{...(A)}$$

$$2\lambda_1 + 2\lambda_3 = 0$$

or $\lambda_1 + \lambda_3 = 0$ ...(B)

and $2\lambda_2 + 3\lambda_3 = 0$ ...(C)

Eq. (A) – Eq. (B), we get

$$\begin{array}{r} \lambda_1 + 2\lambda_2 = 0 \\ \underset{-}{}\lambda_1 \underset{-}{+} \lambda_3 = 0 \\ \hline 2\lambda_2 - \lambda_3 = 0 \end{array} \quad \text{...(D)}$$

Now Eq. (C) – Eq. (D), we get

$$\begin{array}{r} 2\lambda_2 + 3\lambda_3 = 0 \\ \underset{-}{}2\lambda_2 \underset{+}{-} \lambda_3 = 0 \\ \hline 4\lambda_3 = 0 \end{array}$$

$\Rightarrow$ $\lambda_3 - 0$

Putting the value of λ_3 in Eq. (B) and Eq. (C), we get

$\lambda_1 = 0$ and $\lambda_2 = 0$

$\Rightarrow$ $\lambda_1 = \lambda_2 = \lambda_3 = 0$

Hence, the set $\vec{a}_1, \vec{a}_2, \vec{a}_3$ is linearly independent.

Hence, vectors $\vec{a}_1, \vec{a}_2, \vec{a}_3$ form a basis for E^3.

Q18. Show that the collection S_3 of all vectors $\begin{bmatrix} x_1 \\ 0 \\ x_3 \end{bmatrix}$ is a sub space of E^3.

Ans. Let $a_1 = \begin{bmatrix} x_1^1 \\ 0 \\ x_3^1 \end{bmatrix}$ and $a_2 = \begin{bmatrix} x_1^2 \\ 0 \\ x_3^2 \end{bmatrix}$ be any two vectors in S_3.

Then $a_1 + a_2 = \begin{bmatrix} x_1^1 + x_1^2 \\ 0 \\ x_3^1 + x_3^2 \end{bmatrix}$ which is of the form $\begin{bmatrix} y_1 \\ 0 \\ y_3 \end{bmatrix}$ be any two vectors in S_3.

Again $\lambda a = \begin{bmatrix} \lambda x_1 \\ 0 \\ \lambda x_3 \end{bmatrix}$ which is of the form $\begin{bmatrix} x_1 \\ 0 \\ x_3 \end{bmatrix}$ and therefore in S_3.

Therefore the collection of vectors in S_3 is closed under addition and scalar multiplication and hence a sub space.

Q19. If the n × n matrices A and B are non-singular than A + B is non-singular. Is it true? Justify your answer.

Ans. No, it is not true.

Let $A = \begin{bmatrix} 1 & 2 \\ 3 & 2 \end{bmatrix}$ and $B = \begin{bmatrix} 2 & 1 \\ 0 & 1 \end{bmatrix}$ are 2 × 2 matrices.

Now $|A| = 2 - 6 = -4 \neq 0$

and $|B| = 2 - 0 = 2 \neq 0$

Hence, A and B are non-singular matrices.

Now $A + B = \begin{bmatrix} 1+2 & 2+1 \\ 3+0 & 2+1 \end{bmatrix} = \begin{bmatrix} 3 & 3 \\ 3 & 3 \end{bmatrix}$

$\Rightarrow \quad |A + B| = 9 - 9 = 0$

Thus, A + B is singular.

Q20. For what values of k are the following vectors linearly independent?

$$\begin{bmatrix} \mathbf{1} \\ \mathbf{2} \\ \mathbf{1} \end{bmatrix}, \begin{bmatrix} \mathbf{1} \\ \mathbf{k} \\ \mathbf{1} \end{bmatrix}, \begin{bmatrix} \mathbf{k} \\ \mathbf{0} \\ \mathbf{1} \end{bmatrix}$$

[Dec-2014, Q.No.-7(a)]

Ans. Let $\vec{a}_1 = \begin{bmatrix} 1 \\ 2 \\ 1 \end{bmatrix}$, $\vec{a}_2 = \begin{bmatrix} 1 \\ k \\ 1 \end{bmatrix}$, $\vec{a}_3 = \begin{bmatrix} k \\ 0 \\ 1 \end{bmatrix}$

The relation $\lambda_1 \vec{a}_1 + \lambda_2 \vec{a}_2 + \lambda_3 \vec{a}_3 = 0$ gives rise to the following three equations:

$\lambda_1 + 2\lambda_2 + \lambda_3 = 0$ ...(i)

$\lambda_1 + k\lambda_2 + \lambda_3 = 0$ ...(ii)

$$k\lambda_1 + \lambda_3 = 0 \qquad \text{...(iii)}$$

Given vectors are linearly independent, therefore

$\lambda_1 = \lambda_2 = \lambda_3 = 0$

Now, subtracting Eq. (ii) from Eq. (i), we have

$\lambda_2(2-k) = 0$

$\Rightarrow \quad \lambda_2 = 0, \ \ 2-k=0 \Rightarrow k=2$

Now, subtracting Eq. (iii) from Eq. (ii), we have

$\lambda_1(1-k) + k\,\lambda_2 = 0$

$\Rightarrow \quad k = 1 \quad (\text{if } \lambda_2 = 0)$

and $k = 0 \quad (\text{if } \lambda_1 = 0)$

Now, subtracting Eq. (iii) from Eq. (i), we have

$\lambda_1(1-k) + 2\,\lambda_2 = 0$

$\Rightarrow \quad \lambda_1(1-k) = 0$

$\Rightarrow \quad k = 1, \quad \lambda_1 = 0$

Hence, k = 0, 1, 2, ……

Here, k can take any value for which given vectors are linearly independent. Hence,

$k \in \mathbf{R}$

The main aim of GPH book is to provide knowledge as well as good marks in exam.

⌑ ⌑

2 Inequalities and Convex Sets

An Overview

An inequality is a relation that holds between two values when they are different. Any monotonically increasing function may be applied to both sides of an inequality (provided they are in the domain of that function) and it will still hold. Applying a monotonically decreasing function to both sides of an inequality means the opposite inequality now holds.

A convex set is the region such that, for every pair of points within the region, every point on the straight-line segment that joins the pair of points is also within the region. The boundary of a convex set is always a convex curve. The intersection of all convex sets containing a given subset A of Euclidean space is called the convex hull of A. It is the smallest convex set containing A.

2.1 INEQUALITIES

Most of inequalities are of the form

$ax + by \leq c$ or $ax + by \geq c$

In general we can say that a line

$ax + by = c$

divides the XY plane into three regions namely

(1) the set of points (x, y) such that

$ax + by = c,$

that is the line itself;

(2) the set of points (x, y) such that

$ax + by < c,$

i.e., one of the the half planes bounded by the line;

(3) the set of points (x, y) such that

$ax + by > c,$

the other half plane bounded by the line.

2.2 CONVEX SET

A set S is said to be convex if for any two points x_1, x_2 in the set, the line segment joining these points is also in the set. In other words, a set S is said to be convex if for any elements $x_1, x_2 \in S$,

$$\lambda x_2 + (1-\lambda)x_1 \in S \quad \text{for} \quad 0 \leq \lambda \leq 1$$

2.3 EXTREME POINTS

Let S be a convex set. A point $x \in S$ is an extreme point of the convex set S if and only if there do not exist points $x_1, x_2\ (x_1 \neq x_2)$ in the set S such that

$$x = (1-\lambda)x_1 + \lambda x_2 \qquad \text{for} \qquad 0 < \lambda < 1$$

2.4 HYPER PLANE

A hyper plane in E^n is defined to be a set S of points

$$S = \{x \in E^n : c_1x_1 + c_2x_2 + \ldots + c_nx_n = d\}$$

i.e., $S = \{x \in E^n : cx = d\}$

where $c = [c_1, c_2, \ldots, c_n]$ and $x = \begin{bmatrix} x_1 \\ x_2 \\ \vdots \\ x_n \end{bmatrix}$

A hyper plane cx = d in E^n divides E^n into three mutually exclusive and exhaustive regions. These are denoted by the sets

$S_1 = \{x : cx < d\}$

$S_2 = \{x : cx = d\}$

$S_3 = \{x : cx > d\}$

The sets S_1 and S_3 are called **open half spaces**. The sets

$$S_4 = \{x | cx \le d\} \text{ and } S_5 = \{x | cx \ge d\}$$

are called closed half spaces.

Note that $S_4 \cap S_5 = S_2$ which is the hyper-plane cx = d.

2.5 CONVEX COMBINATION

Let $x_1, x_2, ..., x_m$ be a finite number of points in a Euclidean space E^n. A convex combination of points $x_1, x_2, ..., x_m$ is defined as a point

$$x = \sum_{i=1}^{m} \mu_i x_i, \ \mu_i \ge 0, \ i = 1, 2, ..., m$$

where $x = \sum_{i=1}^{m} \mu_i = 1$.

2.6 CONVEX HULL

Suppose A is a set, which is not convex. Then the smallest convex set which contains A is called the Convex Hull of A. That is, the Convex Hull of a set A is the intersection of all Convex sets which contain A.

For example, the Convex Hull of the set

$$A = \{(x, y) : x^2 + y^2 = 1\}$$

is the set

$$S = \{(x, y) : x^2 + y^2 \le 1\}$$

Note: The convex hull of $x_1, x_2, ..., x_m$ is the set

$$S = \left\{ x \in E^n : x = \sum_{i=1}^{m} \mu_i x_i, \text{ all } \mu_i \ge 0, \sum_{i=1}^{m} \mu_i = 1 \right\}$$

The Convex Hull of the finite number of points is called **Convex Polyhedron** spanned by these points. In Fig. 2.1, we have a Convex Polyhedron spanned by five points.

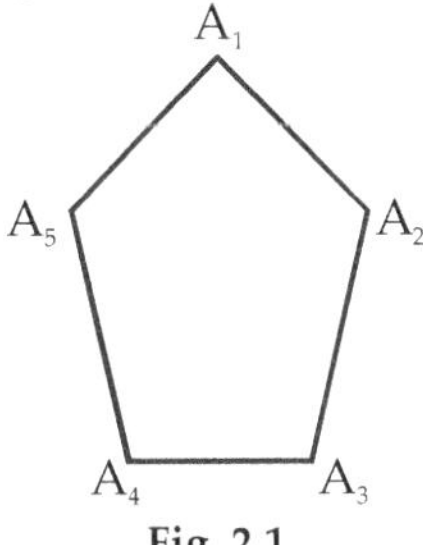

Fig. 2.1

If we consider the convex hull of three points in a plane, it is a triangle.

Theorems

Theorem 1: If S_1 and S_2 are two Convex sets, then their intersection is also a Convex set.

Proof: Suppose $S_3 = S_1 \cap S_2$

Let x_1, x_2 be any two points in S_3. Then $x_1, x_2 \in S_1$ and $x_1, x_2 \in S_2$

Since S_1 and S_2 are Convex, therefore, $\lambda x_2 + (1-\lambda) x_1 \in S_1$ for $0 \le \lambda \le 1$

and

$\lambda x_2 + (1-\lambda) x_1 \in S_2$ for $0 \le \lambda \le 1$

Hence, $\lambda x_2 + (1-\lambda) x_1 \in S_1 \cap S_2$ for $0 \le \lambda \le 1$

This is $\lambda x_2 + (1-\lambda) x_1 \in S_3$, $0 \le \lambda \le 1$

Thus, S_3 is a convex set.

Theorem 2: A hyperplane is a convex set.

Proof: Here, we need to prove that the collection

$$S = \{x \in E^n : cx = d\}$$

is a convex set.

If x_1, x_2 are any two points on the hyper plane cx = d, then $cx_1 = d$ and $cx_2 = d$.

The hyperplane will be convex if the point

$$x = \lambda x_2 + (1-\lambda)x_1 \text{ for } 0 \le \lambda \le 1$$

lies on the hyperplane. Indeed, we have

$$cx = c\left[\lambda x_2 + (1-\lambda) x_1\right] = \lambda cx_2 + (1-\lambda) cx_1 = \lambda d + (1-\lambda)d = d$$

$$\Rightarrow \quad cx = d$$

This shows that the hyperplane is a convex set, which proves the theorem.

Theorem 3: A closed half space is a convex set.

Proof: Consider the closed half space

$$S_4 = \{x : cx \le d\}$$

Suppose $x_1, x_2 \in S_4$, then $cx_1 \le d$, $cx_2 \le d$

Consider $x = \lambda x_2 + (1-\lambda) x_1$, $0 \le \lambda \le 1$

Now $cx = \lambda cx_2 + (1-\lambda) cx_1 \le \lambda d + (1-\lambda)d = d$

i.e., $cx \le d$

This shows that

$$x = \lambda x_2 + (1-\lambda)x_1 \in S \text{ for } 0 \le \lambda \le 1$$

Hence, S is a convex set.

Theorem 4: The set of all convex combinations of a finite number of points, $x_1, x_2, ..., x_m$ in E^n is a convex set that is, the set

$$S = \left\{ x \middle| x = \sum_{i=1}^{m} \mu_i x_i,\ \mu_i \geq 0,\ \sum_{i=1}^{m} \mu_1 = 1 \right\}$$

is convex.

Theorem 5: The convex hull of a finite number of points $x_1, x_2, ..., x_m$ in E^n is the set of all convex combination of $x_1, x_2, ..., x_m$.

Solved Practical Problems

Q1. Draw the graph of the inequality

$2x + 3y \geq 60$

Ans. ***Step I:*** First, we consider a line

$$2x + 3y = 60$$

$$\Rightarrow \quad \frac{2x}{60} + \frac{3y}{60} = 1$$

$$\Rightarrow \quad \frac{x}{30} + \frac{y}{20} = 1$$

Hence, 30 and 20 are the intercepts on the x-axis and y-axis respectively.

Step II: **Region represented by** $2x + 3y \geq 60$:

Point (0, 0) does not satisfy the inequation $2x + 3y \geq 60$. So that region in xy-plane which does not contain the origin is the solution set of this inequation.

Step III: Draw the graph.

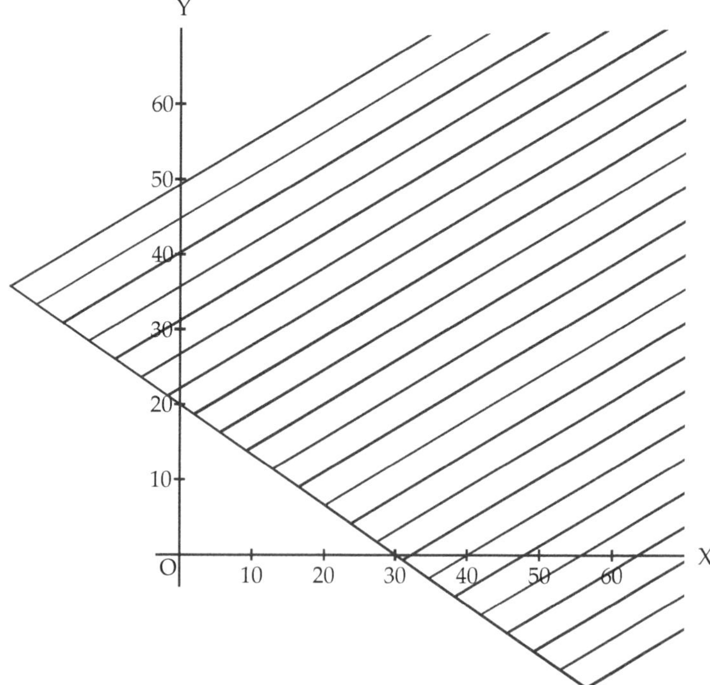

Here, shaded portion represents $2x + 3y \geq 60$.

Q2. Graph the set of points (x, y) satisfying the following three inequalities:

$A = \{(x, y): 3x + y \geq 30\}$

$B = \{(x, y): x \geq 0\}$

and

$C = \{(x, y): y \geq 0\}$

Ans. ***Step I:*** Consider the line

$3x + y = 30$

$\Rightarrow \quad \frac{x}{10} + \frac{y}{30} = 1$

***Step II:* Region represented by** $3x + y \geq 30$ **:** Point (0, 0) does not satisfy the inequation $3x + y \geq 30$. So that region in xy-plane which does not contain the origin is the solution set of this inequation.

Region represented by $x \geq 0, y \geq 0$ **:** Clearly, the region represented by $x \geq 0$ and $y \geq 0$ is the first quadrant in xy-plane.

Step III: Draw the graph.

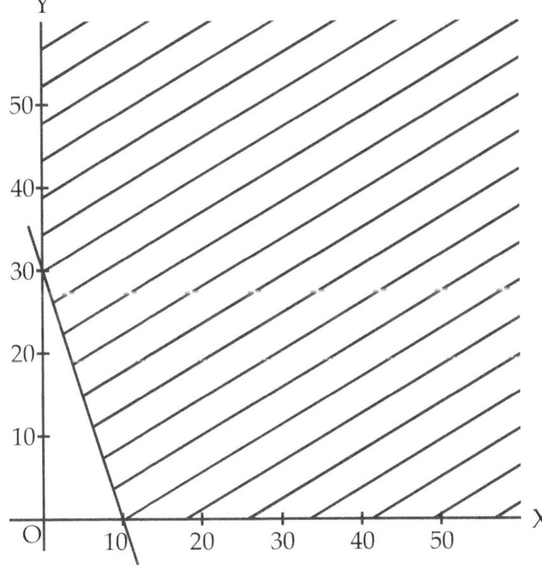

Hence, shaded region represents $3x + y \geq 30$.

Q3. Draw the graph of the inequalities

$3x + 5y \leq 15$

$x, y \geq 0$

Ans. ***Step I:*** Consider the line

$3x + 5y = 15$

$\Rightarrow \quad \frac{x}{5}+\frac{y}{3}=1$

Hence, 5 and 3 are the intercepts of x and y axis respectively.

***Step II:* Region represented by 3x + 5y ≤ 15:** Point (0, 0) satisfies the inequation $3x+5y \le 15$. So, the region containing the origin represents the solution set of this inequation.

Region represented by $x \ge 0$ **and** $y \ge 0$**:** Since, every point in the first quadrant satisfies these inequations then the region represented by $x \ge 0$ and $y \ge 0$ is the first quadrant in xy-plane.

Step III: Draw the graph.

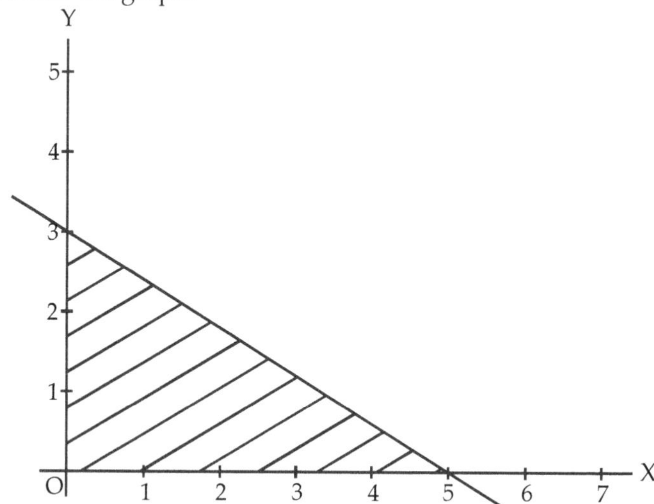

Hence, shaded region represents the given inequality.

Q4. Graph the set of points, which satisfy the inequalities

$\mathbf{3x+2y \le 18}$

$\mathbf{x+2y \le 10}$

$\mathbf{x \ge 0}$

$\mathbf{y \ge 0}$

Ans. Consider,

$3x+2y=18$

$\Rightarrow \quad \frac{x}{6}+\frac{y}{9}=1$

Now, consider

$x+2y=10$

$\Rightarrow \quad \frac{x}{10}+\frac{y}{5}=1$

Since $x, y \ge 0$

Therefore, the set of points will be in the first quadrant. (0, 0) satisfies both the inequalities, $3x + 2y \le 18$ and $x + 2y \le 10$.

Therefore, we can now draw the graph conveniently.

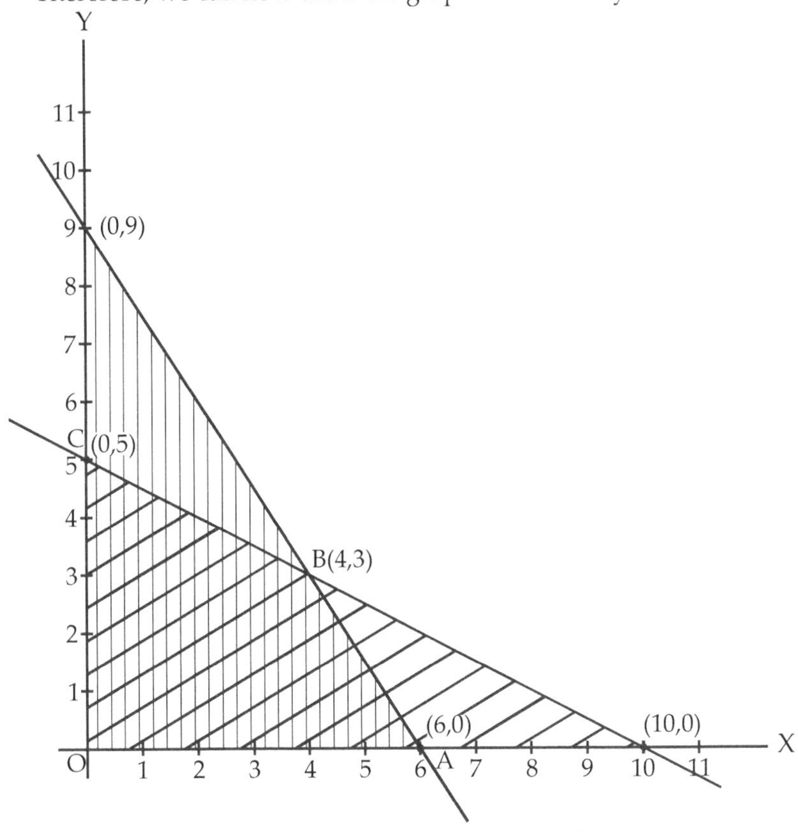

Here, shaded region OABC represents the solution set.

Q5. Graph the set of points, which satisfy the inequalities $x \ge 1$ and $3x + 4y \le 12$

Ans. We can draw the line x = 1, which is a vertical line through the point (1, 0). The line

$$3x + 4y = 12$$

is the line joining the points (4, 0) and (0, 3). The set

$$A = \{(x, y) | (x \ge 1)\}$$

is shaded with horizontal lines and the set

$$B = \{(x, y) | 3x + 4y \le 12\}$$

is the set with vertical shading. Now the set of points, which satisfies both the inequalities, i.e. the set $A \cap B$ of points, is the crosshatched region shown in the following figure:

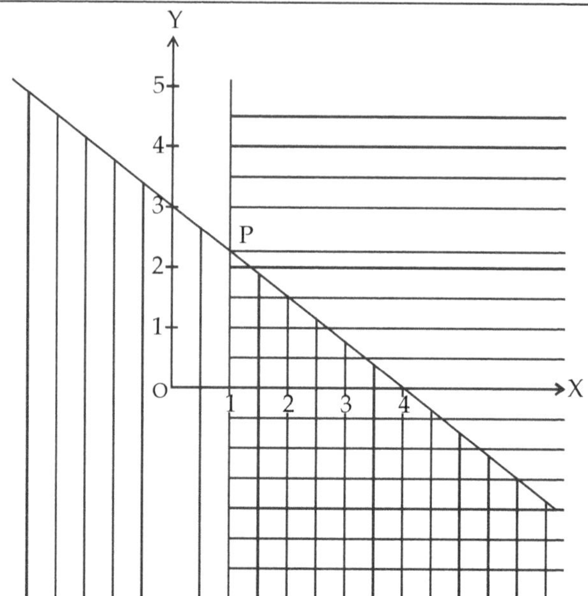

The corner point P is the intersection of lines $x = 1$ and $3x + 4y = 12$. This point is P (1, 9/4).

Q6. Graph the following inequalities

$$\mathbf{x + y \geq 4}$$

$$\mathbf{6x - 12y \geq 12}$$

$$\mathbf{5x + 8y \leq 40}$$

$$\mathbf{x \geq 0}$$

$$\mathbf{y \geq 0}$$

Ans. Consider

$$x + y = 4$$

$$\Rightarrow \quad \frac{x}{4} + \frac{y}{4} = 1$$

Now, $6x - 12y = 12$

$$\Rightarrow \frac{x}{2} - \frac{y}{1} = 1 \text{ or } \frac{x}{2} + \left(\frac{y}{-1}\right) = 1$$

and $5x + 8y = 40$

$$\Rightarrow \quad \frac{x}{8} + \frac{y}{5} = 1$$

Now, we can draw the graph.

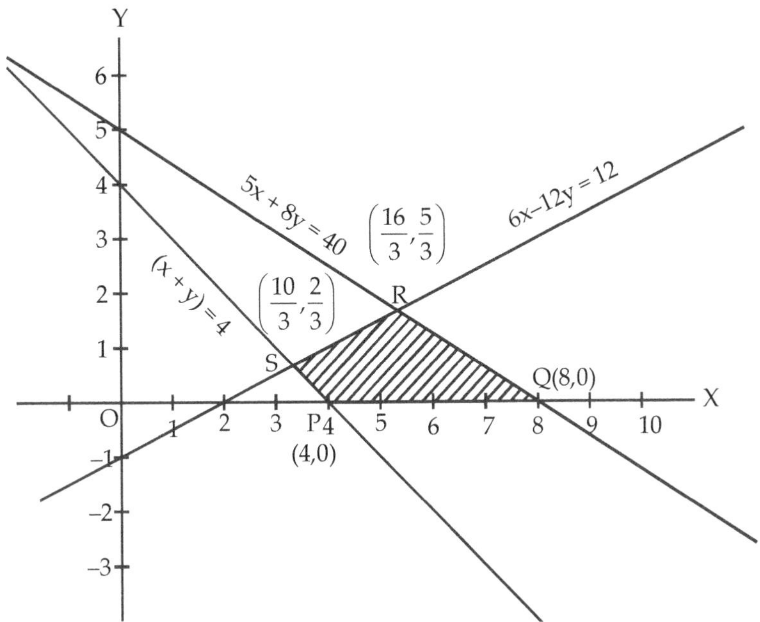

The solution set consists of all the points of the polygon PQRS, which include the points of the boundary as well as the interior region. The vertices of the polygon are

$$P(4,0),\ Q(8,0),\ R\left(\frac{16}{3},\frac{5}{3}\right) \text{ and } S\left(\frac{10}{3},\frac{2}{3}\right).$$

Q7. Graph the set and find its corner points.

$\mathbf{x - y \leq 2}$

$\mathbf{x + 2y \leq 2}$

$\mathbf{2x + y \geq -2}$

Ans. Consider,

$x - y = 2$

$\Rightarrow \quad \frac{x}{2} + \frac{y}{(-2)} = 1$

Now

$x + 2\,y = 2$

$\Rightarrow \quad \frac{x}{2} + \frac{y}{1} = 1$

and $2\,x + y = -2$

$\Rightarrow \quad \frac{x}{-1} + \frac{y}{(-2)} = 1$

Now, we can draw graph.

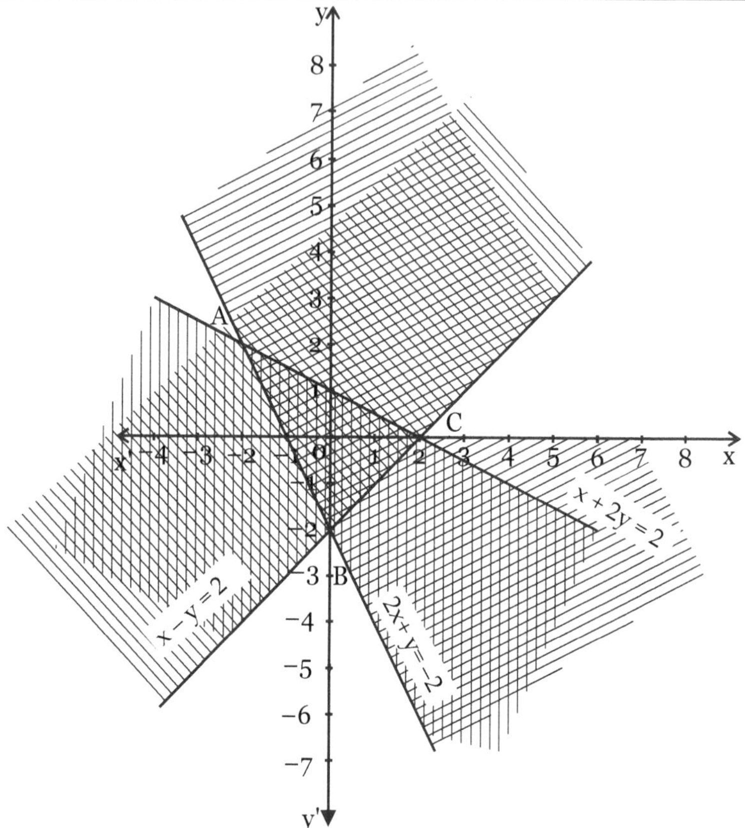

(0, 0) satisfies all the inequalities. Hence, ABC is the solutions set. Corner points are A (–2, 2), B (0, –2) and C (2, 0).

Q8. Show that the set $S = \{(x, y) | 5x^2 + 2y^2 \le 10\}$ is convex.

Ans. Given set is $S = \{(x, y) | 5x^2 + 2y^2 \le 10\}$

Now, suppose $(x_1, y_1) \in S$, $(x_2, y_2) \in S$ are any two points. Then

$$\left.\begin{aligned} & 5x_1^2 + 2y_1^2 \le 10 \\ \text{and } & 5x_2^2 + 2y_2^2 \le 10 \end{aligned}\right\} \quad \text{...(i)}$$

S will be convex if

$$\lambda(x_2, y_2) + (1-\lambda)(x_1, y_1) \in S, \qquad 0 \le \lambda \le 1$$

That is

$$[\lambda x_2 + (1-\lambda)x_1, \lambda y_2 + (1-\lambda)y_1] \in S, \qquad 0 \le \lambda \le 1$$

Consider

$$5[\lambda x_2 + (1-\lambda)x_1]^2 + 2[\lambda y_2 + (1-\lambda)y_1]^2$$

$$=5\left[\lambda^2 x_2^2+(1-\lambda)^2 x_1^2+2\lambda x_2 x_1(1-\lambda)\right]+2\left[\lambda^2 y_2^2+(1-\lambda)^2 y_1^2+2\lambda y_2 y_1(1-\lambda)\right]$$

$$=5\lambda^2 x_2^2+5x_1^2(1-\lambda)^2+10\lambda x_2 x_1(1-\lambda)+2\lambda^2 y_2^2+2y_1^2(1-\lambda)^2+4\lambda y_2 y_1(1-\lambda)$$

$$=\lambda^2\left[5x_2^2+2y_2^2\right]+(1-\lambda)^2\left[5x_1^2+2y_1^2\right]+2\lambda(1-\lambda)(5x_1x_2+2y_1y_2)$$

$$\leq 10\lambda^2+10(1-\lambda)^2+2\lambda(1-\lambda)(5x_1x_2+2y_1y_2)$$

$$\left[\begin{array}{l}\because\ 5x_1^2+2y_1^2\leq 10\\ \text{and } 5x_2^2+2y_2^2\leq 10\end{array}\right]$$

Therefore,

$$5[\lambda x_2+(1-\lambda)x_1]^2+2[\lambda y_2+(1-\lambda)y_1]^2$$

$$\leq 10\lambda^2+10(1-\lambda)^2+2\lambda(1-\lambda)(5x_1x_2+2y_1y_2) \quad \text{...(ii)}$$

Consider

$$5(x_1-x_2)^2+2(y_1-y_2)^2\geq 0$$

$$\Rightarrow (5x_1^2+2y_1^2)+(5x_2^2+2y_2^2)-2(5x_1x_2+2y_1y_2)\geq 0$$

$$\Rightarrow 2(5x_1x_2+2y_1y_2)\leq(5x_1^2+2y_1^2)+(5x_2^2+2y_2^2)\leq 10+10$$

$$\left[\begin{array}{l}\because\ 5x_1^2+2y_1^2\leq 10\\ \text{and } 5x_2^2+2y_2^2\leq 10\end{array}\right]$$

Thus, $2(5x_1x_2+2y_1y_2)\leq 20$

$$\Rightarrow 5x_1x_2+2y_1y_2\leq 10 \quad \text{...(iii)}$$

From Eqs. (ii) and Eq. (iii), we get

$$5[\lambda x_2+(1-\lambda)x_1]^2+2[\lambda y_2+(1-\lambda)y_1]^2\leq 10\lambda^2+10(1-\lambda)^2+20\lambda(1-\lambda)$$

$$=10[\lambda+(1-\lambda)]^2=10$$

Hence,

$$5[\lambda x_2+(1-\lambda)x_1]^2+2[\lambda y_2+(1-\lambda)y_1]^2\leq 10$$

This shows that

$$[\lambda x_2+(1-\lambda)x_1,\ \lambda y_2+(1-\lambda)y_1]\in S$$

Therefore, S is convex set.

Q9. Test the following set for convexity.

$$\mathbf{S=\{(x,y):\ x+y\leq 8\ \text{or}\ 2x+y\leq 10,\ x\geq 0,\ y\geq 0\}}$$

Ans. Suppose, $(x_1, y_1)\in S$, $(x_2, y_2)\in S$

$$\left.\begin{array}{ll}\Rightarrow & x_1+y_1\leq 8\\ \text{and} & x_2+y_2\leq 8\end{array}\right\} \quad \text{...(i)}$$

S will be convex if

$$\lambda(x_2,y_2)+(1-\lambda)(x_1,y_1)\in S, \qquad 0\leq\lambda\leq 1$$

That is

$$\left[\lambda x_2 + (1-\lambda)x_1,\ \lambda y_2 + (1-\lambda)y_1\right] \in S, \qquad 0 \le \lambda \le 1$$

Consider

$$\lambda x_2 + (1-\lambda)x_1 + \lambda y_2 + (1-\lambda)y_1$$

$$= \lambda(x_2 + y_2) + (1-\lambda)(x_1 + y_1) \le 8\lambda + 8(1-\lambda) = 8$$

[using Eq. (i)]

Similarly,

$$\lambda(2x_2 + y_2) + (1-\lambda)(2x_1 + y_1) \le 10\lambda + (1-\lambda)10 = 10$$

Hence, S is convex set.

Q10. Prove algebraically that the set

$$\mathbf{S = \{(x_1, x_2)/2x_1^2 + x_2^2 \le 4\}}$$

is a convex set.

Ans. Let $(x_3, x_4) \in S$, $(x_5, x_6) \in S$ are any two points. Then

$$\left.\begin{aligned} 2x_3^2 + x_4^2 &\le 4 \\ \text{and } 2x_5^2 + x_6^2 &\le 4 \end{aligned}\right\} \qquad \text{...(i)}$$

S will be convex if

$$\lambda(x_5, x_6) + (1-\lambda)(x_3, x_4) \in S, \qquad 0 \le \lambda \le 1$$

$$\Rightarrow \quad \left[\lambda x_5 + (1-\lambda)x_3,\ \lambda x_6 + (1-\lambda)x_4\right] \in S, \ 0 \le \lambda \le 1$$

Now, consider

$$2\left[\lambda x_5 + (1-\lambda)x_3\right]^2 + \left[\lambda x_6 + (1-\lambda)x_4\right]^2$$

$$= 2\left[\lambda^2 x_5^2 + (1-\lambda)^2 x_3^2 + 2x_5x_3\lambda(1-\lambda)\right] + \left[\lambda^2 x_6^2 + (1-\lambda)^2 x_4^2 + 2x_6x_4\lambda(1-\lambda)\right]$$

$$= 2\lambda^2 x_5^2 + 2(1-\lambda)^2 x_3^2 + 4x_5x_3\lambda(1-\lambda) + \lambda^2 x_6^2 + (1-\lambda)^2 x_4^2 + 2x_6x_4\lambda(1-\lambda)$$

$$= \lambda^2(2x_5^2 + x_6^2) + (1-\lambda)^2(2x_3^2 + x_4^2) + 2\lambda(1-\lambda)(2x_5x_3 + x_6x_4)$$

$$\le 4\lambda^2 + 4(1-\lambda)^2 + 2\lambda(1-\lambda)(2x_5x_3 + x_6x_4) \qquad \text{[using Eq. (i)]}$$

Therefore,

$$2\left[\lambda x_5 + (1-\lambda)x_3\right]^2 + \left[\lambda x_6 + (1-\lambda)x_4\right]^2$$

$$\le 4\lambda^2 + 4(1-\lambda)^2 + 2\lambda(1-\lambda)(2x_5x_3 + x_6x_4) \qquad \text{...(ii)}$$

Now, consider

$$2(x_3 - x_5)^2 + (x_4 - x_6)^2 \ge 0$$

$$\Rightarrow \quad 2x_3^2 + 2x_5^2 - 4x_3x_5 + x_4^2 + x_6^2 - 2x_4x_6 \ge 0$$

$$\Rightarrow \quad (2x_3^2 + x_4^2) + (2x_5^2 + x_6^2) - 2(2x_3x_5 + x_4x_6) \ge 0$$

$\Rightarrow \quad 2(2x_3x_5 + x_4x_6) \le (2x_3^2 + x_4^2) + (2x_5^2 + x_6^2) \le 4 + 4$ [using Eq. (i)]

$\Rightarrow \quad 2x_3x_5 + x_4x_6 \le 4$ ...(iii)

From Eq. (ii) and Eq. (iii), we have

$$2[\lambda x_5 + (1-\lambda)x_3]^2 + [\lambda x_6 + (1-\lambda)x_4]^2 \le 4\lambda^2 + 4(1-\lambda)^2 + 2\lambda(1-\lambda)4 = 4$$

Hence,

$$2[\lambda x_5 + (1-\lambda)x_3]^2 + [\lambda x_6 + (1-\lambda)x_4]^2 \le 4$$

This shows that

$$[\lambda x_5 + (1-\lambda)x_3,\ \lambda x_6 + (1-\lambda)x_4] \in S$$

Hence, S is convex set.

Q11. Show that the set S $\{(x, y) : xy \le 1,\ x \ge 0,\ y \ge 0\}$ is not Convex.

Ans. In order to show that S is not convex we will take two points in S and show that their convex combination does not belong to S. Clearly $\left(3, \frac{1}{3}\right)$ and $\left(\frac{1}{2}, 2\right)$ belong to S. Consider the combination of these points, i.e.

$$\lambda(3, 1/3) + (1-\lambda)(1/2, 2) \qquad 0 \le \lambda \le 1$$

i.e. $$\left(3\lambda + \frac{1}{2}(1-\lambda), \frac{\lambda}{3} + 2(1-\lambda)\right) \qquad 0 \le \lambda \le 1$$

i.e. $$\left(\frac{1}{2} + \frac{5}{2}\lambda,\ 2 - \frac{5}{3}\lambda\right) \qquad 0 \le \lambda \le 1$$

S will be convex if

$$\left(\frac{1}{2} + \frac{5}{2}\lambda,\ 2 - \frac{5}{3}\lambda\right) \in S \text{ in all } \lambda \qquad 0 \le \lambda \le 1$$

i.e. $$\left(\frac{1}{2} + \frac{5}{2}\lambda\right)\left(2 - \frac{5}{3}\lambda\right) \le 1 \quad \text{for} \quad 0 \le \lambda \le 1$$

i.e. $$1 + 5\lambda - \frac{5}{6}\lambda - \frac{25}{6}\lambda^2 \le 1 \qquad 0 \le \lambda \le 1$$

$$\frac{25}{6}\lambda - \frac{25}{6}\lambda^2 \le 0 \qquad 0 \le \lambda \le 1 \text{......}$$

This inequality should hold for all values of λ such that $0 \le \lambda \le 1$.

However, if we take $\lambda = \frac{1}{2}$, then we get

$$\frac{25}{6}\lambda - \frac{25}{6}\lambda^2 = \frac{25}{12} - \frac{25}{24} = \frac{25}{24} > 0$$

Thus, the inequality is not satisfied for $\lambda = \frac{1}{2}$.

This contradiction shows that S is not convex.

Q12. Suppose that

$x_1 = (0,0),\ x_2 = (2,0),\ x_3 = (1,1).$

Express the following as convex linear combination of the points x_1, x_2, and x_3 :

(i) $\left(1, \frac{1}{2}\right)$ **(ii)** $\left(\frac{1}{2}, \frac{1}{2}\right)$

Ans. (i) $\left(1, \frac{1}{2}\right) = \frac{1}{4}x_1 + \frac{1}{4}x_2 + \frac{1}{2}x_3$

(ii) $\left(\frac{1}{2}, \frac{1}{2}\right) = \frac{1}{2}x_1 + \frac{1}{2}x_3$

Q13. Which of the following sets are convex:

(i) $S_1 = \left\{(x, y) \middle| x^2 + y^2 \geq 4\right\}$

(ii) $S_2 = \left\{(x, y) \middle| x \geq 3, y \leq 5\right\}$

Verify your result by drawing the graph. [June-2016, Q.No.-7(b)]

Ans. (i) Given, $S_1 = \left\{(x, y) \middle| x^2 + y^2 \geq 4\right\}$

Graph of S_1 is as follows:

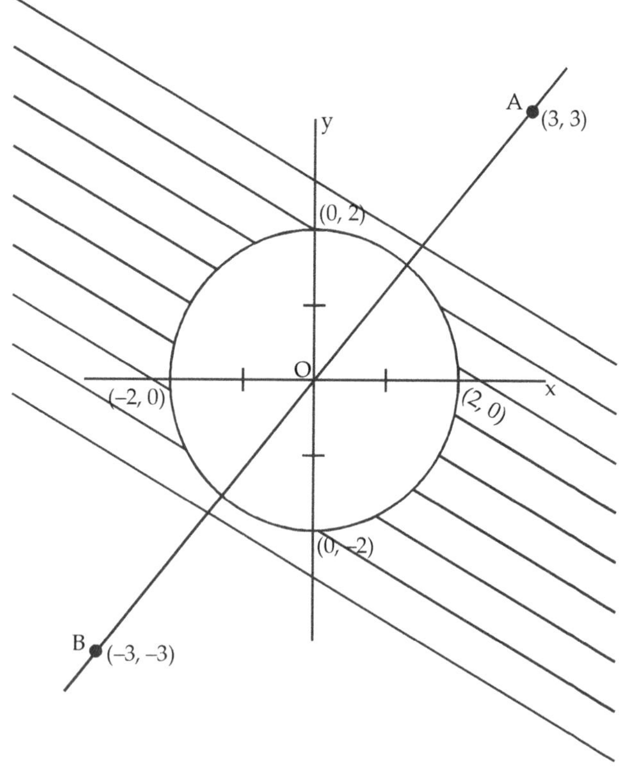

(0, 0) will not satisfy the equation $x^2 + y^2 \geq 4$.

Hence, $S_1 = \{(x, y) | x^2 + y^2 \geq 4\}$ is a circle with its exterior as shown in above figure.

Let we take two points A (3, 3) and B (–3, –3).

$(3)^2 + (3)^2 > 4$ and $(-3)^2 + (-3)^2 > 4$

Therefore, both points belong to S_1. Taking $\lambda = \frac{2}{3}$.

Then, we have

$$\frac{2}{3}(-3, -3) + \left(1 - \frac{2}{3}\right)(3, 3) = (-2, -2) + (1, 1) = (-1, -1)$$

But, $(-1)^2 + (-1)^2 \geq 4$ is wrong.

It means, (–1, –1) does not satisfy $x^2 + y^2 \geq 4$.

It mean, $(-1, -1) \notin S_1$. Thus, S_1 is not convex. In other words, in the graph, the line segment joining the points A and B does not lie in feasible (shaded) region completely. Hence, S_1 is not convex.

(ii) Given

$$S_2 = \{(x, y) | x \geq 3, y \leq 5\}$$

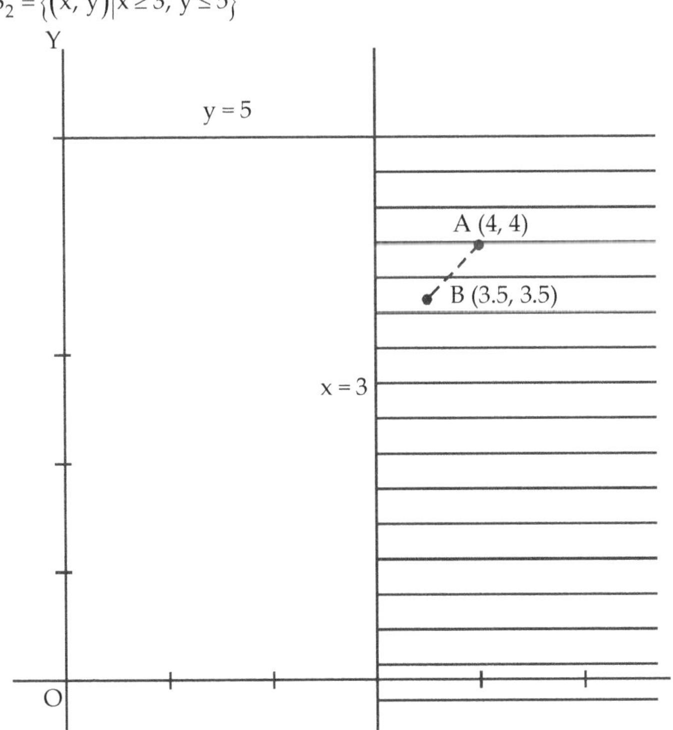

Let A (4, 4) and B (3.5, 4.5) be two points.

Clearly, both points A and B belong to S_2.

Now, let $\lambda = \frac{2}{3}$, then

$$\lambda(3.5, 4.5) + (1-\lambda)(4, 4) = \frac{2}{3}(3.5, 4.5) + \left(1 - \frac{2}{3}\right)(4, 4) = \left(\frac{7}{3}, \frac{9}{3}\right) + \left(\frac{4}{3}, \frac{4}{3}\right)$$

$$= \left(\frac{11}{3}, \frac{13}{3}\right) = (3.66, 4.33) \in S_2$$

Thus, S_2 is convex. In other works, in the graph, shaded region is the feasible region of S_2. The line segment joining the points A and B is in the feasible region, i.e., in the set S_2. Hence, S_2 is convex.

Q14. Without sketching the region, check whether P (0, 0) is in the convex hull of the points A (– 1, – 1), B (1, 0) and C (0, 1). If it is in the region, write P as convex combination of A, B and C.

[June-2014, Q.No.-4(b)]

Ans. The convex combination of the points A (–1, –1), B (1, 0) and C (0, 1) will be a point

$$x = \mu_1(-1, -1) + \mu_2(1, 0) + \mu_3(0, 1)$$

$$= (-\mu_1, -\mu_1) + (\mu_2, 0) + (0, \mu_3)$$

$$= (-\mu_1 + \mu_2, -\mu_1 + \mu_3)$$

Clearly, for all values of μ_1, μ_2 and μ_3, the convex combination will not be (0, 0). Therefore, (0, 0) is not in the set of all convex combination of the points A, B and C. It means, the point P (0, 0) is not in the convex hull of the points A (–1, –1), B (1, 0) and C (0, 1). Best help books for IGNOU students—GPH books.

⌑ ⌑

3 Optimisation in Two Variables

An Overview

Linear programming is the process of taking various linear inequalities relating to some situation, and finding the "best" value obtainable under those conditions. A typical example would be taking the limitations of materials and labor, and then determining the "best" production levels for maximal profits under those conditions.

In "real life", linear programming is part of a very important area of mathematics called "optimisation techniques". This field of study is used every day in the organisation and allocation of resources. These "real life" systems can have dozens or hundreds of variables, or more. Here, we will work with the simple two-variable linear case.

3.1 DEFINITIONS OF LINEAR PROGRAMMING

Definitions of linear programming are as follows:

(1) "Linear programming is the analysis of problems in which a linear function of a number of variables is to be maximised (or minimised) when these variables are subject to a number of constraints in the form of linear inequalities." **– R. Dorfman, P. Samuelson and R. Solow**

(2) "Linear programming is the simpler variety of programming problem in which the objective function as well as the constraint inequalities are all linear." **– Alpha C. Chiang**

(3) "Linear programming is a technique for the formulation and analysis of constrained optimisation problems in which the objective function is a linear function, and is to be maximised or minimises subject to a number of linear inequality constraints." **– David W. Pearce**

3.2 BASIC CONCEPTS OF LINEAR PROGRAMMING

Basic concepts of LPP are as follows:

(1) Objective Function: If $c_1, c_2, ..., c_n$ are constants and $x_1, x_2, ..., x_n$ are variables, then the linear function $Z = c_1x_1 + c_2x_2 + ... + c_nx_n$ which is to be maximised or minimised is called the objective function.

(2) Constraints: The inequations or equations in the variables of a LPP (Linear Programming Problem), which describe the conditions under which the optimisation (maximisation or minimisation) is to be accomplished, are called constraints.

In the constraints given in the general form of a LPP there may be any one of the three signs $\leq, =, \geq$.

(3) Non-negativity Restrictions: The decision variables must not assume negative values, which represent impossible situation. Non-negativity restrictions are those, which assume that there cannot be negative values of the variables involved in the study of linear programming problem. Thus, all variables must take on values equal to or greater than zero.

(4) Feasible Region: The region, which is common to all the constraints of a linear programming problem, is called the feasible region of the given problem. In other words, the graph of the system of linear inequations, comprising of constraints of the problem is the feasible region of the given problem.

(5) Feasible Solution: A feasible solution to a linear programming problem is the set of values of the variables, which satisfies the set of constraints and non-negative restrictions of the problem.

(6) Optimum Solution: A feasible solution that satisfies both the conditions of the problem and also optimise the objective function of the problem is called optimum solution. The optimal solution is the best of the feasible solutions.

3.3 APPLICATIONS OF LINEAR PROGRAMMING

Linear programming is a technique of decision-making mostly used in business, industry and in various other fields. Some of the applications of linear programming are as follows:

(1) Diet Problem: To determine the minimum requirement of nutrients subject to availability of foods and their prices, LPP is used.

(2) Manufacturing Problems: LPP is used to find the number of items of each type that should be manufactured to maximise the profit subject to production restrictions imposed by limitations on the use of machinery and labour.

(3) Transportation Problem: LPP is used to find the least costly way of transporting shipments from the warehouses to customers.

(4) Blending Problems: LPP is used to determine the optimum amount of several constituents to use in producing a set of products while determining the optimum quantity of each product to produce.

(5) Assembling Problems: LPP is used to have the best combination of basic components to produce goods according to certain specifications.

(6) Production Problems: LPP is used to decide the production schedule to satisfy demand and minimise cost in face of fluctuating rates and storage expenses.

(7) Job Assigning Problems: LPP is used to assign job to workers for maximum effectiveness and optimum results subject to restrictions of wages and other costs.

(8) Trim-Loss Problems: LPP is used to determine the best way to obtain a variety of smaller rolls of paper from a standard width of roll that is kept in stock and, at the same time, minimise wastage.

3.4 MATHEMATICAL FORMULATION OF LINEAR PROGRAMMING PROBLEMS

The following algorithm is useful in the formulation of linear programming problems.

Step I: In every LPP, certain decisions are to be made. These decisions are represented by decision variables. These decision variables are those quantities whose values are to be determined. Identify the variables and denote them by $x_1, x_2, x_3, \ldots$

Step II: Identify the objective function and express it as a linear function of the variables introduced in step I.

Step III: In a LPP, the objective function may be in the form of maximising profits or minimising costs. Therefore, after expressing the objective function as a linear function of the decision variables, we must find the type of optimisation, i.e., maximisation or minimisation. Identify the type of the objective function.

Step IV: Identify the set of constraints, stated in terms of decision variables and express them as linear inequations or equations as the case may be.

3.5 GRAPHICAL METHOD FOR SOLVING LINEAR PROGRAMMING PROBLEMS

The graphical method for the solution of the linear programming problem is used when the objective function is a linear function of two variables only. In this method, the following steps are involved:

Step I: Consider the constraints as equalities.

Step II: Sketch these linear constraint equations as straight lines. For example, to draw line $2x_1 + 3x_2 = 6$, put $x_1 = 0$ find x_2 and which is 2 here. Therefore, one point on the line will be (0, 2). Again, put $x_2 = 0$ and find x_1 which is 3 here. Another point on the line is (3, 0). Joining these points, we can find the line represented by the equation $2x_1 + 3x_2 = 6$.

Similarly, for all other linear constraint equations sketch the lines.

Step III: Find the feasible region for the values of the variable, which is the region bounded by the lines drawn in Step-II.

To find permissible region for a constraint $2x_1 + 3x_2 \leq 6$, substitute origin (0, 0) in the corresponding inequation. If the region satisfies the inequation (as in this case $0 \leq 6$ is true), then the left side of the line will be the permissible region, where origin lies. If the origin does not satisfy the inequation, then the right side of the line opposite the origin will be the required region. Generally, for greater than or equal to $(\geq)$ constraints, the feasible region will be the area, which lies above or to the right of the constraint line. For less than or equal to $(\leq)$ constraints, this area is graphically below or to the left of the line drawn.

Step IV: Find the common region satisfied by all the constraints (if any) and shade it.

Step V: Locate the corner points of the region, which may be obtained by simultaneously solving the two linear equations whose point of intersection is the required point.

Step VI: Calculate the value of the objective function at each corner point obtained in previous step. The set of values corresponding to the Max. or Min. values of the objective function is the solution of the LPP.

3.6 SOME EXCEPTIONAL CASES IN LINEAR PROGRAMMING

Some exceptional cases in LPP are as follows:

(1) Infeasible Solution (or No solution): Sometimes the system of constraints in a LPP has no common point, which satisfies all the constraints. In such cases, the LPP is said to have no feasible solution or infeasible solution.

(2) Unbounded Solution: A linear programming problem may have unbounded solution which means that it has no limit on the constraints. It simply means that the common feasible region is not bounded in any respect. The primary variables can take any value in the unbounded region. The objective function can be made infinitely large.

(3) Multiple Optimum Solutions: In certain linear programming problems, situation may arise when there is the possibility of more than one optimum solution.

Solved Practical Problems

Q1. Product–mix Problem:

A person manufactures two types of lamps, say A and B. Both lamps pass through two technicians: first a cutter, and second a finisher. Lamp A requires 2 hours of the cutter's time and 1 hour of the finisher's time. Lamp B requires 1 hour of the cutter's time and 2 hours of the finisher's time. The cutter has 104 hours and the finisher has 76 hours of available time each month. The profit on one lamp A is ₹6.00, and on one lamp B is ₹11.00. Assuming that she can sell all that she produces, formulate the problem of maximisation of profit as an LPP.

Ans. We can tabulate the given LPP as follows:

Product / Time taken by technicians (Hours)	A	B	Total time (Hours)
Cutter	2	1	104
Finisher	1	2	76
Profit (₹)	6	11	

Let time taken for lamp A $= x_1$

and time taken for lamp B $= x_2$

According to the question, cutter takes 2 hours for lamp A and 1 hour for lamp B, hence we have $(2x_1 + x_2)$ and cutter has 104 hours of available time each month, hence we have for maximising

$2x_1 + x_2 \le 104$

Similarly, for finisher, we have

$x_1 + 2x_2 \le 76$

Since, it is not possible to produce a negative quantity, therefore, we restrict the variables x_1, x_2 to have only non-negative values, i.e.,

$x_1 \ge 0,\ x_2 \ge 0$

Now profit is given by $Z = 6x_1 + 11x_2$

Hence, we can formulate the given LPP as follows,

Maximise

$Z = 6x_1 + 11x_2$

Subject to constraints

$2x_1 + x_2 \le 104$

$x_1 + 2x_2 \leq 76$

$x_1 \geq 0$

$x_2 \geq 0$

Q2. Investment Problem:

A dealer wants to purchase a number of fans and sewing machines. He has only ₹5760 to invest and has space for atmost 20 items. A fan costs him ₹ 360 and a sewing machine ₹240. His expectation is that he can sell a fan at a profit of ₹22 and a sewing machine at a profit of ₹18. Assuming that he can sell all the items that he can buy, how should he invest his money in order to maximise his profit?

Ans. Suppose Z denotes the total profit.

Suppose dealer buys x_1 units of fans and x_2 units of sewing machines. As he sells a fan at a profit of ₹22 and a sewing machine at a profit of ₹18, the total profit is given by

$Z = 22x_1 + 18x_2$

As a fan cost him ₹360 and a sewing machine cost ₹240, total amount spent is $360x_1 + 240x_2$. Amount available is ₹5760.

Therefore,

$360x_1 + 240x_2 \leq 5760$

Total number of items he buys $= x_1 + x_2$. Maximum space available is for 20 items. Therefore,

$x_1 + x_2 \leq 20$

Since it is not possible to buy negative quantities, therefore

$x_1 \geq 0,\ x_2 \geq 0$

Thus, the L.P.P. is to find (the decision variables) x_1, x_2 which will maximise (the objective function)

$Z = 22x_1 + 18x_2$

subject to the constraints

$360x_1 + 240x_2 \leq 5760$

$x_1 + x_2 \leq 20$

$x_1, x_2 \geq 0$

Q3. A firm manufactures two products A and B, and has a total production capacity of 9 tonnes per day, A and B requiring the same production capacity. The firm has a permanent contract to supply at least 2 tonnes of A and at least 3 tonnes of B per day to another company. Each tonne of A requires 20 machine-hours production time and each tonne of B requires 50 machine-hours production time, the daily maximum possible number of machine

hours is 360. All the firm's output can be sold, and the profit made is ₹80 per tonne of A and ₹120 per tonne of B. Determine the production schedule for maximum profit.

Ans. Let the production of the product A in tonnes $= x_1$

and the production of the product B in tonnes $= x_2$

First, it is given that the total production capacity of the products A and B is 9 tonnes per day. i.e.,

$$x_1 + x_2 \leq 9$$

Now permanent contract of the product A is at least 2 tonnes and of the product B is at least 3 tonnes. Hence, we have

$$x_1 \geq 2$$

$$x_2 \geq 3$$

Now, 20 machine hours production time is required for A and 50 machine hours production time is required for B. The daily maximum possible number of machine hours is 360. Hence, we get

$$20x_1 + 50x_2 \leq 360$$

Since, it is not possible to produce the negative quantity of the A and B, i.e.,

$$x_1 \geq 0,\ x_2 \geq 0$$

Now the profit is ₹80 per tonne of A and ₹120 per tonne of B, i.e.,

$$Z = 80x_1 + 120x_2$$

Hence, we have

maximise

$$Z = 80x_1 + 120x_2$$

subject to constraints

$$x_1 + x_2 \leq 9$$

$$x_1 \geq 2$$

$$x_2 \geq 3$$

$$20x_1 + 50x_2 \leq 360$$

$$x_1 \geq 0,\ x_2 \geq 0$$

Q4. Diet Problem:

Vitamins A and B are found in two different foods F_1 and F_2. One unit of food F_1 contains 2 units of vitamin A and 3 units of vitamins B. One unit of food F_2 contains 4 units of vitamin A and 2 units of vitamin B. One unit of food F_1 cost ₹3 and one unit of food F_2 costs ₹2.50. The minimum daily requirement for a person of vitamin A and B is 40 and 50 units respectively. Assuming that anything in excess of daily minimum requirement of vitamin A and B is not harmful, find out the

optimal mixture of food F_1 and F_2 at the minimum cost which meats the daily minimum requirement of vitamins A and B.

Ans. We can tabulate the given LPP as follows:

Food items / Resources	F_1	F_2	Total requirement
Vitamin A	2	4	40
Vitamin B	3	2	50
Cost (₹)	3	2.5	

Suppose Z denotes the total cost. Let

x_1 = number of units of food F_1

and

x_2 = number of units of food F_2.

Number of units of vitamin A in x_1 units of food F_1 and x_2 units of food F_2 is $2x_1 + 4x_2$. As the minimum daily requirement of vitamin A is 40 units, therefore, we have

$2x_1 + 4x_2 \geq 40$

Similarly the number of units of vitamin B in F_1 and F_2 is

$3x_1 + 2x_2$

Daily minimum requirement of vitamin B is 50 units, therefore,

$3x_1 + 2x_2 \geq 50$

As the costs of one unit of F_1 and F_2 are ₹3 and ₹2.50 respectively, therefore, total cost is

$Z = 3x_1 + 2.5x_2$

Since negative purchasing of x_1 and x_2 is meaningless, therefore, we must have

$x_1 \geq 0, \ x_2 \geq 0$

Hence, we have the problem as follows:

Minimise

$Z = 3x_1 + 2.5x_2$

Subject to the constraints

$2x_1 + 4x_2 \geq 40$

$3x_1 + 2x_2 \geq 50$

$x_1, \ x_2 \geq 0$

Q5. An Inspection Problem:

A company has two grades of inspectors, I and II, who are to be assigned for a quality control inspection. It is required that at least

2000 pieces be inspected per 8 - hour day. A grade I inspector can check at the rate of 40 per hour with an accuracy of 97 per cent. A grade II inspector checks at the rate of 30 pieces per hour with an accuracy of 95 per cent. The wage rate of a grade I inspector is ₹5 per hour while that of a grade II inspector is ₹4 per hour. An error made by an inspector costs ₹3 to the company. There are only nine grade I inspectors and eleven grade II inspectors available in the company. Formulate the problem of minimising the daily inspection cost as an LPP.

Ans. Let Z denotes the total cost of inspection.

Let x_1 and x_2 denote the number of grade I and grade II inspectors assigned for inspection.

It is given that accuracy of grade I inspector is 97 per cent, i.e.,

$$x_1 \le \frac{97}{100}$$

and the accuracy of grade II inspector is 95 per cent, i.e.,

$$x_1 \le \frac{95}{100}$$

The company requires at least 2000 pieces to be inspected daily, therefore, we get

$$(8\times 40)x_1 + (8\times 30)x_2 \ge 2000$$

$$\Rightarrow 320x_1 + 240x_2 \ge 2000$$

$$\Rightarrow 20x_1 + 15x_2 \ge 125$$

$$\Rightarrow 4x_1 + 3x_2 \ge 25$$

Since the hourly cost of grade I and grade II inspector is ₹ 5 and ₹4 respectively, therefore, total cost $= (5x_1 + 4x_2)\times 8$

i.e., $Z = 40x_1 + 32x_2$

Thus, the LPP becomes

Minimise

$$Z = 40x_1 + 32x_2$$

subject to constraints

$$x_1 \le \frac{97}{100}$$

$$x_2 \le \frac{95}{100}$$

$$4x_1 + 3x_2 \ge 25$$

$$x_1, x_2 \ge 0$$

Q6. A diet for a sick person must contain at least 4000 units of vitamins, 50 units of minerals and 1400 Calories. Two foods A and B are

available at a cost of ₹4 and ₹3 per unit respectively. If one unit of A contains 200 units of vitamins, 1 unit of mineral and 40 calories, and one unit of food B contains 100 units of vitamins, 2 units of minerals and 40 calories, find by graphical method, what combination of foods be used to have least cost?

Ans. We can tabulate the given LPP as

Resources \ Food items	A	B	Requirements
Vitamins	200	100	4000
Minerals	1	2	50
Calories	40	40	1400
Cost (₹)	4	3	

Let Z denotes the total cost.

Let x_1 = number of units in food A

and x_2 = number of units in food B.

Now, according to the table we have

$200x_1 + 100x_2 \geq 4000$

$\Rightarrow \quad 2x_1 + x_2 \geq 40$

Now, $\quad x_1 + 2x_2 \geq 50$

and $\quad 40x_1 + 40x_2 \geq 1400$

$\Rightarrow \quad x_1 + x_2 \geq 35$

Now, we have

$x_1 \geq 0, \ x_2 \geq 0$

Hence, we get LPP as

minimise

$Z = 4x_1 + 3x_2$

subject to constraints

$2x_1 + x_2 \geq 40$

$x_1 + 2x_2 \geq 50$

$x_1 + x_2 \geq 35$

$x_1, x_2 \geq 0$

Now we will find the solution by graphical method of this LPP.

Consider

$2x_1 + x_2 = 40$

$$\Rightarrow \quad \frac{x_1}{20} + \frac{x_2}{40} = 1 \qquad \text{...(i)}$$

Now $x_1 + 2x_2 = 50$

$\Rightarrow \quad \frac{x_1}{50} + \frac{x_2}{25} = 1$ ...(ii)

and $x_1 + x_2 = 35$

$\Rightarrow \quad \frac{x_1}{35} + \frac{x_2}{35} = 1$ ...(iii)

Now, we will plot the graph of Eqs. (i), (ii) and (iii).

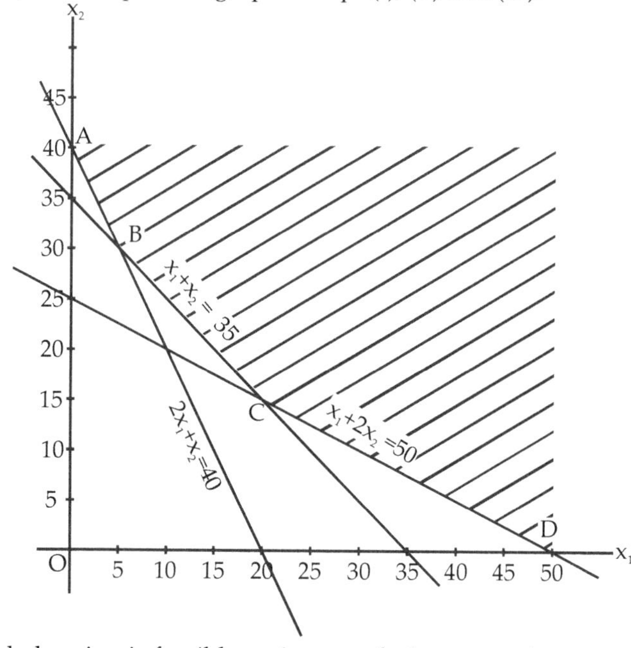

Shaded region is feasible region or solution set region.

Here, feasible region is open with vertices A, B, C and D, i.e., A (0, 40), B (5, 30), C (20, 15) and D (50, 0)

Here, (0, 0) is not a point of the feasible region.

Extreme Point	**Value of** $Z = 4x_1 + 3x_2$
A (0, 40)	$Z = 0 + 3 \times 40 = 120$
B (5, 30)	$Z = 20 + 90 = 110$
C (20, 15)	$Z = 80 + 45 = 125$
D (50, 0)	$Z = 50 \times 4 + 0 = 200$

Minimum value of Z is at B (5, 30).

Hence,

The number of units in food A, $x_1 = 5$,

The number of units in food B, $x_2 = 30$

Hence, this combination (i.e., $x_1 = 5, x_2 = 30$) of foods be used to have least cost.

Q7. Use the graphic method to solve the following LPP: Minimise $Z = -x_1 + 2x_2$ subject to $-x_1 + 3x_2 \le 10$, $x_1 + x_2 \le 6$, $x_1 - x_2 \le 2$, $x_1 \ge 0$ and $x_2 \ge 0$.

Ans. Given LPP is

Minimise

$Z = -x_1 + 2x_2$

subject to

$-x_1 + 3x_2 \le 10$

$x_1 + x_2 \le 6$

$x_1 - x_2 \le 2$

$x_1 \ge 0$

$x_2 \ge 0$

Consider $-x_1 + 3x_2 = 10$

$$\Rightarrow \quad \frac{x_1}{-10} + \frac{x_2}{10/3} = 1 \qquad \text{...(i)}$$

Now $x_1 + x_2 = 6$

$$\Rightarrow \quad \frac{x_1}{6} + \frac{x_2}{6} = 1 \qquad \text{...(ii)}$$

and $x_1 - x_2 = 2$

$$\Rightarrow \quad \frac{x_1}{2} + \frac{x_2}{(-2)} = 1 \qquad \text{...(iii)}$$

Now, we will draw the lines (i), (ii) and (iii) on the graph.

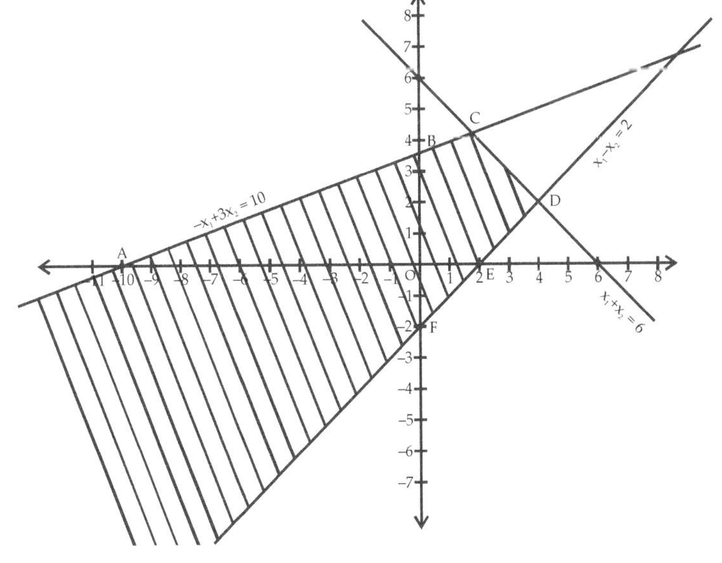

(0, 0) satisfies all $-x_1 + 3x_2 \le 10$, $x_1 + x_2 \le 6$ and $x_1 - x_2 \le 2$. Hence, shaded region is feasible region. Feasible region is unbounded here. The extreme points are

A (–10, 0), B$\left(0, \frac{10}{3}\right)$, C (2, 4), D (4, 2), E (2, 0) and F (0, –2).

At these points, the value of Z is finite. As x_1 and x_2 both can approach to infinity, therefore value of Z approaches to infinity. We say that given LPP is unbounded. The objective function lines indicate that $Z \to \infty$.

Q8. In a solution to a two-dimensional LPP the objective function can assume the same value at two distinct extreme points. Is it true? Justify your answer. **[June-2015, Q.No.-1(a)]**

Ans. Yes, it is true.

Consider the following LPP:

Maximise $Z = 15x_1 + 30x_2$

Subject to the constraints:

$2x_1 + 4x_2 \le 60$

$5x_1 + 2x_2 \le 60$

$x_1, x_2 \ge 0$

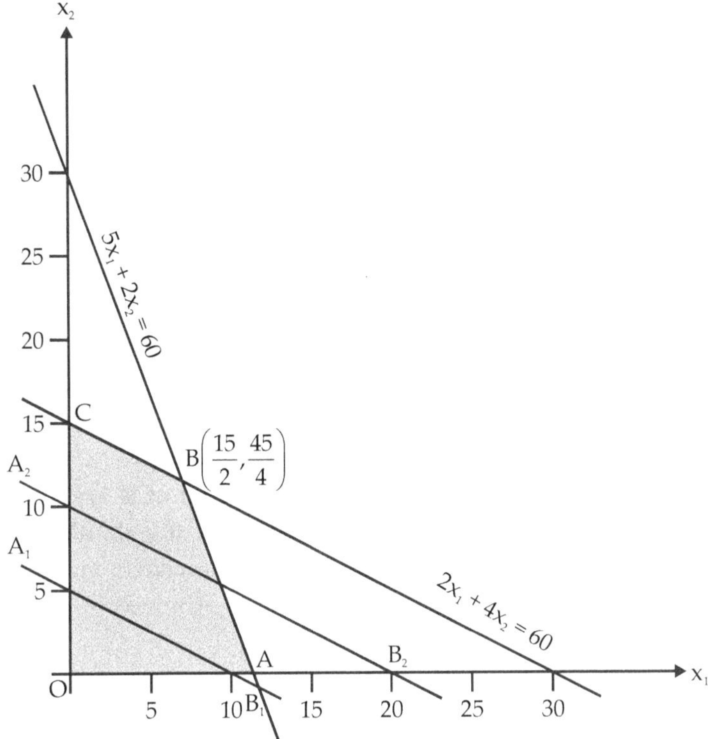

The shaded area OABC represents the set of feasible solutions.

To locate a point on the feasible region, which maximises the objective function, we observe that for a profit of ₹150, the objective function may be written as

$$15x_1 + 30x_2 = 150$$

The line is given by $A_1 B_1$. Now we try a larger value of Z say 300, i.e. $15x_1 + 30x_2 = 300$. The line is $A_2 B_2$. The lines A_1B_1 and A_2B_2 both lie within the feasible region. Increasing the value of Z and drawing different lines, we find that the objective function line finally coincides with the line CB. Hence, every point on the line segment CB of the feasible region provides the optimal value of Z. The extreme points of CB are

$$C\,(0, 15) \quad \text{and} \quad B\left(\frac{15}{2}, \frac{45}{4}\right)$$

and the value of Z at

$$(0, 15) = 15\,(0) + 30\,(15) = 450$$

Value of Z at

$$\left(\frac{15}{2}, \frac{45}{4}\right) = 15 \times \frac{15}{2} + 30 \times \frac{45}{4} = 450$$

i.e., Maximum value of the objective function Z at both the extreme point is same and it is 450.

Q9. A firm plans to purchase at least 200 kg of scrap containing high quality metal X and low quality metal Y. It decided that the scrap to be purchased must contain at least 100 kg of X-metal and not more than 35 kg of Y-metal. The firm can purchase the scrap from two suppliers (A and B) in unlimited quantities. The percentage of X and Y metals in terms of weight in the scrap supplied by A and B is given below:

Metals	Supplier A	Supplier B
X	25%	75 %
Y	10%	20%

The price of A's scrap is ₹200 per kg and that of B is ₹400 per kg. The firm wants to determine the quantities that it should buy from the two suppliers so that the total cost is minimised. Formulate the problem as LPP and solve. [June-2016, Q.No.-5(a)]

Ans. Let scrap purchased from supplier A $= x_1$

Scrap purchased from supplier B $= x_2$

Thus, we have the following LPP:

Minimise $Z = 200x_1 + 400x_2$

Subject to: $x_1 + x_2 \geq 200$

$0.25x_1 + 0.75x_2 \geq 100$

$0.1x_1 + 0.2x_2 \leq 35$

$x_1, x_2 \geq 0$

Now, consider the equations

$x_1 + x_2 = 200$

$\Rightarrow \quad \dfrac{x_1}{200} + \dfrac{x_2}{200} = 1 \quad$ ...(i)

$0.25x_1 + 0.75x_2 = 100$

$\Rightarrow \quad 25x_1 + 75x_2 = 1000$

$\Rightarrow \quad \dfrac{x_1}{400} + \dfrac{x_2}{133.33} = 1 \quad$ ...(ii)

$0.1x_1 + 0.2x_2 = 35$

$\Rightarrow \quad x_1 + 2x_2 = 350$

$\Rightarrow \quad \dfrac{x_1}{350} + \dfrac{x_2}{175} = 1 \quad$ ...(iii)

Now, we have the following graph of Eqs. (i), (ii) and (iii).

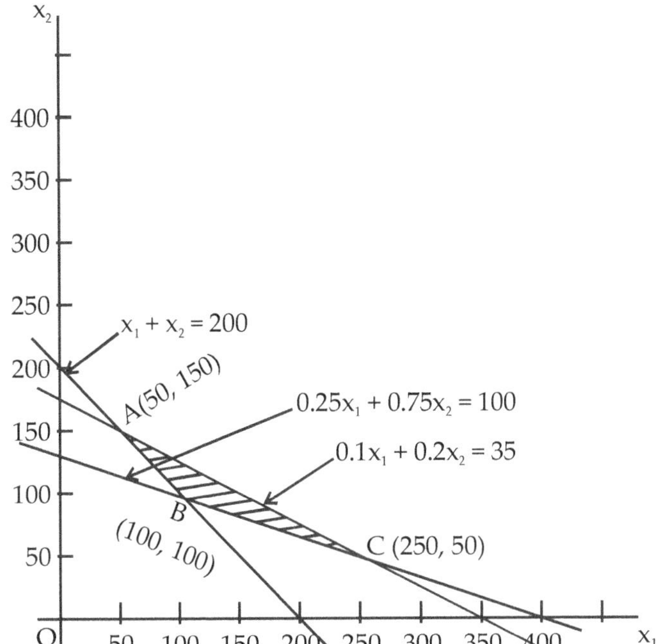

Shaded region ABC is the feasible region.

Now, $Z = 200x_1 + 400x_2$

$\Rightarrow$ Z at (50, 150) = 200 × 50 + 400 × 150 = 70,000

Z at (100, 100) = 200 × 100 + 400 × 100 = 60,000

Z at (250, 50) = 200 × 250 + 400 × 50 = 70,000

Hence, Z is minimum at (100, 100).

Hence, $x_1 = 100$, $x_2 = 100$ and min Z = ₹60,000

Q10. Use the graphical method to solve the following LP problem:

Maximise $z = 2x_1 + 3x_2$

subject to $x_1 + x_2 \le 30$

$x_2 \ge 3$

$0 \le x_2 \le 12$

$0 \le x_1 \le 20$

$x_1 - x_2 \ge 0$ **[June-2014, Q.No.-5(a)]**

Ans. Consider the following equations:

$x_1 + x_2 = 30$ ...(i)

$x_2 = 3$ ...(ii)

$x_2 = 12$ ...(iii)

$x_1 = 20$ ...(iv)

$x_1 - x_2 = 0$ ...(v)

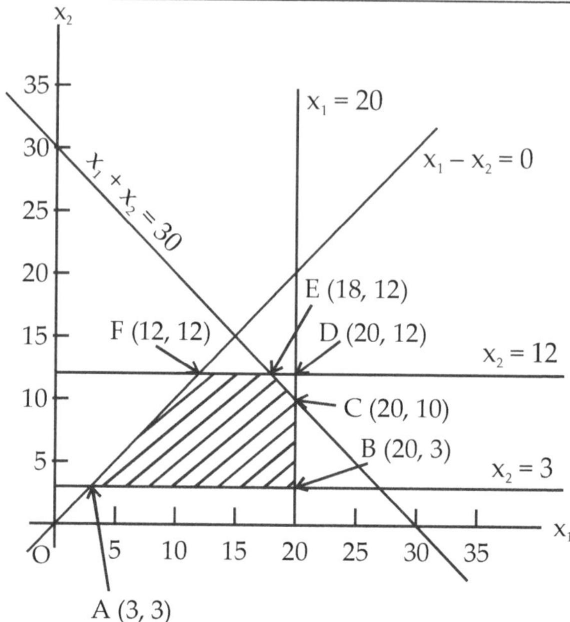

In the above figure, shaded region ABCEF is the feasible region.

Given that

$z = 2x_1 + 3x_2$

Now

z at A (3, 3) = 2 × 3 + 3 × 3 = 15

z at B (20, 3) = 2 × 20 + 3 × 3 = 49

z at C (20, 10) = 2 × 20 + 3 × 10 = 70

z at E (18, 12) = 2 × 18 + 3 × 12 = 72

z at F (12, 12) = 2 × 12 + 3 × 12 = 60

Hence, z is maximum at the point E (18, 12)

$\Rightarrow \quad x_1 = 18,\ x_2 = 12$ and max z = 72

Q11. A businessman has to get 5 cabinets, 12 desks and 18 shelves cleaned. He has two part-time employees, Anjali and Arnav. Anjali can clean 1 cabinet, 3 desks and 3 shelves in a day, while Arnav can clean 1 cabinet, 2 desks and 3 shelves in a day. Arnav is paid ₹22 per day and Anjali is paid ₹25 per day. Formulate the problem of finding the number of days for which Anjali and Arnav have to be employed to get the cleaning done with minimum cost as a linear programming problem. [June-2014, Q.No.-6(a)]

Ans. We can tabulate the given problem as follows:

Furniture \ Employees	Anjali	Arnav	Availability of furniture
Cabinets	1	1	5
Desks	3	2	12
Shelves	3	3	18
Cost	25 ` /day	22 ` /day	

Let Anjali's days of cleaning $= x_1$

and Arnav's days of cleaning $= x_2$

Now, we have the following LPP:

Minimise $Z = 25\,x_1 + 22\,x_2$

subject to $x_1 + x_2 \geq 5$

$3\,x_1 + 2\,x_2 \geq 12$

$3\,x_1 + 3\,x_2 \geq 18$ or $x_1 + x_2 \geq 6$

$x_1,\ x_2 \geq 0$

Q12. A company makes two kinds of leather belts. Belt A is a high quality belt and belt B is of lower quality. The respective profits on A and B are ₹4 and ₹3 per belt. The production of each type A requires twice as much time as a belt of type B, and if all belts were of type B, the company could make 1000 belts per day. The supply of leather is sufficient for only 800 belts per day (both A and B combined). Belt A requires a fancy buckle and only 400 buckles per day are available. There are only 700 buckles a day available for belt B. What should be the daily production of each type of belt? Formulate this problem as an LP model and solve it by the graphical method. [Dec-2014, Q.No.-3(a)]

Ans. Let x_1 = Number of Belt A to be produced

x_2 = Number of Belt B to be produced

Since the objective is to maximise the profit, the objective function is given by

Maximise $Z = 4x_1 + 3x_2$

subject to the constraints

$2x_1 + x_2 \leq 1000$ (Total availability of time)

$x_1 + x_2 \leq 800$ (Total availability of leather)

$x_1 \leq 400$ (Availability of buckles for belt A)

$x_2 \leq 700$ (Availability of buckles for belt B)

$x_1,\ x_2 \geq 0$ (Non-negativity constraint)

Now, we will solve this LPP by graphical method. We have

$2x_1 + x_2 = 1000$

$\frac{x_1}{500} + \frac{x_2}{1000} = 1$ ...(i)

Now, we have

$x_1 + x_2 = 800$

$\Rightarrow \quad \frac{x_1}{800} + \frac{x_2}{800} = 1$ ...(ii)

Finally, we have

$x_1 = 400$ ...(iii)

and $x_2 = 700$ ...(iv)

The graph of Eq (i)-(iv) is as follows:

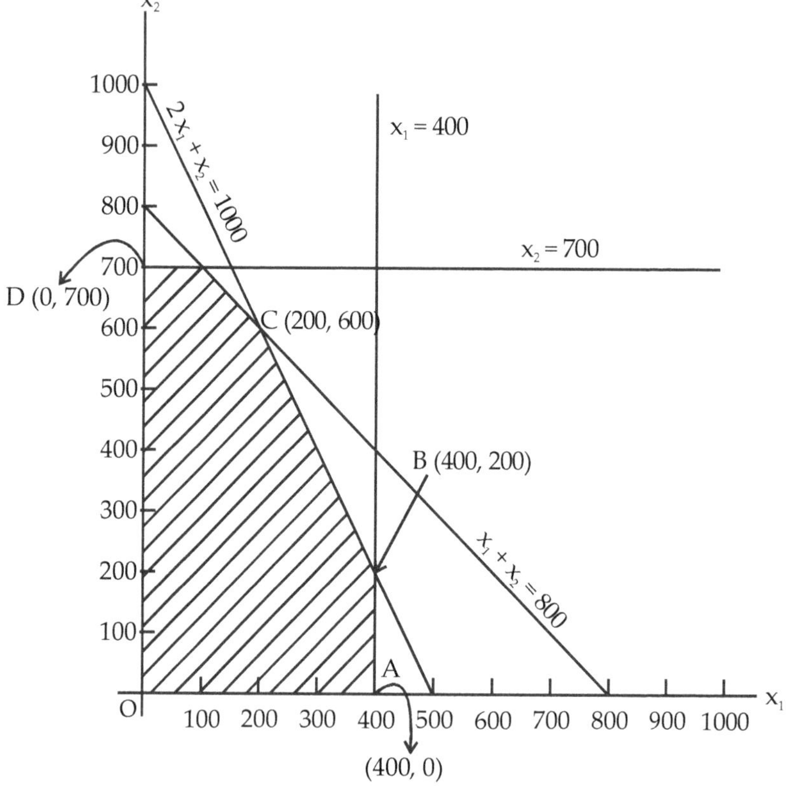

In this figure, shaded region OABCD is the feasible region.

Now, $Z = 4x_1 + 3x_2$

Z at (400, 0) = 4 × 400 + 3 × 0 = 1600

Z at (400, 200) = 4 × 400 + 3 × 200 = 2200

Z at (200, 600) = 4 × 200 + 3 × 600 = 2600

Z at (0, 700) = 4 × 0 + 3 × 700 = 2100

Hence, Z is maximum at (200, 600).

Hence, daily production of belt A = 200

and daily production of belt B = 600

and daily maximum profit Z = ₹2600

Q13. Solve the following linear programming problem by graphical method:

Maximise $z = 5x_1 + 7x_2$

subject to $x_1 + x_2 \leq 4$

$3x_1 + 8x_2 \leq 24$

$10x_1 + 7x_2 \leq 35$

$x_1, x_2 \geq 0$ **[June-2015, Q.No.-4(a)]**

Ans. Consider the equations from the given LPP as follows:

$x_1 + x_2 = 4$

$$\Rightarrow \quad \frac{x_1}{4} + \frac{x_2}{4} = 1 \qquad ...(i)$$

$3x_1 + 8x_2 = 24$

$$\Rightarrow \quad \frac{x_1}{8} + \frac{x_2}{3} = 1 \qquad ...(ii)$$

$10x_1 + 7x_2 = 35$

$$\Rightarrow \quad \frac{x_1}{3.5} + \frac{x_2}{5} = 1 \qquad ...(iii)$$

Graph of these equations is as follows:

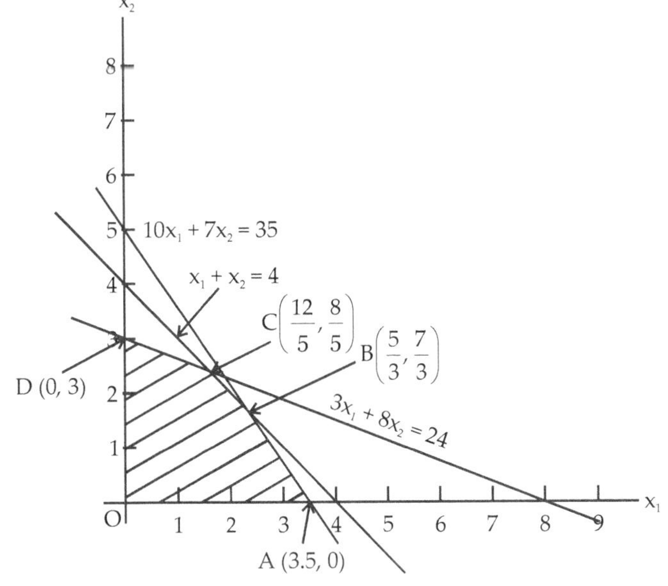

Shaded region OABCD is the feasible region.

Given that $z = 5x_1 + 7x_2$

z at A (3.5, 0) = 5 × 3.5 + 7 × 0 = 17.5

z at $B\left(\frac{5}{3}, \frac{7}{3}\right) = 5 \times \frac{5}{3} + 7 \times \frac{7}{3} = 24.66$

z at $C\left(\frac{12}{5}, \frac{8}{5}\right) = 5 \times \frac{12}{5} + 7 \times \frac{8}{5} = 23.2$

z at D (0, 3) = 5 × 0 + 7 × 3 = 21

Hence, z is maximum at $\left(\frac{5}{3}, \frac{7}{3}\right)$.

Hence, $x_1 = \frac{5}{3}$, $x_2 = \frac{7}{3}$ and max z = 24.66

Q14. A firm manufactures two types of products, A and B, and sells them at a profit of ₹2 on type A and ₹3 on type B. Each product is processed on two machines M_1 and M_2. Type A requires one minute of processing time on M_1 and two minutes on M_2; type B requires one minute on M_1 and one minute on M_2. The machine M_1 is available for not more than 6 hours 40 minutes while machine M_2 is available for 10 hours during any working day. Formulate the problem as LPP. [June-2015, Q.No.-6(a)]

Ans. Given LPP can be tabulated as follows:

Products / Machines	A	B	Total time
M_1	1	1	6 h 40 m = 400 min.
M_2	2	1	10 h = 600 min.
Profit (₹)	2	3	

Let the time for product A is x_1 and for product B is x_2.

Hence, we have the following LPP:

Maximise $2x_1 + 3x_2$

subject to $x_1 + x_2 \le 400$

$2x_1 + x_2 \le 600$

$x_1, x_2 \ge 0$

Q15. Solve the following linear programming problem by graphical method:

Maximise $z = 3x_1 + 2x_2$

subject to $x_1 - x_2 \ge 1$

$x_1 + x_2 \geq 3$

$x_1,\ x_2 \geq 0.$ **[Dec-2015, Q.No.-2(a)]**

Ans. From given LPP, consider the equations

$x_1 - x_2 = 1$

$$\Rightarrow \quad \frac{x_1}{1} + \frac{x_2}{(-1)} = 1 \qquad ...(i)$$

$x_1 + x_2 = 3$

$$\Rightarrow \quad \frac{x_1}{3} + \frac{x_2}{3} = 1 \qquad ...(ii)$$

The graph of Eqs. (i) and (ii) is as follows:

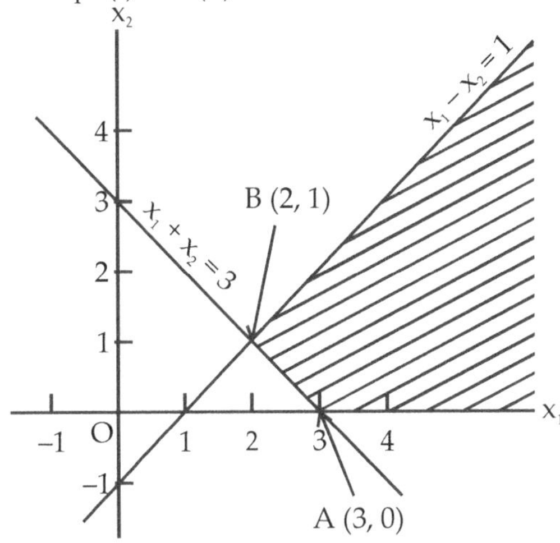

The shaded portion is the feasible region and is unbounded. The extreme points are A (3, 0) and B (2, 1). At these points, the value of z is finite. As x_1 and x_2 both can approach to infinity, therefore value of z approach to infinity. We can say that the given problem is unbounded. Hence, $z \to \infty$.

Q16. A manufacturer of medicines is setting-up a production plant for medicines A and B. There are sufficient ingredients available to make 20,000 bottles of A and 40,000 bottles of B but there are only 45,000 bottles into which either of the medicines can be put. It takes 3 hours to prepare enough material to fill 1000 bottles of A. It takes 1 hour to prepare enough material to fill 1000 bottles of B. There are 66 hours available for this operation. The profit is ₹8 per bottle for A and ₹7 per bottle for B. Formulate this problem as a linear programming problem. **[Dec-2015, Q.No.-5(a)]**

Ans. Let $1000x_1$ be the number of bottles of medicine A and $1000x_2$ be the number of bottles of medicine B. Therefore, we have the following LPP:

Maximise $Z = 8000x_1 + 7000x_2$

subject to $3x_1 + x_2 \leq 66$

$x_1 + x_2 \leq 45$

$x_1 \leq 20$

$x_2 \leq 40$

$x_1,\ x_2 \geq 0$

ꟷ ꟷ

4 Optimisation in More than Two Variables

An Overview

We do not try to graph the feasible region when there are more than two decision variables. Three-dimensional graphs are not that easy to draw and we can forget about making the sketch when there are four or more decision variables.

The table method does not work that well either. Each intersection point is the the solution to a 3×3 system of linear equations. In three dimensions, the inequalities become planes rather than lines as if they were in two dimensions. Each plane can be uniquely identified by setting one of the variables equal to zero.

4.1 GENERAL LINEAR PROGRAMMING PROBLEM

Given a set of m linear inequalities in r variables, we wish to determine non-negative values of these variables, which will satisfy the constraints and maximise or minimise some linear function of the variables.

Mathematically, we have

$$a_{i1}x_1 + a_{i2}x_2 + \ldots\ldots + a_{ir}x_r \{\geq, =, \leq\}\ b_i, \qquad i = 1, 2, \ldots\ldots, m$$

i.e.,

$$a_{11}\ x_1 + a_{12}\ x_2 + a_{13}\ x_3 + \ldots\ldots + a_{1r}\ x_r \{\geq, =, \leq\} b_1$$

$$a_{21}\ x_1 + a_{22}\ x_2 + a_{23}\ x_3 + \ldots\ldots + a_{2r}\ x_r \{\geq, =, \leq\} b_2$$

....

....

$$a_{m1}\ x_1 + a_{m2}\ x_2 + a_{m3}\ x_3 + \ldots\ldots + a_{mr}\ x_r \{\geq, =, \leq\} b_m$$

These are m constraints in r variables each constraints has one and only one sign $\leq$ or $=$ or $\geq$ but the sign may vary from one constraint to another. We want to find the values of the variables x_j satisfying

$$x_j \geq 0, \quad j = 1, 2, \ldots\ldots, r$$

which maximise or minimise a linear function, called the objective function.

$$Z = c_1x_1 + c_2x_2 + \ldots\ldots + c_rx_r$$

The a_{ij}, b_i, c_j are assumed to be known constants.

Solved Practical Problems

Q1. An industrialist produces three types of machine components A, B and C made of steel and brass. The amounts of steel, brass required for each component and the number of man-weeks of labour required to manufacture and assemble one unit of each component are as follows:

	A	B	C	Availability
Steel	7	5	2	95 kg.
Brass	2	3	7	70 kg.
Man-weeks	1	3	2	25 weeks.

This labour is restricted to 25 man-weeks, steel is restricted to 95 kg per week and the brass to 70 kg per week. The industrialist's profit on each unit of A, B and C is ₹5, ₹3 and ₹8 respectively. Give its mathematical formulation as a linear programming problem such that the total profit is maximum.

Ans. Let $x_j, j = 1, 2, 3$ be the number of units of component of A, B and C produce per week. We need to find the values of x_1, x_2, x_3 which maximise the total profit. Since the amount of steel, amount of brass and the labour are limited; we cannot arbitrarily increase the output of any component.

First, consider restriction imposed by the availability of steel. Amount of steel used is

$$7x_1 + 5x_2 + 2x_3$$

per week, because per week, 7 kg are required for each unit of component A, 5 kg are required for each unit of component B and 2 kg for each unit of component C.

Since the total amount of steel available is restricted to 95 kg, therefore,

$$7x_1 + 5x_2 + 2x_3 \leq 95$$

Similarly, for brass, we can have

$$2x_1 + 3x_2 + 7x_3 \leq 70$$

As the labour is restricted to 25 man-weeks, therefore, we must have

$$x_1 + 3x_2 + 2x_3 \leq 25$$

Since we cannot produce negative quantities, that is, we have either a positive amount of any component or none at all. Thus, the additional restrictions $x_1 \geq 0, x_2 \geq 0, x_3 \geq 0$ require that the variables be non-negative. If x_j units of component A, B and C are produced, the weekly profit Z is given by $Z = 5x_1 + 3x_2 + 8x_3$

We need to find the values of the variables, which will satisfy all the constraints, the non-negativity restrictions and maximise Z. Thus, the mathematical formulation of the linear programming problem is as follows:

Maximise $Z = 5x_1 + 3x_2 + 8x_3$

Subject to the constraints $7x_1 + 5x_2 + 2x_3 \leq 95$

$2x_1 + 3x_2 + 7x_3 \leq 70$

$x_1 + 3x_2 + 2x_3 \leq 25$

$x_1, x_2, x_3 \geq 0$

Q2. The annual handmade furniture 'show and sale' occurs next month and the School of Vocational Studies is planning to make furniture for the sale. There are three wood working classes, viz. I year, II year and III year, at the school and they have decided to make three styles of chairs A, B and C. Each chair must receive work in each class and the time in hours required for each chair in each class is given as below:

Chair	I year	II year	III year
A	2	4	3
B	3	3	2
C	2	1	4

During the next month, there will be 120 hours available in the I year class, 160 hours in the II year and 100 hours in the III year class to produce the chairs. The teacher of the wood-working classes feels that a maximum of 40 chairs can be sold at the show. The teacher has determined that the profit from each type of chair will be: ₹ 40 for A type; ₹ 35 for B type and ₹ 30 for C type.

Formulate a linear programming model to determine how many chairs of each type should be made in order to maximise profits at the show and sale programme.

Ans. Let x_1, x_2 and x_3 denote the number of chairs of type A, B and C respectively.

It is given that in the I year class, 2 hours are required for chairs A type, 3 hours for chairs B type and 2 hours for chair C type. Hence, we have $2x_1 + 3x_2 + 2x_3$

and it is also given that there will be 120 hours available in the I year class. Hence, $2x_1 + 3x_2 + 2x_3 \leq 120$

Similarly, for II year class, we have $4x_1 + 3x_2 + x_3 \leq 160$ and for III year class, we have $3x_1 + 2x_2 + 4x_3 \leq 100$

Now, the teacher of the wood-working classes feels that a maximum of 40 chairs can be sold at the show. Hence, we get $x_1 + x_2 + x_3 \leq 40$

Since, we cannot produce negative quantity. Hence, we have

$x_1 \geq 0, x_2 \geq 0, x_3 \geq 0$

Now, given that the teacher has determined that the profit is ₹40 for A type, ₹35 for B type and ₹30 for C type. Hence, we have

$Z = 40x_1 + 35x_2 + 30x_3$

Thus, the mathematical formulation of the linear programming problem is as follows:

Maximise

$Z = 40x_1 + 35x_2 + 30x_3$

Subject to the constraints $2x_1 + 3x_2 + 2x_3 \leq 120$

$4x_1 + 3x_2 + x_3 \leq 160$

$3x_1 + 2x_2 + 4x_3 \leq 100$

$x_1 + x_2 + x_3 \leq 40$

$x_1, x_2, x_3 \geq 0$

Q3. A cold drinks company has three bottling plants, located at two different places. Each plant produces three different drinks A, B and C. The capacities of three plans, in number of bottles per day are as follows:

	Product A	Product B	Product C
Plant I	3000	1000	2000
Plant II	1000	1000	4000
Plant III	2000	500	3000

A market survey indicates that during any particular month there will be a demand of 24,000 bottles of A; 16,000 bottles of B and 48,000 bottles of C. The operating costs, per day, of running plants I, II and III are respectively ₹600, ₹400 and ₹500. Formulate it as a linear programming problem to find the number of days should the company run each plant during the month so that the production is minimised while still meeting the market demand.

Ans. Suppose x_1, x_2, x_3 be the number of days per month in which the company runs the Plants I, II and III respectively. Amount of product A produced by three plant is

$3000x_1 + 1000x_2 + 2000x_3$

The demand of the product A is 24,000 bottles. We need to find x_1, x_2, x_3 such that the market demand must be fulfilled. Therefore, we have $3000x_1 + 1000x_2 + 2000x_3 \geq 24,000$

Similarly, for product B and C, we have

$1000x_1 + 1000x_2 + 500x_3 \geq 16,000$

and

$2000x_1 + 4000x_2 + 3000x_3 \geq 48,000$

As the number of days cannot be negative, therefore, we must have

$x_1 \geq 0, x_2 \geq 0, x_3 \geq 0$

Total cost of running the plants I, II and III is $600x_1 + 400x_2 + 500x_3$

Here, we need to minimise the total cost. Hence, the linear programming problem can be formulated as:

Minimise $Z = 600x_1 + 400x_2 + 500x_3$

Subject to the constraints $3000x_1 + 1000x_2 + 2000x_3 \geq 24,000$

$1000x_1 + 1000x_2 + 500x_3 \geq 16,000$

$2000x_1 + 4000x_2 + 3000x_3 \geq 48,000$

$x_1, x_2, x_3 \geq 0$

Q4. A diet for a sick person must contain at least 400 unit of vitamins, 50 units of minerals and 1400 units of calories. Three goods A, B and C are available at cost of ₹4, ₹3 and ₹3.50 per unit respectively. If one unit of A contains 200 units of vitamin, 2 units of mineral and 40 units of calories, one unit of B contains 100 units of vitamins, 3 units of minerals and 30 units of calories and one unit of C contains 200 units of vitamins, 2 units of minerals and 35 units of calories, formulate it as a linear programming problem to find the combination of food to be used to have the least cost.

Ans. First, we tabulate the given LPP as follows:

Goods / Resources	A	B	C	Total
Vitamins	200	100	200	400
Minerals	2	3	2	50
Calories	40	30	35	1400
Cost (₹)	4	3	3.50	

Let Z denotes the total cost

and x_1 = number of units of good A

x_2 = number of units of good B

x_3 = number of units of good C

It is given that the quantity of vitamins in goods A, B and C is 200, 100 and 200 units respectively and total quantity is 400 units. Hence, we must have $200x_1 + 100x_2 + 200x_3 \geq 400$

Similarly, for minerals, we have $2x_1 + 3x_2 + 2x_3 \geq 50$ and for calories, we have $40x_1 + 30x_2 + 35x_3 \geq 1400$

Since, the number of units cannot be negative. Hence, we have

$x_1 \geq 0, x_2 \geq 0, x_3 \geq 0$

Now total cost for goods A, B and C is ₹ 4, ₹ 3 and ₹ 3.50 per unit respectively. Hence, we get

$Z = 4x_1 + 3x_2 + 3.50x_3$

Hence, the LPP can be formulated as follows:

Minimise

$Z = 4x_1 + 3x_2 + 3.50x_3$

subject to the constraints

$200x_1 + 100x_2 + 200x_3 \geq 400$

$2x_1 + 3x_2 + 2x_3 \geq 50$

$40x_1 + 30x_2 + 35x_3 \geq 1400$

$x_1, x_2, x_3 \geq 0$

Q5. Solve the following LPP

Maximise

$Z - 0.5x_1 + 6x_2 + 5x_3$

Subject to the constraints

$4x_1 + 6x_2 + 3x_3 \leq 24$

$x_1 + 1.5x_2 + 3x_3 \leq 12$

$3x_1 + x_2 \leq 12$

$x_1 \geq 0, x_2 \geq 0, x_3 \geq 0$

Ans. The equations $4x_1 + 6x_2 + 3x_3 = 24$

$x_1 + 1.5x_2 + 3x_3 = 12$

$3x_1 + x_2 = 12$

represent planes.

$3x_1 + x_2 = 12$ is a line in the X_1X_2 plane as shown in the following figure:

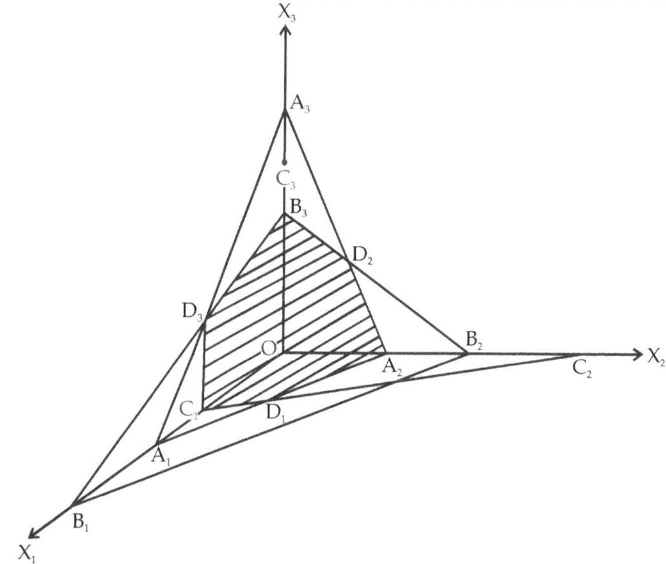

The equation $4x_1 + 6x_2 + 3x_3 = 24$ is represented by the plane $A_1A_2A_3$.

The equation $x_1 + 1.5x_2 + 3x_3 = 12$ is represented by the plane $B_1B_2B_3$.

The equation $3x_1 + x_2 = 12$ represents the plane passing through the line C_1C_2 and perpendicular to the X_1X_2 plane.

The extreme points of the feasible region are

$C_1(4,0,0)$, $D_1\left(\frac{24}{7},\frac{12}{7},0\right)$, $A_2(0,4,0)$, $D_2\left(0,\frac{8}{3},\frac{8}{3}\right)$, $B_3(0,0,4)$, $D_3\left(4,0,\frac{8}{3}\right)$

The objective function Z is maximum at the point $D_2\left(0,\frac{8}{3},\frac{8}{3}\right)$

and the maximum value of the objective function is $Z = \frac{88}{3}$

Q6. Solve graphically the following linear programming problem:

Maximise

$\mathbf{Z = x_1 + 2x_2 + 2x_3}$

subject to the constraints

$\mathbf{2x_1 + x_2 \leq 8}$

$\mathbf{x_3 \leq 10}$

$\mathbf{x_1, x_2, x_3 \geq 0}$

Ans. Given problem is as follows:

Maximise

$Z = x_1 + 2x_2 + 2x_3$

Subject to the constraints

$2x_1 + x_2 \leq 8$

$x_3 \le 10$

$x_1, x_2, x_3 \ge 0$

Now consider $2x_1 + x_2 = 8$ $\Rightarrow \frac{x_1}{4} + \frac{x_2}{8} = 1$

and $x_3 = 10$. Now the graph is

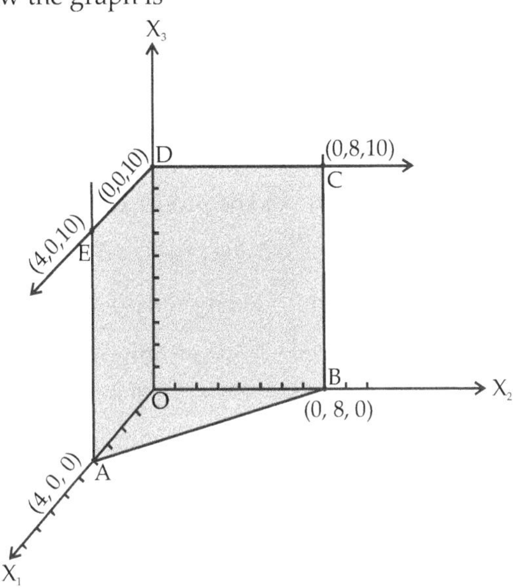

In this figure, shaded region is the feasible region. Extreme points of feasible region are

A (4, 0, 0), B (0, 8, 0), C (0, 8, 10), D (0, 0, 10), E (4, 0, 10)

Now Z at (4, 0, 0) = 4 + 2 (0) + 2 (0) = 4

Z at (0, 8, 0) = 0 + 2 (8) + 2 (0) = 16

Z at (0, 8, 10) = 0 + 2 (8) + 2 (10) = 36

Z at (0, 0, 10) = 0 + 2 (0) + 2 (10) = 20

Z at (4, 0, 10) = 4 + 2 (0) + 2 (10) = 24

Hence, Z = 36 is the maximum at (0, 8, 10).

Hence, $x_1 = 0, x_2 = 8, x_3 = 10$ and maximum Z = 36.

Q7. A company makes four products denoted by P_1, P_2, P_3 and P_4. These products are made using the resources of water, malt, hops and yeast. Company has a free supply of water. Therefore, it is the amount of other resources that restricts production capacity. The following table gives the amount of each resource required in the production of 1 unit of each product, the amount of each resource available, and the revenue received for one unit of each product. The problem faced by the company is to decide how much of each product should it make in order to maximise its revenue. Formulate this problem.

	P_1	P_2	P_3	P_4	Available
Malt	1	1	0	3	50 kg.
Hops	2	1	2	1	150 kg.
Yeast	1	1	1	4	80 kg.
Revenue	₹6	₹5	₹3	₹7	

Ans. Let we choose the following decision variables:

x_1 = No. of units of product P_1 to be produced

x_2 = No. of units of product P_2 to be produced

x_3 = No. of units of product P_3 to be produced

x_4 = No. of units of product P_4 to be produced

Then the revenue Z that results from a given production programme is $Z = 6x_1 + 5x_2 + 3x_3 + 7x_4$

Since, we cannot use more of each resource than is available and only 50 kg of malt is available, therefore, x_1, x_2, x_3 and x_4 must satisfy the constraints $x_1 + x_2 + 0x_3 + 3x_4 \leq 50$

Similarly, we can deduce the other two constraints

$2x_1 + x_2 + 2x_3 + x_4 \leq 150$

$x_1 + x_2 + x_3 + 4x_4 \leq 80$

Finally, we impose the non-negativity restriction on each product, that is, $x_1 \geq 0, x_2 \geq 0, x_3 \geq 0, x_4 \geq 0$

Thus, the problem becomes

Maximise

$Z = 6x_1 + 5x_2 + 3x_3 + 7x_4$

subject to the constraints

$x_1 + x_2 + 3x_4 \leq 50$

$2x_1 + x_2 + 2x_3 + x_4 \leq 150$

$x_1 + x_2 + x_3 + 4x_4 \leq 80$

$x_1, x_2, x_3, x_4 \geq 0$

⌑⌑

5 Standard Forms and Solutions

An Overview

In the standard form of a LPP, all the constraints should be in the form of equations. The conversion from inequalities to equations can be carried out very simply by introducing some additional variables, which are called slack or surplus variables.

Basic solution, basic feasible solution, basic non-feasible solution, degenerate solution, non-degenerate solution, etc. are the types of solutions of LPP.

5.1 GENERAL LINEAR PROGRAMMING MODEL (GLPM)

General Linear Programming Model (GLPM) is as follows:

Maximise (or Minimise) the objective function

$$Z = c_1x_1 + c_2x_2 + \dots + c_nx_n$$

Subject to the constraints

$$a_{11}x_1 + a_{12}x_2 + \dots + a_{1n}x_n (\le, =, \ge) b_1$$

$$a_{21}x_1 + a_{22}x_2 + \dots + a_{2n}x_n (\le, =, \ge) b_2$$

$$\dots\dots\dots\dots\dots\dots\dots\dots\dots\dots$$

$$a_{m1}x_1 + a_{m2}x_2 + \dots + a_{mn}x_n (\le, =, \ge) b_m$$

with the restrictions

$$x_1 \ge 0, x_2 \ge 0, \dots\dots\dots, x_n \ge 0$$

where c_j, b_i, a_{ij} (i = 1, ..., m; j = 1, 2, ..., n) are constants and $x_j, j = 1, 2, \dots\dots\dots, n$ are decision variables. Only one sign $(\le, =, \ge)$ holds for each constraint.

Here,

$$\vec{A}_j = \begin{bmatrix} a_{1j} \\ a_{2j} \\ \vdots \\ a_{mj} \end{bmatrix}, \quad j = 1, 2, 3, \dots\dots, n$$

The vectors $\vec{A}_j$ are called **Activity Vectors.**

The column vector formed by quantities $b_1, b_2, \dots, b_m$ is called the **Requirement Vector** and is denoted by $\vec{B}$. The coefficients $c_1, c_2, \dots, c_n$ in the objective function are known as the **prices** associated with the variables $x_1, x_2, \dots, x_n$ respectively. Also vector $\vec{C} = (c_1, c_2, \dots, c_n)$ is known as the **Price Vector.**

5.2 SLACK AND SURPLUS VARIABLES

Slack Variables

If in any linear programming problem, we have a constraint of the type

$$a_1x_1 + a_2x_2 + \dots\dots\dots + a_nx_n \le b, \; b \ge 0$$

Then, this inequality can be converted into an equation by adding some non-negative variable x_{n+1} to the left hand side. This new variable is called a slack variable and the constraint is transformed into an equation as

$$a_1x_1 + a_2x_2 + \dots\dots\dots + a_nx_n + x_{n+1} = b, \text{ where } x_{n+1} \ge 0$$

Thus, a non-negative variable added to left-hand side of a less than or equal to type of constraint that converts it into an equation is called a slack variable.

Surplus Variables

To understand surplus variables, suppose there is a constraint of the type

$$q_1x_1 + q_2x_2 + \ldots\ldots + q_nx_n \geq q,\ q \geq 0$$

Now something non-negative should be subtracted from the left-hand side to convert this inequality into an equation, i.e., we can have

$$q_1x_1 + q_2x_2 + \ldots\ldots + q_nx_n - x_{n+1} = q$$

where $x_{n+1} \geq 0$ is called a surplus variable.

Thus, a non-negative variable subtracted from the left-hand side of a greater than or equal to type of constraint to convert the constraint into an equation is called a surplus variable.

5.3 UNRESTRICTED VARIABLES

Usually in an LP problem, it is assumed that the variables x_j should have non-negative values. In many practical situations, however, one or more of the variables, x_j can have either positive, negative or zero value. Variables, which can assume positive, negative or zero value are called unrestricted variables. Since the use of the simplex method requires that all the decision variables must have non-negative value at each iteration, in order to convert an LP problem involving unrestricted variables into an equivalent problem having only restricted variables, we have to express of each of unrestricted variables as the difference of two non-negative variables.

Suppose variable x_r be unrestricted in sign. We define two new variables say x_r' and x_r'', such that

$$x_r = x_r' - x_r'';\quad x_r', x_r'' \geq 0$$

when $x_r' \geq x_r''$ then $x_r \geq 0$ and when $x_r' \leq x_r''$ then $x_r \leq 0$. Also if $x_r' = x_r''$, then $x_r = 0$. Hence, depending on the value of x_r' and x_r'', x_r can have any sign.

5.4 STANDARD FORM OF A LPP (LINEAR PROGRAMMING PROBLEM)

A general linear programming problem in its standard form can be stated as follows:

Maximise (or Minimise) $Z = c_1x_1 + c_2x_2 + \ldots + c_nx_n$

subject to $a_{11}x_1 + a_{12}x_2 + \ldots + a_{1n}x_n = b_1$

$a_{21}x_1 + a_{22}x_2 + \ldots + a_{2n}x_n = b_2$

....

$a_{m1}x_1 + a_{m2}x_2 + \ldots + a_{mn}x_n = b_m$

$x_1 \geq 0, x_2 \geq 0, \ldots, x_n \geq 0$

or in the matrix notation, we have:

Maximise (or Minimise) $Z = \vec{C}\vec{X}$

Subject to $\vec{A}\vec{X}=\vec{B}$

$\vec{X}\geq 0$

where $\vec{C}=(c_1,c_2,...,c_n)$, $\vec{X}=\begin{bmatrix} x_1 \\ x_2 \\ \vdots \\ x_n \end{bmatrix}$, $\vec{A}=\begin{bmatrix} a_{11} & a_{12} & \cdots & a_{1n} \\ a_{21} & a_{22} & \cdots & a_{2n} \\ \vdots & \vdots & \vdots & \vdots \\ a_{m1} & a_{m2} & \cdots & a_{mn} \end{bmatrix}$ and $\vec{B}=\begin{bmatrix} b_1 \\ b_2 \\ \vdots \\ b_m \end{bmatrix}$

Characteristics of the Standard Form of a LPP

A standard form of a linear programming problem has the following characteristics:

(1) All constraints are equations.

(2) All variables are non-negative.

(3) Objective function is of the maximisation or of the minimisation type.

(4) The right hand side element of each constraint equation is non-negative.

5.5 THE CANONICAL FORM OF A LPP

The general linear programming problem (GLPP) can always be put in the following form:

Maximise $Z=\sum_{j=1}^{n} c_j x_j$

Subject to $\sum_{j=1}^{n} a_{ij} x_j \leq b_i$, $\quad i = 1, 2, ..., m$

This is called the canonical form.

Characteristics of the Canonical Form of a LPP

(1) all decision variables are non-negative,

(2) all constraints are of the $(\leq)$ type,

(3) the objective function is of the maximisation type.

Elementary Transformations for putting the LPP in the Canonical Form

These transformations are as follows:

(1) The minimisation of the objective function Z is equivalent to the maximisation of the negative expression of this function, – Z.

For example, the linear objective functions,

Minimise $Z=c_1x_1+c_2x_2+\ldots+c_nx_n$,

is equivalent to

Maximise $Z'=-Z=-c_1x_1-c_2x_2-\ldots-c_nx_n$

Consequently, in any linear programming problem the objective function can be put in the maximisation form.

(2) An inequality in one direction $(\leq \text{ or } \geq)$ may be changed to an inequality in the opposite direction $(\geq \text{ or } \leq)$ by multiplying both sides of the inequality by –1. For example, the linear constraint

$$a_1x_1 + a_2x_2 \geq b,$$

is equivalent to

$$-a_1x_1 - a_2x_2 \leq -b,$$

Also, $p_1x_1 + p_2x_2 \leq q,$

is equivalent to

$$-p_1x_1 - p_2x_2 \geq -q$$

(3) An equation may be replaced by two weak inequalities in opposite directions. For example

$$a_1x_1 + a_2x_2 = b$$

is equivalent to the two simultaneous constraints,

$$a_1x_1 + a_2x_2 \leq b \text{ and } a_1x_1 + a_2x_2 \geq b,$$

or

$$a_1x_1 + a_2x_2 \leq b \text{ and } -a_1x_1 - a_2x_2 \leq -b$$

(4) A variable which is unrestricted in sign (that is, positive, negative or zero) is equivalent to the difference between two non-negative variables. Thus, if x is unrestricted in sign, it can be replaced by $(x' - x'')$ where x' and x'' are both non-negative; that is, $x' \geq 0$, and $x'' \geq 0$.

5.6 BASIC SOLUTION AND BASIC FEASIBLE SOLUTION OF LPP

Basic Solution

Consider a system Ax = b of m equations in n unknowns (n > m) and r(A) = r(Ab) = m, i.e., none of the equations is redundant. Redundancy is an issue that relates to individual constraints. In particular, a constraint is said to be redundant, if it can be deleted from the set of constraints without changing the feasible set.

A solution obtained by setting any (n – m) variables to zero is called a basic solution, provided the determinant of the coefficient of the remaining m variables is not zero.

Such m variables (any of them may be zero) are called **basic variables** and remaining (n – m) zero valued variables are called **non-basic variables**.

Thus, for a solution to be basic, at least n – m variables must be zero. Here we note that the matrix formed by the coefficients of the m basic variables, or say formed by the vectors associated to the basic variables is non-singular as its determinant does not vanish. Hence, the vectors associated to the basic variables are **linearly independent (L.I.)**.

Thus, a solution in which the vectors associated to m variables are L.I. and remaining n – m variables are zero is called a basic solution.

Hence, a basic solution can be constructed by selecting the m L.I. vectors out of n and setting the variables associated to the remaining (n – m) columns to zero. If B is the matrix of m L.I. vectors of A and x_B is the vector of the corresponding variables (basic variables), then the basic solution is given by

$$Bx_B = b$$

or $$x_B = B^{-1}b$$

The **number of basic solutions** thus obtained will be at the most $^nC_m = \frac{n!}{m!(n-m)!}$ since m vectors out of n can be selected in ^nC_m ways. Note that a B.S. (Basic Solution) corresponds to some basis. Basic solutions are of two types: Non-degenerate basic solution and degenerate basic solutions.

If any of the basic variables vanishes, the solution is called **degenerate basic solution.** On the other hand, if none of the basic variables vanishes, the solution is called **non-degenerate basic solution.**

Thus, a non-degenerate basic solution contains exactly m non-zero and (n – m) zero variables.

Basis Feasible Solution (B.F.S.)

A B.F.S. is a basic solution, which also satisfies the non-negativity restrictions.

Thus in B.F.S., all basic variables are ≠ 0 and all basic variables are non-negative.

5.7 METHOD OF SOLVING A SYSTEM OF TWO EQUATIONS IN THREE OR MORE VARIABLES

If we are given a system of m-simultaneous equations in n unknown as AX = B where A is an m × n matrix with $\rho(A) = m$ (< n). Select a m × n non-singular submatrix S from A. Set all those components of X, that are not associated with columns of S equal to zero.

Now, partition A into two submatrices S and T where S is m × m non-singular and T consists of those columns of A which have not been included in S. Let X_S and X_T be the vectors of the variables associated with columns of S and T respectively. Then we put the system

$$AX = B$$

as $$(S,T)\begin{pmatrix} X_S \\ X_T \end{pmatrix} = B$$

$$SX_S + TX_T = B \quad \Rightarrow \quad SX_S = B - TX_T \qquad ...(i)$$

Since S is non-singular, therefore S^{-1} exists. If we multiply Eq. (i) by S^{-1}, then we get

$$S^{-1}SX_S = S^{-1}B - S^{-1}TX_T$$

$$X_S = S^{-1}B - S^{-1}TX_T$$

Now set $X_T = O$,

where O is a zero-matrix. Then, it follows that

$$X_S = S^{-1}B$$

This is a basic solution and m-variables included in X_S are basic variables. Non-basic variables in X_T are zero variables. In general, $(X_S, 0)$ is a basic solution of the system of equations AX = B, where 0 is a zero matrix.

5.8 OPTIMAL SOLUTION

Any feasible solution, which optimises the objective function, is called an optimal solution. In other words, a basic feasible solution $(X_S, 0)$ to a linear programming problem

Maximise (or Minimise)

$$Z = CX$$

subject to $AX = B$

$$X \geq 0$$

is said to be optimal if it gives us the maximum (or minimum) value of the objective function.

Theorems

Theorem 1: The set of all feasible solutions to a linear programming problem is a convex set.

Proof: We know that the constraints of a linear programming problem can be converted into equations by means of introduction of slack or surplus variables. Therefore, we consider the constraint system of any given linear programming problem of the form

$$AX = B, \qquad X \geq 0$$

where A is an m × n matrix, X is n × 1 matrix and B is an m × 1 matrix.

Now, we form a set K = (X: AX = B, X ≥ 0). The set K is called the set of all feasible solutions of the linear programming problem AX = B.

To establish convexity of set K, let $X_1, X_2 \in K$. Then we have

$$AX_1 = B,\ X_1 \geq 0,\ AX_2 = B,\ X_2 \geq 0$$

Consider $\lambda X_1 + (1-\lambda)X_2$ for $0 \leq \lambda \leq 1$

and

$$A\left[\lambda X_1 + (1-\lambda)X_2\right] = \lambda AX_1 + (1-\lambda)AX_2 = \lambda B + (1-\lambda)B = B$$

Since $X_1, X_2, \lambda, 1-\lambda$ are all non-negative, therefore

$$\lambda_1 X_1 + (1-\lambda)X_2 \geq 0$$

Thus, $\lambda X_1 + (1-\lambda)X_2 \in K$ for $0 \leq \lambda \leq 1$

which implies the set K is a convex set.

Theorem 2: If there is a feasible solution to the system of constraints

$AX = B$, where $X \geq 0$,

then there also exists a basic feasible solution to this system.

Theorem 3: A basic feasible solution to a linear programming problem corresponds to an extreme point of the Convex set K of feasible solutions and conversely, every extreme point of K corresponds to a basic feasible solution to a linear programming problem.

Theorem 4: The objective function of a linear programming problem attains its maximum (or minimum) at one of the extreme points of K.

Solved Practical Problems

Q1. Given the linear programming problem

Maximise

$Z = 4x_1 + 3x_2$

Subject to $2x_1 + x_2 \leq 3$

$x_1 + 4x_2 \leq 5$

$x_1, x_2 \geq 0$

Reduce its constraints into equations by introducing slack variables.

Ans. Consider the first constraint $2x_1 + x_2 \leq 3$. To convert this inequality into an equation, we introduce a new variable

$x_3 = 3 - 2x_1 - x_2 \geq 0$

x_3 is a slack variable, so that by introduction of a new variable $x_3 \geq 0$, the first constraint reduces to

$2x_1 + x_2 + x_3 = 3$

Similarly, corresponding to the second constraint, we introduce a slack variable $x_4 \geq 0$, and the second constraint reduces to

$x_1 + 4x_2 + x_4 = 5$

The given linear programming problem may now be written as

Maximise $Z = 4x_1 + 3x_2$

Subject to $2x_1 + x_2 + x_3 = 3$

$x_1 + 4x_2 + x_4 = 5$

where $x_1, x_2, x_3, x_4 \geq 0$

Q2. Given the LPP

Maximise $Z = 3x_1 + 2.5x_2$

Subject to $2x_1 + 4x_2 \geq 40$

$3x_1 + 2x_2 \geq 50$

$x_1, x_2 \geq 0$

Reduce its constraints into equations by introducing surplus variables.

Ans. Consider the first constraint

$2x_1 + 4x_2 \geq 40$ or $2x_1 + 4x_2 - 40 \geq 0$

We now introduce a new variable $x_3 \geq 0$ defined by

$x_3 = 2x_1 + 4x_2 - 40$

so that the first constraint reduces to

$2x_1 + 4x_2 - x_3 = 40$

This new variable x_3 is surplus variable. Similarly, we can convert the second constraint into an equation by introducing a surplus variable $x_4 \geq 0$ so that second constraint can now be written as

$3x_1 + 2x_2 - x_4 = 50$

The given problem, then, reduces to

Minimise $Z = 3x_1 + 2.5x_2$

Subject to $2x_1 + 4x_2 - x_3 = 40$

$3x_1 + 2x_2 - x_4 = 50$

where $x_1, x_2, x_3, x_4 \geq 0$

Q3. Rewrite the following inequalities in the form of equations by introducing slack or surplus variables

$\mathbf{x_1 - 2x_2 \leq 6}$

$\mathbf{2x_1 + 5x_2 \geq 8}$

$\mathbf{x_1 - 3x_2 \geq -6}$

$\mathbf{x_1, x_2 \geq 0}$

Ans. By introducing slack variable $x_3 \geq 0$, the first constraint reduced to

$x_1 - 2x_2 + x_3 = 6$

Now, introducing surplus variable $x_4 \geq 0$, second constraint reduces to

$2x_1 + 5x_2 - x_4 = 8$

Now the third constraint is

$x_1 - 3x_2 \geq -6$

We see that R.H.S. is negative. Hence, we can write this constraint as

$-x_1 + 3x_2 \leq 6$ [∵ R.H.S. should be positive]

Now, introducing slack variable $x_5 \geq 0$, we have

$-x_1 + 3x_2 + x_5 = 6$

or $x_1 - 3x_2 - x_5 = -6$

Therefore, the resulting system of equations can be written as

$x_1 - 2x_2 + x_3 = 6$

$2x_1 + 5x_2 - x_4 = 8$

$x_1 - 3x_2 - x_5 = -6$

$x_1, x_2, x_3, x_4, x_5 \geq 0$

Q4. Write the following LPP in a form in which variables are all non-negative.

Maximise $\mathbf{Z = 4x_1 + 2x_2 - 3x_3}$

subject to $\mathbf{2x_1 + 3x_2 + 4x_3 \leq 7}$

$\mathbf{5x_1 + x_2 + 2x_3 \geq 9}$

$\mathbf{x_1, x_2 \geq 0, x_3}$ **is unrestricted.**

Ans. It is given that x_3 is unrestricted.

Hence, we write

$x_3 = x_3' - x_3''$

Hence, we have

Maximise

$Z = 4x_1 + 2x_2 - 3(x_3' - x_3'')$

$\Rightarrow \quad Z = 4x_1 + 2x_2 - 3x_3' + 3x_3''$

subject to

$2x_1 + 3x_2 + 4x_3' - 4x_3'' \leq 7$

$5x_1 + x_2 + 2x_3' - 2x_3'' \geq 9$

$x_1, x_2, x_3', x_3'' \geq 0$

Q5. Maximise $\mathbf{Z = x_1 - 2x_2}$

subject to $\mathbf{3x_1 + 2x_2 \leq 0}$

$\mathbf{x_1 - x_2 \geq -2}$

$\mathbf{-x_1 + 2x_2 = 7}$

$\mathbf{x_1, x_2}$ **are unrestricted.**

Ans. Let $x_1 = x_1' - x_1''$ and $x_2 = x_2' - x_2''$ so that $x_1', x_1'', x_2', x_2'' \geq 0$

The problem reduces to

Maximise $Z = x' - x_1'' - 2x_2' + 2x_2''$

subject to $3x_1' - 3x_1'' + 2x_2' - 2x_2'' \leq 0$

$x_1' - x_1'' - x_2' + x_2'' \geq -2$

$-x_1' + x_1'' + 2x_2' \quad 2x_2'' = 7$

$x_1', x_1'', x_2', x_2'' \geq 0.$

Q6. Put the following linear programming problem into its standard form

Minimise $\mathbf{Z = -3x_1 + 4x_2 - x_3}$

subject to $\mathbf{-x_1 - 3x_2 + 2x_3 \geq -2}$

$\mathbf{2x_1 + x_2 - 4x_3 \leq 10}$

$\mathbf{3x_1 - x_2 + 2x_3 \geq 5}$

$\mathbf{2x_1 + x_2 + 2x_3 = 3}$

$\mathbf{x_1}$ **is unrestricted;** $\mathbf{x_2, x_3 \geq 0.}$

Ans. Multiply the first constraint by (–1) to ensure that all entries on the right hand side of the constraints are positive.

Then problem takes the form

Minimise

$Z = -3x_1 + 4x_2 - x_3$

Subject to $x_1 + 3x_2 - 2x_3 \leq 2$

$2x_1 + x_2 - 4x_3 \leq 10$

$3x_1 - x_2 + 2x_3 \geq 5$

$2x_1 + x_2 + 2x_3 = 3$

x_1 is unrestricted; $x_2, x_3 \geq 0$

Let $x_1 = x_1' - x_1''$, so that $x_1' \geq 0, x_1'' \geq 0$ and problem can be rewritten as

Minimise

$Z = -3x_1' + 3x_1'' + 4x_2 - x_3$

Subject to $x_1' - x_1'' + 3x_2 - 2x_3 \leq 2$

$2x_1' - 2x_1'' + x_2 - 4x_3 \leq 10$

$3x_1' - 3x_1'' - x_2 + 2x_3 \geq 5$

$2x_1' - 2x_1'' + x_2 + 2x_3 = 3$

$x_1', x_1'', x_2, x_3 \geq 0$

Now, we introduce slack variables $x_4 \geq 0$, $x_5 \geq 0$ respectively to the first two constraints and surplus variable $x_6 \geq 0$ to the third constraint, we may rewrite the above problem in the standard form as

Minimise $Z = -3x_1' + 3x_1'' + 4x_2 - x_3$

Subject to $x_1' - x_1'' + 3x_2 - 2x_3 + x_4 = 2$

$2x_1' - 2x_1'' + x_2 - 4x_3 + x_5 = 10$

$3x_1' - 3x_1'' - x_2 + 2x_3 - x_6 = 5$

$2x_1' - 2x_1'' + x_2 + 2x_3 = 3$

$x_1', x_1'', x_2, x_3, x_4, x_5, x_6 \geq 0$

Q7. Reduce the following linear programming problems respectively into their standard forms.

Maximise $Z = 3x_1 - 2x_2 + 4x_3$

Subject to $x_1 - 2x_2 + 3x_3 \leq 2$

$2x_1 + 3x_2 + x_3 \leq -2$

$4x_1 + 2x_2 \leq 2$

$x_1, x_2, x_3 \geq 0$

Ans. We know that the all entries of R.H.S. of all constraints should be positive. Hence, multiply by (–1) in second constraint, then we have the constraints as follows:

$x_1 - 2x_2 + 3x_3 \leq 2$

$-2x_1 - 3x_2 - x_3 \geq 2$

$4x_1 + 2x_2 \le 2$

$x_1, x_2, x_3, \ge 0$

Now, introducing slack variable $x_4 \ge 0$ for first constraint, surplus variable $x_5 \ge 0$ for second constraint and slack variable $x_6 \ge 0$ for third constraint. Then, we have

$x_1 - 2x_2 + 3x_3 + x_4 = 2$

$-2x_1 - 3x_2 - x_3 - x_5 = 2$

or $2x_1 + 3x_2 + x_3 + x_5 = -2$

and $4x_1 + 2x_2 + x_6 = 2$

Thus, we have the standard form of given LPP as follows

Maximise $Z = 3x_1 - 2x_2 + 4x_3$

subject to

$x_1 - 2x_2 + 3x_3 + x_4 = 2$

$2x_1 + 3x_2 + x_3 + x_5 = -2$

$4x_1 + 2x_2 + x_6 = 2$

$x_1, x_2, x_3, x_4, x_5, x_6 \ge 0$

Q8. Write the following LPP in canonical form

Minimise $Z = 8x_1 - 8x_2 + 9x_3$

subject to $2x_1 + 4x_2 + 3x_3 \le 60$

$x_1 + 8x_2 - 7x_3 \ge 70$

$5x_1 + 3x_2 = 30$

$x_1, x_2 \ge 0$

where x_3 is unrestricted in sign.

Ans. We know that in canonical form, all constrains are of $\le$ type and the objective function is of the maximisation type.

Now, it is given that x_3 is unrestricted in sign, so let $x_3 = x_3' - x_3''$, where $x_3', x_3'' \ge 0$

Hence, we have

Minimise $Z = 8x_1 - 8x_2 + 9x_3' - 9x_3''$

subject to $2x_1 + 4x_2 + 3x_3' - 3x_3'' \le 60$

$x_1 + 8x_2 - 7x_3' + 7x_3'' \ge 70$

$5x_1 + 3x_2 = 30$

$x_1, x_2, x_3', x_3'' \ge 0$

Now, third constraint is

$5x_1 + 3x_2 = 30$

It can be written as

$5x_1 + 3x_2 \le 30$

and $-5x_1 - 3x_2 \le -30$

Hence, we have canonical form as follows

Maximise $Z' = (-Z) = -8x_1 + 8x_2 - 9x_3' + 9x_3''$

subject to $2x_1 + 4x_2 + 3x_3' - 3x_3'' \le 60$

$-x_1 - 8x_2 + 7x_3' - 7x_3'' \le -70$

$5x_1 + 3x_2 \le 30$

$-5x_1 - 3x_2 \le -30$

where $x_1, x_2, x_3', x_3'' \ge 0$

Q9. Obtain all basic feasible solutions to the following system of linear equations:

$\mathbf{2x_1 + x_2 - x_3 = 2}$

$\mathbf{3x_1 + 2x_2 + x_3 = 3}$

$\mathbf{x_1, x_2, x_3 \ge 0}$

Or

Check whether the following system of linear equations has degenerate solutions:

$\mathbf{2x_1 + x_2 - x_3 = 2}$

$\mathbf{3x_1 + 2x_2 + x_3 = 3}$

If yes, find all the degenerate basic feasible solutions.

[June-2016, Q.No.-6(a)]

Ans. The given system is of the form

AX = B, where

$$A = \begin{bmatrix} 2 & 1 & -1 \\ 3 & 2 & 1 \end{bmatrix}, \; X = \begin{bmatrix} x_1 \\ x_2 \\ x_3 \end{bmatrix}, \; B = \begin{bmatrix} 2 \\ 3 \end{bmatrix}$$

Here, rank of A, i.e., $\rho(A) = 2$ because $\begin{vmatrix} 2 & 1 \\ 3 & 2 \end{vmatrix} = 1 \ne 0$. Therefore, a basic solution will have at least two components different from zero. Number of basic solutions will be

$$^3C_2 = \frac{3!}{2!(3-2)!} = 3$$

since, m = 2, n = 3.

Here, m = number of equations

and n = number of unknown variable in each equation.

Now, to find all basic solutions, we put n – m = 3 – 2 = 1 variable equal to zero. First, we set $x_3 = 0$. Here, x_3 is the non-basic variable. The system reduces to the form

$$2x_1 + x_2 = 2$$
$$3x_1 + 2x_2 = 3$$

i.e., we have

$$\begin{bmatrix} 2 & 1 \\ 3 & 2 \end{bmatrix} \begin{bmatrix} x_1 \\ x_2 \end{bmatrix} = \begin{bmatrix} 2 \\ 3 \end{bmatrix}$$

Here, $X_T = (x_3) = (0)$, $X_S = \begin{bmatrix} x_1 \\ x_2 \end{bmatrix}$. Therefore

$$\begin{bmatrix} x_1 \\ x_2 \end{bmatrix} = \begin{bmatrix} 2 & 1 \\ 3 & 2 \end{bmatrix}^{-1} \begin{bmatrix} 2 \\ 3 \end{bmatrix}$$

$$\Rightarrow \quad \begin{bmatrix} x_1 \\ x_2 \end{bmatrix} = \begin{bmatrix} 2 & -1 \\ -3 & 2 \end{bmatrix} \begin{bmatrix} 2 \\ 3 \end{bmatrix}$$

$$\Rightarrow \quad \begin{bmatrix} x_1 \\ x_2 \end{bmatrix} = \begin{bmatrix} 4-3 \\ -6+6 \end{bmatrix} = \begin{bmatrix} 1 \\ 0 \end{bmatrix}$$

$$\Rightarrow \quad x_1 = 1,\ x_2 = 0,\ x_3 = 0$$

is a basic solution, where x_1 and x_2 are basic variables.

Now, set $x_2 = 0$, therefore the original system reduces to

$$2x_1 - x_3 = 2$$
$$3x_1 + x_3 = 3$$

$$\Rightarrow \quad \begin{bmatrix} 2 & -1 \\ 3 & 1 \end{bmatrix} \begin{bmatrix} x_1 \\ x_3 \end{bmatrix} = \begin{bmatrix} 2 \\ 3 \end{bmatrix}$$

$$\Rightarrow \quad \begin{bmatrix} x_1 \\ x_3 \end{bmatrix} = \begin{bmatrix} 2 & -1 \\ 3 & 1 \end{bmatrix}^{-1} \begin{bmatrix} 2 \\ 3 \end{bmatrix}$$

$$\Rightarrow \quad \begin{bmatrix} x_1 \\ x_3 \end{bmatrix} = \begin{bmatrix} 1/5 & 1/5 \\ -3/5 & 2/5 \end{bmatrix} \begin{bmatrix} 2 \\ 3 \end{bmatrix}$$

$$\Rightarrow \quad \begin{bmatrix} x_1 \\ x_3 \end{bmatrix} = \begin{bmatrix} \frac{2}{5} + \frac{3}{5} \\ \frac{-6}{5} + \frac{6}{5} \end{bmatrix} = \begin{bmatrix} 1 \\ 0 \end{bmatrix}$$

$$\Rightarrow \quad x_1 = 1,\ x_2 = 0,\ x_3 = 0$$

This is another basic solution to the given system.

Now, set $x_1 = 0$, we then get

$$x_2 - x_3 = 2$$
$$2x_2 + x_3 = 3$$

$$\Rightarrow \quad \begin{bmatrix} 1 & -1 \\ 2 & 1 \end{bmatrix} \begin{bmatrix} x_2 \\ x_3 \end{bmatrix} = \begin{bmatrix} 2 \\ 3 \end{bmatrix}$$

$$\Rightarrow \quad \begin{bmatrix} x_2 \\ x_3 \end{bmatrix} = \begin{bmatrix} 1 & -1 \\ 2 & 1 \end{bmatrix}^{-1} \begin{bmatrix} 2 \\ 3 \end{bmatrix}$$

$$\Rightarrow \quad \begin{bmatrix} x_2 \\ x_3 \end{bmatrix} = \begin{bmatrix} 1/3 & 1/3 \\ -2/3 & 1/3 \end{bmatrix} \begin{bmatrix} 2 \\ 3 \end{bmatrix}$$

$$\Rightarrow \quad \begin{bmatrix} x_2 \\ x_3 \end{bmatrix} = \begin{bmatrix} \frac{2}{3} + \frac{3}{3} \\ \frac{-4}{3} + \frac{3}{3} \end{bmatrix} = \begin{bmatrix} 5/3 \\ -1/3 \end{bmatrix}$$

$$\Rightarrow \quad x_1 = 0,\ x_2 = \frac{5}{3},\ x_3 = \frac{-1}{3}$$

is also a basic solution to the given system of equations.

Hence, we have all the three basic solutions as follows:

$x_1 = 1, \quad x_2 = 0, \quad x_3 = 0$

$x_1 = 1, \quad x_2 = 0, \quad x_3 = 0$

$x_1 = 0, \quad x_2 = 5/3, \quad x_3 = -1/3$

First and second basic solutions satisfy the non-negativity restriction; hence, these are basic **feasible** solutions whereas third basic solution has a negative basic variable $\left(x_3 = -1/3\right)$ so it does not satisfy the non-negativity restriction, so it is **non-feasible**.

Note: First and second basic solutions are **degenerate** because in first solution, basic variable x_2 vanishes, i.e., $x_2 = 0$ and in second solution, basic variable x_3 vanishes, i.e., $x_3 = 0$. Third basic solution is **non-degenerate** because basic variables are non-zero.

Q10. If $A_1 = \begin{bmatrix} 3 \\ 4 \end{bmatrix}, A_2 = \begin{bmatrix} -1 \\ 2 \end{bmatrix}, A_3 = \begin{bmatrix} 1 \\ 4 \end{bmatrix}$, and $B = \begin{bmatrix} 1 \\ 4 \end{bmatrix}$, then determine whether all possible basic solutions exist for the following set of equations $\left[A_1, A_2, A_3\right]X = B$

Ans. Let $A = \left[A_1, A_2, A_3\right],\ X = \begin{bmatrix} x_1 \\ x_2 \\ x_3 \end{bmatrix}$

$$\Rightarrow \quad A = \begin{bmatrix} 3 & -1 & 1 \\ 4 & 2 & 4 \end{bmatrix}$$

Hence, $\left[A_1, A_2, A_3\right]X = B$

$\Rightarrow \quad AX = B$

$$\Rightarrow \quad \begin{bmatrix} 3 & -1 & 1 \\ 4 & 2 & 4 \end{bmatrix} \begin{bmatrix} x_1 \\ x_2 \\ x_3 \end{bmatrix} = \begin{bmatrix} 1 \\ 4 \end{bmatrix}$$

and the system of equations is

$$3x_1 - x_2 + x_3 = 1$$
$$4x_1 + 2x_2 + 4x_3 = 4$$
$$x_1, x_2, x_3 \geq 0$$

Now, rank of A, i.e., $\rho(A) = 2.$ Therefore, a basic solution will have two components different from zero.

Number of basic solutions will be

$$^3C_2 = \frac{3!}{2!1!} = 3$$

Now, set $x_3 = 0$ in the system of equation, i.e.

$$3x_1 - x_2 = 1$$
$$4x_1 + 2x_2 = 4$$

$$\Rightarrow \quad \begin{bmatrix} 3 & -1 \\ 4 & 2 \end{bmatrix} \begin{bmatrix} x_1 \\ x_2 \end{bmatrix} = \begin{bmatrix} 1 \\ 4 \end{bmatrix}$$

$$\Rightarrow \quad \begin{bmatrix} x_1 \\ x_2 \end{bmatrix} = \begin{bmatrix} 3 & -1 \\ 4 & 2 \end{bmatrix}^{-1} \begin{bmatrix} 1 \\ 4 \end{bmatrix}$$

$$\Rightarrow \quad \begin{bmatrix} x_1 \\ x_2 \end{bmatrix} = \begin{bmatrix} 2/10 & 1/10 \\ -4/10 & 3/10 \end{bmatrix} \begin{bmatrix} 1 \\ 4 \end{bmatrix}$$

$$\Rightarrow \quad \begin{bmatrix} x_1 \\ x_2 \end{bmatrix} = \begin{bmatrix} \frac{2}{10} + \frac{4}{10} \\ \frac{-4}{10} + \frac{12}{10} \end{bmatrix} = \begin{bmatrix} \frac{3}{5} \\ \frac{4}{5} \end{bmatrix}$$

$$\Rightarrow \quad x_1 = \frac{3}{5},\ x_2 = \frac{4}{5},\ x_3 = 0$$

This is first set of basic solutions. Now set $x_2 = 0,$ then we have

$$3x_1 + x_3 = 1$$
$$4x_1 + 4x_3 = 4 \text{ or } x_1 + x_3 = 1$$

$$\Rightarrow \quad \begin{bmatrix} 3 & 1 \\ 1 & 1 \end{bmatrix} \begin{bmatrix} x_1 \\ x_3 \end{bmatrix} = \begin{bmatrix} 1 \\ 1 \end{bmatrix}$$

$$\Rightarrow \quad \begin{bmatrix} x_1 \\ x_3 \end{bmatrix} = \begin{bmatrix} 3 & 1 \\ 1 & 1 \end{bmatrix}^{-1} \begin{bmatrix} 1 \\ 1 \end{bmatrix}$$

$$\Rightarrow \quad \begin{bmatrix} x_1 \\ x_3 \end{bmatrix} = \begin{bmatrix} 1/2 & -1/2 \\ -1/2 & 3/2 \end{bmatrix} \begin{bmatrix} 1 \\ 1 \end{bmatrix}$$

$$\Rightarrow \quad \begin{bmatrix} x_1 \\ x_3 \end{bmatrix} = \begin{bmatrix} 1/2 - 1/2 \\ -1/2 + 3/2 \end{bmatrix} = \begin{bmatrix} 0 \\ 1 \end{bmatrix}$$

$$\Rightarrow \quad x_1 = 0,\ x_2 = 0,\ x_3 = 1$$

This is second set of basic solutions.

Now set $x_1 = 0,$ then we have

$$-x_2 + x_3 = 1$$

$$2x_2 + 4x_3 = 4 \text{ or } x_2 + 2x_3 = 2$$

$$\Rightarrow \quad \begin{bmatrix} -1 & 1 \\ 1 & 2 \end{bmatrix} \begin{bmatrix} x_2 \\ x_3 \end{bmatrix} = \begin{bmatrix} 1 \\ 2 \end{bmatrix}$$

$$\Rightarrow \quad \begin{bmatrix} x_2 \\ x_3 \end{bmatrix} = \begin{bmatrix} -1 & 1 \\ 1 & 2 \end{bmatrix}^{-1} \begin{bmatrix} 1 \\ 2 \end{bmatrix}$$

$$\Rightarrow \quad \begin{bmatrix} x_2 \\ x_3 \end{bmatrix} = \begin{bmatrix} -2/3 & +1/3 \\ +1/3 & +1/3 \end{bmatrix} \begin{bmatrix} 1 \\ 2 \end{bmatrix}$$

$$\Rightarrow \quad \begin{bmatrix} x_2 \\ x_3 \end{bmatrix} = \begin{bmatrix} -2/3 + 2/3 \\ 1/3 + 2/3 \end{bmatrix} = \begin{bmatrix} 0 \\ 1 \end{bmatrix}$$

$$\Rightarrow \quad x_1 = 0,\ x_2 = 0,\ x_3 = 1$$

This is third set of basic solutions.

Hence, we have all sets of basic solutions as follows:

$$x_1 = \frac{3}{5}, \quad x_2 = \frac{4}{5}, \quad x_3 = 0$$

$$x_1 = 0, \quad x_2 = 0, \quad x_3 = 1$$

$$x_1 = 0, \quad x_2 = 0, \quad x_3 = 1$$

Q11. Find all the basic solutions of the following system:

$$\mathbf{x_1 + 2x_2 + x_3 = 4}$$

$$\mathbf{2x_1 + x_2 + 5x_3 = 5}$$

Ans. The given system is of the form $AX = B$ where

$$A = \begin{pmatrix} 1 & 2 & 1 \\ 2 & 1 & 5 \end{pmatrix},\ X = \begin{pmatrix} x_1 \\ x_2 \\ x_3 \end{pmatrix},\ B = \begin{pmatrix} 4 \\ 5 \end{pmatrix}.$$

Here $\rho(A) = 2.$ Therefore, a basic solution will have two components different from zero. Number of basic solutions will be

$$^3C_2 = \frac{3!}{2!\ 1!} = 3,$$

Since, m = 2, n = 3.

To find all basic solutions, we first set $x_3 = 0$, the system reduces to the form

$$x_1 + 2x_2 = 4$$
$$2x_1 + x_2 = 5$$

i.e., we have $\begin{pmatrix} 1 & 2 \\ 2 & 1 \end{pmatrix}\begin{pmatrix} x_1 \\ x_2 \end{pmatrix} = \begin{pmatrix} 4 \\ 5 \end{pmatrix}$

Here, $X_T = (x_3) = (0)$, $X_S = \begin{pmatrix} x_1 \\ x_2 \end{pmatrix}$. Therefore,

$$\begin{pmatrix} x_1 \\ x_2 \end{pmatrix} = \begin{pmatrix} 1 & 2 \\ 2 & 1 \end{pmatrix}^{-1}\begin{pmatrix} 4 \\ 5 \end{pmatrix} = \begin{pmatrix} -\frac{1}{3} & \frac{2}{3} \\ \frac{2}{3} & -\frac{1}{3} \end{pmatrix}\begin{pmatrix} 4 \\ 5 \end{pmatrix} = \begin{pmatrix} 2 \\ 1 \end{pmatrix}$$

In other words $x_1 = 2,\ x_2 = 1,\ x_3 = 0$

is a basic solution, where x_1 and x_2 are basic variables.

Now, set $x_2 = 0$, therefore the original system reduces to

$$x_1 + x_3 = 4$$
$$2x_1 + 5x_3 = 5$$

Hence, we have

$$\begin{pmatrix} 1 & 1 \\ 2 & 5 \end{pmatrix}\begin{pmatrix} x_1 \\ x_3 \end{pmatrix} = \begin{pmatrix} 4 \\ 5 \end{pmatrix}$$

or $$\begin{pmatrix} x_1 \\ x_3 \end{pmatrix} = \begin{pmatrix} 1 & 1 \\ 2 & 5 \end{pmatrix}^{-1}\begin{pmatrix} 4 \\ 5 \end{pmatrix} = \begin{pmatrix} \frac{5}{3} & -\frac{1}{3} \\ -\frac{2}{3} & \frac{1}{3} \end{pmatrix}\begin{pmatrix} 4 \\ 5 \end{pmatrix} = \begin{pmatrix} 5 \\ -1 \end{pmatrix}$$

Therefore, $x_1 = 5,\ x_2 = 0,\ x_3 = -1$. This is another basic solution to the given system.

Similarly, we can set $x_1 = 0$ and the system reduces to

$$2x_2 + x_3 = 4$$
$$x_2 + 5x_3 = 5$$

or $$\begin{pmatrix} 2 & 1 \\ 1 & 5 \end{pmatrix}\begin{pmatrix} x_2 \\ x_3 \end{pmatrix} = \begin{pmatrix} 4 \\ 5 \end{pmatrix}$$

$$\begin{pmatrix} x_2 \\ x_3 \end{pmatrix} = \begin{pmatrix} 2 & 1 \\ 1 & 5 \end{pmatrix}^{-1}\begin{pmatrix} 4 \\ 5 \end{pmatrix} = \begin{pmatrix} \frac{5}{9} & -\frac{1}{9} \\ -\frac{1}{9} & \frac{2}{9} \end{pmatrix}\begin{pmatrix} 4 \\ 5 \end{pmatrix} = \begin{pmatrix} \frac{5}{3} \\ \frac{2}{3} \end{pmatrix}$$

and $x_1 = 0,\ x_2 = \frac{5}{3},\ x_3 = \frac{2}{3}$ is a basic solution to the given system. Hence, we have all the three basic solutions as follows:

$$x_1 = 2,\ x_2 = 1,\ x_3 = 0$$

$$x_1 = 5,\ x_2 = 0,\ x_3 = -1$$

$$x_1 = 0,\ x_2 = \frac{5}{3},\ x_3 = \frac{2}{3}.$$

The basic variables in the first and third solutions satisfy the non-negativity restrictions, whereas in the second solution, one of the basic variables is negative. Hence, first and third solutions are basic feasible solutions whereas the second one is basic non-feasible.

Q12. Find all the basic feasible solutions of the following system of linear equations:

$$2x_1 + x_2 - x_3 + 2x_4 = 2$$

$$3x_1 + 2x_2 + x_3 + 4x_4 = 3$$

$$x_1, x_2, x_3, x_4 \geq 0$$

Check if any of them is degenerate solution. Justify your answer.

[Dec-2014, Q.No.-4(b)]

Ans. Here, we have

$$A = \begin{bmatrix} 2 & 1 & -1 & 2 \\ 3 & 2 & 1 & 4 \end{bmatrix},\quad X = \begin{bmatrix} x_1 \\ x_2 \\ x_3 \\ x_4 \end{bmatrix},\quad B = \begin{bmatrix} 2 \\ 3 \end{bmatrix}$$

Number of basic solutions will be

$$^4C_2 = \frac{4!}{2!(4-2)!} = 6$$

Hence, m = 2, n = 4

To find basic solutions, we put n – m = 4 – 2 = 2 variables equal to zero. First, we set $x_3 = x_4 = 0$. Thus, x_1 and x_2 are basic variables and x_3 and x_4 are non-basic variables here. Now, we have

$$2x_1 + x_2 = 2$$

$$3x_1 + 2x_2 = 3$$

Now, we have

$$\begin{bmatrix} 2 & 1 \\ 3 & 2 \end{bmatrix} \begin{bmatrix} x_1 \\ x_2 \end{bmatrix} = \begin{bmatrix} 2 \\ 3 \end{bmatrix}$$

$$\Rightarrow \quad \begin{bmatrix} x_1 \\ x_2 \end{bmatrix} = \begin{bmatrix} 2 & 1 \\ 3 & 2 \end{bmatrix}^{-1} \begin{bmatrix} 2 \\ 3 \end{bmatrix}$$

$$\Rightarrow \quad \begin{bmatrix} x_1 \\ x_2 \end{bmatrix} = \begin{bmatrix} 2 & -1 \\ -3 & 2 \end{bmatrix} \begin{bmatrix} 2 \\ 3 \end{bmatrix}$$

$$\Rightarrow \quad \begin{bmatrix} x_1 \\ x_2 \end{bmatrix} = \begin{bmatrix} 4-3 \\ -6+6 \end{bmatrix} = \begin{bmatrix} 1 \\ 0 \end{bmatrix}$$

Therefore, $x_1 = 1,\ x_2 = 0,\ x_3 = 0,\ x_4 = 0$

This basic feasible solution is degenerate because basic variable x_2 vanishes, i.e., equals to zero.

Now, we set $x_2 = x_3 = 0$, then we have

$$2x_1 + 2x_4 = 2$$

$$\Rightarrow \quad x_1 + x_4 = 1$$

and $3x_1 + 4x_4 = 3$

$$\begin{bmatrix} 1 & 1 \\ 3 & 4 \end{bmatrix} \begin{bmatrix} x_1 \\ x_4 \end{bmatrix} = \begin{bmatrix} 1 \\ 3 \end{bmatrix}$$

$$\Rightarrow \quad \begin{bmatrix} x_1 \\ x_4 \end{bmatrix} = \begin{bmatrix} 1 & 1 \\ 3 & 4 \end{bmatrix}^{-1} \begin{bmatrix} 1 \\ 3 \end{bmatrix}$$

$$\Rightarrow \quad \begin{bmatrix} x_1 \\ x_4 \end{bmatrix} = \begin{bmatrix} 4 & -1 \\ -3 & 1 \end{bmatrix} \begin{bmatrix} 1 \\ 3 \end{bmatrix}$$

$$\Rightarrow \quad \begin{bmatrix} x_1 \\ x_4 \end{bmatrix} = \begin{bmatrix} 4-3 \\ -3+3 \end{bmatrix} = \begin{bmatrix} 1 \\ 0 \end{bmatrix}$$

$$\Rightarrow \quad x_1 = 1,\ x_2 = 0,\ x_3 = 0,\ x_4 = 0$$

This is degenerate solution because basis variable x_4 vanishes, i.e., $x_4 = 0$.

Now, we set $x_1 = x_2 = 0$, then we have

$$-x_3 + 2x_4 = 2$$

$$x_3 + 4x_4 = 3$$

$$\begin{bmatrix} -1 & 2 \\ 1 & 4 \end{bmatrix} \begin{bmatrix} x_3 \\ x_4 \end{bmatrix} = \begin{bmatrix} 2 \\ 3 \end{bmatrix}$$

$$\Rightarrow \quad \begin{bmatrix} x_3 \\ x_4 \end{bmatrix} = \begin{bmatrix} -1 & 2 \\ 1 & 4 \end{bmatrix}^{-1} \begin{bmatrix} 2 \\ 3 \end{bmatrix}$$

$$\Rightarrow \quad \begin{bmatrix} x_3 \\ x_4 \end{bmatrix} = \begin{bmatrix} -\frac{4}{6} & \frac{2}{6} \\ \frac{1}{6} & \frac{1}{6} \end{bmatrix} \begin{bmatrix} 2 \\ 3 \end{bmatrix}$$

$$\Rightarrow \begin{bmatrix} x_3 \\ x_4 \end{bmatrix} = \begin{bmatrix} -\frac{8}{6}+\frac{6}{6} \\ \frac{2}{6}+\frac{3}{6} \end{bmatrix} = \begin{bmatrix} -\frac{1}{3} \\ \frac{5}{6} \end{bmatrix}$$

$$\Rightarrow \quad x_1 = 0,\ x_2 = 0,\ x_3 = -\frac{1}{3},\ x_4 = \frac{5}{6}$$

This is non-degenerate solution because basic variables x_3 and x_4 are non-zero.

Now, we set $x_1 = x_3 = 0$, then we have

$$x_2 + 2x_4 = 2$$

$$2x_2 + 4x_4 = 3$$

$$\begin{bmatrix} x_2 \\ x_4 \end{bmatrix} = \begin{bmatrix} 1 & 2 \\ 2 & 4 \end{bmatrix}^{-1} \begin{bmatrix} 2 \\ 3 \end{bmatrix}$$

$$\Rightarrow \begin{bmatrix} x_2 \\ x_4 \end{bmatrix} = \text{not defined}$$

Hence, there is no solution.

Now, we set $x_2 = x_4 = 0$, then we have

$$2x_1 - x_3 = 2$$

$$3x_1 + x_3 = 3$$

$$\Rightarrow \begin{bmatrix} x_1 \\ x_3 \end{bmatrix} = \begin{bmatrix} 2 & -1 \\ 3 & 1 \end{bmatrix}^{-1} \begin{bmatrix} 2 \\ 3 \end{bmatrix}$$

$$\Rightarrow \begin{bmatrix} x_1 \\ x_3 \end{bmatrix} = \begin{bmatrix} 1/5 & 1/5 \\ -3/5 & 2/5 \end{bmatrix} \begin{bmatrix} 2 \\ 3 \end{bmatrix}$$

$$\Rightarrow \begin{bmatrix} x_1 \\ x_3 \end{bmatrix} = \begin{bmatrix} \frac{2}{5}+\frac{3}{5} \\ -\frac{6}{5}+\frac{6}{5} \end{bmatrix} = \begin{bmatrix} 1 \\ 0 \end{bmatrix}$$

$$\Rightarrow \quad x_1 = 1,\ x_2 = 0,\ x_3 = 0,\ x_4 = 0$$

Here, basic variable $x_3 = 0$, hence it is degenerate solution.

Now, we set $x_1 = x_4 = 0$, then we have

$$x_2 - x_3 = 2$$

$$2x_2 + x_3 = 3$$

$$\begin{bmatrix} x_2 \\ x_3 \end{bmatrix} = \begin{bmatrix} 1 & -1 \\ 2 & 1 \end{bmatrix}^{-1} \begin{bmatrix} 2 \\ 3 \end{bmatrix}$$

$$\Rightarrow \begin{bmatrix} x_2 \\ x_3 \end{bmatrix} = \begin{bmatrix} 1/3 & 1/3 \\ -2/3 & 1/3 \end{bmatrix} \begin{bmatrix} 2 \\ 3 \end{bmatrix}$$

$$\Rightarrow \quad \begin{bmatrix} x_2 \\ x_3 \end{bmatrix} = \begin{bmatrix} \frac{2}{3}+\frac{3}{3} \\ -\frac{4}{3}+\frac{3}{3} \end{bmatrix} = \begin{bmatrix} \frac{5}{3} \\ -\frac{1}{3} \end{bmatrix}$$

$$\Rightarrow \quad x_1 = 0,\ x_2 = \frac{5}{3},\ x_3 = -\frac{1}{3},\ x_4 = 0$$

Finally, we have the following table:

Non-basic variables	Basic variables	Values of Basic Variables	Feasibility	Degenerate or not
$x_3 = x_4 = 0$	x_1, x_2	$x_1 = 1$ $x_2 = 0$	Feasible	Degenerate
$x_2 = x_3 = 0$	x_1, x_4	$x_1 = 1$ $x_4 = 0$	Feasible	Degenerate
$x_1 = x_2 = 0$	x_3, x_4	$x_3 = -\frac{1}{3}$ $x_4 = \frac{5}{6}$	Non–feasible	Non – degenerate
$x_1 = x_3 = 0$	x_2, x_4	No values	Non–feasible	Non – degenerate
$x_2 = x_4 = 0$	x_1, x_3	$x_1 = 1$ $x_3 = 0$	Feasible	Degenerate
$x_1 = x_4 = 0$	x_2, x_3	$x_2 = \frac{5}{3}$ $x_3 = -\frac{1}{3}$	Non–feasible	Non – degenerate

Q13. Consider the system of equations

$$\mathbf{2x_1 + x_2 + 4x_3 = 11}$$

$$\mathbf{3x_1 + x_2 + 5x_3 = 14}$$

A feasible solution is

$$\mathbf{x_1 = 2,\ x_2 = 3,\ x_3 = 1}$$

Reduce this feasible solution to a basic feasible solution.

[Dec-2015, Q.No.-6(c)]

Ans. The given system of equations may be put in matrix notations as

$$\begin{bmatrix} 2 & 1 & 4 \\ 3 & 1 & 5 \end{bmatrix} \begin{bmatrix} x_1 \\ x_2 \\ x_3 \end{bmatrix} = \begin{bmatrix} 11 \\ 14 \end{bmatrix}$$

where AX = B

$$\Rightarrow \quad A = \begin{bmatrix} 2 & 1 & 4 \\ 3 & 1 & 5 \end{bmatrix},\ X = \begin{bmatrix} x_1 \\ x_2 \\ x_3 \end{bmatrix} \text{ and } B = \begin{bmatrix} 11 \\ 14 \end{bmatrix}$$

Let the columns of A be denoted by

$$A_1 = \begin{bmatrix} 2 \\ 3 \end{bmatrix},\ A_2 = \begin{bmatrix} 1 \\ 1 \end{bmatrix},\ A_3 = \begin{bmatrix} 4 \\ 5 \end{bmatrix}$$

Hence, $\rho(A) = 2$, therefore a basic solution to the given system of equations exists with no more than two variables different from zero. In addition, the column vectors A_1, A_2, A_3 are linearly dependent. Therefore, there exist scalars λ_1, λ_2, λ_3 not all zero such that

$$A_1\lambda_1 + A_2\lambda_2 + A_3\lambda_3 = 0$$

$$\Rightarrow \quad \begin{bmatrix} 2 \\ 3 \end{bmatrix}\lambda_1 + \begin{bmatrix} 1 \\ 1 \end{bmatrix}\lambda_2 + \begin{bmatrix} 4 \\ 5 \end{bmatrix}\lambda_3 = 0$$

Hence, we have

$$2\lambda_1 + \lambda_2 + 4\lambda_3 = 0 \qquad ...(i)$$

and $$3\lambda_1 + \lambda_2 + 5\lambda_3 = 0 \qquad ...(ii)$$

Let $\lambda_1 = 1$, then we have

$$\lambda_2 + 4\lambda_3 = -2 \qquad ...(iii)$$

and $$\lambda_2 + 5\lambda_3 = -3 \qquad ...(iv)$$

on solving (iii) and (iv), we get

$$\lambda_2 = 2 \text{ and } \lambda_3 = -1$$

To reduce the number of positive variables, the variable to be driven to zero is found by choosing r for which

$$\frac{x_r}{\lambda_r} = \min_i \left\{ \frac{x_i}{\lambda_i} \middle| \lambda_i > 0 \right\} = \min \left\{ \frac{x_1}{\lambda_1}, \frac{x_2}{\lambda_2}, \frac{x_3}{\lambda_3} \right\} = \min \left\{ \frac{2}{1}, \frac{3}{2}, \frac{1}{-1} \right\}$$

We ignore the negative value.

Hence, $\min \left\{ \frac{2}{1}, \frac{3}{2} \right\} = \frac{3}{2}$

Thus, we can remove vector A_2 for which $\frac{x_2}{\lambda_2} = \frac{3}{2}$ and obtain new solution with not more than two non-negative variables. The values of new variable are as follows:

$$\hat{x}_1 = x_1 - \frac{\lambda_1}{\lambda_2} x_2 = 2 - \frac{1}{2} \times 3 = 2 - \frac{3}{2} = \frac{1}{2}$$

$$\hat{x}_3 = x_3 - \frac{\lambda_3}{\lambda_2} x_2 = 1 + \frac{1}{2} \times 3 = 1 + \frac{3}{2} = \frac{5}{2}$$

Obviously, columns A_1 and A_3 of A corresponding to these non-zero variables are linearly independent. Hence, a basic feasible solution to given system of equations is

$$\boxed{x_1 = \frac{1}{2},\ x_2 = 0,\ x_3 = \frac{5}{2}}$$

Q14. $x_1 = 1, x_2 = 1, x_3 = 1, x_4 = 2$, **is a basic solution for the linear system.**

$$x_1 + x_2 + x_3 = 3$$

$$2x_1 + x_2 + x_4 = 5$$

Is it true? Justify your answer.

Ans. No, it is not true. It is false.

This is not basic solution because in this solution, there is no variable equal to zero. In general, $(X_S, 0)$ is a basic solution of the system of equations AX = B, where 0 is a zero matrix. The given solution is feasible solution. It is not basic solution. The book you can most believe—GPH book.

⌑ ⌑

6 Simplex Method

An Overview

In mathematical optimisation, Dantzig's simplex algorithm (or simplex method) is a popular algorithm for linear programming. The name of the algorithm is derived from the concept of a simplex and was suggested by T. S. Motzkin.

The design of the Simplex method is such so that the process of choosing these two variables allows two things to happen. Firstly, the new objective value is an improvement (or at least equals) on the current one and secondly the new solution is feasible.

6.1 SIMPLEX METHOD

The steps followed in the simplex method are as follows:

Step 1: Set up the inequalities describing the problem constraints.

Step 2: The objective function should be of the maximisation type. Suppose the objective function is of minimisation type, it is converted into maximisation type by using the following relationship

Minimise Z = – (Maximise Z)

Then convert the inequalities to equalities by adding slack variables or surplus variables to derive a standard form of LP problem.

Step 3: Construct initial simplex table and enter the equations in the simplex table.

The simplex table is a convenient way of setting up the problem for simplex computation. This table tells us the following:

(i) The variables in the solution.

(ii) The profit associated with the solution.

(iii) The variables in the solution that add most profit to it.

(iv) The amount of reduction in the variables in the solution that results from introducing one unit of each variable. This amount in called as substitution rate.

Step 4: Compute the Z_j and $Z_j - C_j$ values for this solution. If all $Z_j - C_j \geq 0$, an optimum solution has been obtained and stop the iteration. Otherwise, if all $Z_j - C_j \leq 0$, then the current feasible solution is not optimal. Therefore, the current solution to a given problem should be improved and the procedure should be continued with the step 5.

Step 5: Decide the incoming variable (optimal column) by choosing the most negative all $Z_j - C_j$.

Step 6: In order to decide the leaving variable, compute and select the least positive ratio quantity-column values/their corresponding optimal-column values.

Compute the ratio $\theta = \text{Min}\left\{\frac{X_{B_i}}{a_{ir}}, a_{ir} > 0\right\}$ (i.e., the ratio between the solution column and the entering variable column, by considering only the positive denominators.

Step 7: Calculate the values for the replacing row.

[New pivot equation = old pivot equation + pivot element]

Step 8: Calculate the values for the remaining rows. New equation [all other rows, including $(Z_j - C_j)$ row] = Old equation – (corresponding column coefficient) × (New pivot equation)

Step 9: Calculate Z_j and $Z_j - C_j$ values for this solution. $Z_j = \sum x_i \times C_S$.

Step 10: If all $Z_j - C_j \leq 0$, then the current basic feasible solution is not optimal. Return to step 5.

Step 11: If all $Z_j - C_j \geq 0$, an optimum solution has been obtained.

6.2 ARTIFICIAL VARIABLE METHOD (TWO PHASE METHOD)

Where artificial variables are involved round off error makes and adverse impact on accuracy, it is better to use the Two-Phase Method. This method solves linear programming problems in two phases.

Phase-I: An initial basic feasible solution to a given linear programming problem is obtained in the first phase. Actually, Phase I is used to minimise the sum of the artificial variable with respect to the given constraints and it is known as the auxiliary objective function, wherein a basic feasible solution to the original linear programming problem is obtained. For this the original objective function Z is temporarily set aside during the phase I solution and the new artificial objective function (which is the sum of the artificial variables) is $Z^* = -R_1 - R_2 - R_3 - \ldots - R_n$, where R_i's are artificial variables. Using the simplex method, the artificial objective is minimised thus.

(1) If the minimum value of the artificial problem is zero, first, all the artificial variables are reduced to zero. Then, we derive a basic feasible solution to the given original linear problem.

(2) If the minimum value of the artificial problem is positive, at least one of the artificial variables might be positive or otherwise we have an infeasible solution to the given artificial problem, which will lead to termination of the solution.

(3) If the sum of non negative variable is zero, then each variable should be equal to zero. Thereafter, we go to Phase II.

The schematic procedure of Phase I is summarised as follows:

Step 1: First of all, it is observed that all 'b_i' are non-negative. If not, make them non-negative by multiplying both sides of the equalities and inequalities by (–1).

Step 2: By introducing slack variables, surplus variables, and artificial variables (non-negative variables) in the equations the constraints are expressed in standard form.

Step 3: Assign (–1) to each artificial variable and a cost 0 to all other variables in the objective function.

Step 4: Construct a new objective function Z*.

The new objective is to:

Maximise $Z = R_1 + R_2 + \ldots\ldots\ldots\ldots R_n$

Maximise $Z^* = -R_1 - R_2 - \ldots\ldots\ldots\ldots - R_n$

where R_i (i = 1, 2……., n) are the non-negative artificial variables.

Step 5: Using simplex method minimise the Z* and obtain the basic feasible solution. Any one of the following results may exist during this stage:

(i) If maximise $Z^* < 0$ and at least one artificial variable exists in the current optimum solution at a positive level, the given linear programming problem does not have any basic feasible solution and also stop the procedure.

(ii) If maximise $Z^* = 0$, and at least one artificial variable exists in the current optimum solution at a zero level, Z* can be improved, and Phase II can be started.

(iii) If maximise $Z^* > 0$, and an artificial variable occurs in the current optimum solution, Z* can be improved, and Phase II can be begun.

Phase II: Phase II simply optimises the original objective function by using the basic feasible solution obtained from the final iteration of Phase I.

Step 6: Use the feasible solution obtained in Phase I as an initial basic feasible solution for the original problem. The final table of Phase I becomes the starting table for Phase II. Artificial variables that do not appear in the basic solution may be deleted. Here actual coefficients are assigned to variables in the objective function and zero value is assigned to the artificial variables. Then, the simplex method has to be used to get the optimal basic feasible solution to the given two-phase problem.

Solved Practical Problems

Q1. Solve, by the Simplex Method, the following Linear Programming Problem:

Maximise $Z = 3x_1 + 5x_2 + 4x_3$

Subject to

$2x_1 + 3x_2 \leq 8$

$2x_2 + 5x_3 \leq 10$

$3x_1 + 2x_2 + 4x_3 \leq 15$

$x_1, x_2, x_3 \geq 0$ **[June-2015, Q.No.-2(a)]**

Or

Use the simplex method to solve the following LP problem:

Maximise $z = 3x_1 + 5x_2 + 4x_3$

subject to $2x_1 + 3x_2 \leq 8$

$2x_2 + 5x_3 \leq 10$

$3x_1 + 2x_2 + 4x_3 \leq 15$

$x_1, x_2, x_3 \geq 0.$ **[June-2014, Q.No.-3(a)]**

Ans. ***Step 1:*** **Convert all constraints into equations:**

Adding slack variables x_4, x_5 and x_6 to the constraints, we obtain

$$\left.\begin{aligned} 2x_1 + 3x_2 + x_4 &= 8 \\ 2x_2 + 5x_3 + x_5 &= 10 \\ 3x_1 + 2x_2 + 4x_3 + x_6 &= 15 \end{aligned}\right\} \quad \text{...(i)}$$

Step 2: **Obtain initial basic feasible solution:**

Eq. (i) is of the form

$AX = B$. Then, we have

$$A = \begin{bmatrix} 2 & 3 & 0 & 1 & 0 & 0 \\ 0 & 2 & 5 & 0 & 1 & 0 \\ 3 & 2 & 4 & 0 & 0 & 1 \end{bmatrix}, \quad X = \begin{bmatrix} x_1 \\ x_2 \\ x_3 \\ x_4 \\ x_5 \\ x_6 \end{bmatrix}$$

and

$$B = \begin{bmatrix} 8 \\ 10 \\ 15 \end{bmatrix}$$

Here,

$$A_1=\begin{bmatrix}2\\0\\3\end{bmatrix}, A_2=\begin{bmatrix}3\\2\\2\end{bmatrix}, A_3=\begin{bmatrix}0\\5\\4\end{bmatrix}, A_4=\begin{bmatrix}1\\0\\0\end{bmatrix}, A_5=\begin{bmatrix}0\\1\\0\end{bmatrix}, A_6=\begin{bmatrix}0\\0\\1\end{bmatrix}.$$

Since, rank of A = 3, therefore three of these six columns $A_1, A_2, A_3, A_4, A_5, A_6$ are linearly independent. Hence, a basic solution to this system of equations will have at most three components different from zero.

Now, keep the vectors A_4, A_5, A_6 in the basis, i.e., let

$$S=\begin{bmatrix}1&0&0\\0&1&0\\0&0&1\end{bmatrix}$$

be the initial basis matrix. The corresponding basic variables are x_4, x_5 and x_6 and other three variables x_1, x_2 and x_3 are non-basic variables.

Now putting $x_1 = x_2 = x_3 = 0$ in Eq. (i), we have $x_4 = 8, x_5 = 10$ and $x_6 = 15$

Hence, initial basic feasible solution is $x_1 = 0, x_2 = 0, x_3 = 0, x_4 = 8, x_5 = 10, x_6 = 15$ and $Z = 0$

***Step 3:* Put the problem in a tableau form**

Table 1

	$C_j \rightarrow$	**3**	**5**	**4**	**0**	**0**	**0**	
C_S	**Variables in the basis**	A_1	A_2	A_3	A_4	A_5	A_6	**Solution**
0	x_4	2	[3]	0	1	0	0	$8 \rightarrow$ D.V.
0	x_5	0	2	5	0	1	0	10
0	x_6	3	2	4	0	0	1	15
	Δ_j	$\Delta_1 = -3$	$\Delta_2 = -5$ ↑E.V.	$\Delta_3 = -4$	$\Delta_4 = 0$	$\Delta_5 = 0$	$\Delta_6 = 0$	$Z = 0$

The first column of the tableau gives C_S the coefficients of basic variables x_4, x_5 and x_6 in the objective function. It can be denoted by p_B or C_B also.

The second column tells us which variables are in the basis. Thus, we may see variables x_4, x_5 and x_6 corresponding to slack vectors A_4, A_5 and A_6 are the basic variables.

The last column of the tableau, under the heading 'Solution' gives the current values of the basic variables, together with the value of the objective function for the basic feasible solution described by the given tableau.

Now we find $Y_j = S^{-1}A_j$

Here, $S = \begin{bmatrix} 1 & 0 & 0 \\ 0 & 1 & 0 \\ 0 & 0 & 1 \end{bmatrix} \Rightarrow S^{-1} = \begin{bmatrix} 1 & 0 & 0 \\ 0 & 1 & 0 \\ 0 & 0 & 1 \end{bmatrix}$

$\Rightarrow$ $Y_j = A_j$ for all columns A_j of A.

The last entry in each of these columns gives

$\Delta_j = Z_j - C_j$,

and $Z_j = C_S Y_j = C_S S^{-1} A_j = C_S A_j$, since $S^{-1} = \begin{bmatrix} 1 & 0 & 0 \\ 0 & 1 & 0 \\ 0 & 0 & 1 \end{bmatrix}$.

For computing Δ_1, we first find

$Z_1 = C_S A_1$

Where $C_S = \begin{bmatrix} 0 \\ 0 \\ 0 \end{bmatrix}$ and $A_1 = \begin{bmatrix} 2 \\ 0 \\ 3 \end{bmatrix}$

$\Rightarrow$ $Z_1 = 0 \times 2 + 0 \times 0 + 0 \times 3 = 0$

$\Rightarrow$ $\Delta_1 = Z_1 - C_1 = 0 - 3 = -3$

Similarly, $\Delta_2 = -5$, $\Delta_3 = -4$, $\Delta_4 = 0$, $\Delta_5 = 0$, $\Delta_6 = 0$.

Now, $Z = 0 \times 8 + 0 \times 10 + 0 \times 15 = 0$

Note: $\Delta_1, \Delta_2, \Delta_3, \Delta_4, \Delta_5, \Delta_6$ are called **Relative Cost Coefficients.**

***Step 4:* Apply optimality criteria**

If all $\Delta_j \geq 0$, i.e., if all $\Delta_1, \Delta_2, \Delta_3, \ldots$ are positive or zero, then no further improvement in the value of the objective function would be possible.

However, here Δ_1, Δ_2 and Δ_3 are negative, so we go to next step.

***Step 5:* Choosing a vector to enter the basis**

Here, $\Delta_2 = -5$ is the most negative or smallest. Therefore the vector A_2 enters into the basis and corresponding variable x_2 becomes an **Entering Variable (E.V.)** and hence it is a new basic variable.

Remark: If there is a tie for the minimum value in Δ_j, then any one of the tied vectors can be chosen to enter the basis.

The Entering Column A_2 into the basis is called the **distinguished column or pivot column.**

***Step 6:* Choosing a vector to be removed from the basis**

Now, we divide the elements of Solution Column by the corresponding elements of the Pivot Column and find the minimum positive value. **We ignore the negative values.**

$$\min\left\{\frac{8}{3},\frac{10}{2},\frac{15}{2}\right\}$$

$= \min\{2.67, 5, 7.5\} = 2.67$

The minimum value 2.67 is found by the number 3 of the pivot column. Hence, $\boxed{3}$ is the **pivot element**. Hence, we remove the vector A_4 and corresponding variable x_4 from the basis. x_4 is called **Departing Variable (D.V.).**

Remark: If there is a tie in minimum positive values, then any one of the tied vectors can be removed from the basis.

***Step 7:* Computing the new tableau**

(i) Divide the **pivot row** by the pivot element, i.e., in this case, divide the first row (this is pivot row) by the pivot element $\boxed{3}$.

(ii) Subtract suitable multiple of the **New Row** (First row) from other rows (i.e., second and third rows) of the old table to get zero everywhere else in the pivot column.

Now we have

$R_1(\text{Table 2}) \rightarrow \frac{1}{3}R_1(\text{Table 1})$

$R_2(\text{Table 2}) \rightarrow R_2(\text{Table 1}) - 2R_1(\text{Table2})$

$R_3(\text{Table 2}) \rightarrow R_3(\text{Table 1}) - 2R_1(\text{Table2})$

Table 2

	$C_j \rightarrow$	3	5	4	0	0	0	
C_S	**Variables in the basis**	A_1	A_2	A_3	A_4	A_5	A_6	**Solution**
5	x_2	2/3	1	0	1/3	0	0	8/3
0	x_5	–4/3	0	$\boxed{5}$	–2/3	1	0	14/3 → D.V.
0	x_6	5/3	0	4	–2/3	0	1	29/3
	Δ_j	1/3	0	–4 ↑E.V.	5/3	0	0	40/3

Here, $\Delta_3 = -4$ is most negative. Hence, x_3 is entering variable and A_3 is pivot column.

Now, $\min\left\{\frac{8/3}{0},\frac{14/3}{5},\frac{29/3}{4}\right\} = \frac{14/3}{5}$

Hence, $\boxed{5}$ is pivot element and x_5 is departing variable.

Now, Dividing second row of Table 2 by the pivot element 5 and

$R_3(\text{Table 3}) \rightarrow R_3(\text{Table 2}) - 4R_2(\text{Table 3})$

Table 3

	$C_j \rightarrow$	3	5	4	0	0	0	
C_S	**Variables in the basis**	A_1	A_2	A_3	A_4	A_5	A_6	**Solution**
5	x_2	2/3	1	0	1/3	0	0	8/3
4	x_3	–4/15	0	1	–2/15	1/5	0	14/15
0	x_6	$\boxed{41/15}$	0	0	–2/15	–4/5	1	89/15 → D.V.
	Δ_j	–11/15 ↑E.V.	0	0	17/15	4/5	0	256/15

Here, $\Delta_1 = -11/15$ is most negative. Hence, x_1 is the entering variable and A_1 is pivot column.

Now, $\min\left\{\frac{8/3}{2/3}, \frac{89/15}{41/15}\right\} = \frac{89/15}{41/15}$

Hence, 41/15 is pivot element and x_6 is the departing variable.

Now, divide the third row (i.e. pivot row) of Table 3 by the pivot element 41/15 and

$$R_2(\text{Table 4}) \rightarrow R_2(\text{Table 3}) - \left(\frac{-4}{15}\right)R_3(\text{Table 4})$$

$$R_1(\text{Table 3}) \rightarrow R_1(\text{Table 3}) - \frac{2}{3}R_3(\text{Table 4})$$

Table 4

	$C_j \rightarrow$	3	5	4	0	0	0	
C_S	**Variables in the basis**	A_1	A_2	A_3	A_4	A_5	A_6	**Solution**
5	x_2	0	1	0	15/41	8/41	10/41	50/41
4	x_3	0	0	1	–6/41	5/41	4/41	62/41
3	x_1	1	0	0	–2/41	–12/41	15/41	89/41
	Δ_j	0	0	0	$\frac{45}{41}$	$\frac{24}{41}$	$\frac{111}{41}$	$Z = \frac{765}{41}$ $= 18.66$

Here all Δ_j are zero or positive. Hence, optimal solution is

$x_1 = 89/41, x_2 = 50/41, x_3 = 62/41, x_4 = 0, x_5 = 0, x_6 = 0$ and maximum Z = 18.66

Q2. Solve the following LPP by simplex method.

Maximise

$$Z = 3x_1 + 7x_2 + 29x_3$$

Subject to

$$3x_1 - 3x_2 + 2x_3 \leq 6$$

$$6x_1 + 3x_2 + 13x_3 \leq 39$$

$$-3x_1 + 4x_2 + 16x_3 \leq 8$$

$$(x_1, x_2, x_3) \geq (0, 0, 0)$$

Ans. Adding slack variables x_4, x_5 and x_6 to the constraints, we get

$$\left.\begin{aligned} 3x_1 - 3x_2 + 2x_3 + x_4 = 6 \\ 6x_1 + 3x_2 + 13x_3 + x_5 = 39 \\ -3x_1 + 4x_2 + 16x_3 + x_6 = 8 \end{aligned}\right\} \quad ...(i)$$

Now, the initial basic feasible solution of Eq. (i) is

$x_1 = x_2 = x_3 = 0,\ x_4 = 6,\ x_5 = 39,\ x_6 = 8$

Table 1

	$C_j \rightarrow$	3	7	29	0	0	0	
C_S	**Variables in the basis**	A_1	A_2	A_3	A_4	A_5	A_6	**Solution**
0	x_4	3	–3	2	1	0	0	6
0	x_5	6	3	13	0	1	0	39
0	x_6	–3	4	[16]	0	0	1	8 → D.V.
	Δ_j	–3	–7	–29	0	0	0	0
				↑E.V.				

Here, $\Delta_3 = -29$ is most negative. Hence, x_3 is the entering variable. A_3 is pivot vector and corresponding column of A_3 is pivot column.

Now $\text{Min}\left\{\frac{6}{2}, \frac{39}{13}, \frac{8}{16}\right\} = \frac{8}{16}$

Hence, [16] is the pivot element and x_6 is departing variable.

Table 2

Table 2

	$C_j\rightarrow$	3	7	29	0	0	0	
C_S	**Variables in the basis**	A_1	A_2	A_3	A_4	A_5	A_6	**Solution**
0	x_4	[27/8]	–7/2	0	1	0	–1/8	5 → D.V.
0	x_5	135/16	–1/4	0	0	1	–13/16	65/2
29	x_3	–3/16	1/4	1	0	0	1/16	1/2
	Δ_j	–135/16 ↑E.V.	1/4	0	0	0	29/16	29/2

Here, $\Delta_1 = -135/16$ is negative. Hence, x_1 is the entering variable.

Now, $\text{Min}\left\{\dfrac{5}{27/8}, \dfrac{65/2}{135/16}\right\}$ $\left[\because \text{Ignoring } \dfrac{1/2}{-3/16} \text{ because of } (-)\text{ve value.}\right]$

$= \dfrac{5}{27/8}$

Hence, $\boxed{27/8}$ is the pivot element. Hence, x_4 is the departing variable.

Table 3

	$C_j\rightarrow$	3	7	29	0	0	0	
C_S	**Variables in the basis**	A_1	A_2	A_3	A_4	A_5	A_6	**Solution**
3	x_1	1	–28/27	0	8/27	0	–1/27	40/27
0	x_5	0	[17/2]	0	–5/2	1	–1/2	20 → D.V.
29	x_3	0	1/18	1	1/18	0	1/18	7/9
	Δ_j	0	–17/2 ↑E.V.	0	5/2	0	3/2	27

Here, $\Delta_2 = -17/2$ is most negative. Hence, x_2 is the entering variable.

Now, $\min\left\{\dfrac{20}{17/2}, \dfrac{7/9}{1/18}\right\} = \dfrac{20}{17/2}$

Hence, $\boxed{17/2}$ is the pivot element. Hence, x_5 is the departing variable.

Table 4

	$C_j \rightarrow$	3	7	29	0	0	0	
C_S	Variables in the basis	A_1	A_2	A_3	A_4	A_5	A_6	Solution
3	x_1	1	0	0	–4/459	56/459	–5/51	200/51
7	x_2	0	1	0	–5/17	2/17	–1/17	40/17
29	x_3	0	0	1	11/153	–1/153	1/17	11/17
	Δ_j	0	0	0	0	1	1	47

Here, all $\Delta_j \geq 0$. Hence, solution is

$x_1 = 200/51, x_2 = 40/17, x_3 = 11/17, x_4 = x_5 = x_6 = 0$ and Max $Z = 47$.

This is the optimal solution of given LPP.

Q3. Use Simplex method to solve the following LPP:

Maximise

$\mathbf{Z = 3x_1 + x_2 + 3x_3}$

Subject to

$\mathbf{2x_1 + x_2 + x_3 \leq 2}$

$\mathbf{x_1 + 2x_2 + 3x_3 \leq 5}$

$\mathbf{2x_1 + 2x_2 + x_3 \leq 6}$

$\mathbf{x_1, x_2, x_3 \geq 0}$

Ans. Adding slack variables in the constraints, we have

$$\left.\begin{aligned} 2x_1 + x_2 + x_3 + x_4 = 2 \\ x_1 + 2x_2 + 3x_3 + x_5 = 5 \\ 2x_1 + 2x_2 + x_3 + x_6 = 6 \end{aligned}\right\} \quad \text{...(i)}$$

where x_4, x_5 and x_6 are slack variables.

Now, initial basic feasible solution of Eq. (i) is

$x_1 = x_2 = x_3 = 0,\ x_4 = 2,\ x_5 = 5,\ x_6 = 6$

Table 1

	$C_j \rightarrow$	3	1	3	0	0	0	
C_S	Variables in the basis	A_1	A_2	A_3	A_4	A_5	A_6	Solution
0	x_4	[2]	1	1	1	0	0	2 → D.V.
0	x_5	1	2	3	0	1	0	5
0	x_6	2	2	1	0	0	1	6
	Δ_j	–3 ↑E.V.	–1	–3	0	0	0	0

Here, $\Delta_1 = -3$ and $\Delta_3 = -3$. So, there is a tie in most negative values so any one can be chosen for entering variable.

Here, we choose $\Delta_1 = -3$.

Hence, x_1 is the entering variable.

Now, $\text{Min}\left\{\frac{2}{2}, \frac{5}{1}, \frac{6}{2}\right\} = \frac{2}{2}$

Hence, x_4 is departing variable. Now

Table 2

	$C_j \rightarrow$	3	1	3	0	0	0	
C_S	**Variables in the basis**	A_1	A_2	A_3	A_4	A_5	A_6	**Solution**
3	x_1	1	1/2	1/2	1/2	0	0	1
0	x_5	0	3/2	[5/2]	–1/2	1	0	4 → D.V.
0	x_6	0	1	0	–1	0	1	4
	Δ_j	0	1/2	–3/2 ↑E.V.	3/2	0	0	3

Here, $\Delta_3 = \frac{-3}{2}$, which is negative. Hence, x_3 is entering variables.

Now, $\text{Min}\left\{\frac{1}{1/2}, \frac{4}{5/2}, \frac{4}{0}\right\} = \frac{4}{5/2}$

Hence, $\boxed{5/2}$ is the pivot element. Hence, x_5 is departing variable.

Table 3

	$C_j \rightarrow$	3	1	3	0	0	0	
C_S	**Variables in the basis**	A_1	A_2	A_3	A_4	A_5	A_6	**Solution**
3	x_1	1	1/5	0	3/5	–1/5	0	1/5
3	x_3	0	3/5	1	–1/5	2/5	0	8/5
0	x_6	0	1	0	–1	0	1	4
	Δ_j	0	7/5	0	6/5	3/5	0	27/5

Here, all $\Delta_j \geq 0$. Hence, the solution is

$x_1 = 1/5,\ x_2 = 0,\ x_3 = 8/5,\ x_4 = 0,\ x_5 = 0,\ x_6 = 4$ and Max $Z = 27/5$.

Q4. Solve the following LPP by using Simplex Method (A Case of Alternative Optimal Solutions).

Maximise $Z = 2x_1 + 4x_2 + 6x_3$

Subject to

$x_1 + x_2 \le 5$

$x_1 \le 1$

$x_1 + 2x_2 + 3x_3 \le 10$

$x_1, x_2, x_3 \ge 0.$

Ans. Since all constraints are '≤' type, introducing slack variables x_4, x_5, x_6 the constraints can be put as

$x_1 + x_2 + x_4 = 5$

$x_1 + x_5 = 1$

$x_1 + 2x_2 + 3x_3 + x_6 = 10$

$x_1, \ldots\ldots, x_6 \ge 0$

Hence, initial solution is

$x_1 = 0, x_2 = 0, x_3 = 0, x_4 = 5, x_5 = 1, x_6 = 10$ and Z = 0. Hence, we put the problem into a table form.

Table 1

	$C_j \rightarrow$	2	4	6	0	0	0	
C_S	**Variables in the basis**	A_1	A_2	A_3	A_4	A_5	A_6	**Solution**
0	x_4	1	1	0	1	0	0	5
0	x_5	1	0	0	0	1	0	1
0	x_6	1	2	[3]	0	0	1	10 →
	Δ_j	–2	–4	–6 ↑	0	0	0	0

$\Delta_3 = -6$ is most negative, hence, column A_3 enters the basis, only one entry is +ve in the third column, therefore column corresponding x_6 is to be removed from the basis and [3] is the pivot element. Next table is given by

Table 2

	$C_j \rightarrow$	2	4	6	0	0	0	
C_S	**Variables in the basis**	A_1	A_2	A_3	A_4	A_5	A_6	**Solution**
0	x_4	1	1	0	1	0	0	5
0	x_5	1	0	0	0	1	0	1
0	x_3	1/3	2/3	1	0	0	1/3	10/3
	Δ_j	0	0	0	0	0	2	20

All $\Delta_j \geq 0$, the solution is optimal is given by $x_1 = 0,\ x_2 = 0,\ x_3 = \frac{10}{3}$, Maximum Z = 20

We note that, here $\Delta_1 = 0, x_1$ is non-basic variable and all entries in column 1 are positive. Now we make x_1 a basic variable, i.e. enter A_1 into the basis.

To decide the departing vector, we choose

$$\min\left\{\frac{5}{1}, \frac{1}{1}, \frac{10/3}{1/3}\right\} = \min\{5, 1, 10\} = 1.$$

This shows column corresponding to the basic variable x_5 is to be removed from the basis and new table is

Table 3

	$C_j \rightarrow$	2	4	6	0	0	0	
C_S	**Variables in the basis**	A_1	A_2	A_3	A_4	A_5	A_6	**Solution**
0	x_4	0	1	0	1	–1	0	4
2	x_1	1	0	0	0	1	0	1
6	x_3	0	2/3	1	0	–1/3	1/3	3
	Δ_j	0	0	0	0	0	6	20

Here we note that some Δ_j corresponding to non-basic variables are also zero and some entries y_{ij}'s in those columns are positive. This is an indication to the fact that, we have an alternative optimal solution $x_1 = 1,\ x_2 = 0,\ x_3 = 3$ and max Z = 20 (again)

Similarly for non-basic variable $x_2,\ \Delta_2 = 0,$ and two entries in the column corresponding to x_2 are positive. Therefore, we can make x_2 basic by entering the column A_2 into the basis and we choose

$$\min\left\{\frac{4}{1},\frac{3}{2/3}\right\}=\min\left\{4,\frac{9}{2}\right\}=4.$$

This implies that, we can remove the vector A_4 from the basis and new table is given as

Table 4

	$C_j \rightarrow$	**2**	**4**	**6**	**0**	**0**	**0**	
C_S	**Variables in the basis**	A_1	A_2	A_3	A_4	A_5	A_6	**Solution**
4	x_2	0	1	0	1	–1	0	4
2	x_1	1	0	0	0	1	0	1
6	x_3	0	0	1	–2/3	1/3	1	1/3
	Δ_j	0	0	0	0	0	6	20

Again $\Delta_j \geq 0$ and optimal solution is now given by

$x_1 = 1, x_2 = 4, x_3 = \frac{1}{3}$ and Z = 20 (again)

Also now $\Delta_5 = 0$ and the two entries in the column A_5 are both positive. Therefore, we can enter A_5 and remove x_3 from the basis. New table is given by

Table 5

	$C_j \rightarrow$	**2**	**4**	**6**	**0**	**0**	**0**	
C_S	**Variables in the basis**	A_1	A_2	A_3	A_4	A_5	A_6	**Solution**
4	x_2	0	1	3	–1	0	3	5
2	x_1	1	0	–3	2	$\boxed{0}$	–3	0
0	x_5	0	0	3	–2	1	3	1
	Δ_j	0	0	0	0	0	6	20

Again all $\Delta_j \geq 0$, and optimal solution is now given by

$x_1 = 0,\ x_2 = 5,\ x_3 = 0$ and maximum Z = 20.

Thus, we are able to find four alternative optimal basic feasible solutions given by

$$\left(0,0,\frac{10}{3}\right),(1,0,3),\left(1,4,\frac{1}{3}\right),(0,5,0)$$

with optimal value of the objective function to be the same Z = 20.

Q5. Solve the following LPP by Two Phase Simplex Method.

Minimise

$Z = 3x_1 + 5x_2$

Subject to

$6x_1 + 7x_2 \geq 11$

$4x_1 + 2x_2 \geq 13$

$x_1, x_2 \geq 0$

Ans. We convert the objective function to a maximisation function and introduce surplus variables x_3 and x_4 to convert constraints into equations and problem takes the form

– Maximise

$-Z = -3x_1 - 5x_2$

Subject to

$6x_1 + 7x_2 - x_3 = 11$

$4x_1 + 2x_2 - x_4 = 13$

$x_1, x_2, x_3, x_4 \geq 0$

If we examine the coefficient matrix A of the constraint equations for this problem $A = \begin{bmatrix} 6 & 7 & -1 & 0 \\ 4 & 2 & 0 & -1 \end{bmatrix}$, this coefficient matrix has no identity matrix present, therefore initial basic feasible solution is not available. Therefore, we add artificial variables to the two constrains and we have

$6x_1 + 7x_2 - x_3 + x_1^a = 11$

$4x_1 + 2x_2 - x_4 + x_2^a = 13$

$x_1, \ldots\ldots\ldots, x_4 \geq 0,\ x_1^a,\ x_2^a \geq 0$

Phase I: In phase I of the two phase method we solve the following linear programming problem using Simplex method.

Maximise

$Z^0 = -x_1^a - x_2^a$

Subject to $6x_1 + 7x_2 - x_3 + x_1^a = 11$

$4x_1 + 2x_2 - x_4 + x_2^a = 13$

$x_1, x_2, x_3, x_4, x_1^a, x_2^a \geq 0$

Hence, initial basic feasible solution for this problem is

$x_1 = x_2 = x_3 = x_4 = 0,\ x_1^a = 11,\ x_2^a = 13$ and $Z^0 = -24$

Put the problem in the table form

Table 1

	$C_j^0 \rightarrow$	0	0	0	0	–1	–1	
C_S^0	**Variables in the basis**	A_1	A_2	A_3	A_4	A_1^a	A_2^a	**Solution**
–1	x_1^a	$\boxed{6}$	7	–1	0	1	0	11
–1	x_2^a	4	2	0	–1	0	1	13
	Δ_j^0	–10	–9	1	1	0	0	–24

where C_j^0 is the coefficient of x_j in Z^0 and C_S^0 is the column denoting coefficients of basic variable in Z^0. Most negative Δ_j^0 is –10. Therefore, column A_1 enters the basis. To decide the departing vector we choose minimum $\left\{\frac{11}{6}, \frac{13}{4}\right\} = \frac{11}{6}$ as both entries in column A_1 are positive.

Clearly, vector A_1^a corresponding to artificial variable x_1^a is removed from the basis and in the usual manner we obtain the following new table, in which $\boxed{6}$ is the pivot element.

Table 2

	$C_j^0 \rightarrow$	0	0	0	0	–1	–1	
C_S^0	**Variables in the basis**	A_1	A_2	A_3	A_4	A_1^a	A_2^a	**Solution**
0	x_1	1	$+\frac{7}{6}$	$-\frac{1}{6}$	0	$\frac{1}{6}$	0	$\frac{11}{6}$
–1	x_2^a	0	$-\frac{16}{6}$	$\boxed{\frac{4}{6}}$	–1	$-\frac{4}{6}$	1	$\frac{34}{6} \rightarrow$
	Δ_j^0	0	$\frac{16}{6}$	$-\frac{4}{6}$ ↑	1	$\frac{10}{6}$	0	$-\frac{34}{6}$

Now most negative Δ_j^0 is $-\frac{4}{6}$. Column A_3 enters the basis. We note only one entry in the column A_3 is positive. Therefore, corresponding vector A_2^a is to be removed from the basis and artificial variable x_2^a becomes non-basic and $\boxed{\frac{4}{6}}$ is the pivot element consequently, we obtain the following new table

Table 3

	$C_j^0 \rightarrow$	0	0	0	0	−1	−1	
C_S^0	**Variables in the basis**	A_1	A_2	A_3	A_4	A_1^a	A_2^a	**Solution**
0	x_1	1	$\frac{1}{2}$	0	$-\frac{1}{4}$	0	$\frac{1}{4}$	$\frac{13}{4}$
0	x_3	0	−4	1	$-\frac{3}{2}$	−1	$\frac{3}{2}$	$\frac{17}{2}$
	Δ_j^0	0	0	0	0	1	1	

All $\Delta_j^0 \geq 0$, therefore we have the optimal solution for phase I.

Phase II: Now, we neglect the last two columns, i.e. columns corresponding to artificial vectors as we now have a basic solution in terms of original variables. Now, consider the objective function.

– Maximise

$-Z = -3x_1 - 5x_2$

and initial table for phase II is the final table for phase I without the columns of artificial vectors. Therefore, we now have the following table:

Table 4

	$C_j \rightarrow$	−3	−5	0	0	
C_S	**Variables**	A_1	A_2	A_3	A_4	**Solution**
−3	x_1	1	$\frac{1}{2}$	0	$-\frac{1}{4}$	$\frac{13}{4}$
0	x_3	0	−4	1	$-\frac{3}{2}$	$\frac{17}{2}$
	Δ_j	0	$\frac{7}{2}$	0	$\frac{3}{4}$	$-\frac{39}{4}$

Since $\Delta_j \geq 0$, therefore, we have optimal solution for phase II also.

The optimal solution is given by

$$x_1 = \frac{13}{4},\ x_2 = 0,\ x_3 = \frac{17}{2},\ x_4 = 0,\ \ -\text{Maximum}(-Z) = \frac{-39}{4}.$$

Therefore, Minimum $Z = \frac{39}{4}$.

Q6. Solve the following LP problem by using two-phase simplex method.

Minimise $Z = x_1 - 2x_2 - 3x_3$

subject to $-2x_1 + 3x_2 + 3x_3 = 2$

$$\mathbf{2x_1 + 3x_2 + 4x_3 = 1}$$

$$\mathbf{x_1, x_2, x_3 \geq 0}$$ **[June-2014, Q.No.-7(a)]**

Ans. We convert the objective function to a maximisation function. i.e.,

– Maximise

$$-Z = -x_1 + 2x_2 + 3x_3$$

Subject to

$$-2x_1 + 3x_2 + 3x_3 = 2 \;+$$

$$2x_1 + 3x_2 + 4x_3 = 1$$

$$x_1, x_2, x_3 \geq 0$$

Here, $A = \begin{bmatrix} -2 & 3 & 3 \\ 2 & 3 & 4 \end{bmatrix}$

This coefficient matrix has no identity matrix present; therefore, initial basic feasible solution is not available.

Therefore, we add artificial variables to the constraints and we have

$$-2x_1 + 3x_2 + 3x_3 + x_1^a = 2$$

$$2x_1 + 3x_2 + 4x_3 + x_2^a = 1$$

$$x_1,\ x_2,\ x_3 \geq 0,\ x_1^a,\ x_2^a \geq 0$$

where x_1^a and x_2^a are artificial variables.

Phase I: In phase I, we have

Maximise

$$Z^0 = -x_1^a - x_2^a$$

Subject to

$$-2x_1 + 3x_2 + 3x_3 + x_1^a = 2$$

$$2x_1 + 3x_2 + 4x_3 + x_2^a = 1$$

$$x_1, x_2, x_3 \geq 0,\ x_1^a, x_2^a \geq 0$$

Hence, initial basic feasible solution for this problem is

$x_1 = x_2 = x_3 = 0,\ x_1^a = 2,\ x_2^a = 1$ and $Z^0 = -3$.

Now, putting the problem in Table form as follows:

Table 1

	$C_j^0 \to$	0	0	0	–1	–1	
C_S^0	**Variables in the basis**	A_1	A_2	A_3	A_1^a	A_2^a	**Solution**
–1	x_1^a	–2	3	3	1	0	2
–1	x_2^a	2	3	[4]	0	1	1 → D.V.
	Δ_j^0	0	–6	–7 ↑E.V.	0	0	–3

Here $\Delta_3^0 = -7$ is the most negative. Hence, x_3 is entering variable.

Now $\min\left\{\frac{2}{3}, \frac{1}{4}\right\} = \frac{1}{4}$

Hence, $\boxed{4}$ is the pivot element and x_2^a is departing variable.

Table 2

	$C_j^0 \to$	0	0	0	–1	–1	
C_S^0	**Variables in the basis**	A_1	A_2	A_3	A_1^a	A_2^a	**Solution**
–1	x_1^a	–7/2	[3/4]	0	1	–3/4	5/4 → D.V.
0	x_3	1/2	3/4	1	0	1/4	1/4
	Δ_j^0	7/2	–3/4 ↑ E.V.	0	0	7/4	–5/4

Here, $\Delta_2^0 = -3/4$ is negative. Hence, x_2 is the entering variable.

Here, $\boxed{3/4}$ is the pivot element. Hence, x_1^a is departing variable.

Table 3

	$C_j^0 \to$	0	0	0	–1	–1	
C_S^0	**Variables in the basis**	A_1	A_2	A_3	A_1^a	A_2^a	**Solution**
0	x_2	–14/3	1	0	4/3	–1	5/3
0	x_3	4	0	1	–1	1	–1
	Δ_j^0	0	0	0	1	1	

Here, all $\Delta_j^0 \geq 0$. Therefore, we have the optimal for phase I. Now we neglect last two columns, i.e., columns corresponding to artificial vectors as we now have a basic solution in terms of original variables.

Phase II:

– Maximise

$$-Z = -x_1 + 2x_2 + 3x_3$$

and initial table for phase II is the final table for phase I without the columns of artificial vectors. Hence, the table is

Table 4

	$C_j \rightarrow$	**–1**	**2**	**3**	
C_S	**Variables in the basis**	A_1	A_2	A_3	**Solution**
2	x_2	–14/3	1	0	5/3
3	x_3	4	0	1	–1
	Δ_j	11/3	0	0	1/3

Since, all $\Delta_j \geq 0$. Hence, the solution is

$$x_1 = 0,\ x_2 = {}^5\!/_3,\ x_3 = -1$$

$$-\text{Max}(-Z) = \frac{1}{3}$$

Therefore, minimum $Z = \frac{-1}{3}$.

Q7. Solve the following LPP by two phase simplex method.

Minimise

$$Z = \frac{15}{2}x_1 - 3x_2$$

Subject to

$$3x_1 - x_2 - x_3 \geq 3$$

$$x_1 - x_2 + x_3 \geq 2$$

$$x_1, x_2, x_3 \geq (0,0,0)$$

Ans. Given LPP can be written as

– Maximise

$$-Z = -\frac{15}{2}x_1 + 3x_2$$

Subject to

$$3x_1 - x_2 - x_3 \geq 3$$

$x_1 - x_2 + x_3 \geq 2$

$x_1, x_2, x_3 \geq (0,0,0)$

Now, introducing surplus variables x_4 and x_5. We have

$3x_1 - x_2 - x_3 - x_4 = 3$

$x_1 - x_2 + x_3 - x_5 = 2$

$x_1, x_2, x_3, x_4, x_5 \geq 0$

Here, $A = \begin{bmatrix} 3 & -1 & -1 & -1 & 0 \\ 1 & -1 & 1 & 0 & -1 \end{bmatrix}$

There is no 2 × 2 identity matrix. So, now introducing artificial variables x_1^a and x_2^a, i.e.,

$3x_1 - x_2 - x_3 - x_4 + x_1^a = 3$

$x_1 - x_2 + x_3 - x_5 + x_2^a = 2$

$x_1, x_2, x_3, x_4, x_5, x_1^a, x_2^a \geq 0$

Phase I:

Maximise

$Z^0 = -x_1^a - x_2^a$

Subject to

$3x_1 - x_2 - x_3 - x_4 + x_1^a = 3$

$x_1 - x_2 + x_3 - x_5 + x_2^a = 2$

$x_1, x_2, x_3, x_4, x_5, x_1^a, x_2^a \geq 0$

Table 1

	$C_j^0 \rightarrow$	0	0	0	0	0	–1	–1	
C_S^0	**Variables in the basis**	A_1	A_2	A_3	A_4	A_5	A_1^a	A_2^a	**Solution**
–1	x_1^a	[3]	–1	–1	–1	0	1	0	3 →D.V.
–1	x_2^a	1	–1	1	0	–1	0	1	2
	Δ_j^0	–4 ↑E.V.	2	0	1	1	0	0	–5

$\Delta_1^0 = -4$ is most negative. Hence, x_1 is the entering variable.

Now $\text{Min}\left\{\frac{3}{3}, \frac{2}{1}\right\} = \frac{3}{3}$

$\Rightarrow$ [3] is the pivot element. So, x_1^a is the departing variable.

Table 2

	$C_j^0 \rightarrow$	0	0	0	0	0	−1	−1	
C_S^0	**Variables in the basis**	A_1	A_2	A_3	A_4	A_5	A_1^a	A_2^a	**Solution**
0	x_1	1	−1/3	−1/3	−1/3	0	1/3	0	1
−1	x_2^a	0	−2/3	[4/3]	1/3	−1	−1/3	1	1 → D.V.
	Δ_j^0	0	2/3	−4/3 ↑E.V.	−1/3	1	4/3	0	−1

$\Delta_3^0 = -4/3$ is most negative. Hence, x_3 is the entering variable.

Now $\min\left\{\frac{1}{4/3}\right\} = \frac{1}{4/3}$

$\Rightarrow$ $\boxed{4/3}$ is the pivot element. Hence, x_2^a is the departing variable.

Table 3

	$C_j^0 \rightarrow$	0	0	0	0	0	−1	−1	
C_S^0	**Variables in the basis**	A_1	A_2	A_3	A_4	A_5	A_1^a	A_2^a	**Solution**
0	x_1	1	−1/2	0	−1/4	−1/4	1/4	1/4	5/4
0	x_3	0	−1/2	1	1/4	−3/4	−1/4	3/4	3/4
	Δ_j^0	0	0	0	0	0	1	1	0

Here, all $\Delta_j^0 \geq 0$. Hence, we have the optimal solution for Phase I.

Phase II:

Maximise

$$-Z = \frac{-15}{2}x_1 + 3x_2$$

Table 4

	$C_j \rightarrow$	−15/2	3	0	0	0	
C_s	**Variables in the basis**	A_1	A_2	A_3	A_4	A_5	**Solution**
−15/2	x_1	1	−1/2	0	−1/4	−1/4	5/4
0	x_3	0	−1/2	1	1/4	−3/4	3/4
	Δ_j	0	9/2	0	15/8	15/8	−75/8

Here, all $\Delta_j \geq 0$. Hence, the solution is

$$x_1 = 5/4,\ x_2 = 0,\ x_3 = 3/4,\ x_4 = 0,\ x_5 = 0$$

$$-\text{Max}(-Z) = -75/8$$

$\Rightarrow$ Minimum $Z = 75/8$

Q8. The following table is obtained in the intermediate stage while solving an LPP by simplex method:

	C_i's	30	23	29	0	0	
B	C_B	X_1	X_2	X_3	S_1	S_2	R.H.S.
S_1	0	0	2	–9/2	1	–3/2	31/2
X_1	30	1	1/2	5/4	0	1/4	7/4

Check whether an optimal solution of the LPP will exist or not.

[June-2015, Q.No.-7(a)]

Ans. From given table, we have the following table:

C_B	$C_i \rightarrow$ Variables in the basis	30 x_1	23 x_2	29 x_3	0 S_1	0 S_2	R.H.S.
0	S_1	0	2	–9/2	1	–3/2	31/2
30	X_1	1	1/2	5/4	0	1/4	7/4
	Δ_j	$\Delta_1 = 0$	–8	8.5	0	7.5	52.5

Here, all Δ_j are not zero or positive because $\Delta_2 = -8$ is negative. Hence, optimal solution will not exist here.

¤ ¤

Feedback is the breakfast of Champions.

Ken Blanchard

You can Help other students.

"Inform any error or mistake in this book."

We and Universe

will reward you for Your Kind act.

Email at : feedback@gullybaba.com

or

WhatsApp on 9350849407

7 Primal and Dual

An Overview

The primal-dual method is a standard tool in the design of algorithms for combinatorial optimisation problems. In the linear case, in the primal problem, from each sub-optimal point that satisfies all the constraints, there is a direction or subspace of directions to move that increase the objective function. Moving in any such direction is said to remove slack between the candidate solution and one or more constraints. An infeasible value of the candidate solution is one that exceeds one or more of the constraints.

In the dual problem, the dual vector multiplies the constraints that determine the positions of the constraints in the primal. Varying the dual vector in the dual problem is equivalent to revising the upper bounds in the primal problem. The lowest upper bound is sought. That is, the dual vector is minimised in order to remove slack between the candidate positions of the constraints and the actual optimum.

7.1 FORMULATION OF THE DUAL

Consider the following standard linear programming problem. This will be called as the **primal problem.**

Maximise

$$Z = c_1x_1 + c_2x_2 + ... + c_nx_n$$

Subject to

$$a_{11}x_1 + a_{12}x_2 + ... + a_{1n}x_n \le b_1$$

$$a_{21}x_1 + a_{22}x_2 + ... + a_{2n}x_n \le b_2$$

$$... \quad ... \quad ... \quad ...$$

$$a_{m1}x_1 + a_{m2}x_2 + ... + a_{mn}x_n \le b_m$$

and $x_1 \ge 0, x_2 \ge 0, ..., x_n \ge 0$

The corresponding dual problem is

Minimise

$$D = b_1y_1 + b_2y_2 + ... + b_m y_m$$

Subject to

$$a_{11}y_1 + a_{21}y_2 + ... + a_{m1}y_m \ge c_1$$

$$a_{12}y_1 + a_{22}y_2 + ... + a_{m2}y_m \ge c_2$$

$$... \quad ... \quad ... \quad ...$$

$$a_{1n}y_1 + a_{2n}y_2 + ... + a_{mn}y_m \ge c_n$$

and $y_1 \ge 0, y_2 \ge 0, ..., y_m \ge 0$

The characteristics of the primal and the dual problem

(1) If the primal problem is maximisation, the dual problem is a minimisation, and vice-versa.

(2) The profit constants c_j in the primal problem replace the capacity constants b_i, and vice-versa.

(3) If the primal problem involves $\le$ signs, the dual problem involves $\ge$ signs, and vice-versa.

(4) In the constraints inequalities, the coefficients, which were found by going from left to right, are positioned in the dual from top to bottom, and vice-versa.

(5) A new set of variables appear in the dual problem.

(6) Neglecting the number of non-negativity conditions, if there are n variables and m inequalities in the primal problem, then in the dual problem there will be m variables and n inequalities.

(7) Finally, the dual of the dual problem is the original primal problem itself.

Note:In matrix notation, we may write the dual pair as

Primal	Dual
Maximise	Minimise
$Z = CX$	$D = B^T Y$
Subject to	Subject to
$AX \leq B$	$A^T Y \geq C^T$
$X \geq 0$	$Y \geq 0$

Theorem

Theorem 1: Dual of the dual is the primal.

Proof: Consider the primal as

Maximise CX

Subject to $AX \leq B$

$X \geq 0$

Then the dual is

Minimise $D = B^T Y$

Subject to $A^T Y \geq C^T$

$Y \geq 0$

We write this dual in canonical form, i.e. in a form such that objective function is a maximisation function and constraints are $'\leq'$ type, therefore dual takes the form

– Maximise – $B^T Y$

Subject to $-A^T Y \leq -C^T$

$Y \geq 0$

Now dual to this linear programming problem is

– Maximise $\left(-C^T\right)^T W$

Subject to $\left(-A^T\right)^T W \geq \left(-B^T\right)^T$

$W \geq 0$

Now transpose of the transpose of a vector is the vector itself, therefore, dual of the dual may be put as

– Minimise – CW

Subject to $-AW \geq -B$

$W \geq 0$

which may be rewritten as

Maximise CW

Subject to $AW \leq C$

$W \geq 0$

which is precisely the primal problem.

Solved Practical Problems

Q1. Write the dual of the linear programming problem:

Minimise

$2x_1 + 5x_3$

Subject to the constraints

$x_1 + x_2 \geq 2$

$2x_1 + x_2 + 6x_3 \leq 6$

$x_1 - x_2 + 3x_3 = 4$

$x_1, x_2, x_3 \geq 0$

Ans. First of all, we write the given LPP in the canonical form. i.e.,

$$\left.\begin{array}{l} \text{Maximise } -2x_1 - 5x_3 \\ \text{subject to} \\ \quad -x_1 - x_2 \leq -2 \\ \quad 2x_1 + x_2 + 6x_3 \leq 6 \\ \quad x_1 - x_2 + 3x_3 \leq 4 \\ -x_1 + x_2 - 3x_3 \leq -4 \\ \quad x_1, x_2, x_3 \geq 0 \end{array}\right\} \quad \text{...(i)}$$

This is the canonical form of the given LPP. Now, to write the dual of this LPP, first we write the objective function. The RHS elements of the constraints are the coefficients of the objective function of the dual and the problem is a minimisation problem. Therefore, in the dual, we have to minimise the function

$-2u_1 + 6u_2 + 4u_3 - 4u_4$

The coefficients of x_1 in the constraints in Eq. (i) are –1, 2, 1 and –1, the coefficient of x_1 in the objective function is –2. Therefore, the first constraint in the dual is

$-u_1 + 2u_2 + u_3 - u_4 \geq -2$

Similarly, looking at the coefficients of x_2 in the constraints and in the objective function, the second constraint is

$-u_1 + u_2 - u_3 + u_4 \geq 0$

The third constraint, obtained by looking at the coefficient of x_3 in the constraints and in the objective function is

$6u_2 + 3u_3 - 3u_4 \geq -5$

Putting everything together, the dual of the problem (i) is

Minimise $-2u_1 + 6u_2 + 4u_3 - 4u_4$

Subject to

$-u_1 + 2u_2 + u_3 - u_4 \geq -2$

$-u_1 + u_2 - u_3 + u_4 \geq 0$

$6u_2 + 3u_3 - 3u_4 \geq -5$

$u_1, u_2, u_3, u_4, \geq 0$

Q2. Write the dual of the following LPP.

Minimise

$5x_1 - 6x_2 + 4x_3$

Subject to

$3x_1 + 4x_2 + 6x_3 \geq 9$

$x_1 + 3x_2 + 2x_3 \geq 5$

$2x_1 + 5x_2 - 3x_3 = 3$

$x_1, x_2 \geq 0,\ x_3$ **unrestricted in sign.**

Ans. Canonical form of the given LPP is

Maximise

$-5x_1 + 6x_2 - 4x_3$

Subject to

$-3x_1 - 4x_2 - 6x_3 \leq -9$

$-x_1 - 3x_2 - 2x_3 \leq -5$

$2x_1 + 5x_2 - 3x_3 \leq 3$

$-2x_1 - 5x_2 + 3x_3 \leq -3$

$x_1, x_2 \geq 0$, x_3 is unrestricted in sign.

It is given that x_3 is unrestricted in sign. So, let $x_3 = x_3' - x_3''$

Hence, we have

Maximise

$-5x_1 + 6x_2 - 4x_3' + 4x_3''$

Subject to

$-3x_1 - 4x_2 - 6x_3' + 6x_3'' \leq -9$

$-x_1 - 3x_2 - 2x_3' + 2x_3'' \leq -5$

$2x_1 + 5x_2 - 3x_3' + 3x_3'' \leq 3$

$-2x_1 - 5x_2 + 3x_3' - 3x_3'' \leq -3$

$x_1, x_2, x_3', x_3'' \geq 0$

Now, the Dual of the LPP is

Minimise

$-9u_1 - 5u_2 + 3u_3 - 3u_4$

Subject to

$-3u_1 - u_2 + 2u_3 - 2u_4 \geq -5$

$-4u_1 - 3u_2 + 5u_3 - 5u_4 \geq 6$

$-6u_1 - 2u_2 - 3u_3 + 3u_4 \geq -4$

$6u_1 + 2u_2 + 3u_3 - 3u_4 \geq 4$

$u_1, u_2, u_3, u_4 \geq 0$

Q3. Obtain the dual problem of the following LP problem:

Minimise $Z = x_1 - 3x_2 - 2x_3$

subject to $3x_1 - x_2 + 2x_3 \leq 7$

$2x_1 - 4x_2 \geq 12$

$-4x_1 + 3x_2 + 8x_3 = 10$

$x_1, x_2 \geq 0$, x_3 unrestricted in sign.

Your dual should have only three variables. [June-2014, Q.No.-2(b)]

Ans. Given LPP can be written as

Maximise $-Z = -x_1 + 3x_2 + 2x_3$

subject to $3x_1 - x_2 + 2x_3 \leq 7$

$-2x_1 + 4x_2 \leq -12$

$-4x_1 + 3x_2 + 8x_3 \leq 10$

$4x_1 - 3x_2 - 8x_3 \leq -10$

$x_1, x_2 \geq 0, x_3$ unrestricted in sign

Let $x_3 = x_3' - x_3''$. Hence, the canonical form of given LPP is

Maximise $-Z = -x_1 + 3x_2 + 2x_3' - 2x_3''$

subject to $3x_1 - x_2 + 2x_3' - 2x_3'' \leq 7$

$-2x_1 + 4x_2 \leq -12$

$-4x_1 + 3x_2 + 8x_3' - 8x_3'' \leq 10$

$4x_1 - 3x_2 - 8x_3' + 8x_3'' \leq -10$

$x_1, x_2, x_3', x_3'' \geq 0$

Now, the dual is

Minimise $D = 7y_1 - 12y_2 + 10y_3 - 10y_4$

subject to $3y_1 - 2y_2 - 4y_3 + 4y_4 \geq -1$

$-y_1 + 4y_2 + 3y_3 - 3y_4 \geq 3$

$2y_1 + 8y_3 - 8y_4 \geq 2$

$-2y_1 - 8y_3 + 8y_4 \geq -2$

$y_1, y_2, y_3, y_4 \geq 0$

Now, let $y_3 - y_4 = u$

Hence, the dual will be

Minimise $D = 7y_1 - 12y_2 + 10u$

subject to $3y_1 - 2y_2 - 4u \geq -1$

$-y_1 + 4y_2 + 3u \geq 3$

$2y_1 + 8u \geq 2$

$-2y_1 - 8u \geq -2$

$y_1, y_2 \geq 0$, u is unrestricted.

Q4. Verify that dual of the dual is the primal for the following linear programming problem.

Maximise $Z = 6x_1 - 2x_2 + x_3$

Subject to $4x_1 - 2x_2 - 3x_3 \leq 7$

$2x_1 + x_2 - 4x_3 \geq 5$

$x_1 + x_2 + x_3 = 1$

$x_1, x_2, x_3 \geq 0$

Ans. We shall first put the primal in a canonical form by multiplying second constraint by –1 and putting the third equality constraint in the form of the two inequality constraints, thus we have

Maximise $Z = 6x_1 - 2x_2 + x_3$

Subject to $4x_1 - 2x_2 - 3x_3 \leq 7$

$-2x_1 - x_2 + 4x_3 \leq -5$

$x_1 + x_2 + x_3 \leq 1$

$-x_1 - x_2 - x_3 \leq -1$

$x_1, x_2, x_3 \geq 0$

Dual to this linear programming problem is

Minimise $D = 7y_1 - 5y_2 + y_3 - y_4$

Subject to $4y_1 - 2y_2 + y_3 - y_4 \geq 6$

$-2y_1 - y_2 + y_3 - y_4 \geq -2$

$-3y_1 + 4y_2 + y_3 - y_4 \geq 1$

$y_1, y_2, y_3, y_4 \geq 0$

Now we write this dual in a canonical form, i.e. a maximisation problem with '$\leq$' type of constraints, we therefore have

Maximise $-D = -7y_1 + 5y_2 - y_3 + y_4$

Subject to $-4y_1 + 2y_2 - y_3 + y_4 \leq -6$

$2y_1 + y_2 - y_3 + y_4 \leq 2$

$3y_1 - 4y_2 - y_3 + y_4 \leq -1$

$y_1, y_2, y_3, y_4 \geq 0$

Dual to this linear programming problem is

– Minimise $-P = -6w_1 + 2w_2 - w_3$

Subject to $-4w_1 + 2w_2 + 3w_3 \geq -7$

$2w_1 + w_2 - 4w_3 \geq 5$

$-w_1 - w_2 - w_3 \geq -1$

$w_1 + w_2 + w_3 \geq 1$

$w_1, w_2, w_3 \geq 0$

We can rewrite this linear programming problem as

Maximise $P = 6w_1 - 2w_2 + w_3$

Subject to $4w_1 - 2w_2 - 3w_3 \leq 7$

$2w_1 + w_2 - 4w_3 \geq 5$

$w_1 + w_2 + w_3 = 1$

$w_1, w_2, w_3 \geq 0$

which is precisely the given primal problem. Hence, dual of the dual is the primal.

Q5. Obtain the dual of the following primal LP problem:

Maximise $z = x_1 - 2x_2 + 3x_3$

subject to $-2x_1 + x_2 + 3x_3 = 2$

$2x_1 + 3x_2 + 4x_3 = 1$

$x_1, x_2, x_3 \geq 0$ **[Dec-2014, Q.No.-2(b)]**

Ans. Given primal LPP can be written as follows:

Maximise $Z = x_1 - 2x_2 + 3x_3$

subject to $-2x_1 + x_2 + 3x_3 \leq 2$

$2x_1 - x_2 - 3x_3 \leq -2$

$2x_1 + 3x_2 + 4x_3 \leq 1$

$-2x_1 - 3x_2 - 4x_3 \leq -1$

$x_1,\ x_2,\ x_3 \geq 0$

Thus, dual of this primal LPP is as follows:

Minimise $D = 2y_1 - 2y_2 + y_3 - y_4$

subject to $-2y_1 + 2y_2 + 2y_3 - 2y_4 \geq 1$

$y_1 - y_2 + 3y_3 - 3y_4 \geq -2$

$3y_1 - 3y_2 + 4y_3 - 4y_4 \geq 3$

$y_1,\ y_2,\ y_3,\ y_4 \geq 0$

Q6. An unrestricted primal variable converts into an equality dual constraint. Is it true? **[June-2015, Q.No.-1(c)]**

Ans. True

Let the primal of an LPP is given as follows:

Maximise $x_1 + 2x_2$

subject to $4x_1 + 3x_2 \leq 5$

$x_1 - 2x_2 \leq 2$

x_1, x_2 are unrestricted in sign.

Let $x_1 = x_1' - x_1''$ and $x_2 = x_2' - x_2''$, then we have the primal as follows:

Maximise $x_1' - x_1'' + 2x_2' - 2x_2''$

subject to $4x_1' - 4x_1'' + 3x_2' - 3x_2'' \le 5$

$x_1' - x_1'' - 2x_2' + 2x_2'' \le 2$

$x_1', x_1'', x_2', x_2'' \ge 0$

Now, the dual is

Minimise $5y_1 + 2y_2$

subject to $4y_1 + y_2 \ge 1$

$-4y_1 - y_2 \ge -1$

$3y_1 - 2y_2 \ge 2$

$-3y_1 + 2y_2 \ge -2$

$y_1, y_2 \ge 0$

This Dual can also be written as

Minimise $5y_1 + 2y_2$

subject to $4y_1 + y_2 = 1$

$3y_1 - 2y_2 = 2$

$y_1, y_2 \ge 0$

Here, we can see equality dual constraints. Hence, an unrestricted primal variable converts into an equality dual variable.

Q7. Find the dual of the following LPP:

Maximise $z = 3x_1 + 2x_2$

subject to $x_1 \le 4$

$\mathbf{2x_1 + x_2 \le 6}$

$\mathbf{x_1 + x_2 \le 5}$

$\mathbf{3x_1 - x_2 = -1}$

$x_2 \ge 0$, x_1 is unrestricted. **[Dec-2015, Q.No.-4(a)]**

Ans. Given LPP can be written as follows:

Maximise $z = 3x_1 - 2x_2$

subject to $x_1 \le 4$

$2x_1 + x_2 \le 6$

$x_1 + x_2 \le 5$

$3x_1 - x_2 \le -1$

$-3x_1 + x_2 \le 1$

$x_2 > 0$, x_1 is unrestricted.

Let $x_1 = x_1' - x_1''$, then we have

$z = 3x_1' - 3x_1'' - 2x_2$

subject to $x_1' - x_1'' \le 4$

$2x_1' - 2x_1'' + x_2 \le 6$

$x_1' - x_1'' + x_2 \le 5$

$3x_1' - 3x_1'' - x_2 \le -1$

$-3x_1' + 3x_1'' + x_2 \le 1$

$x_1', x_1'', x_2 \ge 0$

Hence, the dual is

Minimise $D = 4y_1 + 6y_2 + 5y_3 - y_4 + y_5$

subject to $y_1 + 2y_2 + y_3 + 3y_4 - 3y_5 \ge 3$

$-y_1 - 2y_2 - y_3 - 3y_4 + 3y_5 \ge -3$

$y_2 + y_3 - y_4 + y_5 \ge -2$

$y_1, y_2, y_3, y_4, y_5 \ge 0$

⌑ ⌑

Duality Theorems

An Overview

There are two ideas fundamental to duality theory. One is the fact that (for the symmetric dual) the dual of a dual linear programme is the original primal linear programme. Additionally, every feasible solution for a linear programme gives a bound on the optimal value of the objective function of its dual.

The weak duality theorem states that the objective function value of the dual at any feasible solution is always greater than or equal to the objective function value of the primal at any feasible solution. The strong duality theorem states that if the primal has an optimal solution then the dual also has an optimal solution.

8.1 THE PRINCIPLE OF DUALITY

Duality or the duality principle is the principle that optimisation problems may be viewed from either of two perspectives, the primal problem or the dual problem. This is also called the duality principle. The solution to the dual problem provides a lower bound to the solution of the primal (minimisation) problem. However, in general the optimal values of the primal and dual problems need not be equal. Their difference is called the duality gap. For convex optimisation problems, the duality gap is zero under a constraint qualification condition. Hence, we can state the principle of duality as, a solution to the dual problem provides a bound on the value of the solution to the primal problem; when the problem is convex and satisfies a constraint qualification, then the value of an optimal solution of the primal problem is given by the dual problem.

The duality principles can be stated formally in general terms. Let the primal problem be:

Primal:

Maximise $Z = \sum_{j=1}^{n} c_j x_j$,

subject to: $\sum_{j=1}^{n} a_{ij} x_j \le b_i$ (i = 1, 2, ..., m),

$x_j \ge 0$ (j = 1, 2, ..., n)

Associated with this primal problem there is a corresponding dual problem given by:

Dual:

Minimise $D = \sum_{i=1}^{m} b_i y_i$,

subject to: $\sum_{i=1}^{m} a_{ij} y_i \ge c_j$ (j = 1, 2, ..., n),

$y_i \ge 0$ (i = 1, 2, ..., m)

8.2 SIGNIFICANCE OF DUALITY

The significance of the study of dual is as follows:

(1) The right-hand side of the constraint represents the amount of a resource available and the associated dual variable value is interpreted as the maximum amount likely to be paid for additional unit of the resource.

However, such an interpretation is not always correct because of two types of costs involved with each resource: (a) sunk cost that is not affected by the decision made. It will incurred no matter what values the dual variables assume, and (b) relevant cost that depends on the decision made. It will vary with the values of decision variables.

(2) The maximum amount that should be paid for one additional unit of a resource is called its shadow price (also called simplex multiplier).

(3) The total marginal value of the resources equals the optimal objective function value. The dual variables equal the marginal value of resources (shadow prices).

(4) The value of the ith dual variable represents the rate at which the primal objective function value will increase by increasing the right-hand side (resource value) of constraint i, assuming that all other data remain unchanged.

Interpretation of dual variables or Simplex multipliers corresponding to optimal solution of the primal

Consider a general linear programming problem in its standard form

$$\begin{aligned}&\text{Maximise } Z = CX\\&\text{Subject to } AX = B\\&X \geq 0\end{aligned} \quad \text{...(i)}$$

Let $(X_S, 0)$ be the optimal solution to (i) with basis matrix S so that $SX_S = B$ or $X_S = S^{-1}B$. Also $Z_S = C_S X_S$ is the corresponding optimal value of the objective function. We know that an optimal solution to the dual is given by a vector $Y^{OT} = C_S S^{-1}$.

Now we suppose that a small change ΔB in the vector B in Eq. (i) does not cause the optimal basis S to change. Thus, for the changed right hand side in Eq. (i), the optimal solution is given by

$$\begin{aligned}\dot{X}_S &= S^{-1}(B + \Delta B)\\&= S^{-1}B + S^{-1}\Delta B\\&= X_S + \Delta X_S\end{aligned}$$

where $\Delta X_S = S^{-1}\Delta B$

The new value of the objective function corresponding to the solution $\hat{X}_S$ is given by

$$\begin{aligned}\hat{Z}_S &= Z_S + \Delta Z_S = C_S(X_S + \Delta X_S)\\&= C_S X_S + C_S \Delta X_S\end{aligned}$$

or $\Delta Z_S = C_S X_S + C_S \Delta X_S - Z_S$

$$\begin{aligned}&= C_S \Delta X_S \quad (\because Z_S = C_S X_S)\\&= C_S B^{-1}\Delta B \quad = Y^{OT}\Delta B\end{aligned}$$

or $$\frac{\partial Z_S}{\partial b_i} = (Y_0)_i.$$

i.e. rate of change of optimal objective function value Z_S with respect to b_i is the optimal dual variable $(Y_0)_i$.

Hence, we may conclude that the vector Y_0 gives the sensitivity of the optimal cost with respect to small changes in the right hand side vector b of constants, i.e. if the problem (i) was to be solved with B changed to $B + \Delta B$, the change in the optimal value of the objective function would then be $Y \Delta B$. Thus, $(Y_0)_i$ may be considered as the marginal price of the component b_i (since if b_i is changed to $b_i + \Delta b_i$, the optimal objective value changes by $Y_i \ \Delta b_i$, provided optimal basis does not change).

8.3 ADVANTAGES OF DUALITY

Advantages of duality are as follows:

(1) It is advantageous to solve the dual of a primal having less number of constraints, because the number of constraints usually equals the number of iterations required to solve the problem.

(2) It avoids the necessity for adding surplus or artificial variables and solves the problem quickly (the technique is known as the primal-dual method). In economics, duality is useful in the formulation of the input and output systems. It is also useful in physics, engineering, mathematics, etc.

(3) The dual variables provide an important economic interpretation of the final solution of an LP problem.

(4) It is quite useful when investigating changes in the parameters of an LP problem (the technique is known as the sensitivity analysis).

(5) Duality is used to solve an LP problem by the Simplex method in which the initial solution is infeasible (the technique is known as the dual simpler method).

Theorems

Theorem 1: (Weak duality theorem): If primal and dual problems are both feasible with K and E as their respective feasible regions, then

$$Z \le D \quad \text{for every } X \in K \text{ and } Y \in E$$

Proof: Let $X_0 \in K$ and $Y_0 \in E$. Accordingly, we have

$$AX_0 \le B \qquad ...(i)$$

$$X_0 \ge 0 \qquad ...(ii)$$

and $A^T Y_0 \ge C^T$ or $Y_0^T A \ge C$ ...(iii)

$Y_0 \ge 0$ and $Y_0^T \ge 0$ ...(iv)

From (i) and (iv) we have

$$Y_0^T AX_0 \le Y_0^T B \qquad ...(v)$$

Also from (ii) and (iii)

$$Y_0^T AX_0 \ge CX_0 \qquad ...(vi)$$

From (v) and (vi), we have

$$CX_0 \le Y_0^T AX_0 \le Y_0^T B \left(= B^T Y_0\right)$$

or $Z \le D$

Theorem 2: Let primal and dual have feasible solutions X_0 and Y_0 respectively, such that

$$\mathbf{CX_0 = B^T Y_0} \qquad ...(i)$$

then X_0 is the optimal solution for the primal and Y_0 is optimal for the dual.

Proof. Let X be any feasible solution of the primal problem, then according to weak duality theorem, we have

$$CX \le B^T Y, \qquad ...(ii)$$

where Y is any arbitrary feasible solution of the dual.

Now, relation (ii) is true particularly for $Y_0 \in D$

i.e. $CX \le B^T Y_0$

$= CX_0$ (using (i)

$\therefore CX \le CX_0 \quad \forall \quad X \in K$

Therefore X_0 is an optimal solution for the primal. Again, (ii) is true particularly for any $X_0 \in K$, therefore we have

$CX_0 \le B^T Y \quad \forall \quad Y \in E$

or $B^T Y_0 \le B^T Y \quad \forall \quad Y \in E$ (using (i))

$\Rightarrow$ Y_0 is optimal for the dual.

Theorem 3 (Strong Quality theorem): If either of the problems (primal or dual) has a finite optimal solution, then the other problem also has a finite optimal solution and the optimal values of corresponding objective functions are equal.

Solved Practical Problems

Q1. Consider the following dual pair of linear programming problems.

Maximise $Z = 5x_1 + 6x_2 + 4x_3$

Primal

Subject to $x_1 + 2x_2 + x_3 \le 5$

$2x_1 - x_2 + 3x_3 = 2$

$x_1, x_2, x_3 \quad \ge 0$

Dual

Minimise $D = 5y_1 + 2y_2$

Subject to

$y_1 + 2y_2 \ge 5$

$2y_1 - y_2 \ge 6$

$y_1 + 3y_2 \ge 4$

$y_1, \; y_2 \ge 0$

(i) Verify that

$x_1 = 1, x_2 = 1, x_3 = \frac{1}{3}$ **and** $y_1 = 7, y_2 = 2$

are feasible solutions for the two problems respectively.

(ii) Verify the weak duality theorem.

Ans. (i) Taking first constraint of primal,

$x_1 + 2x_2 + x_3 \le 5$

Putting the given values of x_1, x_2 and x_3, we have

$1 + 2(1) + \frac{1}{3} \le 5$

$3.33 \le 5$

Hence, it is satisfied.

Now, taking second constraint of the primal

$2x_1 - x_2 + 3x_3 = 2$

$2(1) - 1 + 3\left(\frac{1}{3}\right) = 2$

$2 = 2$

It is also satisfied.

Similarly, taking the constraints of dual

$y_1 + 2y_2 \ge 5$

$7 + 2(2) \ge 5$

$\Rightarrow \quad 11 \ge 5$

It is satisfied.

Now, $2y_1 - y_2 \geq 6$

$2(7) - 2 \geq 6$

$12 \geq 6$

It is satisfied.

Now, $y_1 + 3y_2 \geq 4$

$7 + 3(2) \geq 4$

$13 \geq 4$

It is also satisfied.

Hence, all the constraints of primal and dual are satisfied by the given values. In addition, these values follow non-negativity restriction, i.e., all the values are positive. Hence, the given solution is the feasible solution.

(ii) Now, $Z = 5x_1 + 6x_2 + 4x_3$

$\Rightarrow \quad Z = 5(1) + 6(1) + 4\left(\frac{1}{3}\right) = \frac{37}{3} = 12.33$

and $D = 5y_1 + 2y_2$

$\Rightarrow \quad D = 5\ (7) + 2\ (2) = 39$

Hence, $Z \leq D$

Hence, weak duality theorem is verified.

Q2. Illustrate strong duality theorem by applying regular Simplex method to the following primal and dual problem.

Maximise $Z = x_1 + x_2 + x_3$

Primal

Subject to

$2x_1 + x_2 + 2x_3 \leq 2$

$4x_1 + 2x_2 + x_3 \leq 2$

$x_1, x_2, x_3 \geq 0$

Minimise $D = 2y_1 + 2y_2$

Dual

Subject to

$2y_1 + 4y_2 \geq 1$

$y_1 + 2y_2 \geq 1$

$2y_1 + y_2 \geq 1$

$y_1, y_2 \geq 0$

Ans. We first solve the primal using Simplex method. Adding slack variables, the constraints of the primal reduce to

$2x_1 + x_2 + 2x_3 + x_4 = 2$

$4x_1 + 2x_2 + x_3 + x_5 = 2$

$x_1, \dots, x_5 \geq 0$

x_4 and x_5 are slack variables, initial solution to this primal problem is

$x_1 = 0, x_2 = 0, x_3 = 0, x_4 = 2, x_5 = 2; Z = 0$

We, therefore, put the primal problem in the tableau form

	$C_j \rightarrow$	1	1	1	0	0	
C_s	**Variables in the basis**	A_1	A_2	A_3	A_4	A_5	**Solution**
0	x_4	2	1	2	1	0	2
0	x_5	4	[2]	1	0	1	2 →
	$Z_j - C_j$	–1	–1 ↑	–1	0	0	0

We notice, all the three non-zero values of $Z_j - C_j$ are equal, i.e. there is a tie, therefore any one of the three vectors A_1, A_2 or A_3 can enter the basis. We let A_2 enter the basis. To decide the departing vector, we compute $\min\left\{\frac{2}{1}, \frac{2}{2}\right\} = \frac{2}{2}$, which indicates vector A_5 is to be removed from the basis and $\boxed{2}$ is the pivot element. Next tableau is given as follows

	$C_j \rightarrow$	1	1	1	0	0	
C_s	**Variables in the basis**	A_1	A_2	A_3	A_4	A_5	**Solution**
0	x_4	0	0	[3/2]	1	–1/2	1 →
1	x_2	2	1	1/2	0	1/2	1
	$Z_j - C_j$	1	0	–1/2 ↑	0	1/2	1

Most negative $Z_j - C_j$ is $-\frac{1}{2}$, therefore column A_3 enters into the basis and $\min\left\{\frac{1}{\frac{3}{2}}, \frac{1}{\frac{1}{2}}\right\} = \min\left\{\frac{2}{3}, 2\right\} = \frac{2}{3}$, vector A_4 is to be removed from the basis and $\boxed{\frac{3}{2}}$ is the pivot element.

Next table is

C_S	$C_j \rightarrow$ Variables in the basis	1 A_1	1 A_2	1 A_3	0 A_4	0 A_5	Solution
1	x_3	0	0	1	2/3	–1/3	2/3
1	x_2	2	1	0	–1/3	2/3	2/3
	$Z_j - C_j$	1	0	0	1/3	1/3	4/3

Since all $Z_j - C_j \geq 0$ we now have the optimal solution which is given by

$x_1 = 0,$ $x_2 = \frac{2}{3},$ $x_3 = \frac{2}{3}$ and maximum $Z = \frac{4}{3}.$

Now, we solve the dual problem using. Two phase Simplex method.

Convert the constraints of the dual into equations by introducing surplus variables y_3, y_4 and y_5 and constraints take form

$$2y_1 + 4y_2 - y_3 = 1$$
$$y_1 + 2y_2 - y_4 = 1$$
$$2y_1 + y_2 - y_5 = 1$$
$$y_1, y_2, y_3, y_4, y_5 \geq 0$$

It is obvious that initial identity matrix is not present in the coefficient matrix of this constraint system, therefore we introduce artificial variables y_1^a, y_2^a and y_3^a and in phase I, we solve

Maximise $D^0 = -y_1^a - y_2^a - y_3^a$

Subject to $2y_1 + 4y_2 - y_3 + y_1^a = 1$

$$y_1 + 2y_2 - y_4 + y_2^a = 1$$
$$2y_1 + y_2 - y_5 + y_3^a = 1$$
$$y_1, \ldots, y_5, y_1^a, y_2^a, y_3^a \geq 0$$

Initial solution is obtained by putting non-basic variables equal to zero, i.e.

$$y_1 = y_2 = y_3 = y_4 = y_5 = 0$$

Therefore, $y_1^a = 1, y_2^a = 1, y_3^a = 1,$ and $y^0 = -3$

We put the problem in the tableau form.

	$C_j^0 \rightarrow$	0	0	0	0	0	–1	–1	–1	
C_S^0	**Variables in the basis**	A_1	A_2	A_3	A_4	A_5	A_1^a	A_2^a	A_3^a	**Solution**
–1	y_1^a	2	[4]	–1	0	0	1	0	0	1
–1	y_2^a	1	2	0	–1	0	0	1	0	1
–1	y_3^a	2	1	0	0	–1	0	0	1	1
	$Z_j^0 - C_j^0$	–5	–7 ↑	1	1	1	0	0	0	–3

Most negative $Z_j^0 - C_j^0$ is –7, therefore column A_2 enters the basis and we choose minimum $\left\{\frac{1}{4}, \frac{1}{2}, \frac{1}{1}\right\} = \frac{1}{4}$. Hence, column of artificial vector y_1^a is to be removed from the basis and [4] is the pivot element. The new table is

	$C_j^0 \rightarrow$	0	0	0	0	0	–1	–1	–1	
C_S^0	**Variables in the basis**	A_1	A_2	A_3	A_4	A_5	A_1^a	A_2^a	A_3^a	**Solution**
0	y_2	1/2	1	1/4	0	0	1/4	0	0	1/4
–1	y_2^a	0	0	1/2	–1	0	–1/2	1	0	1/2
–1	y_3^a	[3/2]	0	1/4	0	–1	–1/4	0	1	3/4 →
	$Z_j^0 - C_j^0$	–3/2 ↑	0	–3/4	1	1	7/4	0	0	–5/4

Most negative $Z_j^0 - C_j^0$ is $-\frac{3}{2}$, therefore column A_1 enters the basis and we choose minimum $\left\{\frac{1/4}{1/2}, \frac{3/4}{3/2}\right\} = \min\left\{\frac{1}{2}, \frac{1}{2}\right\}$, i.e. there is a tie, in this case we decide that artificial vector corresponding to y_3^a is to be removed from the basis and pivot element is $\frac{3}{2}$, again we move to the next table.

	$C_j^0 \rightarrow$	0	0	0	0	0	–1	–1	–1	
C_S^0	**Variables in the basis**	A_1	A_2	A_3	A_4	A_5	A_1^a	A_2^a	A_3^a	**Solution**
0	y_2	0	1	–1/3	0	1/3	1/3	0	–1/3	0
–1	y_2^a	0	0	[1/2]	–1	0	–1/2	1	0	1/2 →
0	y_1	1	0	1/6	0	–2/3	–1/6	0	2/3	1/2
	$Z_j^0 - C_j^0$	0	0	–1/2 ↑	1	0	3/2	0	0	–1/2

Most negative $Z_j^0 - C_j^0$ is $-\frac{1}{2}$, is therefore column vector A_3 enters the basis and choose minimum

That is to say $\left\{\frac{1/2}{1/2}, \frac{1/2}{1/6}\right\} = \min\{1,3\} = 1.$

This implies column corresponding to artificial vector y_2^a is to be removed and $\boxed{\frac{1}{2}}$ is the pivot element. Accordingly the next table is

	$C_j^0 \rightarrow$	0	0	0	0	0	−1	−1	−1	
C_S^0	Variables in the basis	A_1	A_2	A_3	A_4	A_5	A_1^a	A_2^a	A_3^a	Solution
0	y_2	0	1	0	−2/3	1/3	0	2/3	−1/3	1/3
0	y_3	0	0	1	−2	0	−1	2	1	1
0	y_1	1	0	0	1/3	−2/3	0	−1/3	−1/3	1/3
	$Z_j^0 - C_j^0$	0	0	0	0	0	1	1	0	0

Phase I terminates, therefore, we proceed with phase II. Objective function for phase II is.

– Maximise $-D = -2y_1 - 2y_2$.

The final table for phase I gives initial table for phase II (without colums corresponding to artificial vectors)

	$C_j \rightarrow$	−2	−2	0	0	0	
C_S	Variables in the basis	A_1	A_2	A_3	A_4	A_5	Solution
−2	y_2	0	1	0	−2/3	1/3	1/3
0	y_3	0	0	1	−2	0	1
−2	y_1	1	0	0	1/3	−2/3	1/3
	$Z_j - C_j$	0	0	0	2/3	2/3	−4/3

As all $Z_j - C_j \geq 0$, we have reached the optimal and optimal for the dual is given by

$$y_1 = \frac{1}{3}, y_2 = \frac{1}{3}, y_3 = 1, y_4 = 0, y_5 = 0 \text{ and Max } D = -\frac{4}{3}$$

i.e. Minimum $D = \frac{4}{3}$.

Hence, for optimal solutions of primal and dual problems we have

Maximum $Z = \text{Minimum } D = \frac{4}{3}$.

Hence, strong duality theorem is verified.

Q3. Illustrate the principle of duality for the following linear programming problem

Minimise $D = 3y_1 + 2y_2$

Subject to

$7y_1 + 2y_2 \geq 30$

$5y_1 + 4y_2 \geq 20$

$2y_1 + 8y_2 \geq 16$

$y_1, \ y_2 \geq 0$

Ans. Dual of the given LPP is

Maximise $Z = 30x_1 + 20x_2 + 16x_3$

Subject to $7x_1 + 5x_2 + 2x_3 \leq 3$

$2x_1 + 4x_2 + 8x_3 \leq 2$

$x_1, x_2, x_3 \geq 0$

Now, we solve it by simplex method.

Adding slack variables, constraints reduce to

$7x_1 + 5x_2 + 2x_3 + x_4 = 3$

$2x_1 + 4x_2 + 8x_3 + x_5 = 2$

$x_1, x_2, x_3, x_4, x_5 \geq 0$

Initial solution is

$x_1 = x_2 = x_3 = 0, \ x_4 = 3, \ x_5 = 2$

Now, putting the problem in the table form as

	$C_j \rightarrow$	**30**	**20**	**16**	**0**	**0**	
C_S	**Variables in the basis**	A_1	A_2	A_3	A_4	A_5	**Solution**
0	x_4	[7]	5	2	1	0	$3 \rightarrow$
0	x_5	2	4	8	0	1	2
	$Z_j - C_j$	–30 ↑	–20	–16	0	0	0

–30 is most negative. Hence, entering variable is x_1. Entering column is A_1.

Now $\min\left\{\frac{3}{7}, \frac{2}{2}\right\} = \frac{3}{7}$

Hence, 7 is pivot element and x_4 is departing variable. Hence, new table is

C_S	$C_j \rightarrow$ Variables in the basis	30 A_1	20 A_2	16 A_3	0 A_4	0 A_5	Solution
30	x_1	1	5/7	2/7	1/7	0	3/7
0	x_5	0	18/7	[52/7]	–2/7	1	8/7→
	$Z_j - C_j$	0	10/7	–52/7 ↑	30/7	0	90/7

Now, $\min\left\{\frac{3/7}{2/7}, \frac{8/7}{52/7}\right\}$

$= \frac{8/7}{52/7}$

C_S	$C_j \rightarrow$ Variables in the basis	30 A_1	20 A_2	16 A_3	0 A_4	0 A_5	Solution
30	x_1	1	56/91	0	2/13	–1/26	5/13
16	x_3	0	9/26	1	–1/26	7/52	2/13
	$Z_j - C_j$	0	4	0	4	1	14

Since, all $Z_j - C_j \geq 0$, hence we have the optimal solution of dual is

$x_1 = \frac{5}{13}, x_2 = 0, x_3 = \frac{2}{13}$ and Max Z = 14

Now, $Z_j - C_j$ corresponding to the columns of slack variables, provides us with the values of the primal variables, i.e.,

$y_1 = Z_4 - C_4 = 4$

and $y_2 = Z_5 - C_5 = 1$

and Min D = 14

This is the duality pri nciple.

Hence, optimal solutions of primal and dual are

$y_1 = 4, y_2 = 1$; $x_1 = \frac{5}{13}, x_2 = 0, x_3 = \frac{2}{13}$

Min D = Max Z = 14.

Q4. A chemical-dye manufacturing firm is considering the production of two new products. Each product requires manufacturing time on two machines A and B given in a table below. The profits per unit of the products I and II are respectively ₹5 and ₹6. Find the units of each product that should be manufactured every week so that the

profit is maximum. Also, give economic interpretation of the optimal values of primal and dual variables.

Data for manufacture of two products.

Product	Hours needed on machine A per unit of the product	Hours needed on machine B per unit of the product
I	2	1
II	3	1
Total time available (Hours/week)	24	10

Ans. We assume that number of units manufactured is x_1 for the first and x_2 for the second product. The mathematical formulation of the given problem is

Maximise $Z = 5x_1 + 6x_2$

Subject to $2x_1 + 3x_2 \leq 24$

$x_1 + x_2 \leq 10$

$x_1, x_2 \geq 0$

where Z represents the profit in rupees; first and second constraints reflect the time restrictions (in hours) place on the production of two products on machines A and B respectively. The last two constraints express the fact that negative number of units of either product cannot be produced. Optimal solution of this primal problem is given by

$x_1^0 = 6,\ x_2^0 = 4$ and maximum $Z = 54$

Dual to the above linear programming problem is:

Minimise $D = 24y_1 + 10y_2$

Subject to $2y_1 + y_2 \geq 5$

$3y_1 + y_2 \geq 6$

$y_1, y_2 \geq 0$

Optimal solution to this dual problem is given by

$y_1^0 = 1,\ y_2^0 = 3$ and Minimum $D = 54$

We can now have an economic interpretation of the dual problem. Now Minimum D = Maximum Z and the primal objective function is evaluated in rupees, therefore, the dual objective function may also be evaluated in rupees. The constants in the primal objective function Z are the profits in rupees. Also, right hand-side constants in the primal constraints are in hours and these become constant in Y, the dual variables y_1 and y_2 must be the costs incurred (or implicit prices) paid in rupees for using machines A and B, respectively, for an hour.

According to strong duality theorem, there is an equilibrium set of activities $y_i^{'S}$ and a set of prices $y_i^{'S}$ where the maximum production profit is equal to the minimum rental cost.

Now, we look for the interpretation of the optimal prices y_1^0 and y_2^0 as follows. Since $y_1^0 = 1$, the increase in the optimal value Z is ₹1 if the time available on machine A is increased by 1 hr (i.e. from 24 hrs to 25 hrs) provided machine B is available only for 10 hrs and the optimal basis to the primal does not change. Similarly, the increase in profit (i.e. the value of Z) by increasing time available on machine B by one hour is ₹3$\left(= y_2^0\right)$ provided machine A is available only for 24 hrs and the optimal basis to the primal does not change.

We note here that if the time available on machine B is kept at 10 hrs, it does not necessarily mean that the profit will increase by $hy_1^0 (= h)$ if the time available on machine A is increased to (24 + h) hours. This is so because the optimal basis to the primal might change if h is not small enough. For primal problem the optimal basis is

$$S = \begin{pmatrix} 2 & 3 \\ 1 & 1 \end{pmatrix}$$

$b = (24, 10)^T$ – the vector of right hand side constants in the primal constraints – is changed to $(24 + h, 10)^T$, the basis matrix S remains optimal if the basis solution provided by S is feasible, i.e. if

$$\begin{pmatrix} 2 & 3 \\ 1 & 1 \end{pmatrix}^{-1} \begin{pmatrix} 24 + h \\ 10 \end{pmatrix} = \begin{pmatrix} 6 - h \\ 4 + h \end{pmatrix} \geq 0$$

Thus, if h > 6 then the optimal basis does not remain the same. The optimal primal value x_i^0, i = 1, 2 represents the rate of change of D when right hand side constant in the ith constraint of the **dual** is changed, provided this change does not change the optimal basis of the dual problem. To be a top scorer — Read only GPH Books.

⌑⌑

9 Transportation Problems

An Overview

Transportation theory is a name given to the study of optimal transportation and allocation of resources. The problem was formalised by the French mathematician Gaspard Monge in 1781.

It deals with sources where a supply of some commodity is available and destinations where the commodity is demanded. The classic statement of the transportation problem uses a matrix with the rows representing sources and columns representing destinations. The algorithms for solving the problem are based on this matrix representation. The costs of shipping from sources to destinations are indicated by the entries in the matrix.

9.1 MATHEMATICAL FORMULATION OF A TRANSPORTATION PROBLEM

Let there be m sources of supply, $S_1, S_2, \ldots, S_m$ having $a_i\,(i = 1, 2, \ldots, m)$ units of supply (or capacity) respectively, to be transported among n destinations, $D_1, D_2, \ldots, D_n$ with $b_j\,(j = 1, 2, \ldots, n)$ units of demand (or requirement) respectively. Let C_{ij} be the cost of shipping one unit of the commodity from source i to destination j for each route. If x_{ij} represents number of units shipped per route from source i to destination j, the problem is to determine the transportation schedule so as to minimise the total transportation cost while satisfying the supply and demand conditions. Mathematically, the problem, in general, may be stated as follows:

Minimise (total cost) $Z = \sum_{i=1}^{m} \sum_{j=1}^{n} C_{ij} x_{ij}$ ...(i)

subject to the constraints

$$\sum_{j=1}^{n} x_{ij} = a_i,\ i = 1, 2, \ldots, m \text{ (supply constraints)} \quad \text{...(ii)}$$

$$\sum_{i=1}^{m} x_{ij} = b_j,\ j = 1, 2, \ldots, n \text{ (demand constraints)} \quad \text{...(iii)}$$

and $x_{ij} \geq 0$ for all i and j ...(iv)

Note: Transportation problems for which

$$\sum_{i=1}^{m} a_i = \sum_{j=1}^{n} b_j$$

are called **balanced problems** otherwise they are **unbalanced.**

9.2 TABULAR REPRESENTATION OF A TP (TRANSPORTATION PROBLEM)

We can tabulate the given TP as follows:

Table 9.1

To / From	D_1	D_2	...	D_n	Supply a_i
S_1	c_{11}	c_{12}	...	c_{1n}	a_1
S_2	c_{21}	c_{22}	...	c_{2n}	a_2
⋮	⋮	⋮		⋮	⋮
S_m	c_{m1}	c_{m2}	...	c_{mn}	a_m
Demand b_j	b_1	b_2	...	b_n	$\sum_{i=1}^{m} a_i = \sum_{j=1}^{n} b_j$

9.3 SPECIAL STRUCTURE OF THE TRANSPORTATION PROBLEM

Consider the following data of a TP:

$$m = 3 \quad n = 4$$

$$a_1 = 15 \quad a_2 = 20 \quad a_3 = 30$$

$$b_1 = 10 \quad b_2 = 15 \quad b_3 = 22 \quad b_4 = 18$$

$$C_{11} = 5 \quad C_{12} = 7 \quad C_{13} = 2 \quad C_{14} = 1$$

$$C_{21} = 2 \quad C_{22} = 4 \quad C_{23} = 3 \quad C_{24} = 6$$

$$C_{31} = 1 \quad C_{32} = 3 \quad C_{33} = 7 \quad C_{34} = 4$$

The mathematical model of this data is

Minimise

$$Z = 5x_{11} + 7x_{12} + 2x_{13} + x_{14} + 2x_{21} + 4x_{22} + 3x_{23}$$

$$+6x_{24} + x_{31} + 3x_{32} + 7x_{33} + 4x_{34} = \sum_{i=1}^{3}\sum_{j=1}^{4} C_{ij} x_{ij}$$

subject to

$$\left.\begin{aligned} x_{11} + x_{12} + x_{13} + x_{14} &= 15 \\ x_{21} + x_{22} + x_{23} + x_{24} &= 20 \\ x_{31} + x_{32} + x_{33} + x_{34} &= 30 \end{aligned}\right\} \qquad \text{...(i)}$$

and

$$\left.\begin{aligned} x_{11} + x_{21} + x_{31} &= 10 \\ x_{12} + x_{22} + x_{32} &= 15 \\ x_{13} + x_{23} + x_{33} &= 22 \\ x_{14} + x_{24} + x_{34} &= 18 \end{aligned}\right\} \qquad \text{...(ii)}$$

$$x_{ij} \geq 0, \qquad i = 1, 2, 3 \text{ and } j = 1, 2, 3, 4.$$

The observations are as follows:

(1) The total number of constraints is 7 viz 3 + 4 where 3 is number of sources and 4 is number of destinations. Thus, in general TP with 'm' sources and 'n' destinations, the total number of constraints is (m + n) and table consists of m rows and n columns.

Row constraints or source constraints: Those constraints which arise from availability restriction at the source are called row constraints or source constraints.

The constraints of Eq. (i) are source constraints, i.e., there are three source constraints in the mathematical model of the given data.

Column constraints or destination constraints: Those constraints which arise from demand needed at the destination are called column constraints or destination constraints.

The constraints of Eq. (ii) are destination constraints, i.e., there are four destination constraints in the mathematical model of the given data.

(2) If a transportation problem (TP) consists of 'm' sources and 'n' destinations, it has a total of (m + n) constraints. First 'm' constraints are source constraints and next 'n', i.e., $(m+1)^{th}, (m+2)^{th}, ...(m+n)^{th}$ are destination constraints. A variable x_{ij} occurs in i^{th} source constraints and j^{th} destination constraints which is $(m+j)^{th}$. The coefficients of each variable x_{ij} are '1' each.

For example, x_{13} occurs in 1st source constraint and 3rd destination constraint which is $(3+3)^{th} = 6^{th}$ constraint.

(3) For a general TP, **activity vector** of any variable x_{ij} is a m + n vector. For example, x_{31} occurs in 3rd constraints with coefficient 1 and in the $(3+1)^{th} = 4^{th}$ constraint with coefficient 1 and with zero coefficient in remaining constraints. Its activity vector is

$$\begin{matrix} m=1 \\ m=2 \\ m=3 \\ n=1 \\ n=2 \\ n=3 \\ n=4 \end{matrix} \begin{bmatrix} 0 \\ 0 \\ 1 \\ \cdots \\ 1 \\ 0 \\ 0 \\ 0 \end{bmatrix}$$

Similarly, activity vectors of the variables x_{23} and x_{14} are

$$\begin{matrix} m=1 \\ m=2 \\ m=3 \\ n=1 \\ n=2 \\ n=3 \\ n=4 \end{matrix} \begin{bmatrix} 0 \\ 1 \\ 0 \\ \cdots \\ 0 \\ 0 \\ 1 \\ 0 \end{bmatrix}, \begin{bmatrix} 1 \\ 0 \\ 0 \\ \cdots \\ 0 \\ 0 \\ 0 \\ 1 \end{bmatrix}$$

respectively.

(4) We can write matrix of coefficients A from the given TP. We write activity vectors in the order to give us a 7×12 matrix. (7 is the number of constraints and 12 is the number of variables) .Thus, A is as follows:

$$A = \begin{bmatrix} 1 & 1 & 1 & 1 & 0 & 0 & 0 & 0 & 0 & 0 & 0 & 0 \\ 0 & 0 & 0 & 0 & 1 & 1 & 1 & 1 & 0 & 0 & 0 & 0 \\ 0 & 0 & 0 & 0 & 0 & 0 & 0 & 0 & 1 & 1 & 1 & 1 \\ 1 & 0 & 0 & 0 & 1 & 0 & 0 & 0 & 1 & 0 & 0 & 0 \\ 0 & 1 & 0 & 0 & 0 & 1 & 0 & 0 & 0 & 1 & 0 & 0 \\ 0 & 0 & 1 & 0 & 0 & 0 & 1 & 0 & 0 & 0 & 1 & 0 \\ 0 & 0 & 0 & 1 & 0 & 0 & 0 & 1 & 0 & 0 & 0 & 1 \end{bmatrix}$$

We can exhibit this structure as

$$\begin{bmatrix} \textcircled{1} & 0 & 0 \\ 0 & \textcircled{1} & 0 \\ 0 & 0 & \textcircled{1} \\ I_{4\times4} & I_{4\times4} & I_{4\times4} \end{bmatrix}$$

Hence, for a general $m \times n$ TP, 1 is a n-vector with element 1 each, 0 is a n-vector with element 0 each. $I_{m\times n}$ is a $m \times n$ unit matrix.

(5) For any given $m \times n$ TP, A is an $(m + n) \times mn$ matrix and its rank is $(m + n) - 1$.

In the given TP, the rank of the matrix A is $(3 + 4) - 1 = 6$.

Solved Practical Problems

Q1. Write the mathematical model (LPP Model) of the following TP:

$m = 3 \quad n = 4$

$a_1 = 70 \quad a_2 = 50 \quad a_3 = 90$

$b_1 = 50 \quad b_2 = 40 \quad b_3 = 50 \quad b_4 = 70$

$C_{11} = 5 \quad C_{12} = 7 \quad C_{13} = 6 \quad C_{14} = 4$

$C_{21} = 2 \quad C_{22} = 8 \quad C_{23} = 3 \quad C_{24} = 1$

$C_{31} = 1 \quad C_{32} = 7 \quad C_{33} = 4 \quad C_{34} = 5$

Ans. Mathematical model of the given TP is as follows:

Minimise

$$Z = 5x_{11} + 7x_{12} + 6x_{13} + 4x_{14} + 2x_{21} + 8x_{22} + 3x_{23} + x_{24} + x_{31} + 7x_{32} + 4x_{33} + 5x_{34}$$

Subject to the constraints

$x_{11} + x_{12} + x_{13} + x_{14} = 70, \qquad x_{11} + x_{21} + x_{31} = 50$

$x_{21} + x_{22} + x_{23} + x_{24} = 50, \qquad x_{12} + x_{22} + x_{32} = 40$

$x_{31} + x_{32} + x_{33} + x_{34} = 90, \qquad x_{13} + x_{23} + x_{33} = 50$

$x_{14} + x_{24} + x_{34} = 70$

$x_{ij} \geq 0, \quad i = 1, 2, 3$ and $j = 1, 2, 3, 4.$

The constraints can also be written as

$$\sum_{j=1}^{4} x_{1j} = 70, \qquad \sum_{i=1}^{3} x_{i1} = 50$$

$$\sum_{j=1}^{4} x_{2j} = 50, \qquad \sum_{i=1}^{3} x_{i2} = 40$$

$$\sum_{j=1}^{4} x_{3j} = 90, \qquad \sum_{i=1}^{3} x_{i3} = 50$$

$$\sum_{i=1}^{3} x_{i4} = 70$$

$x_{ij} \geq 0, \quad i = 1, 2, 3$ and $j = 1, 2, 3, 4.$

Q2. Represent the following data of a TP in tabular form:

$m = 3 \quad n = 4$

$a_1 = 15 \quad a_2 = 20 \quad a_3 = 30$

$b_1 = 10 \quad b_2 = 15 \quad b_3 = 22 \quad b_4 = 18$

$C_{11} = 5 \quad C_{12} = 7 \quad C_{13} = 2 \quad C_{14} = 1$

$C_{21} = 2 \quad C_{22} = 4 \quad C_{23} = 3 \quad C_{24} = 6$

$C_{31} = 1 \quad C_{32} = 3 \quad C_{33} = 7 \quad C_{34} = 4$

Ans. Following is the required tabular form of the given TP:

	D_1	D_2	D_3	D_4	$a_i\downarrow$
S_1	5	7	2	1	15
S_2	2	4	3	6	20
S_3	1	3	7	4	30
$b_j\rightarrow$	10	15	22	18	

Q3. Give the tabular form of the following TP:

$m = 4 \quad n = 3$

$a_1 = 45 \quad a_2 = 30 \quad a_3 = 25 \quad a_4 = 50$

$b_1 = 40 \quad b_2 = 20 \quad b_3 = 90$

$C_{11} = 4 \quad C_{12} = 3 \quad C_{13} = 2$

$C_{21} = 3 \quad C_{22} = 7 \quad C_{23} = 5$

$C_{31} = 7 \quad C_{32} = 2 \quad C_{33} = 9$

$C_{41} = 2 \quad C_{42} = 6 \quad C_{43} = 7$

Ans.

	D_1	D_2	D_3	$a_i\downarrow$
S_1	4	3	2	45
S_2	3	7	5	30
S_3	7	2	9	25
S_4	2	6	7	50
$b_j\rightarrow$	40	20	90	

Q4. Consider the following data of a TP,

$m = 4 \quad n = 3$

$a_1 = 40 \quad a_2 = 35 \quad a_3 = 50 \quad a_4 = 25$

$b_1 = 70 \quad b_2 = 30 \quad b_3 = 80$

$C_{11} = 5 \quad C_{12} = 3 \quad C_{13} = 6$

$C_{21} = 8 \quad C_{22} = 9 \quad C_{23} = 7$

$C_{31} = 2 \quad C_{32} = 6 \quad C_{33} = 3$

$C_{41} = 7 \quad C_{42} = 6 \quad C_{43} = 4$

(i) **Write the matrix of coefficients A**

(ii) **Write the activity vector of the variables** x_{13}, x_{33}, x_{21} **and** x_{23}.

(iii) **Write the rank of the matrix A**

(iv) Write the non-singular matrix D of A of order 6 × 6.

Ans. (i) $$A = \begin{bmatrix} 1 & 1 & 1 & 0 & 0 & 0 & 0 & 0 & 0 & 0 & 0 & 0 \\ 0 & 0 & 0 & 1 & 1 & 1 & 0 & 0 & 0 & 0 & 0 & 0 \\ 0 & 0 & 0 & 0 & 0 & 0 & 1 & 1 & 1 & 0 & 0 & 0 \\ 0 & 0 & 0 & 0 & 0 & 0 & 0 & 0 & 0 & 1 & 1 & 1 \\ 1 & 0 & 0 & 1 & 0 & 0 & 1 & 0 & 0 & 1 & 0 & 0 \\ 0 & 1 & 0 & 0 & 1 & 0 & 0 & 1 & 0 & 0 & 1 & 0 \\ 0 & 0 & 1 & 0 & 0 & 1 & 0 & 0 & 1 & 0 & 0 & 1 \end{bmatrix}$$

(ii) $$\begin{bmatrix} 1 \\ 0 \\ 0 \\ 0 \\ \cdots \\ 0 \\ 0 \\ 1 \end{bmatrix}, \begin{bmatrix} 0 \\ 0 \\ 1 \\ 0 \\ \cdots \\ 0 \\ 0 \\ 1 \end{bmatrix}, \begin{bmatrix} 0 \\ 1 \\ 0 \\ 0 \\ \cdots \\ 1 \\ 0 \\ 0 \end{bmatrix} \text{ and } \begin{bmatrix} 0 \\ 1 \\ 0 \\ 0 \\ \cdots \\ 0 \\ 0 \\ 1 \end{bmatrix}$$

(iii) Rank of the matrix $A = (4 + 3) - 1$
$= 6$

(iv) Non-singular matrix

$$D = \begin{bmatrix} 1 & 0 & 0 & 0 & 1 & 1 \\ 0 & 1 & 0 & 0 & 0 & 0 \\ 0 & 0 & 1 & 0 & 0 & 0 \\ 0 & 0 & 0 & 1 & 0 & 0 \\ 0 & 0 & 0 & 0 & 1 & 0 \\ 0 & 0 & 0 & 0 & 0 & 1 \end{bmatrix} = \begin{bmatrix} I_{4\times4} & B \\ O & I_{2\times2} \end{bmatrix}$$

where, $I_{4\times4}$ is a unit matrix of order 4, $I_{2\times2}$ is a unit matrix of order 2, O is a zero matrix of order 2 × 4, and

$$B = \begin{bmatrix} 1 & 1 \\ 0 & 0 \\ 0 & 0 \\ 0 & 0 \end{bmatrix}$$

Here $|D| = 1 \neq 0$

Q5. Represent the following TP in tabular form:

Max $Z = (4x_{11} + 3x_{12} + 2x_{13}) + (3x_{21} + 7x_{22} + 5x_{23})(7x_{31} + 2x_{32} + 9x_{33})$

Subject to $x_{11} + x_{12} + x_{13} = 45$

$x_{21} + x_{22} + x_{23} = 20$

$x_{31} + x_{32} + x_{33} = 25$

$x_{11} + x_{21} + x_{31} = 40$

$x_{12} + x_{22} + x_{32} = 25$

$x_{13} + x_{23} + x_{33} = 35$

$x_{ij} \geq 0, \quad i = 1, 2, 3 ; j = 1, 2, 3.$

Ans. From the given TP,

We have

$m = 3 \quad n = 3$

$a_1 = 45 \quad a_2 = 30 \quad a_3 = 25$

$b_1 = 40 \quad b_2 = 25 \quad b_3 = 35$

$C_{11} = 4 \quad C_{12} = 3 \quad C_{13} = 2$

$C_{21} = 3 \quad C_{22} = 7 \quad C_{23} = 5$

$C_{31} = 7 \quad C_{32} = 2 \quad C_{33} = 9$

Now, the table is

	D_1	D_2	D_3	$a_i\downarrow$
S_1	4	3	2	45
S_2	3	7	5	30
S_3	7	2	9	25
$b_j\rightarrow$	40	25	35	

⌑ ⌑

10 Feasible Solutions of Transportation Problems

An Overview

Feasible solution to a transportation problem can be found by some methods such as North-West corner method, Matrix-Minima method etc.

The North-West corner method is a method for computing a basic feasible solution of a transportation problem, where the basic variables are selected from the North-West corner (i.e., top left corner). Matrix minima (Least cost) method is a method for computing a basic feasible solution of a transportation problem, where the basic variables are chosen according to the unit cost of transportation. This method is very useful because it reduces the computation and the time required to determine the optimal solution.

10.1 AN INITIAL BASIC FEASIBLE SOLUTION OF TRANSPORTATION PROBLEM

An initial basic feasible solution of a TP corresponds to a solution with all integer values that satisfies all the constraints. Here, we are giving two methods to find an initial basic feasible solution to a transportation problem.

(1) North-West Corner Method

(2) Matrix-Minima Method

10.2 NORTH-WEST CORNER METHOD

The steps of this method are as follows:

Step 1: Select the upper left hand corner cell of the given transportation table and allocate as much as possible in such a way that either the capacity of the first row is exhausted or the first column of demand is satisfied, i.e. $x_{11} = \min(a_1, b_1)$.

Step 2: (i) If $b_1 > a_1$, move vertically down to second row and make the second allocation $x_{21} = \min(a_2, b_2 - x_{11})$.

(ii) If $b_1 < a_1$, move horizontally right to second column and make the second allocation $x_{12} = \min(a_1 - x_{11}, b_2)$.

(iii) If $b_1 = a_1$, one can choose any one of the following allocations:

$$x_{12} = \min(a_1 - a_1, b_1) = 0$$

or $$x_{21} = \min(a_2, b_1 - b_1) = 0$$

Step 3: Repeat step 1 and step 2 while moving down towards the lower right corner of the table.

10.3 MATRIX-MINIMA METHOD (LEAST COST METHOD)

The steps of this method are as follows:

Step 1: Select the smallest cost value in the given cost matrix of transportation problem, say C_{ij}. Then, allocation will be $\min(a_i, b_j)$.

Step 2: (i) If allocation is equal to supply (a_i), cross the ith row and decrease b_j (demand) by a_i.

(ii) If allocation is equal to demand (b_j), cross the jth column and decrease a_i by b_j.

(iii) If allocation is equal to both demand and supply, cross any one of them (either column or row).

Step 3: Repeat the above steps for finally reduced transportation table.

10.4 CLOSED CHAIN RULE

A rule for checking whether a given feasible solution is basic, i.e., cells are in linearly independent positions is called closed chain rule. In other words, a given set of columns from the coefficient matrix of a $m \times n$ transportation problem forms a linearly independent set if and only if the set of corresponding cells in the $m \times n$ transportation array does not contain a closed chain.

10.5 DEGENERATE BASIC FEASIBLE SOLUTION

A basic feasible solution in which the total number of non-negative allocations is less than $m + n - 1$ is called degenerate basic feasible solution.

In other words, a basic feasible solution is said to be degenerate if certain basic variables (one or more) are at zero level, i.e., number of positive variables is less than $m + n - 1$.

Rule to identify the additional basic variable at zero level: Select a variable as a candidate for basic variable at zero level. The cell of this candidate is called candidate cell. Start joining it by horizontal lines and vertical lines alternately to basic variable cells with circled allocation.

In this process, if we can come back to the candidate cell, this is disqualified. Because they form a linearly dependent set. Otherwise, we can put a zero in the cell and circle it as ⓪.

Solved Practical Problems

Q1. Find the initial solution of the following transportation problem using north-west corner method.

	D	E	F	G	Supply
A	11	13	17	14	250
B	16	18	14	10	300
C	21	24	13	10	400
Demand	200	225	275	250	

Ans. Solving according to the algorithm of north-west corner method:

Step 1: Start with the upper left corner of cost table and allocate as much as possible according to demand. The upper left is C_{11}, where the demand is 200 and supply is 250, hence demand could meet with supply. So allocate 200 in C_{11}.

	D	E	F	G	Supply
A	11 (200)	13 (50)	17	14	250
B	16	18 (175)	14 (125)	10	300
C	21	24	13 (150)	10 (250)	400
Demand	200	225	275	250	

Step 2: Now, we will move horizontally to the next cell C_{12}. Here demand is 225 and supply is 250 – 200 = 50, so we will allocate only 50 to cell C_{12}.

Step 3: Now, we will move vertically to the next cell C_{22}. Here demand is 225 – 50 = 175 and supply is 300. So, we will allocate 175 to cell C_{22}.

Step 4: Now, we will move horizontally to the next cell C_{23}. Here demand is 275 and supply is 300 – 175 = 125, so we will allocate 125 to cell C_{23}.

Step 5: Now, we will move vertically down to the next cell C_{33}. Here demand is 275 – 125 = 150 and supply is 400, so allocate 150 to cell C_{33}.

Step 6: Now, we will move horizontally to the next cell C_{34}. Here demand is 250 and supply is 400 – 150 = 250, so we will allocate 250 in this cell.

Hence, the initial basic feasible solution has been obtained as follows:

$x_{11} = 200, x_{12} = 50, x_{22} = 175, x_{23} = 125, x_{33} = 150, x_{34} = 250$

The number of basic variables is 6 over here because in the given problem there are 3 rows and 4 columns and the number of basic variables is (3 + 4 –1) = 6.

Total cost = (200 × 11) + (50 × 13) + (175 × 18) + (125 × 14) + (150 × 13) + (250 × 10) = ₹12,200

Q2. Using matrix-minima method, find the initial basic feasible solution to the following TP:

	D_1	D_2	D_3	
S_1	1	7	6	40
S_2	4	2	3	30
S_3	3	5	4	20
S_4	2	1	8	30
	45	40	35	

Ans. ***Step 1:*** Minimum cost of the given table is 1 in C_{11} and C_{42}. We can take any one of them. We take C_{11} here. Here demand is 45 and supply is 40. We allocate minimum of demand and supply. We allocate 40 here. We cross the remaining entries of first row because supply has been completed, which is 40.

Step 2: Now, 1 in C_{42} is minimum among the uncrossed numbers in the table. The allocation in C_{42} is 30. We cross the remaining entries of fourth row because supply has been completed.

We repeat these steps until we get the initial basic feasible solution as follows:

$$x_{11} = 40,\ x_{22} = 10,\ x_{23} = 20,\ x_{31} = 5,\ x_{33} = 15,\ x_{42} = 30$$

	D_1	D_2	D_3	
S_1	1 (40)	7 ×	6 ×	40
S_2	4 ×	2 (10)	3 (20)	30
S_3	3 (5)	5 ×	4 (15)	20
S_4	2 ×	1 (30)	8 ×	30
	45	40	35	

Q3. Check whether the given feasible solution of the transportation problem is basic, i.e., cells are in linearly independent positions.

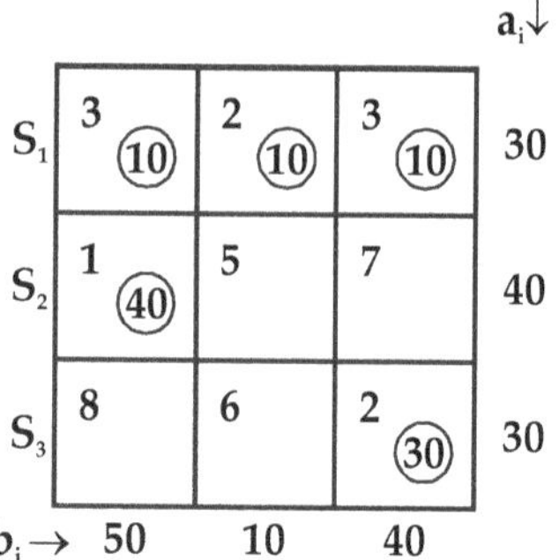

Ans. Here, basic cells are C_{11} or (1, 1), C_{12} or (1, 2), C_{13} or (1, 3), C_{21} or (2, 1) and C_{33} or (3, 3).

Taking (1, 1), (1, 2) and (2, 1), we have the figure below:

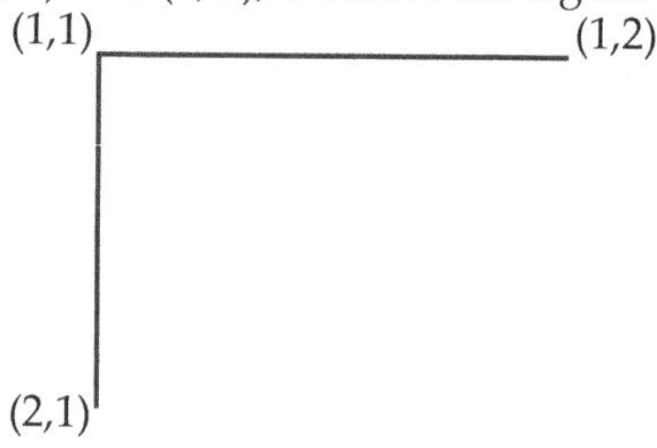

Hence, (1, 1), (1, 2) and (2, 1) do not form a closed chain.

Now taking the cells (1, 2), (1, 3) and (3, 3),

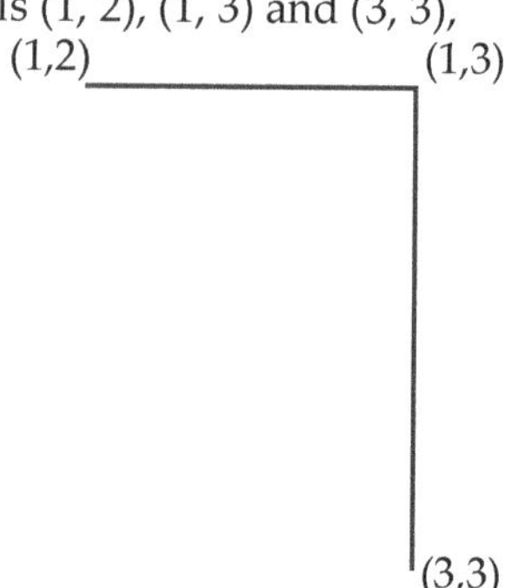

(1, 2), (1, 3) and (3, 3) do not form a closed chain.

Similarly, not all basic cells form a closed chain. Hence, the given feasible solution $x_{11} = 10, x_{12} = 10, x_{13} = 10, x_{21} = 40$ and $x_{33} = 30$ is basic, i.e., cells are in linearly independent positions.

Q4. In the following transportation problem check if there is a closed chain in the set of starred cells. Starred cells are the feasible solution of the transportation problem.

	D_1	D_2	D_3	D_4	D_5	Supply
S_1	C_{11} *	C_{12}	C_{13} *	C_{14}	C_{15}	a_1
S_2	C_{21} *	C_{22}	C_{23}	C_{24} *	C_{25} *	a_2
S_3	C_{31}	C_{32}	C_{33} *	C_{34} *	C_{35}	a_3
Demand	b_1	b_2	b_3	b_4	b_5	

Ans. Taking all the starred cells,

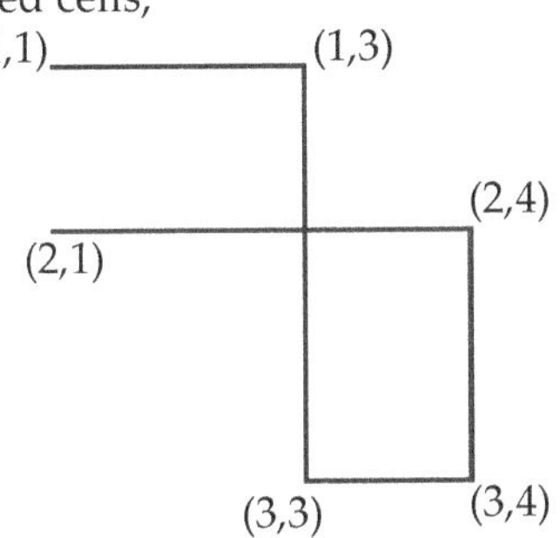

Closed chain is formed. Hence, given feasible is not basic, i.e., cell are in linearly dependent position.

Q5. In the following TP, circled numbers are the basic feasible solutions obtained by matrix-minima method. Indicate the basic variables at zero level.

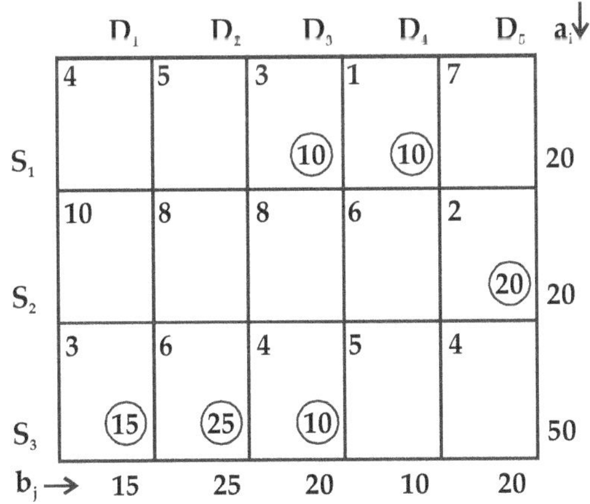

	D_1	D_2	D_3	D_4	D_5	$a_i \downarrow$
S_1	4	5	3 (10)	1 (10)	7	20
S_2	10	8	8	6	2 (20)	20
S_3	3 (15)	6 (25)	4 (10)	5	4	50
$b_j \rightarrow$	15	25	20	10	20	

Ans. Number of basic variables needed is (5 + 3) – 1 = 7. We find only 6 of these, in the process. Thus, an addition basic variable at zero level is to be identified.

We see that (1, 1) does not qualify as we have the following closed chain.

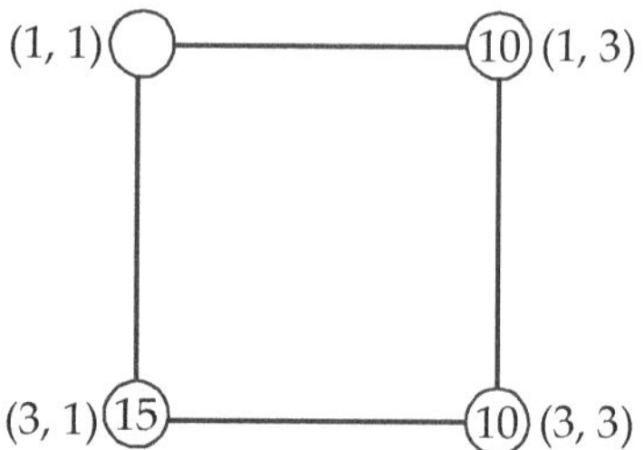

Thus, (1, 1) forms a closed chain with basic cells or variables at (1, 3), (3, 3) and (3, 1).

(1, 2) also does not qualify as it forms a closed chain as shown below.

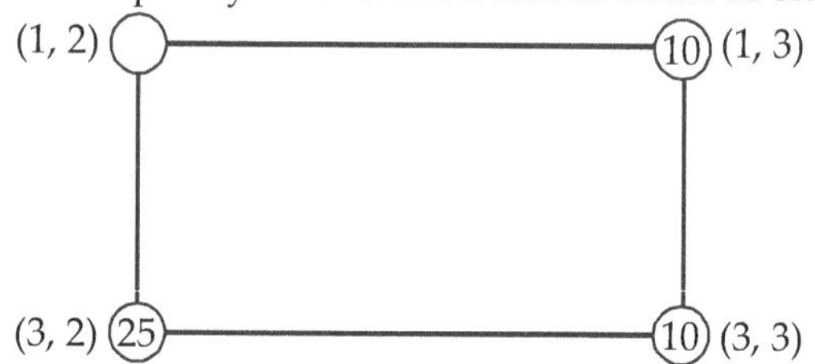

We note that (1, 5) qualifies as it does not form a closed chain.

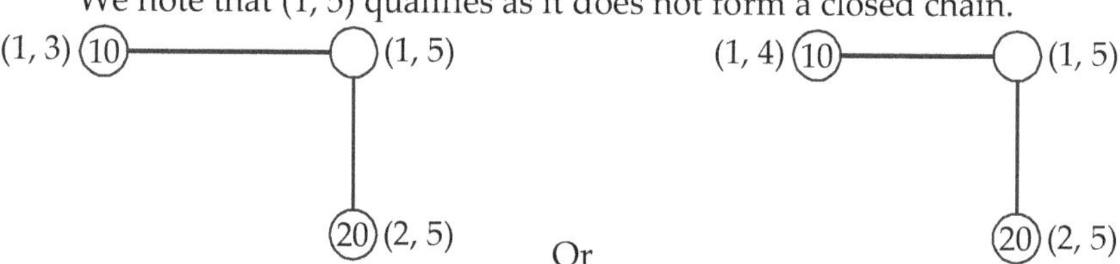

We may similarly discover that (2, 1), (2, 2), (2, 3), (2, 4) and (3, 5) qualify and (3, 4) does not. Thus, we can put a zero or (0) in any of these cells (1, 5), (2, 1), (2, 2), (2, 3), (2, 4), (3, 5) but not in (1, 1) (1, 2) and (3, 4).

Hence, basic variables at zero level are $x_{15} = 0, x_{21} = 0, x_{22} = 0, x_{23} = 0, x_{24} = 0, x_{35} = 0$.

Q6. A dairy firm has three plants located in a state. The daily milk production at each plant is as follows:

Plant 1: 6 thousand litres

Plant 2: 1 thousand litres

Plant 3: 10 thousand litres

Each day, the firm must fulfil the needs of its four distribution centres. Minimum requirement at each centre is as follows:

Distribution centre 1: 7 thousand litres

Distribution centre 2: 5 thousand litres

Distribution centre 3: 3 thousand litres

Distribution centre 4: 2 thousand litres

Cost in hundreds of rupees of shipping one thousand litres from each plant to each distribution centre is given in the following table:

Distribution Centre

		D_1	D_2	D_3	D_4
	P_1	2	3	11	7
Plant	P_2	1	0	6	1
	P_3	5	8	15	9

Find initial basic feasible solution for the given problem by using North-West corner method, and Matrix-Minima method. Which of the two solutions is better? Justify your answer.

[June-2014, Q.No.-2(a)]

Ans. We have the following transportation problem:

	D_1	D_2	D_3	D_4	
P_1	200	300	1100	700	6000
P_2	100	0	600	100	1000
P_3	500	800	1500	900	10000
	7000	5000	3000	2000	

Using North-west corner method, we have the following table:

	D_1	D_2	D_3	D_4	
P_1	200 (6000)	300	1100	700	6000
P_2	100 (1000)	0	600	100	1000
P_3	500 (0)	800 (5000)	1500 (3000)	900 (2000)	10000
	7000	5000	3000	2000	

Initial basic feasible solution is $x_{11} = 6000,\ x_{21} = 1000,\ x_{31} = 0,\ x_{32} = 5000$

$x_{33} = 3000,\ x_{34} = 2000$

Now, we use the matrix-minima method, and we have the following table:

	D_1	D_2	D_3	D_4	
P_1	200 (6000)	300	1100	700	6000
P_2	100	0 (1000)	600	100	1000
P_3	500 (1000)	800 (4000)	1500 (3000)	900 (2000)	10000
	7000	5000	3000	2000	

Initial basic feasible solution is

$x_{11} = 6000,\ x_{22} = 1000,\ x_{31} = 1000$

$x_{32} = 4000,\ x_{33} = 3000,\ x_{34} = 2000$

Matrix-minima method is better than north-west corner method because in matrix-minima method we transport starting with cheapest route and using the routes in ascending order of costs of transportation. The main aim of GPH book is to provide knowledge as well as good marks in exam.

⌑ ⌑

11 Computational Method for Transportation Problems

An Overview

An optimal solution for the transportation problem provides the allocations which suit the best for the problem cannot be further reduced. To do this, we have to calculate every unoccupied cell in terms of an opportunity of reducing the total cost. Then the cell which has the largest negative value of opportunity cost is selected and is exchanged by an already occupied cell in a unique loop (closed) whose allocation will become zero at the first move as more units there is no negative opportunity cost which indicated the sign of optimal solution. This whole process is done by a method known as MODI (Modified Distribution) method. It is also known as U-V method. This is the computational method for the transportation problem.

11.1 METHOD TO SOLVE A BALANCED TRANSPORTATION PROBLEM

Modified Distribution (MODI) Method Or u-v Method

The MODI Method is used for optimality test of an initial basic feasible solution of a transportation problem.

This method follows the following steps:

Step 1: Find the initial basic feasible solution using north-west corner method or matrix-minima method.

Step 2: Find the values of u_i and v_i.

Step 3: Determine the values of Δ_{ij}, i.e., net evaluations. If all $\Delta_{ij} \le 0$, then solution is optimal. If all Δ_{ij} are not equal to or less than zero then go to next step.

Step 4: Determine the cell to enter the basis.

Step 5: Determine the cell to leave the basis. In this step, we take entering cell or indentified cell as +ve (positive) and each occupied cell at the corner of the path alternatively $-ve, +ve, -ve$ and so on. Repeat step $2 \to 5$ each time till we get all $\Delta_{ij} \le 0$, i.e., optimal solution.

11.2 METHOD TO SOLVE AN UNBALANCED TRANSPORTATION PROBLEM

The transportation problems in which, $\sum_{i=1}^{m} a_i \ne \sum_{j=1}^{n} b_j$ are called unbalanced transportation problems. The two possibilities of an unbalanced transportation problem are that either $\sum_{i=1}^{m} a_i < \sum_{j=1}^{n} b_j$ or $\sum_{i=1}^{m} a_i > \sum_{j=1}^{n} b_j$.

Case I: When $\sum_{i=1}^{m} a_i < \sum_{j=1}^{n} b_j$

Here the total availability at all the sources is less than the total demand of all the destinations. In such cases, we do the following:

(i) Create an artificial sources S_{m+1} with availability

$a_{m+1} = \sum_{j=1}^{n} b_j - \sum_{i=1}^{m} a_i$.

This gives us a new problem with (m + 1) sources and n destinations, and of course is balanced.

(ii) Set C_{ij}'s in cells corresponding to this artificial source S_{m+1}, equal to zero, i.e. $C_{m+1,\, j} = 0$ for j = 1, 2, ..., n.

(iii) Solve the balanced transportation problem thus obtained by 'u – v method'. Optimal solution of this balanced transportation problem with variables $x_{m+1, j}$ (j = 1, 2, ... n) deleted, give an optimal solution for the original unbalanced problem.

***Case II*:** When $\sum_{i=1}^{m} a_i > \sum_{j=1}^{n} b_j$

Here the total availability at all the sources is more than the total demand of all the destinations. In such cases we do the following:

(i) Create an artificial destination D_{n+1} with demand $b_{n+1} = \sum_{i=1}^{m} a_i - \sum_{j=1}^{n} b_j$. This gives us a new problem with m sources and (n + 1) destinations, and of course is balanced.

(ii) Set C_{ij}'s for all cells corresponding to the artificial destination D_{n+1}, equal to zero, i.e. $C_{i,\ n+1} = 0$ for i = 1, 2, ..., m.

(iii) Solve the above balanced transportation problem by 'u–v method'. Optimal solution of this problem, with variables $x_{i,\ n+1}$ (i = 1, 2, ..., m) corresponding to the artificial destination D_{n+1} deleted give an optimal solution for the given unbalanced transportation problem.

Solved Practical Problems

Q1. Solve the following transportation problem by u–v method and obtain the optimal solution and the optimal cost.

	D_1	D_2	D_3	D_4	Supply
S_1	9	16	15	9	15
S_2	2	1	3	5	25
S_3	6	4	7	3	20
Demand	10	15	25	10	

Ans. *Step 1:* We have the given transportation problem with transportation array also showing the North-West corner solution for the problem.

Table 1

	D_1	D_2	D_3	D_4	Supply
S_1	9 (10)	16 (5)	15	9	15
S_2	2	1 (10)	3 (15)	5	25
S_3	6	4	7 (10)	3 (10)	20
Demand	10	15	25	10	

Step 2: Finding the values of $\mathbf{u}_i$ and $\mathbf{v}_j$:

(a) As maximum number of basic cells exist in the 1st, 2nd and 3rd rows, we can start by putting any one of u_1, u_2 and u_3 equal to zero. We put $u_3 = 0$.

(b) For basic cells, we know that $\Delta_{ij} = u_i + v_j - C_{ij}$

Putting Δ_{ij} equal to zero, then we have $u_i + v_j = C_{ij}$

Hence, we have

$u_1 + v_1 = 9,$ $\quad u_2 + v_3 = 3$

$u_1 + v_2 = 16,$ $\quad u_3 + v_3 = 7$

$u_2 + v_2 = 1,$ $\quad u_3 + v_4 = 3$

Now, taking $u_3 = 0$, we have

$u_3 + v_3 = 7$

$\Rightarrow \quad 0 + v_3 = 7$

$\Rightarrow \quad v_3 = 7$

and $u_3 + v_4 = 3$

$\Rightarrow \quad 0 + v_4 = 3$

$\Rightarrow \quad v_4 = 3$

Similarly, we can find

$u_1 = 11, \quad u_2 = -4, \quad v_1 = -2, v_2 = 5$

Step 3: Determining the net evaluations

Table 2

	D₁	**D₂**	**D₃**	**D₄**	**Supply**	$u_i \downarrow$
S_1	9 (10)	16 (5)	15 / $\Delta_{13}=3$	9 / 5	**15**	**11**
S_2	2 / –8	1 (10)	3 (15)	5 / –6	**25**	**–4**
S_3	6 / –8	4 / 1	7 (10)	3 (10)	**20**	**0**
Demand	**10**	**15**	**25**	**10**		
$v_j \rightarrow$	**–2**	**5**	**7**	**3**		

For all non-basic cells (i, j), i.e., cells where allocations has not been made, we calculate

$\Delta_{ij} = u_i + v_j - C_{ij}$

The cell (1, 3) yields

$\Delta_{13} = u_1 + v_3 - C_{13} = 11 + 7 - 15 = 3$

Similarly,

$\Delta_{14} = u_1 + v_4 - C_{14} = 11 + 3 - 9 = 5$

Similarly, we have

$\Delta_{21} = -8, \ \Delta_{24} = -6, \ \Delta_{31} = -8$ and $\Delta_{32} = 1$

In this way Δ_{ij} for all non-basic cells are evaluated and recorded in right-bottom of each cell as shown in Table-2.

Step 4: Determining the cell to enter the basis:

Calculate Max. $\left\{\Delta_{ij} \middle| \Delta_{ij} > 0\right\}$, i.e.,

$\Delta_{14} = 5$ is the maximum. Therefore, cell (1, 4) enters the basis.

Step 5: Determination of cell to leave the basis:

For this, we construct a chain or path. We start from the cell of the entering variable, i.e., x_{14}. We find a path with horizontal and vertical edges and having corners at only those cells where allocations have been made.

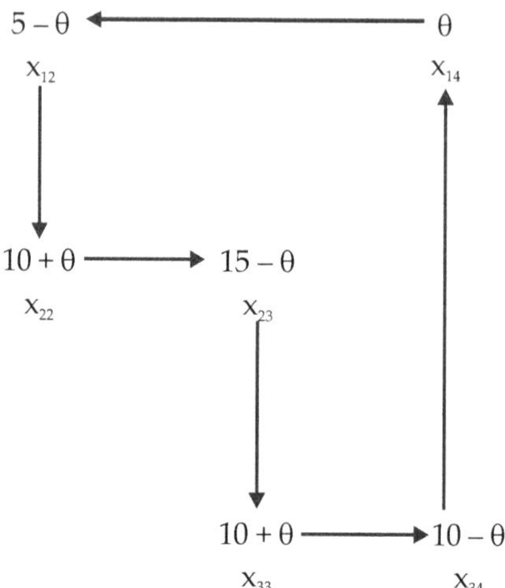

Hence, the direction of the path is

$(u_1, v_4) \to (u_1, v_2) \to (u_2, v_2) \to (u_2, v_3) \to (u_3, v_3) \to (u_3, v_4) \to (u_1, v_4).$

Now, the value of θ,

if $5-\theta=0 \Rightarrow \theta=5$

if $10+\theta=0 \Rightarrow \theta=-10$

if $15-\theta=0 \Rightarrow \theta=15$

if $7+\theta=0 \Rightarrow \theta=-7$

if $10-\theta=0 \Rightarrow \theta=10$

The value of allocation cannot be negative.

Now, taking $\theta = \min\{5, 15, 10\} = 5$

Now, if $\theta = 5$, then entry at x_{12} will be 0. Hence, x_{12} is Leaving Variable. Now, putting the value of θ, we get new improved BFS (Basic Feasible Solution) as

$x_{11}=10,\ x_{14}=5,\ x_{22}=10+5=15$

$x_{23}=15-5=10,\ x_{33}=10+5=15$

$x_{34}=10-5=5$

"We repeat steps $2 \rightarrow 5$ each time with improved BFS till we get optimal solution, i.e., till we get all entries ≤ 0, in the right bottom of the cells."

Now, we have

Table 3

	D_1	D_2	D_3	D_4	Supply	$u_i \downarrow$
S_1	9 (10)	16 / –5	15 / –2	9 (5)	15	6
S_2	2 / –3	1 (15)	3 (10)	5 / –6	25	–4
S_3	6 / –3	4 / 1	7 (15)	3 (5)	20	0
Demand	10	15	25	10		
$v_j \rightarrow$	3	5	7	3		

We have,

$u_1 + v_1 = 9$

$u_1 + v_4 = 9$

$u_2 + v_2 = 1$

$u_2 + v_3 = 3$

$u_3 + v_3 = 7$

$u_3 + v_4 = 3$

Taking $u_3 = 0$, we have

$u_1 = 6,\ u_2 = -4,\ v_1 = 3,\ v_2 = 5,\ v_3 = 7,\ v_4 = 3$

In, table 3, x_{32} is entering variable and x_{33} is leaving variable. Now we can find the values of $u_1, u_2, u_3, v_1, v_2, v_3$ and v_4 using the procedure in Step 2.

Table 4

	D_1	D_2	D_3	D_4	Supply	$u_i \downarrow$
S_1	9 (10)	16 / –6	15 / –3	9 (5)	15	6
S_2	2 / –2	1 (0)	3 (25)	5 / –5	25	–3
S_3	6 / –3	4 (15)	7 / –1	3 (5)	20	0
Demand	10	15	25	10		
$v_j \rightarrow$	3	4	6	3		

Here, we can see that all entries in the right bottom are ≤ 0.

Hence, optimal solution is

$x_{11} = 10,\ x_{14} = 5,\ x_{22} = 0,\ x_{23} = 25,\ x_{32} = 15,\ x_{34} = 5$

Now, optimal cost

$9 \times 10 + 9 \times 5 + 1 \times 0 + 3 \times 25 + 4 \times 15 + 3 \times 5 = 285$

Q2. Solve the transportation problem

	D_1	D_2	D_3	D_4	$a_i \downarrow$
S_1	25	17	25	14	30
S_2	15	10	18	24	50
S_3	16	20	8	13	60
$b_j \rightarrow$	30	30	50	50	

Ans. The given transportation problem is unbalanced as $\sum_{i=1}^{3} a_i (= 140) < \sum_{j=1}^{4} b_j (= 160)$. As total demand is more than total availability, we introduce an artificial source S_4 with availability $a_4 = \sum_{j=1}^{4} b_j - \sum_{i=1}^{3} a_i = 20$ costs C_{ij}'s for all cells corresponding to artificial source S_4 are taken as zeros. By this, we have the following balanced transportation problem.

Table 1

	D_1	D_2	D_3	D_4	$a_i \downarrow$
S_1	25	17	25	14	30
S_2	15	10	18	24	50
S_3	16	20	8	13	60
S_4	0	0	0	0	20
$b_j \rightarrow$	30	30	50	50	

Solving this balanced transportation problem by the 'u-v method', the optimal solution is given as:

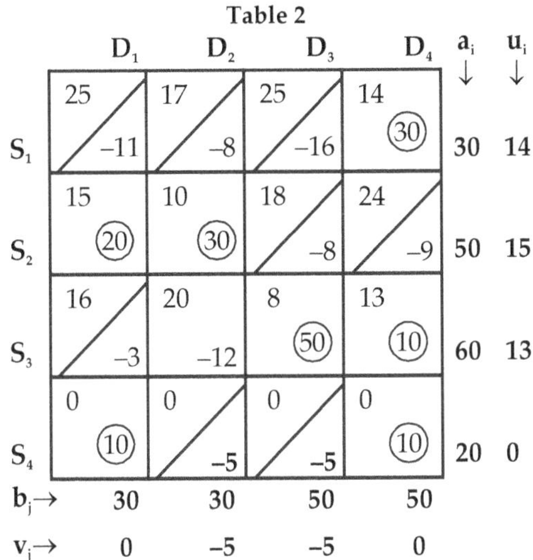

From this, the optimal solution of the original unbalanced transportation problem is given by:

$x_{14} = 30,\ x_{21} = 20,\ x_{22} = 30,\ x_{33} = 50,\ x_{34} = 10$

and the minimum cost of transportation is given by

$Z = (14 \times 30) + (15 \times 20) + (10 \times 30) + (8 \times 50) + (13 \times 10) = 1550$

Q3. Solve the following transportation problem to maximize profit:

Destination

		I	II	III	IV	Supply
Source	A	40	25	22	33	100
	B	44	35	30	30	30
	C	38	38	28	30	70
Demand		40	20	60	30	

[June-2016, Q.No.-3(b)]

Ans. Since the given problem is a maximisation problem, we have to convert it into a minimisation problem by subtracting each element of profit matrix from the biggest element (44), producing the matrix as follows:

Table 1

Destinations

Source	I	II	III	IV	Supply
A	4	19	22	11	100
B	0	9	14	14	30
C	6	6	16	14	70
Demand	40	20	60	30	

This is unbalanced TP. We make it balanced as follows:

Table 2

	I	II	III	IV	V	$a_i \downarrow$
A	4	19	22	11	0	100
B	0	9	14	14	0	30
C	6	6	16	14	0	70
$b_j \rightarrow$	40	20	60	30	50	

Using matrix-minima method, we have the initial basic feasible solution of the TP.

Table 3

	I	II	III	IV	V	$a_i \downarrow$
A	4 (10)	19 ×	22 (10)	11 (30)	0 (50)	100
B	0 (30)	9 ×	14 ×	14 ×	0 ×	30
C	6 ×	6 (20)	16 (50)	14 ×	0 ×	70
$b_j \rightarrow$	40	20	60	30	50	

From Table 3, we have

$u_1 + v_1 = 4, \quad u_1 + v_3 = 22, \quad u_1 + v_4 = 11, \quad u_1 + v_5 = 0$

$u_2 + v_1 = 0, \quad u_3 + v_2 = 6, \quad u_3 + v_3 = 16$

Putting $u_3 = 0$, we have

$u_1 = 6, \quad u_2 = 2, \quad v_1 = -2, \quad v_2 = 6, \quad v_3 = 16$

$v_4 = 5, \quad v_5 = -6$

Therefore, we have the following table:

Table 4

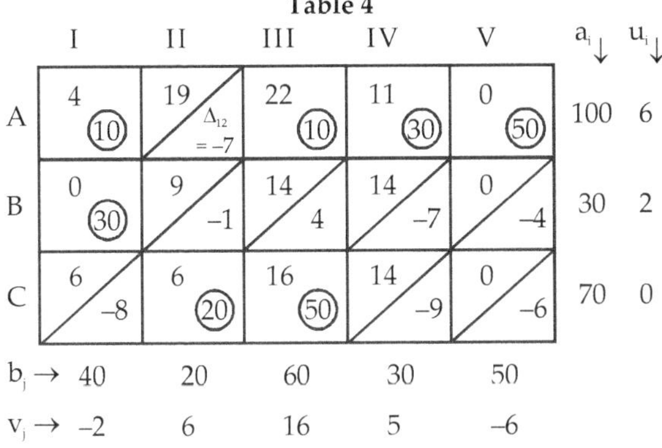

	I	II	III	IV	V	$a_i \downarrow$	$u_i \downarrow$
A	4 (10)	19 $\Delta_{12} = -7$	22 (10)	11 (30)	0 (50)	100	6
B	0 (30)	9 / −1	14 / 4	14 / −7	0 / −4	30	2
C	6 / −8	6 (20)	16 (50)	14 / −9	0 / −6	70	0
$b_j \rightarrow$	40	20	60	30	50		
$v_j \rightarrow$	−2	6	16	5	−6		

In Table 4, all Δ_{ij} are not negative, therefore, this is not optimal solution.

$\Delta_{23} = 4$ is maximum. Therefore, cell (2, 3) enters the basis. We have the following path starting from the cell of entering variable x_{23}:

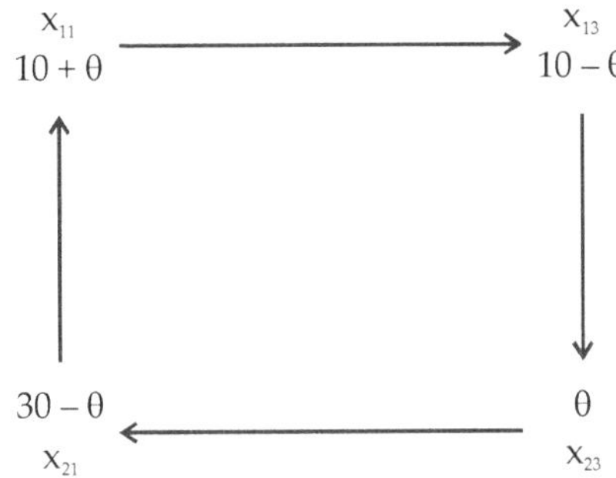

Hence, direction of path is

$(u_2, v_3) \rightarrow (u_2, v_1) \rightarrow (u_1, v_1) \rightarrow (u_1, v_3) \rightarrow (u_2, v_3)$

Now the value of θ are as follows:

if $30 - \theta = 0 \Rightarrow \theta = 30$

if $10 + \theta = 0 \Rightarrow \theta = -10$

if $10 - \theta = 0 \Rightarrow \theta = 10$

The value of allocation cannot be negative.

Now, taking $\theta = \min\{30, 10\} = 10$

If $\theta = 10$, then entry at x_{13} will be zero. Hence, x_{13} is leaving variable.

Now, putting the value of θ, we get improved BFS (Basic feasible solution) as follows:

$x_{11} = 10 + \theta = 10 + 10 = 20$

$x_{14} = 30, \quad x_{15} = 50$

$x_{21} = 30 - 10 = 20, \quad x_{32} = 20, \quad x_{33} = 50$

and $x_{23} = \theta = 10$

Now, we have the following table

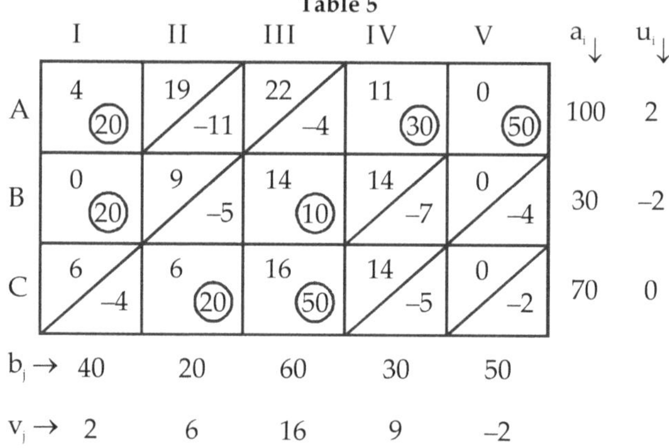

Here, all $\Delta_{ij} \le 0$. Hence, this is the optimal solution set, which is as follows:

$x_{11} = 20,\ x_{14} = 30,\ x_{15} = 50,\ x_{21} = 20,\ x_{23} = 10,\ x_{32} = 20$ and $x_{33} = 50$

Maximum profit $= 20 \times 40 + 30 \times 33 + 20 \times 44 + 10 \times 30 + 20 \times 38 + 50 \times 28$
$= 800 + 990 + 880 + 300 + 760 + 1400 =$ ₹ 5130

Q4. Find the initial basics feasible solution of the following transportation problem using North-West Corner method.

90	**90**	**100**	**110**	**200**
50	**70**	**130**	**85**	**50**
75	**100**	**100**	**30**	

[Dec-2014, Q.No.-3(b)]

Ans. In the given TP,

$$\sum_{i=1}^{2} a_i = 200 + 50 = 250$$

$$\sum_{j=1}^{4} b_j = 75 + 100 + 100 + 30 = 305$$

Therefore, $\sum_{i=1}^{2} a_i < \sum_{j=1}^{4} b_j$

We introduce an artificial source with availability $a_3 = 305 - 250 = 55$. Hence, we have

				$a_i \downarrow$
90	90	100	110	200
50	70	130	85	50
0	0	0	0	55
$b_j \rightarrow$ 75	100	100	30	

Using North-west corner method, we have the following table:

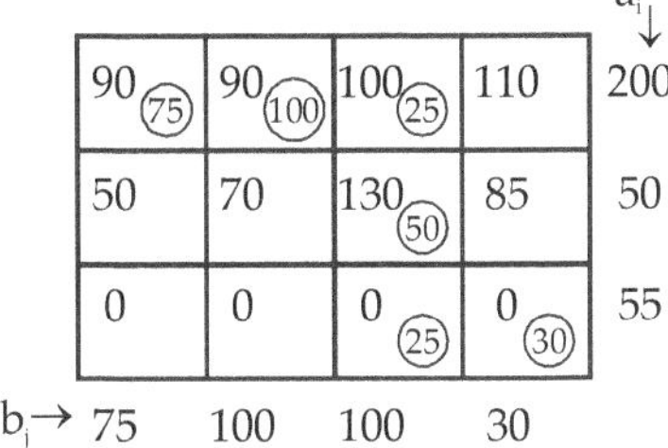

Hence, initial basic feasible solution is as follows:

$x_{11} = 75,\ x_{12} = 100,\ x_{13} = 25$

$x_{23} = 50,\ x_{33} = 25,\ x_{34} = 30$

Q5. Is following statement true or false? Give a short proof or a counter-example in support of your answer.

An unbalanced transportation model requires the addition of both a dummy source and a dummy destination to effect balancing.

[Dec-2015, Q.No.-1(a)]

Ans. False.

For example, we have the following balanced transportation problem:

	D_1	D_2	D_3	$a_i \downarrow$
S_1	4	3	1	4
S_2	2	6	2	6
$b_j \rightarrow$	2	3	5	

If we make an addition in dummy source only, then we have the following table:

	D_1	D_2	D_3	$a_i \downarrow$
S_1	4	3	1	4
S_2	2	6	2	6
S_3	1	4	5	3
$b_j \rightarrow$	2	3	5	

Here, $\sum a_i \neq \sum b_j$, i.e., this TP is unbalanced

Thus, it is not necessary to make addition in both dummy source and dummy destination to effect balancing.

⌑ ⌑

12 Assignment Problems

An Overview

The assignment problem is one of the fundamental combinatorial optimisation problems in the branch of optimisation or operations research in mathematics. It consists of finding a maximum weight matching (or minimum weight perfect matching) in a weighted bipartite graph.

The Hungarian algorithm is one of many algorithms that have been devised that solve the linear assignment problem within time bounded by a polynomial expression of the number of agents. Other algorithms include adaptations of the primal simplex algorithm, and the auction algorithm. The assignment problem is a special case of the transportation problem, which is a special case of the minimum cost flow problem, which in turn is a special case of a linear programme.

12.1 FORMULATION OF AN ASSIGNMENT PROBLEM

Assume a scenario where assignment of n resources is required to n activities, to minimize the overall cost or time or to maximise the total profit, in such a way that each resource can only associated to one activity. The problem in the form of matrix is as follows:

	Activity							Available
	A_1	A_2	A_3	...	...	...	A_n	
Resource R_1	a_{11}	a_{12}	a_{13}	...	...	...	a_{1n}	1
R_2	a_{21}	a_{22}	a_{23}	...	...	...	a_{2n}	1
...	...	...	...	...	...	...	...	...
...	...	...	...	...	...	...	...	...
...	...	...	...	...	...	...	...	...
R_n	a_{n1}	a_{n2}	a_{n3}	...	...	...	a_{nn}	1
Required	1	1	1				1	

Let $x_{ij} = 1$, if resource i is assigned to activity j

0, if other case

Then, the mathematical formulation of the assignment problem is:

Minimise

$$Z = \sum_{i=1}^{n} \sum^{n} C_{ij} x_{ij}$$

subject to constraints

$$\sum_{i=1}^{n} x_{ij} = 1 \text{ and } \sum_{j=1}^{n} x_{ij} = 1, \; x_{ij} = 0 \text{ or } 1$$

for all i = 1, 2, ..., n and j = 1, 2, ..., n, where C_{ij} represents to the cost of assignment of resource i to activity j.

Note: Assigning a non-negative integer value to x_{ij} is equivalent to assigning values 0 or 1 to x_{ij}. For this, one has only to see the constraints of the problem. This also justifies the way x_{ij}, s have been defined.

An assignment problem is known from its cost-matrix $\left[C_{ij}\right]$, which is given is:

$$\begin{bmatrix} C_{11} & C_{12} & \cdots & C_{ij} & \cdots & C_{1n} \\ C_{21} & C_{22} & \cdots & C_{2j} & \cdots & C_{2n} \\ \vdots & & & & & \\ C_{i1} & C_{i2} & \cdots & C_{ij} & \cdots & C_{in} \\ \vdots & & & & & \\ C_{n1} & C_{n2} & \cdots & C_{nj} & \cdots & C_{nn} \end{bmatrix}$$

If each row refers to a job and each column refers to a machine, then C_{ij} is the cost of processing i^{th} job on j^{th} machine. Clearly $\left[C_{ij}\right]$ is a square matrix of order n.

Assignment Problem as a special case of Transportation Problem

Consider an m × n transportation problem:

$$\left.\begin{aligned} &\text{Minimise} \quad Z = \sum_{i=1}^{m} \sum_{j=1}^{n} C_{ij}\, x_{ij} \\ &\text{Subject to} \quad \sum_{i=1}^{n} x_{ij} = b_j \qquad (j = 1, 2, \ldots, n) \\ &\qquad\qquad\quad \sum_{j=1}^{n} x_{ij} = a_i \qquad (i = 1, 2, \ldots, n) \\ &\qquad\qquad\qquad x_{ij} \geq 0, \end{aligned}\right] \text{TP-1}$$

where a_i = availability at i^{th} source

b_j = demand of jth destination

C_{ij} = per unit transportation cost from i^{th} source to j^{th} destination

and x_{ij} = number of units transported from i^{th} source to j^{th} destination.

We state a well known result here that wherever a_i and b_j in TP-1 are integers, then every basic feasible solution to TP-1 has integrated values.

Assignment problem can be viewed as a special case of transportation problem. What we have to do is only to regard 'jobs' as 'sources' and 'machines' as 'destinations'. As each $a_i = 1$ and each $b_j = 1$, therefore $\sum_{i=1}^{m} a_i = m$ and $\sum_{j=1}^{n} b_j = n$. In order to solve a transportation problem we 'balance' it, in case it is not already so. For this, we require m = n, i.e. the number of jobs are taken equal to the number of machines. This is what we do in an assignment problem, i.e. we take the number of jobs equal to the number of machines. Thus, we see that an assignment problem is a special case of transportation problem.

12.2 HUNGARIAN METHOD TO SOLVE THE ASSIGNMENT PROBLEM

Step 1: (i) Subtract the minimum element of each row from all elements of that row.

(ii) Subtract the minimum element of each column from all elements of that column.

The reduced matrix thus obtained, contains at least one zero in each row and each column.

Step 2: Cover all the zeros in the reduced cost-matrix by minimum number of horizontal and vertical lines. Let the least number of such lines needed to cover all the zeros be r. If r = n, an optimal assignment can be made at this stage in this case go to Step 4. If r < n, an optimal assignment can not be made at this stage. In this case, go to Step 3.

Step 3: Here, the least number of lines needed to cover all the zeros is less than the order of the assignment problem.

Pick the minimum element not covered by these r covering-lines and,

(i) Subtract it from all uncovered elements,

(ii) Add to all elements at intersection of two covering lines, and

(iii) Leave all other covered elements unchanged.

Thus, we get a new reduced cost-matrix. Go to step 2.

Step 4: Here the minimum number of lines needed to cover all the zeros is exactly equal to the order of the assignment.

An optimal assignment shall be made now.

(i) Examine the rows successively until a row with exactly one zero is found. Encircle this zero and cross all other zeros in its column.

(ii) Similarly, examine the columns successively until a column with exactly one zero is found. Encircle this zero and cross all other zeros in its row.

Repeating the above steps, either of the following situations is encountered:

(i) Each row and each column has an encircled zero. In this case an optimal assignment has been made and the process terminates.

(ii) There lie more than one zero in some rows and columns which are not encircled. In such a case, encircle any one of the zeros which is not encircled arbitrarily and cross all other zeros in its row and column, both.

Continuing in this way, we shall have exactly one encircled zero in each row and each column.

Assignments are made corresponding to each encircled zero.

Step 5: For obtaining the minimum cost, refer to the original cost-matrix of the given problem. Optimum cost is obtained by adding costs C_{ij}'s at all the encircled-zero positions.

Theorem

Theorem 1: The optimal solution of an assignment problem remains the same, if a constant is added or subtracted from any row or column of the cost matrix.

Proof: Let $\left[C_{ij}\right]$ and $\left[C^*_{ij}\right]$ with $C^*_{ij} = C_{ij} \pm u_i \pm v_j$ represent respectively the original assignment problem, obtained after adding or subtracting constants u_i's and v_j's from its rows and columns. Here, u_i is the constant added or subtracted from all the elements of ith row of matrix $\left[C_{ij}\right]$; and v_j is the constant added or subtracted from all the elements of the jth column of the matrix $\left[C_{ij}\right]$. Let $Z = \sum_{i=1}^{n} \sum_{j=1}^{n} C_{ij} x_{ij}$ be the objective function of the original problem with cost matrix $\left[C_{ij}\right]$. The objective function Z* for the resulting assignment problem with cost matrix $\left[C^*_{ij}\right]$ is given by,

$$Z^* = \sum_{i=1}^{n} \sum_{j=1}^{n} C^*_{ij} x_{ij} = \sum_{i=1}^{n} \sum_{j=1}^{n} \left(C_{ij} \pm u_i \pm v_j\right) x_{ij}$$

$$= \sum_{i=1}^{n} \sum_{j=1}^{n} C_{ij} x_{ij} \pm \sum_{i=1}^{n} \left(u_i \sum_{j=1}^{n} x_{ij}\right) \pm \sum_{j=1}^{n} \left(v_j \sum_{i=1}^{n} x_{ij}\right)$$

$$= Z \pm \sum_{i=1}^{n} u_i \pm \sum_{j=1}^{n} v_j, \qquad \because \sum_{i=1}^{n} x_{ij} = 1 = \sum_{j=1}^{n} x_{ij}$$

$$= Z \pm K \text{ where } \pm \sum_{i=1}^{n} u_i \pm \sum_{j=1}^{n} v_j = \pm K.$$

This shows that the minimisation of the original objective function Z yields the same solution as the minimisation of Z*. Only the optimal values differ.

Solved Practical Problems

Q1. Solve the following cost-minimising assignment problem.

	I	II	III	IV	V
A	2	9	2	7	1
B	6	8	7	6	1
C	4	6	5	3	1
D	4	2	7	3	1
E	5	3	9	5	1

[June-2016, Q.No.-2(b)]

Or

Solve the following assignment problem:

	A	B	C	D	E
I	2	9	2	7	1
II	6	8	7	6	1
III	4	6	5	3	1
IV	4	2	7	3	1
V	5	3	9	5	1

[June-2015, Q.No.-6(b)]

Ans. We have the assignment problem

	I	II	III	IV	V
A	2	9	2	7	1
B	6	8	7	6	1
C	4	6	5	3	1
D	4	2	7	3	1
E	5	3	9	5	1

Step 1: (i) Subtracting the minimum element of each row from all elements of that row, we get

	I	II	III	IV	V
A	1	8	1	6	0
B	5	7	6	5	0
C	3	5	4	2	0
D	3	1	6	2	0
E	4	2	8	4	0

(ii) Subtracting the minimum elements of each column from elements all of that column, we get

	I	II	III	IV	V
A	0	7	0	4	0
B	4	6	5	3	0
C	2	4	3	0	0
D	2	0	5	0	0
E	3	1	7	2	0

Step 2: Cover all the zeros by minimum number of horizontal and vertical lines. A systematic approach for this is to look for a row or column containing the maximum number of zeros.

	I	II	III	IV	V
A	0	7	0	4	0
B	4	6	5	3	0
C	2	4	3	0	0
D	2	0	5	0	0
E	3	1	7	2	0

Here, we can cover all the zeros by 4 lines only. So, r = 4 < 5 = n, so we go to step 3.

Step 3: 1 is the least uncovered element.

(i) Subtract 1 from all uncovered elements.

(ii) Add 1 to elements at intersection of the covering lines, viz. 0 at position (1, 5), 0 at position (3, 5) and 0 at position (4, 5).

(iii) Leave other covered elements unchanged. The reduced cost-matrix so obtained is,

	I	II	III	IV	V
A	0	7	0	4	1
B	3	5	4	2	0
C	2	4	3	0	1
D	2	0	5	0	1
E	2	0	6	1	0

Again r < n. Hence, we have

	I	II	III	IV	V
A	0	9	0	6	3
B	1	5	2	2	0
C	0	4	1	0	1
D	0	0	3	0	1
E	0	0	4	1	0

Here, r = n = 5. Now, we will go for step 4.

Step 4: For making assignments, we proceed as follows:

(i) 2nd row has only one zero in position (2, 5), so encircle this zero and cross all other zeros in its column, i.e., in fifth column.

(ii) Now, no row has exactly one zero. Therefore, we shall look column wise now. 3rd column has exactly one zero, so encircle this and cross all other zeros in its row.

(iii) Now no column has exactly one zero.

(iv) Third row has two zeros. We can encircle any zero according to our choice and cross all other zeros in its column.

Here, we encircle zero at position (3, 4) and cross the zero at the position (4, 4). We follow this procedure till we get all zeros either encircled or crossed.

Each row and each column has an encircled zero. Thus, we have the following table:

	I	II	III	IV	V
A	0 (crossed)	9	(0)	6	3
B	1	5	2	2	(0)
C	0 (crossed)	4	1	(0)	1
D	0 (crossed)	(0)	3	0 (crossed)	1
E	(0)	0 (crossed)	4	1	0 (crossed)

In this table, we can see that each row and each column has a single encircled zero. The optimal assignment is given by

A–III, B–V, C–IV, D–II, E–I

Step 5: The minimum assignment cost is read from the original cost matrix as

$$C_{13} + C_{25} + C_{34} + C_{42} + C_{51} = 2+1+3+2+5 = 13$$

Q2. The profit achieved on assigning 5 different jobs to 5 different people are given below. Find the assignment that maximises the profit, and the maximum profit.

$$\begin{bmatrix} 1 & 5 & 7 & 3 & 8 \\ 9 & 0 & 4 & 4 & 5 \\ 8 & 3 & 2 & 9 & 5 \\ 0 & 1 & 3 & 4 & 1 \\ 5 & 9 & 6 & 5 & 9 \end{bmatrix}$$

Ans. From linear programming, we know that a maximum problem can be converted into a minimisation problem by replacing the costs with their negatives. It is also known that an assignment problem is a linear programming problem. Therefore, we can convert the given maximising assignment problem into the usual minimising assignment problem, by replacing costs with their negatives and proceed with the Hungarian Method. The corresponding minimising assignment problem has the cost-matrix given below:

People

Jobs		I	II	III	IV	V
	A	–1	–5	–7	–3	–8
	B	–9	0	–4	–4	–5
Jobs	C	–8	–3	–2	–9	–5
	D	0	–1	–3	–4	–1
	E	–5	–9	–6	–5	–9

Step 1: (i) Subtract minimum element –8 from all elements of 1st row. Similarly, subtract –9, –9, –4, and –9 respectively from all elements of 2nd, 3rd, 4th and 5th rows. The reduced matrix is

	I	II	III	IV	V
A	7	3	1	5	0
B	0	9	5	5	4
C	1	6	7	0	4
D	4	3	1	0	3
E	4	0	3	4	0

(ii) Subtract the minimum element of each column from all elements of that column. The reduced matrix so obtained is,

	I	II	III	IV	V
A	7	3	0	5	0
B	0	9	4	5	4
C	1	6	6	0	4
D	4	3	0	0	3
E	4	0	2	4	0

Step 2: Cover all zeros by minimum number of horizontal and vertical lines.

	I	II	III	IV	V
A	7	3	0	5	0
B	0	9	4	5	4
C	1	6	6	0	4
D	4	3	0	0	3
E	4	0	2	4	0

Here, number of lines, r = 5 which is equal to the order of cost-matrix, n = 5

Hence, optimal assignment can be made at this stage. So, we go to step 4.

Step 3: There is no need of step 3.

Step 4: Now, we have

	I	II	III	IV	V
A	7	3	⊠	5	(0)
B	(0)	9	4	5	4
C	1	6	6	(0)	4
D	4	3	(0)	⊠	3
E	4	(0)	2	4	⊠

Hence, optimal assignment is

A - V, B - I, C - IV, D - III, E - II

Step 5: Adding costs corresponding to these assignments from the original profit maximising matrix we get the maximum profit as

$$C_{15} + C_{21} + C_{34} + C_{43} + C_{52} = 8 + 9 + 9 + 3 + 9 = 38$$

Q3. The owner of a small machine shop has 4 mechanists available to do 4 jobs. Jobs are offered with expected profits for each mechanist as follows:

Machanists

Jobs		I	II	III	IV
	A	6	7	5	2
	B	4	3	2	8
	C	2	4	9	4
	D	5	3	1	7

Find by using the assignment method, the assignment of mechanists to jobs that will result in a maximum profit.

Ans. The corresponding minimising assignment problem has the cost-matrix given below:

	I	II	III	IV
A	–6	–7	–5	–2
B	–4	–3	–2	–8
C	–2	–4	–9	–4
D	–5	–3	–1	–7

Step 1: (i) Subtract the minimum element –7 from all elements of 1st row. Similarly, subtract –8, –9 and –7 respectively from all elements of 2nd, 3rd and 4th rows. The reduced matrix is,

	I	II	III	IV
A	1	0	2	5
B	4	5	6	0
C	7	5	0	5
D	2	4	6	0

(ii) Subtract the minimum element of each column from all elements of that column. The recorded matrix so obtained is,

	I	II	III	IV
A	0	0	2	5
B	3	5	6	0
C	6	5	0	5
D	1	4	6	0

Step 2: Cover all the zeros by minimum number of horizontal and vertical lines. Observe that only 3 lines can cover all the zeros. So, r = 3. As 3 = r < n = 4, so we go to step 3.

	I	II	III	IV
A	0	0	2	5
B	3	5	6	0
C	6	5	0	5
D	1	4	6	0

Step 3: The minimum uncovered element is 1, so

(i) Subtracting 1 from all uncovered elements

(ii) Adding 1 to elements at intersection of horizontal and vertical lines, viz. elements at positions (1, 4) and (3, 4).

(iii) Leaving all other covered elements unchanged, we get,

	I	II	III	IV
A	0	0	2	6
B	2	4	5	0
C	6	5	0	6
D	0	3	5	0

Observe that now we require exactly 4 lines to cover all the zeros, i.e. now r = n. So, we can go to step 4, and make optimal assignment.

Step 4: (i) There is a single zero in 2nd row in the position (2, 4). Encircle this zero and cross all zeros in its column, i.e. 4th column.

(ii) There is a single zero in 3rd in the position (3, 3). Encircle this zero and cross all other zeros (if any) in its columns, i.e. 3rd column.

(iii) Now, there is only one unmarked zero in 4th row in the position (4, 1). Encircle this zero and cross all other zeros in its column, i.e. 1st column.

	I	II	III	IV
A	~~0~~	(0)	2	6
B	2	4	5	(0)
C	6	5	(0)	6
D	(0)	3	5	~~0~~

(iv) There is now a single zero in 1st row in the position (1, 2). Encircle it to get the optimal assignment as A - II, B - IV, C - III, D - I.

Step 5: Adding costs corresponding to these assignments from the original profit maximising matrix we get the maximum profit as, 7 + 8 + 9 + 5 = 29.

Q4. If 10 is added to each of the entries of the cost matrix of a 3 × 3 assignment problem, then the total cost of an optimal assignment for the changed cost matrix will increase by 10. True or false?

[Dec-2014, Q.No.-1(c)] [June-2015, Q.No.-1(e)]

Ans. False.

Let the 3 × 3 assignment problem is

	M_1	M_2	M_3
J_1	2	4	2
J_2	5	2	3
J_3	4	2	5

and the optimal solution of this assignment problem is J_1M_1, J_2M_3, J_3M_2.

Hence, the total cost will be

2 + 3 + 2 = 7

If 10 is added to each of the entries of the cost matrix of the assignment problem, then we have

	M_1	M_2	M_3
J_1	12	14	12
J_2	15	12	13
J_3	14	12	15

We know that the optimal solution of an assignment problem remains the same, if a constant is added or subtracted from any row or column of the cost matrix. Hence, the optimal solution will be J_1M_1, J_2M_3, J_3M_2.

Now, the total cost will be

$12 + 13 + 12 = 37$

Hence, the total cost will not increase by 10. The book you can most believe—GPH book.

⌑ ⌑

13 Games with Pure strategy

An Overview

Game theory is the study of mathematical models of conflict and co-operation between intelligent rational decision-makers. Game theory is mainly used in economics, political science, and psychology, as well as logic, computer science, biology and poker. Originally, it addressed zero-sum games, in which one person's gains result in losses for the other participants.

A pure strategy provides a complete definition of how a player will play a game. In particular, it determines the move a player will make for any situation he or she could face.

13.1 BASIC DEFINITIONS

Game

A game is defined to be a competitive activity between two or more persons each, of whom makes decisions to defeat others adding a set of rules and at the end of which each player gets some benefit or suffers a loss.

In other words,

A competitive situation is called a Game if it has the following properties:

(1) The number of competitors called **players** is finite.

(2) Each player has a finite number of choices called **strategies**. The number of choices need not be the same for each player.

(3) All relevant informations, i.e. the different strategies of each player and the amount of gain on an individual's move (strategy) is known to each player in advance.

(4) Each player acts rationally to maximise his gain. A play of the game results when each player makes a set of moves according to this principle.

(5) The outcome of the play determines a set of payments which may be positive, negative or zero.

Two-Person Game

When the game takes place between two competitors only, it is called a Two-Person Game. In two-person game each player may have a number of possible choices for each play of the game.

n-Person Game

When the game takes place between n competitors, it is called an n-Person Game. An n-person game can be regarded as a two-person game of n-persons and it can be divided into two groups of identical interests.

Two-Person Zero-Sum Game

A Two-Person Zero-Sum Game is a game in which the gain of one player after a play equals the net loss of his opponent. It means, in a two-person zero-sum game, the algebraic sum of the gains to both the players after a play is bound to be zero.

Pay-off Matrix

The matrix, which shows the outcome of the game as the player select their particular strategies, is known as the Pay-off Matrix.

The pay-off matrix of a rectangular game given by

$$
\begin{array}{c c} & \text{Player B} \\ & \begin{array}{ccccc} B_1 & B_2 & B_3 & \cdots & B_n \end{array} \\ \text{Player A} \begin{array}{c} A_1 \\ A_2 \\ A_3 \\ \vdots \\ A_m \end{array} & \begin{bmatrix} a_{11} & a_{12} & a_{13} & \cdots & a_{1n} \\ a_{21} & a_{22} & a_{23} & \cdots & a_{2n} \\ a_{31} & a_{32} & a_{33} & \cdots & a_{3n} \\ \vdots & \vdots & \vdots & & \vdots \\ a_{m1} & a_{m2} & a_{m3} & \cdots & a_{mn} \end{bmatrix} \end{array}
$$

may be interpreted as

(1) The player A has m strategies, namely $A_1, A_2, ..., A_m$ and the player B has n strategies.

(2) The pay-off a_{ij} is the gain of A if he adopts the ith strategy and B adopts the jth strategy.

(3) The pay-off a_{ij} is the loss of B if he adopts the jth strategy when A adopts the ith strategy.

Note: a_{ij} may be positive, negative or zero.

Strategy

A strategy of a player is a rule or programme, which tells the player what to do in each personal move depending on the situation at hand.

Pure Strategy

If a player knows in advance that, of all plays, he will choose only one particular course of action, then the decision of selecting the same course of action is called a Pure Strategy.

For example, the player X has three courses of action (i.e. strategies) and player Y has two courses of action. If for some reason, at each play of the game, player X selects strategy 1, but player Y selects strategy 2, then we say that player X uses the pure strategy 1 and player Y uses the pure strategy 2.

Maximin and Minimax Principle

According to this principle, the player adopts a pessimistic attitude and plays safe, i.e. this strategy is always that which results in the best of the worst outcomes. In other words, the player X (the maximising player) decides to play that strategy which corresponds to the maximum of the minimum gain for his different courses of action. This is known as **Maximin principle**.

Similarly, the player Y (the minimising player) would also like to play safe and in that case he selects that strategy which corresponds to the minimum of the maximum losses for his different courses of action and this is known as the **Minimax Principle**.

In other words, the maximising player adopts the maximin criterion, while the minimising player adopts the minimax criterion, for their optimal strategy.

To explain these principles, we choose a 3 × 4 pay-off matrix table as follows:

$$\begin{array}{cc} & \text{Player B} \\ & \begin{array}{cccc} B_1 & B_2 & B_3 & B_4 \end{array} \\ \text{Player A} \begin{array}{c} A_1 \\ A_2 \\ A_3 \end{array} & \begin{bmatrix} 1 & 4 & 3 & 1 \\ 3 & 2 & 5 & 7 \\ 0 & 3 & 4 & 2 \end{bmatrix} \end{array}$$

Maximin a_{ij} = max {1, 2, 0} = 2, minimax a_{ij} = {3, 4, 5, 7} = 3.

Observe for the player A, the strategies are A_1, A_2, and A_3. For the strategy A_1, the player B must choose B_1, for A_2 the choice of B will be B_2 as 2 is the minimum of the row, for A_3, the choice of B will be B_1, as 0 is the minimum. Now for A, therefore, the best choice will be A_2 since 2 is the maximum of {1, 2, 0}. Thus, the choice is made based on the maximum principle.

Similarly, the best choice of B will be determined by the minimax principle. Here min {maximum of each column} = min {3, 4, 5, 7} = 3 which corresponds to the strategy B_1 for the player B.

We observe from the above example:

maximin $a_{ij} \leq$ minimax a_{ij}

13.2 SADDLE POINT OF A PAY-OFF MATRIX

The saddle point in a pay off matrix is one, which is the smallest value in its row and the largest value in its column. The saddle point is also known as equilibrium point in the theory of games.

In other words, **a saddle point is the point of intersection of the optimal pure strategies of the two players.**

In case of pure strategy game, the maximising player arrives at his optimal strategy on the basis of maximin criterion while the minimising player's strategy is based on the minimax criterion. If the maximin value is equal to the minimax value, then the game is said to have a saddle point or equilibrium and the best strategy for both players will be those, which corresponds to row and column through the saddle point. The amount of pay off at the saddle point is known as the **value of the game**. This, in order to solve a pure strategy game or game with saddle point, one has to find the saddle point.

Methods to find saddle point

The saddle point is detected as follows:

(i) Select the minimum value of each row of the pay off matrix and put a circle ◯ around it.

(ii) Select the maximum value of each column of the pay off matrix and put square □ around it.

(iii) If there appears a value in the pay off matrix marked with both circle ○, and square □, that value is a saddle point of the pay off matrix.

Note:

(i) A matrix may not have any saddle point. In this case, the game is not a game of pure strategies.

(ii) A matrix may have more than one saddle point. In that case, the game will have more than one optimum solution.

13.3 VALUE OF THE GAME

If the maximin value for X (the maximising player) equals the minimax value for Y (the minimising player) then the game is said to have a saddle point or equilibrium point and the corresponding strategies are called optimal strategies. The amount of pay-off at an equilibrium point is known as the value of the game and is denoted by v.

However, if the two values, maximin value for X and the minimax value for Y are not equal then there will be no saddle point and the maximin value for X is called the lower value of the game and is denoted by $\underline{v}$, while the minimax value for Y is called the upper value of the game and is denoted by $\bar{v}$. Suppose a_{ij} denote the elements of the pay-off matrix, then

$$\underline{v} = \max_i \min_j a_{ij} = \text{maximum of the row minima}$$

and $$\bar{v} = \min_j \max_i a_{ij} = \text{minimum of the column maxima}$$

A game is **strictly determinable** if $\underline{v} = \bar{v} = v$. v is the value of the game.

Note: A game is called **fair** if its value is zero.

Solved Practical Problems

Q1. (a) Find the maximin and minimax value of the following pay-off matrix:

$$\text{Player A}\quad \begin{array}{c} \\ A_1 \\ A_2 \\ A_3 \end{array}\overset{\text{Player B}}{\begin{array}{cccc} B_1 & B_2 & B_3 & B_4 \\ \hline 35 & 65 & 25 & 5 \\ 30 & 20 & 15 & 0 \\ 55 & 60 & 10 & 15 \end{array}}$$

Ans. It may be noted that the player A will get at least 5 if he plays the A_1 strategy, will get at least 0 if he plays the A_2 strategy and will get at least 10 if he plays A_3 strategy. Out of these three strategies, he would like to play safe by adopting the strategy A_3 in which he gets the maximum (10) out of his minimum gains of 5, 0 and 10.

Hence, Row minima is as follows:

		Player B				
		B_1	B_2	B_3	B_4	Row minima
	A_1	35	65	25	5	5
Player A	A_2	30	20	15	0	0
	A_3	55	60	10	15	10

Hence, maximin value = max (5, 0, 10)
= 10

Now, the game is considered from the player B's point of view. The maximum loss to player B when he plays the strategy B_1 is 55, and 65, 25 and 15 when he plays the B_2,B_3 and B_4 strategies respectively. Now out of these maximum losses of 55, 65, 25, 15 he would like to play safe and accordingly would select that strategy which corresponds to the minimum of the maximum losses, i.e., 15 which corresponds to his B_4 strategy and he would therefore, decide to play the B_4 strategy throughout the game.

Hence, column maxima is as follows:

		B_1	B_2	B_3	B_4
	A_1	35	65	25	5
Player A	A_2	30	20	15	0
	A_3	55	60	10	15
Column maxima		55	65	25	15

Hence, minimax value = min (55,65, 25, 15)
= 15

(b) **Two companies A and B are competing for their competitive product. To improve its market share, the company A adopts the following strategies:**

A_1 – Home delivery service

A_2 – Mail order service

A_3 – Free gift for customer

while the company B adopts to use media advertising as

B_1 – Radio

B_2 – Magazine

B_3 – Newspaper

Past experiences show that the pay-off matrix for the company A is given as

$$\begin{array}{c} \text{Company B} \\ \begin{array}{cc} & \begin{array}{ccc} B_1 & B_2 & B_3 \end{array} \\ \text{Company A} \begin{array}{c} A_1 \\ A_2 \\ A_3 \end{array} & \begin{bmatrix} -2 & 12 & -4 \\ 1 & 4 & 8 \\ -5 & 2 & 3 \end{bmatrix} \end{array} \end{array}$$

what is the optimal strategy for both the companies?

Ans. The optimal strategies are A_2 for the company A and B_1 for the company B. Thus, the optimal strategies $S_0 = (A_2, B_1)$.

Q2. Find the saddle point of the following pay-off matrices:

(a)

$$\begin{array}{c} \text{Player B} \\ \begin{array}{cc} & \begin{array}{cc} B_1 & B_2 \end{array} \\ \text{Player A} \begin{array}{c} A_1 \\ A_2 \\ A_3 \end{array} & \begin{bmatrix} -1 & 6 \\ 2 & 4 \\ -2 & -6 \end{bmatrix} \end{array} \end{array}$$

(b)

$$\begin{array}{c} \text{Player B} \\ \begin{array}{cc} & \begin{array}{ccc} B_1 & B_2 & B_3 \end{array} \\ \text{Player A} \begin{array}{c} A_1 \\ A_2 \\ A_3 \end{array} & \begin{bmatrix} 1 & 3 & 1 \\ 0 & -4 & -3 \\ 1 & 5 & -1 \end{bmatrix} \end{array} \end{array}$$

Ans. (a) In the given matrix, we encircle the minimum of each row and put a square $\square$ on the maximum of each column,

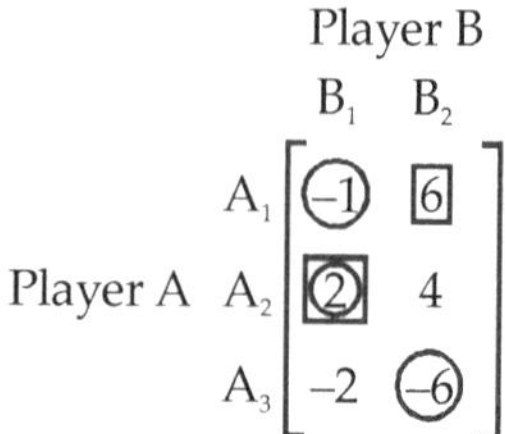

Thus, the maximin value and the minimax value each is 2, which occurs at the intersection of the 2nd row and Ist column. Thus, the saddle point is at the position (2, 1), i.e. the best strategy for the player A is A_2 and the best strategy for the player B is B_1.

(b) In the given matrix, we encircle the minimum of teach row and put a square $\square$ on the maximum of each column,

$$\begin{array}{ccc} & & \text{Player B} \\ & & \begin{array}{ccc} B_1 & B_2 & B_3 \end{array} \\ & \begin{array}{c} A_1 \\ A_2 \\ A_3 \end{array} & \begin{bmatrix} \boxed{\textcircled{1}} & 3 & \boxed{\textcircled{1}} \\ 0 & \textcircled{-4} & -3 \\ \boxed{1} & \boxed{5} & \textcircled{-1} \end{bmatrix} \end{array}$$

Player A

Thus, we have here two saddle points, since we have encircled and put squares on the two elements which are at the intersection on the 1st row and 1st column and at the intersection of the 1st row and the third column. Thus, the saddle points are at (A_1, B_1) and (A_1, B_3).

Q3. Solve the game whose pay-off matrices are given below:

(a)

$$\begin{array}{cc} & \textbf{Player B} \\ & \begin{array}{ccc} Y_1 & Y_2 & Y_3 \end{array} \\ \textbf{Player A} \begin{array}{c} X_1 \\ X_2 \\ X_3 \end{array} & \begin{bmatrix} -3 & -2 & 6 \\ 2 & 0 & 2 \\ 5 & -2 & -4 \end{bmatrix} \end{array}$$

Ans. We encircle the minimum of each row and put a square on the maximum of each column as

$$\begin{array}{cc} & \text{Player Y} \\ & \begin{array}{ccc} Y_1 & Y_2 & Y_3 \end{array} \\ \text{Player X} \begin{array}{c} X_1 \\ X_2 \\ X_3 \end{array} & \begin{bmatrix} \textcircled{-3} & -2 & \boxed{6} \\ 2 & \boxed{\textcircled{0}} & 2 \\ \boxed{5} & -2 & \textcircled{-4} \end{bmatrix} \end{array}$$

We find that both the circle and the square are on the element 0, which is at the intersection of the 2nd row and the 2nd column. Thus, the saddle point occurs at (2, 2), i.e. the best strategy for the player X is X_2 and also the best strategy for the player Y is Y_2 and the value of the game is 0. Thus, the game is a fair game.

(b)

Player B

		B_1	B_2	B_3	B_4
Player A	A_1	–5	2	0	7
	A_2	5	6	4	8
	A_3	4	0	2	–3

Ans. We encircle the minimum of each row and put a square on the maximum of each column as

Player B

		B_1	B_2	B_3	B_4
Player A	A_1	(–5)	2	0	7
	A_2	[5]	[6]	[(4)]	[8]
	A_3	4	0	2	(–3)

We find here both the symbols ◯ and the □ are only at 4, which lies at the intersection of the 2nd row and 3rd column. Thus, the best strategy for the player A is A_2 and the best strategy for the player B is B_3 i.e. the optimum strategies for A and B are $S_0 = (A_2, B_3)$ and the value of the game v = 4.

Thus, the value of the game is 4 for the player A and –4 for the player B and since the value of the game is not zero, it is not a fair game though it is strictly determinable.

Q4. Do the following pay-off matrices have saddle point? If they do, what is a solution and value of the corresponding game? Indicate which game is a fair game.

(a) **Player B**

		B_1	B_2
Player A	A_1	5	0
	A_2	0	2

(b) **Player B**

		B_1	B_2
Player A	A_1	0	2
	A_2	–1	4

(c) **Player B**

		B_1	B_2
Player A	A_1	1	1
	A_2	1	1

(c) **Player B**

		B_1	B_2	B_3
Player A	A_1	7	3	4
	A_2	6	4	5

Ans. (a) We encircle the minimum of each row and put a square on the maximum of each column as

Player B

Player A	B_1	B_2
A_1	$\boxed{5}$	(0)
A_2	(0)	$\boxed{2}$

It does not have saddle point.

Lower value of the game, $\underline{v}$ = Maximin value for Player A

$\Rightarrow \quad \underline{v} = 0$

Upper value of the game, $\bar{v}$ = minimax value for Player B

$\Rightarrow \quad \bar{v} = 2$

(b) We have

Player B

Player A	B_1	B_2
A_1	$\boxed{(0)}$	2
A_2	(−1)	$\boxed{4}$

Hence, optimum strategies $S_0 = (A_1, B_1)$.

Value of game, v = 0

This is a fair game.

(c) We have

Player B

Player A	B_1	B_2
A_1	$\boxed{(1)}$	$\boxed{(1)}$
A_2	$\boxed{(1)}$	$\boxed{(1)}$

Hence, optimum strategies $S_0 = (A_i, B_j)$

where i = 1, 2 and j = 1, 2.

Value of the game, v = 1

(d) We have

Player B

Player A	B_1	B_2	B_2
A_1	$\boxed{7}$	(3)	4
A_2	6	$\boxed{(4)}$	$\boxed{5}$

Hence, optimum strategies $S_0 = (A_2, B_2)$.

Value of the game, v = 4.

Q5. Solve the game whose pay-off matrix is given by,

$$\begin{array}{c c} & \textbf{Player B} \\ & \begin{array}{ccccc} B_1 & B_2 & B_3 & B_4 & B_5 \end{array} \\ \textbf{Player A} \begin{array}{c} A_1 \\ A_2 \\ A_3 \\ A_4 \end{array} & \begin{bmatrix} 9 & 3 & 1 & 8 & 0 \\ 6 & 5 & 4 & 6 & 7 \\ 2 & 4 & 3 & 3 & 8 \\ 5 & 6 & 2 & 2 & 1 \end{bmatrix} \end{array}$$

Ans. We have

$$\begin{array}{c c} & \text{Player B} \\ & \begin{array}{ccccc} B_1 & B_2 & B_3 & B_4 & B_5 \end{array} \\ \text{Player A} \begin{array}{c} A_1 \\ A_2 \\ A_3 \\ A_4 \end{array} & \begin{bmatrix} \boxed{9} & 3 & 1 & \boxed{8} & \textcircled{0} \\ 6 & 5 & \boxed{\textcircled{4}} & 6 & 7 \\ \textcircled{2} & 4 & 3 & 3 & \boxed{8} \\ 5 & \boxed{6} & 2 & 2 & \textcircled{1} \end{bmatrix} \end{array}$$

Hence, the optimum strategies are $S_0 = (A_2, B_3)$.

The value of the game, $v = 4$.

Q6. If value of the 2 × 2 matrix game $\begin{bmatrix} 1 & 2 \\ p & 4 \end{bmatrix}$ is 4, then $p \geq 4$. True or false? **[Dec-2014, Q.No.-1(b)]**

Ans. True.

If $p = 4$, then

$$\begin{bmatrix} \textcircled{1} & 2 \\ \boxed{\textcircled{4}} & \boxed{4} \end{bmatrix}$$

The value of the game = 4

If $p = 5 > 4$, then

$$\begin{bmatrix} \textcircled{1} & 2 \\ \boxed{5} & \boxed{\textcircled{4}} \end{bmatrix}$$

The value of the game = 4

Hence, if $p \geq 4$, the value of the given game remains 4.

Q7. Two breakfast food manufacturers ABC and XYZ are competing for an increased market share. The pay-off matrix, shown in the following table, describes the increase in market share for ABC and

decrease in market share for XYZ. Determine optimal strategies for both the manufacturers and the value of the game.

ABC \ XYZ	B_1	B_2	B_3	B_4
A_1	2	–2	4	1
A_2	6	–5	12	3
A_3	–3	–2	0	6
A_4	2	–2	7	1

[Dec-2014, Q.No.-4(a)]

Ans. We will find the saddle point as follows:

ABC \ XYZ	B_1	B_2	B_3	B_4
A_1	2	(–2) [boxed]	4	1
A_2	6 [boxed]	(–5)	12 [boxed]	3
A_3	(–3)	–2 [boxed]	0	6 [boxed]
A_4	2	(–2) [boxed]	7	1

It has two saddle points. Hence, optimal strategies for ABC and XYZ are

$S_0 = (A_1, B_2)$ and (A_4, B_2)

Value of the game $v = -2$

Q8. Find the range of values of p and q which will render the entry (2, 2), a saddle point for the following game:

	Player B		
Player A	2	4	5
	10	7	q
	4	p	6

[June-2015, Q.No.-7(c)]

Ans. First, ignore the values of p and q in the payoff matrix, and then determine the maximin and minimax values in the usual manner, as shown in the following table.

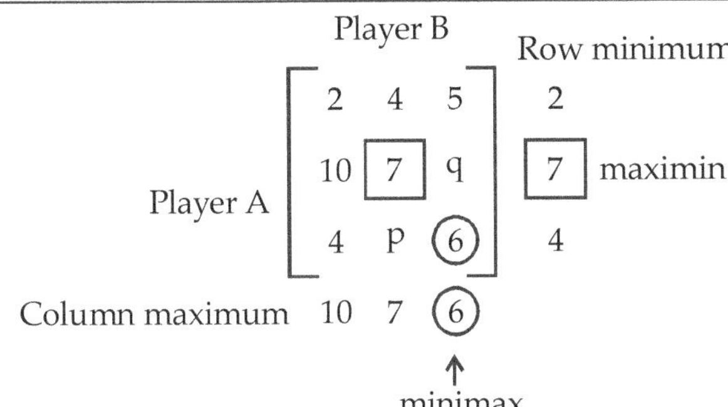

As shown in above table, since there exists no unique saddle point, therefore, the saddle point will exist at the position (2, 2) only when $p \leq 7$ and $q > 7$.

¤ ¤

14 Games with Mixed Strategy

An Overview

A mixed strategy is an assignment of a probability to each pure strategy. This allows a player to select randomly a pure strategy. Since probabilities are continuous, there are infinitely many mixed strategies available to a player.

Mixed strategies are best understood in the context of repeated games, where each player's aim is to keep the other player(s) guessing, for example: Rock, Scissors, and Paper. If each player in an n-player game has a finite number of pure strategies strategies, then there then there exists at least one equilibrium equilibrium in (possibly) mixed strategies.

14.1 MIXED STRATEGIES

For a two-person zero-sum game the existence of a saddle point asserts the existence of pure strategies for both the players, namely the maximising player and the minimising player, but when a saddle point does not exist, no single strategy will be adequate to fetch maximum benefit out of a play of the game and the same is true for the minimising player to minimise his loss. In such a situation, a combination of the several pure strategies, which we call a mixed strategy, will fulfil their objectives.

In other words,

If a player does not obey to the same strategy throughout the game but mixes the strategies in such a way that his opponent is not in a position to guess it and moreover he himself does not know what his next move would be, then the game is said to be played with mixed strategies. Thus, a game with mixed strategies is the game where the saddle point does not exist.

Meaning of Mixed Strategy

Consider a rectangular game with pay-off matrix

$$\text{Player X} \overset{\text{Player Y}}{\begin{bmatrix} a_{11} & a_{12} & \cdots & a_{1n} \\ a_{21} & a_{22} & \cdots & a_{2n} \\ \vdots & & & \\ a_{m1} & a_{m2} & \cdots & a_{mn} \end{bmatrix}}$$

Here the player X has m strategies (1, 2,..., m) and the player Y has n strategies (1, 2,..., n). If the above matrix has a saddle point

i.e. $\underset{i}{\text{Max}}\,\underset{j}{\text{Min}}\; a_{ij} = \underset{j}{\text{Min}}\,\underset{i}{\text{Max}}\; a_{ij} = a_{hk}$ then the best strategy for player X is the pure strategy h, the best strategy for player Y is the pure strategy k and the value of the game is a_{hk}.

If, i.e. $\underset{i}{\text{Max}}\,\underset{j}{\text{Min}}\; a_{ij} \neq \underset{j}{\text{Min}}\,\underset{i}{\text{Max}}\; a_{ij} = a_{hk}$, then there are no optimal pure strategies for the players and then we define a Mixed Strategy.

Mixed Strategy for player X is a vector $x = (x_1, ..., x_m)$ of m non-negative real numbers that satisfies the condition $\sum_{i=1}^{m} x_i = 1$ where x_i may be interpreted as the probability with which player X chooses the strategy i. Similarly, a Mixed Strategy for player Y is a vector $y = (y_1, ..., y_n)$ of n non-negative real numbers satisfying the condition $\sum_{j=1}^{n} y_j = 1$ where y may be interpreted as the probability with which player y chooses the strategy j.

The set of mixed strategies includes the set of pure strategies. In fact, a pure strategy k for player X is a special cases of a mixed strategy x = (0, 0,..., 1, ..., 0) where $x_k = 1$ and all other $x_i = 0$. The set of all mixed strategies for player X will be denoted by S and that of all mixed strategies for player Y by T. In other words

$$S = \left\{ x \mid x = (x_1, \ldots, x_m), \ \sum_{i=1}^{m} x_i = 1, \ \ x_i \geq 0, \ \ i = 1, \ldots, m \right\}$$

$$T = \left\{ y \mid y = (y_1, \ldots, y_n), \ \sum_{j=1}^{n} y_j = 1, \ \ y_j \geq 0, \ \ j = 1, \ldots, n \right\}$$

Expected Value

If Player X uses the mixed strategy $x = (x_1, \ldots, x_i, \ldots x_m)$ and player Y uses the mixed strategy $y = (y_1, \ldots, y_j, \ldots, y_n)$, then we need to know a way of evaluating the outcome.

For this, we use the concept of 'expected value' from probability theory. In probability theory, the expected value of an event is defined to be the sum of the values of each possible outcome of the event times the probability that the outcome occurs. Therefore, if Player X chooses the mixed strategy $x = (x_1, \ldots, x_i, \ldots, x_m)$ and player Y chooses the mixed strategy $y = (y_1, \ldots, y_j, \ldots, y_n)$ then the outcome a_{ij} will occur with probability $x_i\, y_j$ since this is the probability of both the Player X choosing strategy i and the Player Y choosing strategy j. Thus, the expected value for the game is the sum of all the products $x_i\, a_{ij}\, y_j$, that is, the sum

$$\sum_{j=1}^{n} \sum_{i=1}^{m} x_i\, a_{ij}\, y_j$$

i.e. $$(x_1, \ldots, x_m) \begin{pmatrix} a_{11} & \cdots & a_{1j} & \cdots & a_{1n} \\ \cdots & \cdots & \cdots & \cdots & \cdots \\ a_{i1} & \cdots & a_{ij} & \cdots & a_{in} \\ \cdots & \cdots & \cdots & \cdots & \cdots \\ a_{m1} & \cdots & a_{mj} & \cdots & a_{mn} \end{pmatrix} \begin{pmatrix} y_1 \\ \vdots \\ y_n \end{pmatrix}$$

i.e. $x\, A\, y^T$

Observe that if Player X selects the mixed strategy $x = (x_1, \ldots, x_m)$ and Player Y selects the pure strategy j (i.e. mixed strategy y = (0, 0,..., 1, ..., 0) where 1 occurs at j[th] place only)

Then the expected value $= \sum_{i=1}^{m} x_i\, a_{ij}$

Similarly if Player X selects the pure strategy i, i.e. mixed strategy x = (0, 0,..., 1,..., 0) where '1' occurs in the ith position only) and Player Y selects the mixed strategy $y = (y_1,...,y_n)$, then the expected value $= \sum_{j=1}^{n} a_{ij} y_j$.

Value of the Game

Consider a game with pay-off matrix A of order m × n. For each mixed strategy $x = (x_1,...,x_m)$, Player X must determine the worst possible outcome of the game allowing that Player Y also has available mixed strategies $y = (y_1,...,y_n)$. This would be then $\underset{y}{\text{Min}}\ xAy^T$.

This minimum represents expected minimum gain of Player X if he were to choose strategy x. Since he wants to maximise his gain, therefore Player X should seek a strategy that attains the maximum of these minima, that is, strategy x* such that

$$\underset{y \in T}{\text{Min}}\ x^* Ay^t = \underset{x \in S}{\text{Max}}\ \underset{y \in T}{\text{Min}}\ xAy^t$$

Similarly, for each strategy $y = (y_1,...,y_n)$, Player Y should be prepared for the worst possible outcome of the game knowing that Player X also has mixed strategies $x = (x_1,...,x_m)$, which would be used to maximise his earnings. This shows that Player Y should be ready to concede Max xAy^t to Player Y. Since the objective of Player Y is to minimise the gain to Player X, therefore player Y seeks a strategy y* such the

$$\underset{x \in S}{\text{Max}}\ xAy^{*t} = \underset{y \in T}{\text{Min}}\ \underset{x \in S}{\text{Max}}\ xAy^t$$

At this stage, it is possible to define the strategic saddle point of the game with mixed strategy.

$$\text{if } \underset{x \in S}{\text{max}}\ \underset{y \in T}{\text{min}}\ xAy^t = \underset{y \in T}{\text{min}}\ \underset{x \in S}{\text{max}}\ xAy^t = x^* Ay^{*t}$$

then (x*, y*) is called the **strategic saddle point** of the game where x* and y* define the optimal strategies and $v = x^* Ay^{*t}$ is the value of the game.

14.2 ALGEBRAIC METHOD TO SOLVE A GAME WITH MIXED STRATEGIES

A game in which both players have two alternative strategies is known as 2 × 2 game. If the game does not have a saddle point, the two largest elements of the matrix must constitute one of the diagonals. Thus, both players used mixed strategies. In this case, the task is to determine the probabilities with which both players choose their course of action. Considering a general case as following:

		Player Y	
		I	II
		q	1–q
Player X	I	a	b
	II	c	d
	1 – p		

Suppose player-X chooses action-I with probability p and therefore chooses action-II with a probability 1 – p. If the player-Y selects strategy I, the expected gain to player-X for this game can be given by

$$ap + c\,(1 - p) \qquad \text{...(i)}$$

On the other hand, if player-Y selects strategy II, then player Y's expected gain is

$$bp + d\,(1 - p) \qquad \text{...(ii)}$$

However, for player-X to be indifferent to which strategy player-Y selects, the optimal plan player-X requires that its expected gain to be equal for each of player Y's possible strategies. Thus, equating equations (i) and (ii).

i.e., $ap + c\,(1 - p) = bp + d\,(1 - p)$

or $p\,(a - b) + c - cp = d - dp$

or $p\,(a - b) + p\,(d - c) = d - c$

or $p\,[a + d - (b + c)] = d - c$

or $$p = \frac{d - c}{a + d - (b + c)} \qquad \text{...(iii)}$$

Similarly, if player-Y selects strategy I and II with a probability of q and 1 – q respectively, the expected loss to Y when player-X adopts I and II, respectively are

$$aq + b\,(1 - q) \qquad \text{...(iv)}$$

and $$cq + d\,(1 - q) \qquad \text{...(v)}$$

By equating expected losses of player-Y, regardless of what player-X would choose, we have

$$aq + b\,(1 - q) = cq + d\,(1 - q)$$

$$q = \frac{d - b}{a + d - (b + c)} \qquad \text{...(vi)}$$

The value of game V is found by substituting the value of p in one of the expressions for the expected gains of player-X

e.g., $V = ap + c\,(1 - p)$

$$= \frac{a(d-c)}{a+d-(b+c)} + c\left[1 - \frac{d-c}{a+d-(b+c)}\right]$$

$$= \frac{ad-bc}{a+d-(b+c)} \qquad \text{...(vii)}$$

The solution of the game is

X player's (p, 1 – p) where $p = \frac{d-c}{a+d-(b+c)}$

Y player's (q, 1 – q) where $q = \frac{d-b}{a+d-(b+c)}$

and the value of the game V is $= \frac{ad-bc}{a+d-(b+c)}$

14.3 SUB-GAME METHOD FOR M × 2 OR 2 × N GAMES

In this method we sub-divide the given game (2 × n or m × 2) into a number of 2 × 2 games. Now each of these 2 × 2 games can be solved and then optimal strategies are selected. These are games when one of the player has 2 alternatives, where as the other player has more than two alternatives. When there is no saddle point the sub-games method is very useful. It is suitable when the number of alternatives is limited to 4. In case of large number of alternatives, the solution becomes lengthy and complicated. It follows the following procedure.

Step 1: Divide the 2 × n or m × 2 game matrix in 2 × 2 matrix sub games.

Step 2: Take up each game one by one and find out if a saddle point exists. Such a sub-game has pure strategies.

Step 3: If the sub-game has no saddle point, then use short-cut method to solve the sub game.

Step 4: Select the best sub-game out of all the sub games from the point of view of the player who has more than two alternatives.

Step 5: Find out the strategies of this selected sub game. This is applicable to both the players and for the entire game.

Step 6: Find out the value of the selected sub-game, this will be the value of the whole game.

Solved Practical Problems

Q1. Solve the game by algebraic method whose pay-off matrix are given by

$$\begin{array}{c} \quad \textbf{B} \\ \textbf{A}\begin{bmatrix} 2 & -9 \\ -7 & -1 \end{bmatrix} \end{array}$$

Ans. We can write the given pay-off matrix as

$$\begin{array}{ccc} & & \text{Player B} \\ & & \begin{array}{cc} B_1 & B_2 \end{array} \\ \text{Player A} & \begin{array}{c} A_1 \\ A_2 \end{array} & \begin{bmatrix} 2 & -9 \\ -7 & -1 \end{bmatrix} \end{array}$$

Suppose player A chooses strategy A_1 with probability p and therefore chooses strategy A_2 with a probability (1 – p). If the player B selects strategy B_1, the expected gain to player-A for this game can be given by

$$2p + (-7)(1 - p) \qquad ...(i)$$

On the other hand, if player B selects strategy B_2, then expected gain to player A for the game would be

$$-9p + (-1)(1 - p) \qquad ...(ii)$$

Now in order that the player A may be indifferent to the strategy B selects, the optimal plan for the player A should be such that

$$2p + (-7)(1 - p) \geq v$$

$$-9p + (-1)(1 - p) \geq v$$

where v is the value of the game. If the inequalities are satisfied as equations, then we have

$$2p + (-7)(1 - p) = -9p + (-1)(1 - p)$$

$$\Rightarrow \quad 2p - 7(1 - p) = -9p - (1 - p)$$

$$\Rightarrow \quad 2p - 7 + 7p = -9p - 1 + p$$

$$\Rightarrow \quad 2p + 7p + 9p - p = -1 + 7$$

$$\Rightarrow \quad 17p = 6$$

$$\Rightarrow \quad p = \frac{6}{17} = 0.35$$

and $(1 - p) = 1 - 0.35 = 0.65$ or $\frac{11}{17}$

Hence, the player A would select the strategy A_1 with probability $\frac{6}{17}$ and the strategy A_2 with a probability $\frac{11}{17}$.

Similarly, if player B selects strategies B_1 and B_2 with probabilities q and
(1 – q) respectively, then the expected pay-off or expected loss to player B when the player A adopts the strategy A_1 throughout the game would be

$$2q + (-9)(1 - q) \quad \text{...(iii)}$$

and the expected pay-off or expected loss to player B, when the player A adopts the strategy A_2 throughout the game would be

$$-7q + (-1)(1 - q) \quad \text{...(iv)}$$

Now, we have

$$2q + (-9)(1 - q) \le v$$

and $-7q + (-1)(1 - q) \le v$

Hence, we have

$$2q + (-9)(1 - q) = -7q + (-1)(1 - q)$$

$\Rightarrow \quad 2q - 9(1 - q) = -7q - (1 - q)$

$\Rightarrow \quad 2q - 9 + 9q = -7q - 1 + q$

$\Rightarrow \quad 2q + 9q + 7q - q = -1 + 9$

$\Rightarrow \quad 17q = 8$

$\Rightarrow \quad q = \frac{8}{17} = 0.47$

and $(1 - q) = 1 - \frac{8}{17} = \frac{9}{17} = 0.53$

Hence, the player B would select the strategies B_1 and B_2 with probabilities $\frac{8}{17}$ and $\frac{9}{17}$ respectively.

The value of game is determined by substituting the value of p or q in any of the expected value.

Now using equations (i) and (ii), we have

Expected gain to Player A

(i) $2 \times \frac{6}{17} + (-7) \times \frac{11}{17} = \frac{-65}{17}$

(ii) $-9 \times \frac{6}{17} + (-1) \times \frac{11}{17} = \frac{-65}{17}$

Now using equations (iii) and (iv), we have expected loss to Player B

(i) $2 \times \frac{8}{17} + (-9) \times \frac{9}{17} = \frac{-65}{17}$

(ii) $-7 \times \frac{8}{17} + (-1) \times \frac{9}{17} = \frac{-65}{17}$

Hence, the strategies for player A and B are $\left(\frac{6}{17}, \frac{11}{17}\right)$ and $\left(\frac{8}{17}, \frac{9}{17}\right)$. The value of the game $= \frac{-65}{17}$.

Alternative for short-cut method

If the original game consists of a pay-off matrix of order 2 × 2 and there is no saddle point in it, then the strategies, to which each player would resort, can be determined as follows:

Let the original game be

$$\begin{array}{cc} & B \\ A & \begin{bmatrix} 2 & -9 \\ -7 & -1 \end{bmatrix} \end{array}$$

Step 1: Subtract the smaller pay-off in each row from the larger one and the smaller pay-off in each column from the larger one as

$$\begin{array}{cccc} & \multicolumn{2}{c}{B} & \\ A & \begin{bmatrix} 2 & -9 \\ -7 & -1 \end{bmatrix} & \begin{array}{l} 2-(-9)=11 \\ -1-(-7)=6 \end{array} \\ & \begin{array}{cc} 2-(-7) & -1-(-9) \\ =9 & =8 \end{array} & \end{array}$$

Step 2: Interchange each of these pairs of subtracted numbers found in step 1, as

$$\begin{array}{ccc} & B & \\ A & \begin{bmatrix} 2 & -9 \\ -7 & -1 \end{bmatrix} & \begin{array}{c} 6 \\ 11 \end{array} \\ & \begin{array}{cc} 8 & 9 \end{array} & \end{array}$$

Step 3: Put each of the interchanged numbers over the sum of the pair of numbers, as

$$\begin{array}{ccc} & B & \\ A & \begin{bmatrix} 2 & -9 \\ -7 & -1 \end{bmatrix} & \begin{array}{c} \frac{6}{6+11} \\ \frac{11}{6+11} \end{array} \\ & \begin{array}{cc} \frac{8}{8+9} & \frac{9}{8+9} \end{array} & \end{array}$$

Step 4: Simplify the fraction to obtain the required strategies

$$\begin{array}{ccc} & B & \\ A & \begin{bmatrix} 2 & -9 \\ -7 & -1 \end{bmatrix} & \begin{array}{c} \frac{6}{17} \\ \frac{11}{17} \end{array} \\ & \begin{array}{cc} \frac{8}{17} & \frac{9}{17} \end{array} & \end{array}$$

Step 5: Value of the game can be determined from the viewpoint of the player by finding his expected value. For player A – the expected value (expected gain) is obtained as

(i) $2 \times \frac{6}{17} + (-7) \times \frac{11}{17} = \frac{-65}{17}$

(ii) $-9 \times \frac{6}{17} + (-1) \times \frac{11}{17} = \frac{-65}{17}$

For player B – the expected value (the expected loss) is obtained as

(i) $2 \times \frac{8}{17} + (-9) \times \frac{9}{17} = \frac{-65}{17}$

(ii) $-7 \times \frac{8}{17} + (-1) \times \frac{9}{17} = \frac{-65}{17}$

Hence, the value of the game = v $= \frac{-65}{17}$

Note: The short-cut method can be applied only when the pay-off matrix of a game is of order 2 × 2 and there is no saddle point in it.

Q2. Solve a game of order 4 × 2 with the following pay-off matrix concerning 2 persons:

$$\mathbf{A}\overset{\mathbf{B}}{\begin{bmatrix} -6 & -2 \\ -3 & -4 \\ 2 & -9 \\ -7 & -1 \end{bmatrix}}$$

Ans. There is no saddle point in the given game. Moreover, since Player B has got only two alternatives to play, the Player A will also use two strategies. Accordingly, Player A can actually think of this 4 × 2 game as being of six sub-games each of size 2 × 2. The six sub-games can be described as follows:

(i) $A \quad \overset{\displaystyle B}{\begin{array}{c} \\ A_1 \\ A_2 \end{array}\begin{array}{c} \begin{array}{cc} B_1 & B_2 \end{array} \\ \begin{bmatrix} -6 & -2 \\ -3 & -4 \end{bmatrix} \end{array}}$

(ii) $A \quad \overset{\displaystyle B}{\begin{array}{c} \\ A_1 \\ A_3 \end{array}\begin{array}{c} \begin{array}{cc} B_1 & B_2 \end{array} \\ \begin{bmatrix} -6 & -2 \\ 2 & -9 \end{bmatrix} \end{array}}$

(iii) $A \quad \overset{\displaystyle B}{\begin{array}{c} \\ A_1 \\ A_4 \end{array}\begin{array}{c} \begin{array}{cc} B_1 & B_2 \end{array} \\ \begin{bmatrix} -6 & -2 \\ -7 & -1 \end{bmatrix} \end{array}}$

(iv) $A \quad \overset{\displaystyle B}{\begin{array}{c} \\ A_2 \\ A_3 \end{array}\begin{array}{c} \begin{array}{cc} B_1 & B_2 \end{array} \\ \begin{bmatrix} -3 & -4 \\ 2 & -9 \end{bmatrix} \end{array}}$

(v) $A \quad \overset{\displaystyle B}{\begin{array}{c} \\ A_2 \\ A_4 \end{array}\begin{array}{c} \begin{array}{cc} B_1 & B_2 \end{array} \\ \begin{bmatrix} -3 & -4 \\ -7 & -1 \end{bmatrix} \end{array}}$

(vi) $A \quad \overset{\displaystyle B}{\begin{array}{c} \\ A_3 \\ A_4 \end{array}\begin{array}{c} \begin{array}{cc} B_1 & B_2 \end{array} \\ \begin{bmatrix} 2 & -9 \\ -7 & -1 \end{bmatrix} \end{array}}$

Now, we solve the six-sub games by Pure strategy or in the absence of saddle point by Mixed strategies (short-cut method) as follows:

Sub-game: (i) There is no saddle point and therefore the mixed strategies are determined as:

$$\begin{array}{cc|cc|l} & & \multicolumn{2}{c}{B} & \\ & & B_1 & B_2 & \\ \hline & & & & 1/5 \\ A & A_1 & -6 & -2 & \\ & A_2 & -3 & -4 & \\ & & & & 4/5 \\ \hline & & 2/5 & 3/5 & \end{array}$$

and $v = -2 \times \frac{1}{5} - 4 \times \frac{4}{5} = -\frac{18}{5} = -3.60$

Sub-game: (ii) There is no saddle point and the mixed strategies are calculated as:

$$\begin{array}{cc|cc|l} & & \multicolumn{2}{c}{B} & \\ & & B_1 & B_2 & \\ \hline & & & & 11/15 \\ A & A_1 & -6 & -2 & \\ & A_3 & 2 & -9 & \\ & & & & 4/15 \\ \hline & & 7/15 & 8/15 & \end{array}$$

and $v = (-2)\left(\frac{11}{15}\right) + (-9)\left(\frac{4}{15}\right) = -\frac{58}{15} = -3.87$

Sub-game: (iii)

$$\begin{array}{cc|cc|} & & \multicolumn{2}{c}{B} \\ & & B_1 & B_2 \\ A & A_1 & -6 & -2 \\ & A_4 & -7 & -1 \end{array}$$

There is a saddle point and the value of the game is –6.

Sub-game: (iv)

$$\begin{array}{cc|cc|} & & \multicolumn{2}{c}{B} \\ & & B_1 & B_2 \\ A & A_2 & -3 & -4 \\ & A_3 & 2 & -9 \end{array}$$

there is a saddle point and the value of the game is –4.

Sub-game: (v) There is no saddle point in it and the mixed strategies are calculated as:

$$\begin{array}{cc|cc|l} & & \multicolumn{2}{c}{B} & \\ & & B_1 & B_2 & \\ & & & & 6/7 \\ A & A_2 & -3 & -4 & \\ & A_4 & -7 & -1 & \\ & & & & 1/7 \\ & & 3/7 & 4/7 & \end{array}$$

and $v = (-4)\left(\frac{6}{7}\right) + (-1)\left(\frac{1}{7}\right) = -\frac{25}{7} \approx -3.57$

Sub-game: (vi) There is no saddle point in it and the mixed strategies are calculated as

$$\begin{array}{cc|cc|l} & & \multicolumn{2}{c}{B} & \\ & & B_1 & B_2 & \\ & & & & 6/17 \\ A & A_3 & 2 & -9 & \\ & A_4 & -7 & -1 & \\ & & & & 11/17 \\ & & 8/17 & 9/17 & \end{array}$$

and $v = (-9)\left(\frac{6}{17}\right) + (-1)\left(\frac{11}{17}\right) = -\frac{65}{17} = -3.82$

If we look at the values of all the six sub-games, we find that all of them are negative, i.e. the Player B wins and Player A looses in all the six sub-games. Thus, the Player A would like to play the safest and accordingly, he would choose that sub-game which gives the maximum value of all the six values, –3.6, –3.87, –6, –4, –3.57 and –3.82. Accordingly, Player A would play the sub-game (v) whose value is –3.57 and the strategies for A and B would be

$$\left(0,\ \frac{6}{7},\ 0,\ \frac{1}{7}\right) \text{ and } \left(\frac{3}{7}, \frac{4}{7}\right)$$

⌑ ⌑

15 Graphical Method and Dominance

An Overview

Game theory deals with decisions under uncertainty involving two or more intelligent opponents in which each opponent aspires to optimise his own decision at the expense of the other opponents. To solve the matrix of game theory, graphical method is the easiest compared to other methods such as dominance property, matrix method etc. In the graphical method, it is assumed that there is no saddle point. However, till now graphical method is restricted to $(2\times n)$ or $(m\times 2)$ matrix only.

In game theory, dominance occurs when one strategy is better than another strategy for one player, no matter how that player's opponents may play.

15.1 GRAPHICAL SOLUTION OF 2 × N GAME

Algorithm for solving $2 \times n$ matrix games is as follows:

(1) Draw two vertical axes 1 unit apart. The two lines are $x_1 = 0, x_1 = 1$

(2) Take the points of the first row in the payoff matrix on the vertical line $x_1 = 1$ and the points of the second row in the payoff matrix on the vertical line $x_1 = 0$.

(3) The point a_{1j} on axis $x_1 = 1$ is then joined to the point a_{2j} on the axis $x_1 = 0$ to give a straight line. Draw 'n' straight lines for j= 1, 2, ..., n and determine the highest point of the lower envelope obtained. This will be the **maximin point.**

(4) The two or more lines passing through the maximin point determines the required 2 × 2 payoff matrix. This in turn gives the optimum solution by making use of short-cut method.

15.2 GRAPHICAL SOLUTION OF M × 2 GAME

Algorithm for solving m × 2 matrix games is as follows:

(1) Draw two vertical axes 1 unit apart. The two lines are $x_1 = 0, x_1 = 1$.

(2) Take the points of the first row in the payoff matrix on the vertical line $x_1 = 1$ and the points of the second row in the payoff matrix on the vertical line $x_1 = 0$.

(3) The point a_{1j} on axis $x_1 = 1$ is then joined to the point a_{2j} on the axis $x_1 = 0$ to give a straight line. Draw 'n' straight lines for j= 1, 2... n and determine the lowest point of the upper envelope obtained. This will be the **minimax point.**

(4) The two or more lines passing through the minimax point determines the required 2 × 2 payoff matrix. This in turn gives the optimum solution by making use of short-cut method.

15.3 DOMINANCE PROPERTY

For a pay-off matrix of large size, the dominance property can be used to reduce its size by carefully eliminating redundant strategies (certain rows and/or columns) prior to final analysis to determine the optimum strategy to be selected by each player.

This property (or the set of rules associated with it) comes to our rescue particularly when the game does not have any saddle point because large pay-off matrices are not amenable to algebraic/arithmetic/graphical/LP treatment required to clinch the value of the game.

Rules for Dominance

(1) If all the elements of a row (say i^{th} row) of a pay-off matrix are less than or equal to the corresponding elements of the other row (say j^{th} row), then the Player A (maximising player) will never choose the ith strategy or in other words, the ith strategy is dominated by the jth strategy.

(2) If all the elements of a column (say r^{th} column) of a pay-off matrix are greater than or equal to the corresponding elements of the other column (say s^{th} column), then the Player B (minimising player) will never choose the rth strategy or in other words the rth strategy is dominated by the $s\text{-}^{th}$ strategy.

15.4 MODIFIED DOMINANCE PROPERTY

The dominance property is not always based on the inferiority of pure strategies only. Sometimes a given strategy may be inferior to a convex combination of two or more pure strategies. As a particular case, the given, strategy may be inferior to the average of two or more pure strategies. In such cases, if the given strategy is inferior to the average of two or more pure strategies, then the inferior strategy is deleted from the pay-off matrix and the size of the matrix is reduced considerably. Thus, the dominance is not only recognised in case of pure strategies but also made applicable on the basis of mixed strategies, since the average of two or more pure strategies is a case of mixed strategies. This type of dominance property is known as the modified dominance property.

Solved Practical Problems

Q1. Use graphical method to solve the following game:

		Player B			
		B_1	B_2	B_3	B_4
Player A	A_1	2	2	3	–2
	A_2	4	3	2	6

[June-2014, Q.No.-3(b)]

Ans. Since in the given matrix there is no one value which is smallest in its row and the largest in its columns, the game does not possess a saddle point. Accordingly, the player A would resort to mixed strategies.

Let the player A play the strategy A_1 with probability p and hence the strategy A_2 with probability (1 – p), since the sum of the probabilities of two strategies should be 1.

Now we calculate the Expected pay-offs for Player A, against any pure move of player B, that is, against strategies B_1, B_2, B_3 or B_4 of player B as:

B's strategy	**Expected pay-off for A**
B_1	$E_1(p) = 2p + 4(1-p) = -2p + 4$
B_2	$E_2(p) = 2p + 3(1-p) = -p + 3$
B_3	$E_3(p) = 3p + 2(1-p) = p + 2$
B_4	$E_4(p) = -2p + 6(1-p) = -8p + 6$

Now we plot the graphs of E_1, E_2, E_3 and E_4 against p. For this, we draw two vertical parallel lines at unit distance apart and mark a scale on each of them. The two lines A_1 and A_2 represent A's strategies A_1 and A_2 respectively and the distance between these lines has been taken as unity because the value of the probability cannot exceed 1. We draw lines to represent each of B's strategies.

Now, taking $E_1(p) = -2p + 4$

If p = 0, then $E_1(0) = 4$ (point on A_2 – axis)

If p = 1, then $E_1(1) = 2$ (point on A_1 – axis)

Now, taking $E_2(p) = -p + 3$

If p = 0, then $E_2(0) = 3$ (point on A_2 – axis)

If p = 1, then $E_2(1) = 2$ (point on A_1 – axis)

Now, taking $E_3(p) = p + 2$

If $p = 0$, then $E_3(0) = 2$ (point on A_2 – axis)

If $p = 1$, then $E_3(1) = 3$ (point on A_1 – axis)

Now, taking $E_4(p) = -8p + 6$

If $p = 0$, then $E_4(0) = 6$ (point on A_2 – axis)

If $p = 1$, then $E_4(1) = -2$ (point on A_1 – axis)

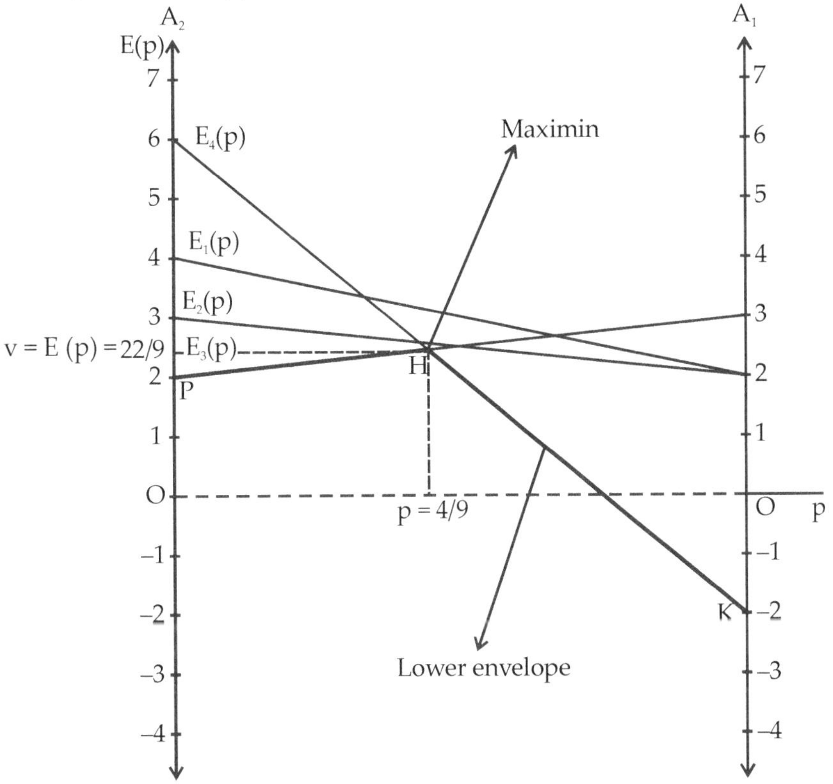

A_2 A_1
E(p)
$E_4(p)$
Maximin
$E_1(p)$
$E_2(p)$
v = E (p) = 22/9 $E_3(p)$
H
P
O
p = 4/9
O p
K
Lower envelope

The lower envelope is shown by the dark line PHK and the highest point H gives the maximum of the minimum pay-offs. H is the intersection of the lines $E_3(p)$ and $E_4(p)$, which corresponds to the matrix

$$\begin{array}{cc} & \begin{array}{cc} & B \\ & \begin{array}{cc} B_3 & B_4 \end{array} \end{array} \\ A & \begin{array}{c} A_1 \\ A_2 \end{array} \begin{bmatrix} 3 & -2 \\ 2 & 6 \end{bmatrix} \end{array} \quad \ldots(i)$$

Now the game can be solved with the help of short-cut method.

Step 1: Subtracting the pay-off's

$$A\quad \begin{array}{c} \\ A_1 \\ A_2 \\ \\ \end{array} \overset{\displaystyle B}{\begin{array}{cc} B_3 & B_4 \\ \left[\begin{array}{c} 3 \\ 2 \end{array}\right. & \left.\begin{array}{c} -2 \\ 6 \end{array}\right] \\ 3-2 & 6-(-2) \\ =1 & =8 \end{array}} \begin{array}{c} \\ 3-(-2)=5 \\ 6-2=4 \\ \\ \end{array}$$

Step 2: Interchanging the pairs

$$A\quad \begin{array}{c} \\ A_1 \\ A_2 \\ \\ \end{array} \overset{\displaystyle B}{\begin{array}{cc} B_3 & B_4 \\ \left[\begin{array}{c} 3 \\ 2 \end{array}\right. & \left.\begin{array}{c} -2 \\ 6 \end{array}\right] \\ 8 & 1 \end{array}} \begin{array}{c} \\ 4 \\ 5 \\ \\ \end{array}$$

Step 3: Putting the pairs over their sum

$$A\quad \begin{array}{c} \\ A_1 \\ A_2 \\ \\ \end{array} \overset{\displaystyle B}{\begin{array}{cc} B_3 & B_4 \\ \left[\begin{array}{c} 3 \\ 2 \end{array}\right. & \left.\begin{array}{c} -2 \\ 6 \end{array}\right] \\ 8/9 & 1/9 \end{array}} \begin{array}{c} \\ 4/9 \\ 5/9 \\ \\ \end{array}$$

Step 4: Value of the game

$$v = 3\left(\frac{4}{9}\right) + 2\left(\frac{5}{9}\right)$$

$$\Rightarrow \quad v = \frac{12}{9} + \frac{10}{9}$$

$$\Rightarrow \quad v = \frac{22}{9}$$

Thus, the strategies for B are given by

$$S_B = \begin{bmatrix} B_1 & B_2 & B_3 & B_4 \\ 0 & 0 & \frac{8}{9} & \frac{1}{9} \end{bmatrix}$$

and A's strategies are given by

$$S_A = \begin{bmatrix} A_1 & A_2 \\ 4/9 & 5/9 \end{bmatrix}$$

Note: This game (i) could be solved directly by equating the two values of E_3 and E_4 since the point H is the intersection of lines E_3 and E_4, as

$$E_3(p) = E_4(p)$$

$$\Rightarrow \quad p + 2 = -8p + 6 \qquad \Rightarrow 9p = 4 \qquad \Rightarrow p = \frac{4}{9}$$

Thus, $1 - p = 1 - \frac{4}{9} = \frac{5}{9}$

Hence, value of the game $v = 3\left(\frac{4}{9}\right) + 2\left(\frac{5}{9}\right) = \frac{22}{9}$

Hence, strategies for plays A

$$S_A = \begin{bmatrix} A_1 & A_2 \\ \frac{4}{9} & \frac{5}{9} \end{bmatrix}$$

Strategies B_3 and B_4 for players B could be found out by considering the probability of B_3 as q and thus the probability of B_4 as (1-q) and by finding the minimum of the maximum expected pay-off to player B. Accordingly, if the player A selects the strategy A_1 and plays with it throughout the game then the player B's expected pay-off will be

$3q + (-2)(1 - q)$

and similarly if the player A selects the strategy A_2 and plays with it throughout the game, the expected pay-off to player B will be

$2q + 6(1 - q)$

Equating the two pay-offs, we have

$3q + (-2)(1 - q) = 2q + 6(1 - q)$

$3q - 2 + 2q = 2q + 6 - 6q$

$3q + 2q - 2q + 6q = 6 + 2$

$\Rightarrow \quad 9q = 8 \quad \Rightarrow q = \frac{8}{9}$

Thus, $1 - q = 1 - \frac{8}{9} = \frac{1}{9}$

Hence, we have

$$S_B = \begin{bmatrix} B_1 & B_2 & B_3 & B_4 \\ 0 & 0 & \frac{8}{9} & \frac{1}{9} \end{bmatrix}$$

Q2. Solve (a particular case of a game of order m × 2) a game of order 4 × 2

		B	
		B_1	**B_2**
A	**A_1**	**2**	**1**
	A_2	**1**	**0**
	A_3	**0**	**3**
	A_4	**–2**	**2**

by the graphical method.

Ans. Since there is no saddle point in the game, the Player B would resort to mixed strategies. Let the Player B play the strategy B_1 with probability q and hence the strategy B_2 with probability (1–q).

Now the expected pay-offs for Player B for any pure strategy of Player A i.e. for any one of the pure strategies A_1, A_2, A_3, A_4 of Player A would be given by:

A's strategy	**Expected pay-off for B**
A_1	$E_1(q) = 2q + 1(1-q) = q + 1$
A_2	$E_2(q) = 1.q + 0(1-q) = q$
A_3	$E_3(q) = 0.q + 3(1-q) = 3 - 3q$
A_4	$E_4(q) = -2.q + 2(1-q) = -4q + 2$

Now we plot the graphs of $E_1(q)$, $E_2(q)$, $E_3(q)$ and $E_4(q)$ against q.

As in the case of game of order 2 × 4, we draw two vertical parallel lines called B_1 and B_2 at a unit distance and draw the graphs of E_1, E_2, E_3 and E_4 against q as has been drawn in the case of $E_1(p)$, $E_2(p)$ etc. against p.

Now for mixed strategies the Player B should follow the minimax principle and select the value of q in such a way that he gets the minimum of his maximum expected pay-offs. The upper boundary of the lines E_1, E_2, E_3 and E_4 i.e. the upper envelope will give the maximum expected pay-offs and the lowest point on this upper envelope, will then give the minimum value of the maximum expected pay-offs. In the graph, the upper envelope is shown by thick line KLM and the lowest point L (the point of intersection of E_1 and E_3) gives the minimum value of the maximum pay-offs of B, the point L corresponds to the matrix

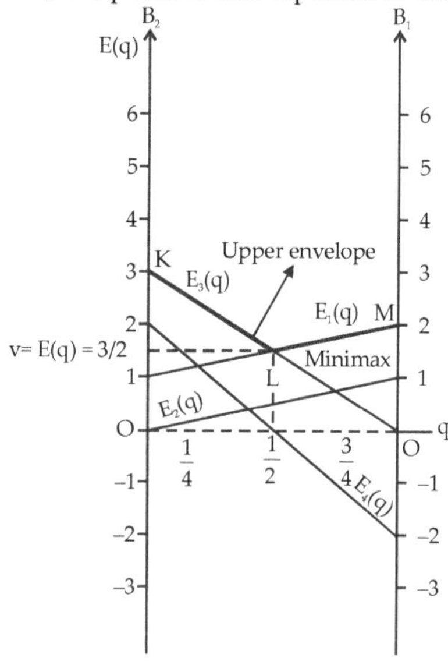

$$\begin{array}{cc} & B \\ & \begin{array}{cc} B_1 & B_2 \end{array} \\ A \begin{array}{c} A_1 \\ A_3 \end{array} & \begin{bmatrix} 2 & 1 \\ 0 & 3 \end{bmatrix} \end{array}$$

Thus, we have reduced the size of the game from 4 × 2 to that of 2 × 2 and the game could now be solved by the short-cut method. The mixed strategies for player B and A are given by

$$S_B \begin{bmatrix} B_1 & B_2 \\ \frac{1}{2} & \frac{1}{2} \end{bmatrix} \text{ and } S_A = \begin{bmatrix} A_1 & A_2 & A_3 & A_4 \\ \frac{3}{4} & 0 & \frac{1}{4} & 0 \end{bmatrix}$$

and value of the game $v = 0.\frac{2}{4} + 3.\frac{2}{4} = \frac{6}{4} = \frac{3}{2}$

Q3. Consider the following game and reduce the pay-off matrix by applying the principle of dominance:

	Player B				
Player A	**B_1**	**B_2**	**B_3**	**B_4**	**B_5**
A_1	3	5	4	9	6
A_2	5	6	3	7	8
A_3	8	7	9	8	7
A_4	4	2	8	5	3

Ans. The game has a saddle point at (A_3, B_2) and the value of the game is 7. However, we shall reduce the pay-off matrix by applying the principle of dominance. If we look at the columns of the given pay-off matrix, we observe that the elements of the fourth column are greater than or equal to the corresponding elements of the first column and also the elements of the fifth column are greater than or equal to the corresponding elements of the second column. Hence, by applying the principle of dominance, the fourth column and the fifth column being inferior strategies can be deleted and the pay-off matrix reduces to

	Player B		
Player A	B_1	B_2	B_3
A_1	3	5	4
A_2	5	6	3
A_3	8	7	9
A_4	4	2	8

Again, we observe that the elements of the first, second and the fourth rows are less than the corresponding elements of the third row.

Thus, the third row dominates all the other three rows and accordingly the first, second and fourth rows are deleted.

The pay-off matrix reduces to

$$\text{Player A} \quad \begin{array}{c} \\ A_3 \end{array} \overset{\text{Player B}}{\begin{array}{ccc} B_1 & B_2 & B_3 \\ \end{array}} \begin{bmatrix} 8 & 7 & 9 \end{bmatrix}$$

Again, the elements of the first column and the third column are greater than the corresponding elements of the second column. Thus, the second column dominates the first and the third column. The first and the third columns are deleted and we are left with the matrix

$$\text{Player A} \quad A_3 \overset{\substack{\text{Player B} \\ B_2}}{\begin{bmatrix} 7 \end{bmatrix}}$$

Thus, the solution of the game is given by

(i) Player A should play with strategy A_3.

(ii) Player B should play with strategy B_2, and

(iii) The value of the game is 7.

Q4. The following pay-off matrix is given for the two firms A and B. Use the dominance property to find the best mixed strategies for both the firms and find out the value of the game.

$$\textbf{Firm A} \quad \begin{array}{c} A_1 \\ A_2 \\ A_3 \end{array} \overset{\substack{\textbf{Firm B} \\ B_1 \quad B_2 \quad B_3}}{\begin{bmatrix} 60 & 50 & 40 \\ 70 & 70 & 50 \\ 80 & 60 & 75 \end{bmatrix}}$$

Ans. The given game has no saddle point. If we look at the columns of the pay-off matrix, it is observed that the elements of the first column are greater or equal to the corresponding elements of the second column, thus the first column is dominated by the second column and we are left with the matrix

$$\text{Firm A} \quad \begin{array}{c} A_1 \\ A_2 \\ A_3 \end{array} \overset{\substack{\text{Firm B} \\ B_2 \quad B_3}}{\begin{bmatrix} 50 & 40 \\ 70 & 50 \\ 60 & 75 \end{bmatrix}}$$

Again, the elements of the first row are less than the corresponding elements of the second and third rows, hence the first row is deleted from the matrix and we are left with a matrix of order 2 × 2 as given below

$$\text{Firm A}\;\begin{matrix} \\ A_2 \\ A_3\end{matrix}\overset{\text{Firm B}}{\begin{matrix} B_2 & B_3 \\ \end{matrix}}\!\!\!\!\!\!\!\!\begin{bmatrix} 70 & 50 \\ 60 & 75 \end{bmatrix}$$

The game can now be solved with the help of short-cut method as:

Step 1: Subtracting the pay-offs

$$\begin{array}{cccc} & & \text{Firm B} & \\ & B_2 & B_3 & \\ \text{Firm A}\quad A_2 & 70 & 50 & 70-50=20 \\ \phantom{\text{Firm A}}\quad A_3 & 60 & 75 & 75-60=15 \\ & 70-60 & 75-50 & \\ & =10 & =25 & \end{array}$$

Step 2: Interchanging the pairs and putting the pairs over their sums and simplifying

$$\begin{array}{cccc} & & \text{Firm B} & \\ & B_2 & B_3 & \\ \text{Firm A}\quad A_2 & 70 & 50 & \dfrac{15}{15+20}=\dfrac{3}{7} \\ \phantom{\text{Firm A}}\quad A_3 & 60 & 75 & \dfrac{20}{15+20}=\dfrac{4}{7} \\ & \dfrac{25}{10+25} & \dfrac{10}{10+25} & \\ & =\dfrac{5}{7} & =\dfrac{2}{7} & \end{array}$$

Thus, the optimal mixed strategies for the firms A and B are given by

$$S_A = \begin{bmatrix} A_1 & A_2 & A_3 \\ 0 & \frac{3}{7} & \frac{4}{7} \end{bmatrix} \text{ and } S_B = \begin{bmatrix} B_1 & B_2 & B_3 \\ 0 & \frac{5}{7} & \frac{2}{7} \end{bmatrix}$$

and the value of the game $v = 50 \times \frac{3}{7} + 75 \times \frac{4}{7} = \frac{450}{7}$.

Q5. Using the principle of dominance, solve the game whose pay-off matrix is given below:

Player B

Player A	B_1	B_2	B_3	B_4
A_1	4	3	5	1
A_2	4	5	3	5
A_3	5	3	5	1
A_4	1	5	1	9

[June-2014, Q.No.-4(a)]

Ans. The game does not possess the saddle point. The elements of the first row are less than or equal to the corresponding elements of the third row, hence the first row is dominated by the third row, and the game is reduced to

Player B

		B_1	B_2	B_3	B_4
	A_2	4	5	3	5
Player A	A_3	5	3	5	1
	A_4	1	5	1	9

Further, the elements of the first column are greater than or equal to the corresponding elements of the third column. Hence, the first column is dominated by the third column and the matrix is reduced to

Player B

		B_2	B_3	B_4
	A_2	5	3	5
Player A	A_3	3	5	1
	A_4	5	1	9

Now in this matrix, no row or column dominates its another row or column. Therefore, we use modified dominance property. In the above matrix the convex combination of the elements (average of the elements) of the second and third column are $\left[\frac{3+5}{2}, \frac{5+1}{2}, \frac{1+9}{2}\right]$, i.e. [4, 3, 5], and the elements so obtained are less than or equal to the corresponding element of the first column. Therefore, the player B would prefer to play the convex combination of B_3 and B_4 in comparison to his strategy B_2. Accordingly, strategy B_2 is deleted and the game is reduced to

Player B

		B_3	B_4
	A_2	3	5
Player A	A_3	5	1
	A_4	1	9

Again, the convex combination (the average of the elements) of A_3 and A_4 is given by

$$\left[\frac{5+1}{2}, \frac{1+9}{2}\right] \text{ i.e. } [3, 5]$$

Thus, the elements of the first row are equal to the corresponding elements of the average of A_3 and A_4 strategies and accordingly player A would prefer to play the convex combination of A_3 and A_4 and as such strategy A_2 is deleted and we are left with 2×2 matrix.

		Player B	
		B_3	B_4
Player A	A_3	5	1
	A_4	1	9

Now, we will solve it by short cut method.

Step 1:

		Player B		
		B_3	B_4	
Player A	A_3	5	1	5–1=4
	A_4	1	9	9–1=8
		5 – 1 = 4	9 – 1 = 8	

Step 2:

		Player B		
		B_3	B_4	
Player A	A_3	5	1	8
	A_4	1	9	4
		8	4	

Step 3:

		Player B		
		B_3	B_4	
Player A	A_3	5	1	8/12 = 2/3
	A_4	1	9	4/12 = 1/3
		8/12 = 2/3	4/12 = 1/3	

Step 4: Value of the game

$$v = 5\left(\frac{2}{3}\right) + 1\left(\frac{1}{3}\right) = \frac{11}{3}$$

The optimal strategies are given by

$$\begin{bmatrix} A_1 & A_2 & A_3 & A_4 \\ 0 & 0 & \frac{2}{3} & \frac{1}{3} \end{bmatrix} \text{ and } \begin{bmatrix} B_1 & B_2 & B_3 & B_4 \\ 0 & 0 & \frac{2}{3} & \frac{1}{3} \end{bmatrix}$$

Q6. Reduce following two person zero sum game to 2 × 2 game using principle of dominance. And hence solve the game.

		Player B	
		B_1	B_2
Player A	A_1	1	–3
	A_2	3	5
	A_3	–1	6
	A_4	4	1
	A_5	2	2
	A_6	–5	0

[Dec-2014, Q.No.-2(a)]

Ans. The given game does not have the saddle point. The elements of first row are less than the corresponding elements of the second row. Hence, first row is dominated by second row. Thus, we have the reduced game as follows:

$$\text{Player A}\quad \begin{array}{c} \\ A_2 \\ A_3 \\ A_4 \\ A_5 \\ A_6 \end{array}\overset{\text{Player B}}{\begin{array}{cc} B_1 & B_2 \\ \left[\begin{matrix} 3 & 5 \\ -1 & 6 \\ 4 & 1 \\ 2 & 2 \\ -5 & 0 \end{matrix}\right. & \left.\right] \end{array}}$$

Fifth row is dominated by fourth row. Hence, we have

$$\text{Player A}\quad \begin{array}{c} \\ A_2 \\ A_3 \\ A_4 \\ A_5 \end{array}\overset{\text{Player B}}{\begin{array}{cc} B_1 & B_2 \\ \left[\begin{matrix} 3 & 5 \\ -1 & 6 \\ 4 & 1 \\ 2 & 2 \end{matrix}\right. & \left.\right] \end{array}}$$

Now, fourth row is dominated by first row, hence, we have

$$\text{Player A}\quad \begin{array}{c} \\ A_2 \\ A_3 \\ A_4 \end{array}\overset{\text{Player B}}{\begin{array}{cc} B_1 & B_2 \\ \left[\begin{matrix} 3 & 5 \\ -1 & 6 \\ 4 & 1 \end{matrix}\right. & \left.\right] \end{array}}$$

Now, in this matrix, no row or column dominates its another row or column. Moreover, the modified dominance property also does not help us to reduce the size of the game. Therefore, we use the graphical method.

Let the player B plays the strategy B_1 with probability q and hence the strategy B_2 with probability (1 – q). Now, we have

A's strategy	Expected pay-off for B
A_2	$E_2(q) = 3q + 5(1-q) = -2q + 5$
A_3	$E_3(q) = -1(q) + 6(1-q) = -7q + 6$
A_4	$E_4(q) = 4q + 1(1-q) = 3q + 1$

Taking, $E_2(q) = -2q + 5$

If $q = 0$, then $E_2(0) = 5$ (point on B_2 – axis)

If $q = 1$, then $E_2(1) = 3$ (point on B_1 – axis)

Now, we have $E_3(q) = -7q + 6$

then $E_3(0) = 6$ and $E_3(1) = -1$

Now, $E_4(q) = 3q + 1$

$\Rightarrow \quad E_4(0) = 1$ and $E_4(1) = 4$

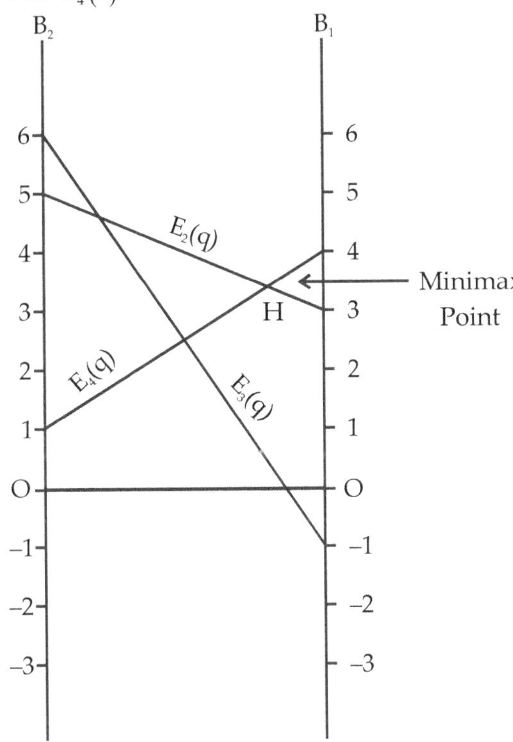

In this graph, H is the minimax point. Hence, we have the reduced matrix as follows:

$$\text{Player A} \quad \begin{array}{c} \\ A_2 \\ A_4 \end{array} \overset{\text{Player B}}{\begin{array}{cc} B_1 & B_2 \\ \end{array}} \hspace{-4em} \begin{array}{c} \\ \begin{bmatrix} 3 & 5 \\ 4 & 1 \end{bmatrix} \end{array}$$

Applying the short-cut method, we have

$$\begin{array}{cc} & \text{Player B} \\ & \begin{array}{cc} B_1 & B_2 \end{array} \\ \text{Player A} \begin{array}{c} A_2 \\ \\ A_4 \end{array} & \begin{bmatrix} 3 & 5 \\ & \\ 4 & 1 \end{bmatrix} \begin{array}{c} \frac{3}{5} \\ \\ \frac{2}{5} \end{array} \\ & \begin{array}{cc} \frac{4}{5} & \frac{1}{5} \end{array} \end{array}$$

Value of the game $v = 3 \times \frac{3}{5} + 4 \times \frac{2}{5} = \frac{9}{5} + \frac{8}{5} = \frac{17}{5}$

The optimal mixed strategies are as follows:

$$S_A = \begin{bmatrix} A_1 & A_2 & A_3 & A_4 & A_5 & A_6 \\ 0 & \frac{3}{5} & 0 & \frac{2}{5} & 0 & 0 \end{bmatrix}, \quad S_B = \begin{bmatrix} B_1 & B_2 \\ \frac{4}{5} & \frac{1}{5} \end{bmatrix}$$

⌑ ⌑

16 Games and Linear Programming

An Overview

This relationship between linear programming and games was first pointed out by J. von Neumann in the fall of 1947 in informal discussions with the author. He showed that the central mathematical problem associated with a matrix game could be stated as a linear programme and he conjectured that the converse was true. A. W. Tucker and his groups at Princeton in early-1948 undertook a systematic study of the interrelations between the two fields in order to place the theory on a rigorous foundation [Gale, Kuhn, and Tucker, 1951-1]. It is the purpose of this chapter to bring out these connections.

Game theory is concerned with finding the best "strategies" for solving conflict situations. In the abstract, these may be characterised as situations where the participants of the contest each control some but not all the actions that can take place. This, together with chance events (if present), determines the outcome upon which the participants may place widely differing values.

16.1 ALGEBRAIC METHOD WHEN THE PAY-OFF IS A SQUARE MATRIX

If the pay-off matrix is of order 4 × 4, then the problem is to determine 4 probabilities p_1, p_2, p_3, p_4 for player A with which he must mix his 4 pure strategies to get the mixed strategies and also 4 probabilities q_1, q_2, q_3, q_4 for Player B with which he should mix his 4 pure strategies to get the mixed strategies.

16.2 REDUCING THE RECTANGULAR MATRIX GAME TO THAT OF A LINEAR PROGRAMMING PROBLEM (LINEAR PROGRAMMING METHOD)

A two person zero-sum game can also be solved by linear programming approach. The major advantage of using linear programming technique is that it solves mixed strategy of any size.

To illustrate the connection between a game problem and linear programming we consider (m × n) pay off matrix (a_{ij}) for player A.

$$\text{Let } S_A = \begin{bmatrix} A_1 & \cdots & A_m \\ p_1 & \cdots & p_m \end{bmatrix} \text{ and } S_B = \begin{bmatrix} B_1 & \cdots & B_n \\ q_1 & \cdots & q_n \end{bmatrix}$$

be the optimum strategies for player A and player B respectively.

$$\text{Then, } \sum_{i=1}^{m} p_i = \sum_{j=1}^{n} q_i = 1$$

Then, the expected gains $g_j(j = 1,...,n)$ of player A against B's pure strategies will be

$$g_1 = a_{11}p_1 + a_{21}p_2 + ... + a_{m1}\ p_m$$
$$g_2 = a_{12}p_1 + a_{22}p_2 + ... + a_{m2}\ p_m$$
$$\vdots$$
$$g_m = a_{1n}p_1 + a_{2n}p_2 + ... + a_{mn}\ p_m$$

and the expected loss $l_i(i = 1,...,n)$ of player B against A's pure strategies will be

$$l_1 = a_{11}q_1 + a_{21}q_2 + ... + a_{1n}\ q_n$$
$$l_2 = a_{12}q_1 + a_{22}q_2 + ... + a_{2n}\ q_n$$
$$\vdots$$
$$l_n = a_{m1}q_1 + a_{m2}q_2 + ... + a_{mn}\ q_n$$

The objective of player A is to select $p_i(i = 1,2,...,m)$ such that he can maximise his minimum expected gains and the player B desires to select $q_j(j = 1,2,...,n)$ that will minimise his expected loss.

Thus, if we let $\quad u = \min_j \sum_{i=1}^{m} a_{ij}\ p_i \quad (j = 1, 2, ... n)$

and, $\quad v = \max_i \sum_{j=1}^{n} a_{ij}\ q_j \quad (i = 1, 2, ... m)$

The problem of two players could be written as

Player A: Maximise u = minimise $\frac{1}{u} = \sum_{i=1}^{m} \frac{p_i}{u}$

subject to the constraints

$$\sum_{i=1}^{m} a_{ij}\, p_i \geq u \text{ and } \sum p_i = 1$$

$$p_i \geq 0 \qquad (i = 1, 2, ..., m)$$

Player B: Minimise v = maximise $\frac{1}{v} = \sum_{j=1}^{n} \frac{q_j}{v}$

subject to the constraints

$$\sum_{j=1}^{n} a_{ij}\, q_j \leq v \text{ and } \sum q_j = 1$$

$$q_j \geq 0 \qquad (j = 1, 2, ..., n)$$

Assuming u > 0, v > 0, introduce a new variable defined by $p_i^1 = \frac{p_i}{u}$ and $q_j^1 = \frac{q_j}{v}$, where i = 1, 2, ..., m, j = 1, 2, ..., n

Then, the pair of linear programming problem can be rewritten as

Player A: Minimise $p_0 = p_1^1 + p_2^1 + ... + p_m^1$

subject to $\quad a_{1j}\, p_1^1 + a_{2j}\, p_2^1 + ... + a_{mj}\, p_m^1 \geq 1$

$\quad p_i^1 \geq 0$ (i = 1 to m and j = 1 to n)

Player B: Maximise $q_0 = q_1^1 + ... + q_n^1$

subject to constraints $\quad a_{i1}\, q_1^1 + a_{i2}\, q_2^1 + ... + a_{in}\, q_n^1 \leq 1$

$\quad q_j^1 \geq 0$ (i = 1 to m, j = 1 to n)

Note that the LPPs of the 2 players represent a primal dual pair. Therefore, by fundamental theorem of duality one can read the optimum solution of one player, just from the optimum simplex table of the opponent. That is, solve one player's LPP.

Remark: In case there are negative elements in the pay off matrix add a suitable constant, then value of the game = value of the game – constant.

16.3 IMPORTANT PROPERTIES OF OPTIMAL MIXED STRATEGIES

There are three important properties of Optimal Mixed Strategies:

(1) If one of the two players adheres to his optimal mixed strategy and the other player deviates from his optimal strategy, then the deviating player can only decrease his yield and cannot increase it in any case. At the most, the yield may equal the value of the game.

(2) If one of the two players adheres to his optimal strategy, then the value of the game does not alter if the other player uses his supporting strategies either singly or in any mixture.

Proof: Let $g_1, g_2, g_3, \ldots, g_m$ be the pay-offs (gains) of Player A, when he uses his optimal mixed strategy and Player B uses his pure supporting strategies $B_1, B_2, B_3, \ldots, B_n$ respectively. Now as B uses his pure strategies with probabilities $y_1^*, y_2^*, y_3^*, \ldots, y_n^*$ (B's optimal strategies), then we have

$$v = g_1 y_1^* + g_2 y_2^* + g_3 y_3^* + \ldots + g_n y_n^* \qquad \ldots(i)$$

In objective of player B is to minimise his loss,

therefore, $v = g_1 y_1^* + \ldots + g_n y_n^* = \underset{y_1, \ldots, y_n}{\text{Min}} \left[g_1 y_1 + \ldots + g_n y_n\right]$.

In particular for different values of k = 1, ..., n, if we set $y_j = 0 \ \forall \ j \neq k$ and $y_k = 1$, we have $v \leq g_k$, k = 1, ..., n ...(ii)

Thus if player b selects any other mixed strategy $(y_1, \ldots, y_n)$, then from Eq. (ii), we have $\sum_{k=1}^{n} y_k g_k \geq v \sum_{k=1}^{n} y_k$

i.e., $y_1 g_1 + \ldots + y_n g_n \geq v$ showing that the Player B cannot decrease his loss.

Similarly, we can show that the result holds if B adheres to his optimal strategy.

(3) If a fixed number C is added to each element of the pay-off matrix, the optimal strategies remain unchanged while the value of the game increases by C.

Proof: Let the pay-off matrix be $(a_{ij})_{m \times n}$ and let a fixed number C be added to each element of the pay-off matrix. Thus, the element a_{ij} becomes $(a_{ij} + C)$.

Now if $E_1(x, y)$ be the pay-off function for the original pay-off matrix $(a_{ij})_{m \times n}$, then

$$E_1(x, y) = \sum_{i=1}^{m} \sum_{j=1}^{n} x_i a_{ij} y_j$$

and if $E_2(x, y)$ be the pay-off function for the new pay-off matrix $(a_{ij} + C)_{m \times n}$ then

$$E_2(x, y) = \sum_{i=1}^{m} \sum_{j=1}^{n} x_i (a_{ij} + C) y_j$$

$$= \sum_{i=1}^{m} \sum_{j=1}^{n} x_i a_{ij} y_i + C \sum_{i=1}^{m} \sum_{j=1}^{n} x_i y_j$$

$$= E_1(x, y) + C.1 \qquad \left[\because \sum_{i=1}^{m} x_i = \sum_{j=1}^{n} y_j = 1\right]$$

Thus, addition of C does not change the nature of $E_1(x,y)$. Therefore, the optimal strategies for the two games, are the same.

So,

$$\underset{x}{\text{Min}}\ E_2(x,y) = \underset{x}{\text{Min}}\left(E_1(x,y)+C\right)$$

$$= \underset{x}{\text{Min}}\ E_1(x,y)+C$$

$$\underset{y}{\text{Max}}\ \underset{x}{\text{Min}}\, E_2(x,y) = \underset{y}{\text{Max}}\ \underset{x}{\text{Min}}\, E_1(x,y)+C$$

Similarly, we have

$$\underset{y}{\text{Min}}\ \underset{x}{\text{Max}}\ E_2(x,y) = \underset{y}{\text{Min}}\ \underset{x}{\text{Max}}\, E_1(x,y)+C$$

So, $v_2 = v_1 + C$ where v_1 is the value of the game corresponding to the matrix (a_{ij}) and v_2 is the value of the corresponding too $(a_{ij}+C)$.

Also, if x*, y* are the optimal strategies for two games, then

$$E_2(x^*, y^*) = E_1(x^*, y^*)+C$$

Value of the new game = v + C

Hence, the value of the game only increases by an amount C, if a fixed constant C is added to each element of the pay-off matrix.

Theorem

Theorem 1: (Fundamental Theorem of Game Theory): Let $(a_{ij})_{m\times n}$ be the pay-off matrix of a 2-person, zero sum and rectangular game. Assume that both the players play rationally. Let

$$S=\left\{(x_1, x_2,...,x_m) \mid 0\le x_i\le 1, \sum_{i=1}^{m} x_i = 1\right\}$$

be the set of mixed strategies for the maximising player and

$$T=\left\{(y_1, y_2,...,y_n) \mid 0\le y_j\le 1, \sum_{j=1}^{n} y_j = 1\right\}$$

be the set of mixed strategies for the minimising player. Then, there always exist strategies $x=(x_1^0,...,x_m^0)$ and $y_0=(y_1^0, y_2^0,...,x_n^0)$ such that

$$\underset{x\in S}{\text{Max}}\ \underset{y\in T}{\text{Min}}\ xAy^t = \underset{y\in T}{\text{Min}}\ \underset{x\in S}{\text{Max}}\ xAy^t = x^0\,Ay^{0t}$$

Solved Practical Problems

Q1. Solve the following game, by the Algebraic Method, whose pay-off matrix of order 3 × 3 is given bellow:

$$\text{Player A}\begin{matrix} \\ A_1 \\ A_2 \\ A_3 \end{matrix}\overset{\text{Player B}}{\begin{matrix} B_1 & B_2 & B_3 \\ \end{matrix}}\begin{bmatrix} -1 & 2 & 1 \\ 1 & -2 & 2 \\ 3 & 4 & -3 \end{bmatrix}$$

Ans. Let the mixed optimal strategies for players A and B be S_A and S_B respectively so that

$$S_A = \begin{bmatrix} A_1 & A_2 & A_3 \\ p_1 & p_2 & p_3 \end{bmatrix} \text{ and } S_B = \begin{bmatrix} B_1 & B_2 & B_3 \\ q_1 & q_2 & q_3 \end{bmatrix}$$

where $p_1 + p_2 + p_3 = 1, q_1 + q_2 + q_3 = 1$ and $p_i(i = 1, 2, 3) \geq 0;\ q_j(j = 1,2,3) \geq 0.$

Let v be the value of the game. The Player A now selects his strategies with probabilities $p_i(i = 1,2,3)$ that will maximise his minimum expected pay-offs (gains) for any one of B's pure strategies, while Player B selects his strategies with probabilities $q_j(j = 1,2,3)$ that will minimise his maximum expected pay-offs (losses) for any one of A's pure strategies in the pay-off matrix.

Since Player A would like to maximise his gains or would like to have the gains at least equal to the value of the game v, the expected gains of Player A against any one of the pure strategies of Player B are given by the following relations:

$$g_1 = -p_1 + p_2 + 3p_3 \geq v$$
$$g_2 = 2p_1 - 2p_2 + 4p_3 \geq v$$
$$g_3 = p_1 + 2p_2 - 3p_3 \geq v$$

Similarly, the expected pay-offs (losses) of Player B against A's any one pure strategy should be less than or at least equal to the value of the game since B would like to minimise his losses or at the most he can have the loss equal to v. Therefore,

$$l_1 = -q_1 + 2q_2 + q_3 \leq v$$
$$l_2 = q_1 - 2q_2 + 2q_3 \leq v$$
$$l_3 = 3q_1 + 4q_2 - 3q_3 \leq v$$

Now considering the above relations as strict equations, we have

$$-p_1 + p_2 + 3p_3 = v \quad \text{...(i)}$$
$$2p_1 - 2p_2 + 4p_3 = v \quad \text{...(ii)}$$

$$p_1 + 2p_2 - 3p_3 = v \quad \text{...(iii)}$$

$$-q_1 + 2q_2 + q_3 = v \quad \text{...(iv)}$$

$$q_1 - 2q_2 + 2q_3 = v \quad \text{...(v)}$$

$$3q_1 + 4q_2 - 3q_3 = v \quad \text{...(vi)}$$

$$p_1 + p_2 + p_3 = 1 \quad \text{...(vii)}$$

$$q_1 + q_2 + q_3 = 1 \quad \text{...(viii)}$$

From Eqs. (i) and (ii) and from Eqs. (ii) and (iii), we have

$$3p_1 - 3p_2 + p_3 = 0$$

and $p_1 - 4p_2 + 7p_3 = 0$

By cross multiplication and with the principle of ratio and proportion, we have

$$\frac{p_1}{-21+4} = \frac{p_2}{1-21} = \frac{p_3}{-12+3} = \frac{p_1 + p_2 + p_3}{-(17+20+9)} = \frac{1}{-46} \quad \text{(from Eq. (vii))}$$

or $\frac{p_1}{17} = \frac{p_2}{20} = \frac{p_3}{9} = \frac{1}{46}$

$\Rightarrow$ $p_1 = \frac{17}{46},\ p_2 = \frac{20}{46},\ p_3 = \frac{9}{46}$

Similarly, from Eqs. (iv) and (v) and from Eqs. (v) and (vi), we have

$$2q_1 - 4q_2 + q_3 = 0$$

and $2q_1 + 6q_2 - 5q_3 = 0$

By cross multiplication and simplification, we have

$$\frac{q_1}{20-6} = \frac{q_2}{2+10} = \frac{q_3}{12+8} = \frac{q_1 + q_2 + q_3}{14+12+20} = \frac{1}{46} \quad \text{(from Eq. (viii))}$$

$\Rightarrow$ $q_1 = \frac{14}{46}, q_2 = \frac{12}{46}$ and $q_3 = \frac{20}{46}$

Now, substituting the values of p_1, p_2 and p_3 in Eq. (i) or the values of q_1, q_2 and q_3 in Eq. (iv), we get,

$$v = -p_1 + p_2 + 3p_3 = -\frac{17}{46} + \frac{20}{46} + \frac{27}{46} = \frac{30}{46} = \frac{15}{23}$$

$$= -q_1 + 2q_2 + q_3 = -\frac{14}{46} + \frac{24}{46} + \frac{20}{46} = \frac{30}{46} = \frac{15}{23}$$

Hence the optimum mixed strategies for players A and B are given by

$$S_A = \begin{bmatrix} A_1 & A_2 & A_3 \\ \frac{17}{46} & \frac{20}{46} & \frac{9}{46} \end{bmatrix} \text{ and } S_B = \begin{bmatrix} B_1 & B_2 & B_3 \\ \frac{14}{46} & \frac{12}{46} & \frac{20}{46} \end{bmatrix}$$

The value of the game $v = \frac{15}{23}$.

Q2. For the following pay-off matrix, transform the zero-sum game into an equivalent linear programming problem:

		Player B		
		B_1	B_2	B_3
	A_1	1	–1	3
Player A	A_2	3	5	–3
	A_3	6	2	–2

[June-2014, Q.No.-6(b)]
[Dec-2014, Q.No.-5(b)]

Or

Transform the following zero-sum game into an equivalent linear programming problem:

	B_1	B_2	B_3
A_1	1	–1	3
A_2	3	5	–3
A_3	6	2	–2

[Dec-2015, Q.No.-4(b)]

Ans. The given game has no saddle point. The maximin value for player A is –1 and the minimax value for B is 3. Therefore, we have

Maximin value for A < value of the game < Minimax value for B

Hence, the value of the game lies between –1 and 3.

Let player A plays his strategies A_1, A_2, A_3 with probabilities p_1, p_2, p_3 and player B plays his strategies B_1, B_2, B_3 with probabilities q_1, q_2, q_3 respectively to get their optimum mixed strategies, so that

$$S_A = \begin{bmatrix} A_1 & A_2 & A_3 \\ p_1 & p_2 & p_3 \end{bmatrix} \text{ and } S_B = \begin{bmatrix} B_1 & B_2 & B_3 \\ q_1 & q_2 & q_3 \end{bmatrix}$$

such that

$$p_1 + p_2 + p_3 = 1 \text{ and } q_1 + q_2 + q_3 = 1$$

where

$$p_1 + p_2 + p_3 \geq 0$$

and $q_1 + q_2 + q_3 \geq 0$

The expected pay-offs (gains) of A, when he plays strategies A_1, A_2 and A_3 against any pure strategy B_1, B_2 and B_3 of B are given by (g_1, g_2, g_3, g_4) as follow:

$$g_1 = p_1 + 3p_2 + 6p_3$$
$$g_2 = -p_1 + 5p_2 + 2p_3$$
$$g_3 = 3p_1 - 3p_2 - 2p_3$$

where $p_1 + p_2 + p_3 = 1$

The expected pay-offs (losses) of B when he plays strategies B_1, B_2, B_3 against any pure strategy A_1, A_2 and A_3 of A, are given by (l_1, l_2, l_3) as follows:

$$l_1 = q_1 - q_2 + 3q_3$$
$$l_2 = 3q_1 + 5q_2 - 3q_3$$
$$l_3 = 6q_1 + 2q_2 - 2q_3$$

where $q_1 + q_2 + q_3 = 1$

Now, let the minimum expected gain of player A is

$$u = \min[g_1, g_2, g_3]$$

and the maximum expected loss of player B is

$$v = \max[l_1, l_2, l_3]$$

In the given game, maximin value $u = -1$ and the minimax value $v = 3$.

Now, we have

$$\frac{g_1}{u} = \frac{p_1}{u} + \frac{3p_2}{u} + \frac{6p_3}{u} \geq \frac{u}{u}$$

$$\frac{g_2}{u} = \frac{-p_1}{u} + \frac{5p_2}{u} + \frac{2p_3}{u} \geq \frac{u}{u}$$

$$\frac{g_3}{u} = \frac{3p_1}{u} - \frac{3p_2}{u} - \frac{2p_3}{u} \geq \frac{u}{u}$$

$$\frac{p_1}{u} + \frac{p_2}{u} + \frac{p_3}{u} = \frac{1}{u}$$

and

$$\frac{l_1}{v} = \frac{q_1}{v} - \frac{q_2}{v} + \frac{3q_3}{v} \leq \frac{v}{v}$$

$$\frac{l_2}{v} = \frac{3q_1}{v} + \frac{5q_2}{v} - \frac{3q_3}{v} \leq \frac{v}{v}$$

$$\frac{l_3}{v} = \frac{6q_1}{v} + \frac{2q_2}{v} - \frac{2q_3}{v} \leq \frac{v}{v}$$

$$\frac{q_1}{v} + \frac{q_2}{v} + \frac{q_3}{v} = \frac{1}{v}$$

We now define new variables

$$x_1 = \frac{p_1}{u}, x_2 = \frac{p_2}{u}, x_3 = \frac{p_3}{u}$$

and $y_1 = \frac{q_1}{v}, y_2 = \frac{q_2}{v}, y_3 = \frac{q_3}{v}$

that $x_1 + x_2 + x_3 = \frac{1}{u}$, $y_1 + y_2 + y_3 = \frac{1}{v}$

The problem of A, therefore, becomes

maximise u = minimise $\frac{1}{u} = x_1 + x_2 + x_3$

subject to

$$\left.\begin{array}{l} x_1 + 3x_2 + 6x_3 \ge 1 \\ -x_1 + 5x_2 + 2x_3 \ge 1 \\ 3x_1 - 3x_2 - 2x_3 \ge 1 \\ x_1, x_2, x_3 \ge 0 \end{array}\right\} \quad ...(i)$$

While the problem of B becomes as

minimise v = maximise $\frac{1}{v} = y_1 + y_2 + y_3$

subject to

$$\left.\begin{array}{l} y_1 - y_2 + 3y_3 \le 1 \\ 3y_1 + 5y_2 - 3y_3 \le 1 \\ 6y_1 + 2y_2 - 2y_3 \le 1 \\ y_1, y_2, y_3 \ge 0 \end{array}\right\} \quad ...(ii)$$

The problem of A given in Eq. (i) and the problem of B given in Eq. (ii) are the linear programming problems and if one is the primal, then the other is its dual.

Q3. Solve the following game by using simplex method

Player B

$$\textbf{Player A} \begin{bmatrix} 1 & -1 & 3 \\ 3 & 5 & -3 \\ 6 & 2 & -2 \end{bmatrix}$$

Ans. Since some of the entries in the pay off matrix are negative, we add a suitable constant, say c = 4 to each element.

Player B

$$\text{Player A} \begin{bmatrix} 5 & 3 & 7 \\ 7 & 9 & 1 \\ 10 & 6 & 2 \end{bmatrix}$$

Let the strategies for 2 players be

$$S_A = \begin{bmatrix} A_1 & A_2 & A_3 \\ p_1 & p_2 & p_3 \end{bmatrix}$$

$$S_B = \begin{bmatrix} B_1 & B_2 & B_3 \\ q_1 & q_2 & q_3 \end{bmatrix}$$

where $p_1 + p_2 + p_3 = 1, q_1 + q_2 + q_3 = 1$

The linear programming problem for B is

Minimise v = maximise $\frac{1}{v} = y_1 + y_2 + y_3$

subject to

$5y_1 + 3y_2 + 7y_3 \le 1,$

$7y_1 + 9y_2 + y_3 \le 1,$

$10y_1 + 6y_2 + 2y_3 \le 1,$

$y_j \ge 0, \ j = 1,2,3$ where $y_j = q_j/v, \quad j = 1, 2, 3$

Introduce slack variables $s_1 \ge 0, s_2 \ge 0, s_3 \ge 0$

Now, we have the following simples table:

Table 1

	$C_j \rightarrow$	**1**	**1**	**1**	**0**	**0**	**0**	
C_S	**Variables in the basis**	y_1	y_2	y_3	s_1	s_2	s_3	**Solution**
0	s_1	5	3	[7]	1	0	0	1 →
0	s_2	7	9	1	0	1	0	1
0	s_3	10	6	2	0	0	1	1
	$\Delta_j = Z_j - C_j$	–1	–1	–1 ↑	0	0	0	

From the above table, we observe that y_3 enters into the basis and s_1 leaves the basis. Hence, we have the following table:

Table 2

	$C_j \rightarrow$	**1**	**1**	**1**	**0**	**0**	**0**	
C_S	**Variables in the basis**	y_1	y_2	y_3	s_1	s_2	s_3	**Solution**
–1	y_3	5/7	3/7	1	1/7	0	0	1/7
0	s_2	44/7	[60/7]	0	–1/7	1	0	6/7 →
0	s_3	60/7	36/7	0	–2/7	0	1	5/7
	$\Delta_j = Z_j - C_j$	–2/7	–4/7 ↑	0	1/7	0	0	

From the above table, we observe that y_2 enters into the basis and s_2 leaves the basis. Hence, we have the following table:

Table 3

	$C_j \rightarrow$	1	1	1	0	0	0	
C_s	**Variables in the basis**	y_1	y_2	y_3	s_1	s_2	s_3	**Solution**
1	y_3	2/5	0	1	3/20	–1/20	0	1/10
1	y_2	11/15	1	0	–1/60	7/60	0	1/10
0	s_3	24/5	0	0	–1/5	–3/5	1	1/5
	$\Delta_j = Z_j - C_j$	2/5	0	0	2/15	1/15	0	1/5

Since all $Z_j - C_j \geq 0$ the current solution is optimum. Here,

$$\frac{1}{v} = \frac{1}{5} \qquad \therefore \quad v = 5$$

The value of the game = v – c = v – 4 = 5 – 4 = 1

Optimum strategies for B are

$$q_1^1 = 0,\ q_2^1 = \frac{1}{10} \times 5 = \frac{1}{2},\ q_3^1 = \frac{1}{10} \times 5 = \frac{1}{2}$$

Making use of duality, the optimum strategies for player A are obtained as

$$p_1^1 = \frac{2}{15} \times 5 = \frac{2}{3},\ p_2^1 = \frac{1}{10} \times 5 = \frac{1}{2},\ p_3^1 = 0$$

⌑ ⌑

Question Papers

Linear Programming : MTE-12

June, 2014

Note: *Question no. 1 is compulsory. Do any four questions out of question nos. 2 to 7. Calculators are not allowed.*

Q1. State which of the following statements are true and which are false. Give reasons for your answer with a short proof or counter example.

(a) A constraint in an LP problem restricts the use of available resource.

Ans. True.

A constraint in an LP problem restricts the value of objective function, value of a decision variable and the use of the available resource.

(b) When maximin value of the game is less than or equal to minimax values of the game, then saddle point exists.

Ans. False.

When maximin value of the game is equal to minimax value of the game, then saddle point exists.

(c) The solution to a transportation problem with m-rows (supplies) and n-columns (destinations) is feasible if number of positive allocations are m + n.

Ans. False.

The solution to a transportation problem with m-rows (supplies) and n-columns (destinations) is feasible if number of positive allocations are (m + n) – 1.

(d) $S = \{(x, y) : 2x + y \le 4 \text{ or } x + 2y \le 4\}$ **is a convex set.**

Ans. Same as Chapter-2, Q.No.-9 [Solved Practical Problem]

(e) If the dual LPP is unbounded, then the primal LPP is bounded.

Ans. False.

If the primal LPP has feasible solution as well as the bounded optimal solution then by the fundamental theorem of duality, the dual LPP has also a feasible solution. But this contradicts the hypothesis that the dual has not feasible solution. Hence, the primal can not have a bounded optimal solution.

Q2. (a) A dairy firm has three plants located in a state. The daily milk production at each plant is as follows:

Plant 1: 6 thousand litres

Plant 2: 1 thousand litres

Plant 3: 10 thousand litres

Each day, the firm must fulfil the needs of its four distribution centres. Minimum requirement at each centre is as follows:

Distribution centre 1: 7 thousand litres

Distribution centre 2: 5 thousand litres

Distribution centre 3: 3 thousand litres

Distribution centre 4: 2 thousand litres

Cost in hundreds of rupees of shipping one thousand litres from each plant to each distribution centre is given in the following table:

		Distribution Centre			
		D_1	D_2	D_3	D_4
	P_1	2	3	11	7
Plant	P_2	1	0	6	1
	P_3	5	8	15	9

Find initial basic feasible solution for the given problem by using North-West corner method, and Matrix-Minima method. Which of the two solutions is better? Justify your answer.

Ans. Refer to Chapter-10, Q.No.-6 [Solved Practical Problem]

(b) Obtain the dual problem of the following primal LP problem:

Miniimise $z = x_1 - 3x_2 - 2x_3$

subject to $3x_1 - x_2 + 2x_3 \leq 7$

$2x_1 - 4x_2 \geq 12$

$-4x_1 + 3x_2 + 8x_3 = 10$

$x_1, x_2 \geq 0$, x_3 **unrestricted in sign.**

Your dual should have only three variables.

Ans. Refer to Chapter-7, Q.No.-3 [Solved Practical Problem]

Q3. (a) Use the simplex method to solve the following LP problem:

Maximise $z = 3x_1 + 5x_2 + 4x_3$

subject to $2x_1 + 3x_2 \leq 8$

$2x_2 + 5x_3 \leq 10$

$3x_1 + 2x_2 + 4x_3 \leq 15$

$x_1, x_2, x_3 \geq 0.$

Ans. Refer to Chapter-6, Q.No.-1 [Solved Practical Problem]

(b) **Use graphical method to solve the following game:**

		Player B			
		B_1	B_2	B_3	B_4
Player A	A_1	2	2	3	–2
	A_2	4	3	2	6

Ans. Refer to Chapter-15, Q.No.-1 [Solved Practical Problem]

Q4. (a) Using the principle of dominance, solve the game whose pay-off matrix is given below:

		Player B			
		B_1	B_2	B_3	B_4
Player A	A_1	4	3	5	1
	A_2	4	5	3	5
	A_3	5	3	5	1
	A_4	1	5	1	9

Ans. Refer to Chapter-15, Q.No.-5 [Solved Practical Problem]

(b) **Without sketching the region, check whether P (0, 0) is in the convex hull of the points A (– 1, – 1), B (1, 0) and C (0, 1). If it is in the region, write P as convex combination of A, B and C.**

Ans. Refer to Chapter-2, Q.No.-14 [Solved Practical Problem]

Q5. (a) Use the graphical method to solve the following LP problem:

Maximise $z = 2x_1 + 3x_2$

subject to $x_1 + x_2 \leq 30$

$x_2 \geq 3$

$0 \leq x_2 \leq 12$

$0 \leq x_1 \leq 20$

$x_1 - x_2 \geq 0$

Ans. Refer to Chapter-3, Q.No.-10 [Solved Practical Problem]

(b) **Solve the following cost minimisation assignment problem:**

		Job				
		P	Q	R	S	T
	A	85	75	65	125	75
	B	90	78	66	132	78
Machine	C	75	66	57	114	69
	D	80	72	60	120	72
	E	76	64	56	112	68

Ans. Same as Chapter-12, Q.No.-1 [Solved Practical Problem]

Q6. (a) A businessman has to get 5 cabinets, 12 desks and 18 shelves cleaned. He has two part-time employees, Anjali and Arnav. Anjali can clean 1 cabinet, 3 desks and 3 shelves in a day, while Arnav can clean 1 cabinet, 2 desks and 3 shelves in a day. Arnav is paid ₹22 per day and Anjali is paid ₹25 per day. Formulate the problem of finding the number of days for which Anjali and Arnav have to be employed to get the cleaning done with minimum cost as a linear programming problem.

Ans. Refer to Chapter-3, Q.No.-11 [Solved Practical Problem]

(b) For the following pay-off matrix, transform the zero-sum game into an equivalent linear programming problem:

		Player B		
		B_1	B_2	B_3
	A_1	1	–1	3
Player A	A_2	3	5	–3
	A_3	6	2	–2

Ans. Refer to Chapter-16, Q.No.-2 [Solved Practical Problem]

Q7. (a) Solve the following LP problem by using two-phase simplex method:

Minimise $z = x_1 - 2x_2 - 3x_3$

subject to $-2x_1 + 3x_2 + 3x_3 = 2$

$2x_1 + 3x_2 + 4x_3 = 1$

$x_1, x_2, x_3 \geq 0.$

Ans. Refer to Chapter-6, Q.No.-6 [Solved Practical Problem]

(b) The initial basic feasible solution of a transportation problem is given below:

	W_1	W_2	W_3	Supply
F_1	16 (180)	20	12 (20)	200
F_2	14	8 (120)	18 (40)	160
F_3	26	24	16 (90)	90
Demand	180	120	150	450

Check whether the given solution is optimal. If it is not, then find the optimal solution.

Ans. In the given TP, we have

$u_1 + v_1 = 16$, $u_2 + v_3 = 18$

$u_1 + v_3 = 12$, $u_3 + v_3 = 16$

$u_2 + v_2 = 8$

Now, taking $u_3 = 0$, we have

$v_3 = 16$

$\Rightarrow$ $u_1 = 12 - 16 = -4$

$\Rightarrow$ $v_1 = 16 + 4 = 20$

$\Rightarrow$ $u_2 = 18 - 16 = 2$

$\Rightarrow$ $v_2 = 8 - 2 = 6$

Now, we have the following table:

	W_1	W_2	W_3	Supply	$u_i \downarrow$
F_1	16 (180)	20 / $\Delta_{12} = -18$	12 (20)	200	−4
F_2	14 / 8	8 (120)	18 (40)	160	2
F_3	26 / −6	24 / −18	16 (90)	90	0
Demand	180	120	150	450	
$v_j \rightarrow$	20	6	16		

This is not optimal solution because all entries in the right bottom (i.e., Δ_{ij}) are not negative. In the above table, $\Delta_{21} = 8$ is positive.

Now, Same as Chapter-11, Q.No.-1

¤ ¤

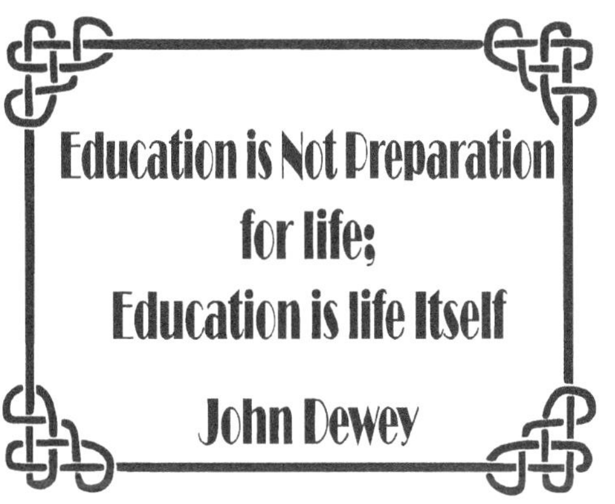

Linear Programming : MTE-12
December, 2014

Note: *Question no. 1 is compulsory. Do any four questions out of questions no. 2 to 7. Use of calculators is not allowed.*

Q1. State which of the following statements are true and which are false. Give reasons for your answer with a short proof or a counter example.

(a) The intersection of finite number of convex sets is not convex.

Ans. False. Now, Refer to Chapter 2 (Theorem 1)

(b) If value of the 2 × 2 matrix game $\begin{bmatrix} 1 & 2 \\ p & 4 \end{bmatrix}$ **is 4, then** $p \geq 4$.

Ans. True. Now, Refer to Chapter-13, Q.No.-6 [Solved Practical Problem]

(c) If 10 is added to each of the entries of the cost matrix of a 3 × 3 assignment problem, then the total cost of an optimal assignment for the changed cost matrix will increase by 10.

Ans. False. Now, Refer to Chapter-12 to Q.No.-4 [Solved Practical Problem]

(d) For maximisation LP model, the simplex method is terminated when all values $c_j - z_j \geq 0$.

Ans. False.

For maximisation LP model, the simplex method is terminated when all values $z_j - c_j \geq 0$.

(e) The dummy source or destination in a transportation problem is added to prevent solution from becoming degenerate.

Ans. False.

The dummy source or destination in a transportation problem is added to satisfy rim conditions (supply and demand condition).

Q2. (a) Reduce following two person zero sum game to 2 × 2 game using principle of dominance. And hence solve the game.

		Player B	
		B_1	B_2
Player A	A_1	1	–3
	A_2	3	5
	A_3	–1	6
	A_4	4	1
	A_5	2	2
	A_6	–5	0

Ans. Refer to Chapter-15, Q.No.-6 [Solved Practical Problem]

(b) Obtain the dual of the following primal LP problem:

Maximise $z = x_1 - 2x_2 + 3x_3$

subject to $-2x_1 + x_2 + 3x_3 = 2$

$2x_1 + 3x_2 + 4x_3 = 1$

$x_1, x_2, x_3 \geq 0$

Ans. Refer to Chapter-7, Q.No.-5 [Solved Practical Problem]

Q3. (a) A company makes two kinds of leather belts. Belt A is a high quality belt and belt B is of lower quality. The respective profits on A and B are ₹4 and ₹3 per belt. The production of each type A requires twice as much time as a belt of type B, and if all belts were of type B, the company could make 1000 belts per day. The supply of leather is sufficient for only 800 belts per day (both A and B combined). Belt A requires a fancy buckle and only 400 buckles per day are available. There are only 700 buckles a day available for belt B. What should be the daily production of each type of belt? Formulate this problem as an LP model and solve it by the graphical method.

Ans. Refer to Chapter-3, Q.No.-12 [Solved Practical Problem]

(b) Find the initial basics feasible solution of the following transportation problem using North-West Corner method.

90	90	100	110	200
50	70	130	85	50
75	100	100	30	

Ans. Refer to Chapter-11, Q.No.-4 [Solved Practical Problem]

Q4. (a) Two breakfast food manufacturers ABC and XYZ are competing for an increased market share. The pay-off matrix, shown in the following table, describes the increase in market share for ABC and decrease in market share for XYZ. Determine optimal strategies for both the manufacturers and the value of the game.

		XYZ			
		B_1	B_2	B_3	B_4
	A_1	2	–2	4	1
	A_2	6	–5	12	3
ABC	A_3	–3	–2	0	6
	A_4	2	–2	7	1

Ans. Refer to Chapter-13, Q.No.-7 [Solved Practical Problem]

(b) Find all the basic feasible solutions of the following system of linear equations:

$$2x_1 + x_2 - x_3 + 2x_4 = 2$$

$$3x_1 + 2x_2 + x_3 + 4x_4 = 3$$

$$x_1, x_2, x_3, x_4 \geq 0$$

Check if any of them is degenerate solution. Justify your answer.

Ans. Refer to Chapter-5, Q.No.-2 [Solved Practical Problem]

Q5. (a) A department has five employees with five jobs to be performed. The time (in hours) each employees will take to perform each job is given in the following matrix. How should the jobs be allocated, one per employee, so as to minimise the total man hours?

		Employees				
		I	II	III	IV	V
	A	10	5	13	15	16
	B	3	9	18	13	6
Jobs	C	10	7	2	2	2
	D	7	11	9	7	12
	E	7	9	10	4	12

Ans. Same as Chapter-12, Q.No.-1 [Solved Practical Problem]

(b) For the following pay-off matrix, transform the zero-sum game into an equivalent linear programming problem:

		Player B		
		B_1	B_2	B_3
	A_1	1	–1	3
Player A	A_2	3	5	–3
	A_3	6	2	–2

Ans. Refer to Chapter-16, Q.No.-12 [Solved Practical Problem]

Q6. (a) Using matrix - minima method, find the initial basic feasible solution of the following transportation problem:

4	6	8	8	40
6	8	6	7	60
5	7	6	8	50
20	30	50	50	

Hence find the optimal solution.

Ans. Using matrix-minima method, we have the following table:

4 (20)	6 (20)	8	8	40
6	8	6 (50)	7 (10)	60
5	7 (10)	6	8 (40)	50
20	30	50	50	

Therefore, initial basic feasible solution is

$x_{11} = 20,\ x_{12} = 20,\ x_{23} = 50,\ x_{24} = 10$

$x_{32} = 10,\ x_{34} = 40$

Now, Same as Chapter-11, Q.No.-1

(b) Check whether the following set is convex:

$S = \{(x,y) : x^2 + y^2 \leq 1, y^2 \geq x\}$

Ans. Same as Chapter-2, Q.No.-8 and Q.No.-9 [Solved Practical Problem]

Q7. (a) For what values of k are the following vectors linearly independent?

$$\begin{bmatrix}1\\2\\1\end{bmatrix}, \begin{bmatrix}1\\k\\1\end{bmatrix}, \begin{bmatrix}k\\0\\1\end{bmatrix}$$

Ans. Refer to Chapter-1, Q.No.-20 [Solved Practical Problem]

(b) Solve the following LP problem using simplex method:

Maximise $z = 6x_1 + 4x_2$

subject to $2x_1 + 3x_2 \leq 30$

$3x_1 + 2x_2 \leq 24$

$x_1 + x_2 \geq 3$

$x_1, x_2 \geq 0$

Ans. Same as Chapter-6, Q.No.-1 [Solved Practical Problem]

⌑⌑

Linear Programming : MTE-12

June, 2015

Note: *Question no. 1 is compulsory. Answer any four questions out of questions no. 2 to 7. Use of calculators is not allowed.*

Q1. Which of the following statements are true and which are false? Give a short proof or a counter-example in support of your answer.

(a) In a two-dimensional LPP solution, the objective function can assume the same value at two distinct extreme points.

Ans. True. Now, Refer to Chapter-3, Q.No.-8 [Solved Practical Problem]

(b) Both the primal and dual of an LPP can be infeasible.

Ans. True.

For example, if the primal is

Maximise $x_1 + 3x_2$

subject to $x_1 + 2x_2 = 1$

$x_1 + 2x_2 = 2$

then dual is

Minimise $y_1 + 2y_2$

subject to $y_1 + y_2 = 1$

$2y_1 + 2y_2 = 3$

Here, primal and dual are both infeasible.

(c) An unrestricted primal variable converts into an equality dual constraint.

Ans. Refer to Chapter-7, Q.No.-6 [Solved Practical Problem]

(d) In a two-person zero-sum game, if the optimal solution requires one player to use a pure strategy, the other player must do the same.

Ans. True.

In a two-person zero-sum game, if the optimal solution requires one player to use a pure strategy, the other player must do the same because the optimal solution selects one strategy for each player such that any change in the chosen strategies does not improve the payoff to either player.

(e) If 10 is added to each entry of a row in the cost matrix of an assignment problem, then the total cost of an optimal assignment for the changed cost matrix will also increase by 10.

Ans. True. Now, Refer to Chapter-12, Q.No.-4 [Solved Practical Problem]

Q2. (a) Solve the following linear programming problem using simplex method:

Maximise $z = 3x_1 + 5x_2 + 4x_3$

subject to $2x_1 + 3x_2 \leq 8$

$2x_2 + 5x_3 \leq 10$

$3x_1 + 2x_2 + 4x_3 \leq 15$

$x_1, x_2\ x_3 \geq 0$

Ans. Refer to Chapter-6, Q.No.-1 [Solved Practical Problem]

(b) Using the principle of dominance, reduce the size of the following game:

$$\begin{bmatrix} -1 & -2 & 8 \\ 7 & 5 & -1 \\ 6 & 0 & 12 \end{bmatrix}$$

Hence solve the game.

Ans. Same as Chapter-15, Q.No.-4 [Solved Practical Problem]

Q3. (a) Find all basic feasible solutions for the following set of equations:

$2x_1 + 6x_2 + 2x_3 + x_4 = 3$

$6x_1 + 4x_2 + 4x_3 + 6x_4 = 2$

$x_1, x_2, x_3, x_4 \geq 0$

Ans. Same as Chapter-5, Q.No.-12 [Solved Practical Problem]

(b) Examine convexity of the following sets:

(i) $S_1 = \{(x_1, x_2) \in R^2 \mid 4x_1 + 3x_2 \leq 6,\ x_1 + x_2 \geq 1\}$

Ans. Same as Chapter-2, Q.No.-9

(ii) $S_2 = \{(x, y) \in R^2 \mid x^2 + y^2 \geq 1\}$

Ans. Same as Chapter-2, Q.No.-8 [Solved Practical Problem]

Q4. (a) Solve the following linear programming problem by graphical method:

Maximise $z = 5x_1 + 7x_2$

subject to $x_1 + x_2 \leq 4$

$3x_1 + 8x_2 \leq 24$

$10x_1 + 7x_2 \leq 35$

$x_1, x_2 \geq 0$

Ans. Refer to Chapter-3, Q.No.-13 [Solved Practical Problem]

(b) Find the dual of the following LPP:

Maximise $z = x_1 + x_2 + x_3$

subject to $x_1 - 3x_2 + 4x_3 = 5$

$x_1 - 2x_2 \leq 3$

$2x_2 - x_3 \geq 4$

$x_1, x_2 \geq 0$ **and** x_3 **is unrestricted in sign.**

Ans. Same as Chapter-7, Q.No.-1 [Solved Practical Problem]

Q5. (a) Find the initial basic feasible solution of the following transportation problem using matrix-minima method:

		Destinations			Supply
		I	II	III	
Sources	A	2	7	4	5
	B	3	3	1	8
	C	5	4	7	7
	D	1	6	2	14
Demand		7	9	18	34

Also, find the optimal solution.

Ans. Same as Dec-2014, Q.No.-6(a) [Solved Practical Problem]

(b) Solve the following game graphically:

		Play 'B'	
		B_1	B_2
Play 'A'	I	2	7
	II	3	5
	III	11	2

Ans. Same as Chapter-15, Q.No.-2 [Solved Practical Problem]

Q6. (a) A firm manufactures two types of products, A and B, and sells them at a profit of ₹ 2 on type A and ₹ 3 on type B. Each product is processed on two machines M_1 and M_2. Type A requires one minute of processing time on M_1 and two minutes on M_2; type B requires one minute on M_1 and one minute on M_2. The machine M_1 is available for not more than 6 hours 40 minutes while machine M_2 is available for 10 hours during any working day.

Formulate the problem as LPP.

Ans. Refer to Chapter-3, Q.No.-14 [Solved Practical Problem]

(b) **Solve the following assignment problem:**

	A	B	C	D	E
I	2	9	2	7	1
II	6	8	7	6	1
III	4	6	5	3	1
IV	4	2	7	3	1
V	5	3	9	5	1

Ans. Refer to Chapter-12, Q.No.-1 [Solved Practical Problem]

Q7. (a) The following table is obtained in the intermediate stage while solving an LPP by simplex method:

	C_i's	30	23	29	0	0	
B	C_B	X_1	X_2	X_3	S_1	S_2	R.H.S.
S_1	0	0	2	–9/2	1	–3/2	31/2
X_1	30	1	1/2	5/4	0	1/4	7/4

Check whether an optimal solution of the LPP will exist or not.

Ans. Refer to Chapter-6, Q.No.-8 [Solved Practical Problem]

(b) Write the LPP model of the following transportation problem:

5	7	6	4	70
2	8	3	1	50
1	7	4	5	90
50	40	50	70	

Ans. From given TP, we have the following:

$m = 3$ $n = 4$

$a_1 = 70$ $a_2 = 50$ $a_3 = 90$

$b_1 = 50$ $b_2 = 40$ $b_3 = 50$ $b_4 = 70$

$C_{11} = 5$ $C_{12} = 7$ $C_{13} = 6$ $C_{14} = 4$

$C_{21} = 2$ $C_{22} = 8$ $C_{23} = 3$ $C_{24} = 1$

$C_{31} = 1$ $C_{32} = 7$ $C_{33} = 4$ $C_{34} = 5$

Now, Same as Chapter-9, Q.No.-1

(c) **Find the range of values of p and q which will render the entry (2, 2), a saddle point for the following game:**

Player B

Player A	2	4	5
	10	7	q
	4	p	6

Ans. Refer to Chapter-13, Q.No.-8 [Solved Practical Problem]

⌑ ⌑

Linear Programming : MTE-12

December, 2015

Note: *Question no. 1 is compulsory. Attempt any four questions out of questions no. 2 to 7. Use of calculators is not allowed.*

Q1. Which of the following statements are true and which are false? Give a short proof or a counter-example in support of your answer.

(a) An unbalanced transportation model requires the addition of both a dummy source and a dummy destination to effect balancing.

Ans. False. Now, Refer to Chapter-11, Q.No.-5 [Solved Practical Problem]

(b) If the coefficients of the objective function of a LPP are changed, then optimal values of the variables are also changed.

Ans. False.

For example, we have the following LPP:

Maximise $Z = 3x_1 + 5x_2 + 4x_3$

subject to $2x_1 + 3x_2 \le 8$

$2x_2 + 5x_3 \le 10$

$3x_1 + 2x_2 + 4x_3 \le 15$

$x_1, x_2, x_3 \ge 0$

The optimal solution of this LPP is as follows:

$x_1 = 89/41,\ x_2 = 50/41,\ x_3 = 62/41,\ x_4 = x_5 = x_6 = 0$

and maximum $Z = 18.66$

If we change the coefficients of objective function then, clearly, the value of objective function will be changed but the optimal values of the variables will not be changed.

(c) The dual of the dual is the primal.

Ans. True. Now, Refer to Chapter-7 (Theorem 1)

(d) In a LPP, degeneracy can be avoided if redundant constraints are deleted.

Ans. False.

We know that a LPP is degenerate if in a basic feasible solution, one of the basic variables takes on a zero value. Degeneracy is caused by redundant constraints (s) and could cost simplex method

extra iterations. Constraints are either redundant or necessary; redundant constraints are constraints that may be deleted from the set without changing the region defined by the set.

(e) **In a two-person zero-sum game, if the optimal solution requires one player to use a mixed strategy, the other player must do the same.**

Ans. False.

A game with mixed strategies is the game where the saddle point does not exist. Therefore, none of the players would play the same strategy.

Q2. **(a) Solve the following linear programming problem by graphical method:**

Maximise $z = 3x_1 + 2x_2$

subject to $x_1 - x_2 \geq 1$

$x_1 + x_2 \geq 3$

$x_1,\ x_2 \geq 0$.

Ans. Refer to Chapter-3, Q.No.-15 [Solved Practical Problem]

(b) **Solve the following assignment problem:**

	I	II	III	IV
A	2	3	4	5
B	4	5	6	7
C	7	8	9	8
D	3	5	8	4

Ans. Same as Chapter-12, Q.No.-1 [Solved Practical Problem]

Q3. **(a) A manufacturer has two products P_1 and P_2, both of which are produced in two steps by machines M_1 and M_2. The process time per hundred for the products on the machines are:**

	M_1	M_2	Profit (per 100 units)
P_1	4	5	10
P_1	5	2	5
Available hours	100	80	

The manufacturer can sell as much as he can produce of both products. Formulate the problem as LP model. Determine optimum solution, using simplex method.

Ans. Let process time for $P_1 = x_1$ and process time for $P_2 = x_2$

Therefore, we have the following LPP:

Maximise $Z = 10x_1 + 5x_2$

subject to $4x_1 + 5x_2 \leq 100$

$5x_1 + 2x_2 \leq 80$

$x_1, x_2 \geq 0$

Now, Same as Chapter-6, Q.No.-1

(b) Using graphical method, solve the game whose pay-off matrix is given as:

A \ B	I	II	III	IV
I	1	3	–3	7
II	2	5	4	–6

Ans. Same as Chapter-15, Q.No.-1 [Solved Practical Problem]

Q4. (a) Find the dual of the following LPP:

Maximise $z = 3x_1 + 2x_2$

subject to $x_1 \leq 4$

$2x_1 + x_2 \leq 6$

$x_1 + x_2 \leq 5$

$3x_1 - x_2 = -1$

$x_2 \geq 0$, x_1 **is unrestricted.**

Ans. Refer to Chapter-7, Q.No.-7 [Solved Practical Problem]

(b) Transform the following zero-sum game into an equivalent linear programming problem:

	B_1	B_2	B_3
A_1	1	–1	3
A_2	3	5	–3
A_3	6	2	–2

Ans. Refer to Chapter-16. Q.No.-2 [Solved Practical Problem]

Q5. (a) A manufacturer of medicines is setting-up a production plant for medicines A and B. There are sufficient ingredients available to make 20,000 bottles of A and 40,000 bottles of B but there are only 45,000 bottles into which either of the medicines can be put. It takes 3 hours to prepare enough material to fill 1000 bottles of A. It takes 1 hour to prepare enough material to fill 1000 bottles of B. There are 66 hours available for this operation. The profit is ₹ 8 per bottle for A and ₹ 7 per bottle for B. Formulate this problem as a linear programming problem.

Ans. Refer to Chapter-3, Q.No.-16 [Solved Practical Problem]

(b) Find the initial basic feasible solution of the following transportation problem using North-West corner method:

	P_1	P_2	P_3	P_4	Requirement
M_1	19	11	23	11	11
M_2	15	16	12	21	13
M_3	30	25	16	39	19
Availability	6	10	12	15	113

Also, find the optimal solution.

Ans. Same as Chapter-11, Q.No.-1 [Solved Practical Problem]

Q6. (a) Show that the set $S = \{(x, y) \mid 3x^2 + 5y^2 \leq 15\}$ **is convex.**

Ans. Same as Chapter-2, Q.No.-8 and Q.No.-10 [Solved Practical Problem]

(b) Show that the set of vectors a_1, a_2 **and** a_3 **forms a basis for** E^3**:**

$$a_1 = \begin{bmatrix} 1 \\ 2 \\ 0 \end{bmatrix}, \; a_2 = \begin{bmatrix} 2 \\ 0 \\ 2 \end{bmatrix}, \; a_3 = \begin{bmatrix} 0 \\ 2 \\ 3 \end{bmatrix}$$

Ans. Refer to Chapter-1, Q.No.-17 [Solved Practical Problem]

(c) Consider the system of equations

$$2x_1 + x_2 + 4x_3 = 11$$

$$3x_1 + x_2 + 5x_3 = 14$$

A feasible solution is $x_1 = 2,\ x_2 = 3,\ x_3 = 1$. **Reduce this feasible solution to a basic feasible solution.**

Ans. Refer to Chapter-5, Q.No.-13 [Solved Practical Problem]

Q7. (a) Solve the game whose pay-off matrix is

$$\begin{bmatrix} -1 & -2 & 8 \\ 7 & 5 & 1 \\ 6 & 0 & 12 \end{bmatrix}$$

Ans. Same as Chapter-16, Q.No.-1 [Solved Practical Problem]

(b) 5 jobs are to be assigned on 5 available machines. The following matrix shows the profit obtained (in ₹) on assigning various jobs to different machines:

	M_1	M_2	M_3	M_4	M_5
J_1	5	11	10	12	14
J_2	2	4	6	3	5
J_3	3	12	5	14	6
J_4	6	14	4	11	7
J_5	7	9	8	12	5

Determine an assignment which maximises the total profit.

Ans. Same as Chapter-12, Q.No.-2 [Solved Practical Problem]

⌑ ⌑

Linear Programming : MTE-12

June, 2016

Note: *Question no. 1 is compulsory. Attempt any four questions out of questions no. 2 to 7. Use of calculators is not allowed.*

Q1. Which of the following statements are true and which are false? Give reasons for your answers.

(a) If S_1 and S_2 are two convex sets, then their intersection is also a convex set.

Ans. True. Now, Refer to Chapter-2 (Theorem 1)

(b) Dual of a dual is a primal problem.

Ans. True. Now, Refer to Chapter-7 (Theorem 1)

(c) A saddle point in a game is the point of intersection of the optimal pure strategies of the two players.

Ans. True. Now, Refer to Chapter-13 (Theory 13.2)

(d) The vectors $e_1 = \begin{bmatrix} 1 \\ 0 \end{bmatrix}$ and $e_2 = \begin{bmatrix} 0 \\ 1 \end{bmatrix}$ constitute a basis for E^3.

Ans. False.

$e_1 = \begin{bmatrix} 1 \\ 0 \end{bmatrix}$ and $e_2 = \begin{bmatrix} 0 \\ 1 \end{bmatrix}$ do not constitute a basis for E^3 because e_1 and e_2 are in two-dimensional and E^3 is three-dimensional space. Therefore,

$$e_1 = \begin{bmatrix} 1 \\ 0 \\ 0 \end{bmatrix}, \quad e_2 = \begin{bmatrix} 0 \\ 1 \\ 0 \end{bmatrix}, \quad e_3 = \begin{bmatrix} 0 \\ 0 \\ 1 \end{bmatrix}$$

will constitute a basis for E^3.

(e) The solution to a transportation problem with m-rows and n-columns is feasible if number of positive allocations is m + n.

Ans. False.

The solution to a TP with m-rows and n-columns is feasible if the number of positive allocation is m + n – 1.

Q2. (a) Solve the following linear programming problem by Simplex method:

Maximise $z = x_1 + 4x_2 + 5x_3$

Subject to

$3x_1 + 3x_3 \leq 22$

$x_1 + 2x_2 + 3x_3 \leq 14$

$3x_1 + 2x_2 \leq 14$

$x_1, x_2, x_3 \geq 0.$

Ans. Same as Chapter-6, Q.No.-1 [Solved Practical Problem]

(b) Solve the following cost minimising assignment problem:

	I	II	III	IV	V
A	2	9	2	7	1
B	6	8	7	6	1
C	4	6	5	3	1
D	4	2	7	3	1
E	5	3	9	5	1

Ans. Refer to Chapter-12, Q.No.-1[Solved Practical Problem]

Q3. (a) In a game of two players, given the payoff matrix for player A, obtain the optimum strategies for both the players and determine the value of the game:

$$\begin{array}{c} \\ \text{Player A} \end{array} \overset{\textbf{B}}{\begin{bmatrix} 6 & -3 & 7 \\ -3 & 0 & 4 \\ 1 & -5 & 2 \end{bmatrix}}$$

Ans. Same as Chapter-16, Q.No.-1 [Solved Practical Problem]

(b) Solve the following transportation problem to maximise profit:

		Destination				
		I	II	III	IV	Supply
Source	A	40	25	22	33	100
	B	44	35	30	30	30
	C	38	38	28	30	70
Demand		40	20	60	30	

Ans. Refer to Chapter-11, Q.No.-3 [Solved Practical Problem]

Q4. (a) Convert the following game problem, involving two person 'zero-sum' game in an equivalent linear programming problem:

Player B

Player A				
	8	20	–3	1
	6	25	4	2
	0	–8	12	9
	16	9	21	0

Ans. Same as Chapter-16, Q.No.-2 [Solved Practical Problem]

(b) Write the mathematical model of the following transportation problem:

Distribution Centre

		D_1	D_2	D_3	D_4	Capacity
	P_1	19	30	50	12	7
Plant	P_2	70	30	40	60	10
	P_3	40	10	60	20	18
Demand		5	8	7	15	

Ans. From the given TP, we have the following:

$m = 3 \quad n = 4$

$a_1 = 7 \quad a_2 = 10 \quad a_3 = 18$

$b_1 = 5 \quad b_2 = 8 \quad b_3 = 7 \quad b_4 = 15$

$C_{11} = 19 \quad C_{12} = 30 \quad C_{13} = 50 \quad C_{14} = 12$

$C_{21} = 70 \quad C_{22} = 30 \quad C_{23} = 40 \quad C_{24} = 60$

$C_{31} = 40 \quad C_{32} = 10 \quad C_{33} = 60 \quad C_{34} = 20$

Mathematical model of this TP is as follows:

Minimise

$$Z = 19x_{11} + 30x_{12} + 50x_{13} + 12x_{14} + 70x_{21} + 30x_{22} + 40x_{23}$$
$$+ 60x_{24} + 40x_{31} + 10x_{32} + 60x_{33} + 20x_{34}$$

Subject to the constraints

$x_{11} + x_{12} + x_{13} + x_{14} = 7, \qquad x_{11} + x_{21} + x_{31} = 5$

$x_{21} + x_{22} + x_{23} + x_{24} = 10, \qquad x_{12} + x_{22} + x_{32} = 8$

$x_{31} + x_{32} + x_{33} + x_{44} = 18, \qquad x_{13} + x_{23} + x_{33} = 7$

$x_{14} + x_{24} + x_{34} = 15$

$x_{ij} \geq 0, \quad i = 1, 2, 3$ and $j = 1, 2, 3, 4$

Q5. (a) A firm plans to purchase at least 200 kg of scrap containing high quality metal X and low quality metal Y. It decided that the scrap to be purchased must contain at least 100 kg of X-metal and not more than 35 kg of Y-metal. The firm can purchase the scrap from two

suppliers (A and B) in unlimited quantities. The percentage of X and Y metals in terms of weight in the scrap supplied by A and B is given below:

Metals	Supplier A	Supplier B
X	25%	75 %
Y	10%	20%

The price of A's scrap is ₹200 per kg and that of B is ₹400 per kg. The firm wants to determine the quantities that it should buy from the two suppliers so that the total cost is minimised. Formulate the problem as LPP and solve.

Ans. Refer to Chapter-3, Q.No.-9 [Solved Practical Problem]

(b) **Write the dual of the following linear programming problem:**

Minimise $z = x_1 + x_2 + x_3$

Subject to

$x_1 - 3x_2 + 4x_3 = 5$

$x_1 - 2x_2 \leq 3$

$2x_2 - x_3 \geq 4$

$x_1, x_2 \geq 0$, x_3 **is unrestricted.**

Your dual must contain one unrestricted variable.

Ans. Same as Chapter-7, Q.No.-3 [Solved Practical Problem]

Q6. **(a) Check whether the following system of linear equations has degenerate solutions:**

$2x_1 + x_2 - x_3 = 2$

$3x_1 + 2x_2 + x_3 = 3$

If yes, find all the degenerate basic feasible solutions.

Ans. Refer to Chapter-5, Q.No.-9 [Solved Practical Problem]

(b) **Using two-phase method, solve the following linear programming problem:**

Minimise $z = x_2 - 3x_3 + 2x_5$

Subject to

$x_1 + 3x_2 - x_3 + 2x_5 = 7$

$-2x_2 + 4x_3 + x_4 = 12$

$-4x_2 + 3x_3 + 8x_5 + x_6 = 10$

$x_1, x_2, x_3, \ldots x_6 \geq 0$.

Ans. Same as Chapter-6, Q.No.-6 [Solved Practical Problem]

Q7. (a) Solve the following game using graphical method:

	B		
A	6	4	3
	2	4	8

Ans. Same as Chapter-15, Q.No.-1 [Solved Practical Problem]

(b) Which of the following sets are convex?

(i) $S_1 = \{(x, y) | x^2 + y^2 \geq 4\}$

(ii) $S_2 = \{(x, y) | x \geq 3, y \leq 5\}$

Verify your result by drawing the graph.

Ans. Refer to Chapter-2, Q.No.-13 [Solved Practical Problem]

¤¤

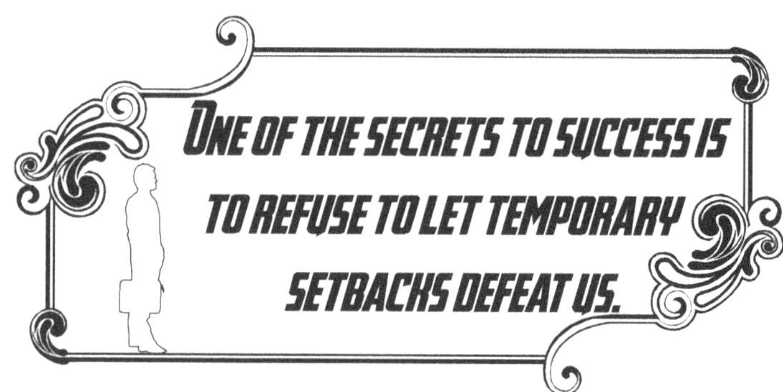

Linear Programming : MTE-12

December, 2016

Note: *Question no. 1 is compulsory Attempt any four questions out of questions no. 2 to 7. Use of calculators is not allowed.*

Q1. Which of the following statements are True and which are False? Give reasons for your answers.

(a) Assignment problem is a special structure of Linear Programming Problem.

(b) A hyperplane is a convex set.

(c) A game in which maximum value for the maximizing player is equal to the minimum value for the minimizing player, is called a game with a saddle point.

(d) If the primal LPP is unbounded, then the dual LPP is bounded.

(e) Two-phase simplex method can be used to solve the system of linear equations.

Q2. (a) Two firms are competing for business under the condition that one firm's gain is another firm's loss. Firm A's pay-off matrix is given below:

		Firm B (Advertising)		
		No	Medium	Heavy
Firm A	No Advertising	10	5	–2
	Medium Advertising	13	12	15
	Heavy Advertising	16	14	10

Suggest optimal strategies for the two firms and the net outcome thereof.

(b) Solve the following LPP graphically:

Minimize $z = 5x_1 + 8x_2$

subject to

$$x_1 \leq 4$$

$$x_2 \geq 2$$

$x_1 + x_2 \leq 5$

$x_1 \geq 0,\ x_2 \geq 0.$

Q3. (a) Solve the following LPP by simplex method:

Maximize $z = 50x_1 + 70x_2$

subject to

$120x_1 + 120x_2 \leq 8400$

$x_1 + 2x_2 \leq 100$

$2x_1 + x_2 \leq 120$

$x_1, x_2 \geq 0.$

(b) Write the mathematical model of the following assignment problem:

Job → / Man ↓	I	II	III	IV
A	5	3	2	8
B	7	9	2	6
C	6	4	5	7
D	5	7	7	8

Q4. (a) A dairy firm has two milk plants with daily milk production of 6 thousand litres and 9 thousand litres, respectively. Each day the firm must fulfil the needs of its three distribution centres which have milk requirements of 7, 5 and 3 thousand litres, respectively. Cost of shipping one thousand litres of milk from each plant to each distribution centre is given (in hundreds of rupees) below. Formulate the LPP model to minimize the transportation cost.

Distribution Centres

		1	2	3	Supply
Plants	1	2	3	11	6
	2	1	9	6	9
Demand		7	5	3	

(b) Solve the following LP problem by simplex method:

Maximize $z = x_1 + 2x_2 + 3x_3 - x_4$

subject to

$x_1 + 2x_2 + 3x_3 = 15$

$$2x_1 + x_2 + 5x_3 = 20$$
$$x_1 + 2x_2 + x_3 + x_4 = 10$$
$$x_1, x_2, x_3, x_4 \geq 0.$$

Q5. (a) Check whether the vectors

$$a_1 = \begin{bmatrix} 1 \\ 3 \\ 2 \end{bmatrix}, a_2 = \begin{bmatrix} 5 \\ -2 \\ 1 \end{bmatrix} \text{ and } a_3 = \begin{bmatrix} -7 \\ 13 \\ 4 \end{bmatrix}$$

are linearly dependent. If so, find a relation between them.

(b) A company has three factories F_1, F_2 and F_3 which supply to three warehouses W_1, W_2 and W_3. Weekly factory capacities are 200, 160 and 90 units, respectively. Weekly warehouse requirements are 180, 120 and 150 units, respectively. Unit shipping costs (in ₹) are as follows:

Warehouse

		W_1	W_2	W_3	Supply
Factory	F_1	16	20	12	200
	F_2	14	8	18	160
	F_3	26	24	16	90
	Demand	180	120	150	450

Determine the optimal distribution for this company to minimize total shipping cost.

Q6. (a) Obtain the dual of the following LPP:

Maximize $z = 4x_1 + 3x_2 - x_3 + x_4 + 4x_5$

subject to

$$2x_1 - x_2 + 3x_3 + x_4 - x_5 = 2$$
$$x_1 + x_2 + 2x_3 + x_4 - 9x_5 = 6$$
$$x_1, x_2, x_3, x_4 \geq 0, x_5 \text{ unrestricted.}$$

(b) Use graphical method to solve the following game and find the value of the game:

Player B

		B_1	B_2	B_3	B_4
Player A	A_1	2	2	3	–2
	A_2	4	3	2	6

Q7. **(a) A company has one surplus truck in each of the cities A, B, C, D, and E and one deficit truck in each of the cities 1, 2, 3, 4, 5 and 6. The distance between the cities in km is shown in the matrix below. Find the assignment of trucks from cities in surplus to cities in deficit so that the total distance covered by the vehicles is minimum.**

	1	2	3	4	5	6
A	12	10	15	22	18	8
B	10	18	25	15	16	12
C	11	10	3	8	5	9
D	6	14	10	13	13	12
E	8	12	11	7	13	10

(b) Find the range of values of p and q which will render the entry (2, 2) a saddle point for the game.

	Player B		
Player A	B_1	B_2	B_3
A_1	2	4	5
A_2	10	7	q
A_3	4	p	6

⌑⌑

Linear Programming : MTE-12

June, 2017

Note: *Question no. 1 is compulsory. Do any four questions out of questions no. 2 to 7. Use of calculators is not allowed.*

Q1. **State which of the following statements are true and which are false. Give reasons for your answer with a short proof or a counter-example.**

(a) The LPP, maximizing $z = -5x_2$ subject to $x_1 + x_2 \leq 1, 0 \cdot 5x_1 + 5x_2 \geq 0$ and $x_1 \geq 0, x_2 \geq 0$, has no feasible solution.

(b) If a negative value appears in the solution column (x_B) of the simplex method, then the basic solution is unbounded.

(c) If the variables in a primal problem are all greater than, or equal to zero, then the variables in the dual problem would be less than or equal to zero.

(d) The value of the game

	I	II	III	IV
I	−5	3	1	5
II	5	5	0	6
III	−4	−2	4	5
IV	7	2	6	8

is 6.

(e) The minimum number of lines covering all zeros in a reduced cost matrix of order n in an assignment problem can be at least n.

Q2. (a) Formulate the dual of the following LPP:

Maximize $z = 2x_1 + x_2$

subject to the constraints

$$x_1 + 5x_2 \leq 10$$
$$x_1 + 3x_2 \geq 6$$
$$2x_1 + 2x_2 \leq 8$$
$$x_2 \geq 0 \text{ and } x_1 \text{ unrestricted.}$$

The dual must have exactly two constraints and three variables.

(b) Solve graphically the following LPP:

Maximize $z=3x_1+2x_2$

subject to the constraints

$$-2x_1+x_2\le 1$$
$$x_1\le 2$$
$$x_1+x_2\le 3$$
$$x_1, x_2\ge 0.$$

Q3. (a) Use simplex method to solve the following LPP:

Maximize $z=x_1+2x_2+3x_3$

subject to the constraints

$$x_1+2x_2+3x_3\le 10$$
$$x_1+x_2\le 5$$
$$x_1, x_2, x_3\ge 0.$$

Also, compute one more alternate optimal solution if it exists.

(b) Solve the following game graphically:

$$\begin{bmatrix} -2 & 0 \\ 3 & -1 \\ -3 & 2 \\ 5 & -4 \end{bmatrix}$$

Q4. (a) Five men are available to do five different jobs. From past records, the time (in hours) that each man takes to do the job is known and given in the following table:

		Jobs				
		I	II	III	IV	V
	A	2	9	2	7	1
	B	6	8	7	6	1
Men	C	4	6	5	3	1
	D	5	3	9	5	1
	E	4	2	7	3	1

Find the assignment of men to jobs that will minimize the total time taken. Also, compute the time.

(b) Solve the following LPP using the two phase simplex method:

Maximize $z=3x_1+2x_2+x_3$

subject to the constraints

$$-3x_1 + 2x_2 + x_3 = 8$$
$$-3x_1 + 4x_2 + x_3 = 7$$
$$x_1, x_2, x_3 \geq 0.$$

Q5. (a) Use dominance principle to solve the game whose pay-off matrix is given by

Player B

		I	II	III	IV
Player A	I	5	6	4	2
	II	5	6	4	6
	III	6	4	6	2
	IV	2	4	2	10

Also, find the value of the game.

(b) A Chemistry laboratory uses raw material I and II to produce two domestic cleaning solutions A and B. The daily availability of raw materials I and II are 150 and 145 units respectively. One unit of solution A consumes $0 \cdot 5$ units of raw material I and $0 \cdot 6$ units of raw material II and one unit of solution B uses $0 \cdot 5$ units of raw material I and $0 \cdot 4$ units of raw material II. The profit per unit of solutions A and B are ₹8 and ₹10 respectively. The daily demand for solution A lies between 30 and 150 units and that for B between 40 and 200 units. Formulate the above data as LPP.

Q6. (a) For the following problem in the game theory, formulate the problem of finding the optimal strategies for player A and player B as linear programming problem:

Player B

$$\text{Player A} \begin{bmatrix} 1 & 2 & 2 \\ 0 & -2 & 6 \\ -4 & 2 & 6 \end{bmatrix}$$

(b) Find the initial basic feasible solution of the following transportation problem to minimize the cost using matrix-minima method:

Warehouses

		W_1	W_2	W_3	W_4	Capacity
Factories	F_1	5	7	3	8	300
	F_2	4	6	9	5	500
	F_3	3	6	4	5	200
Demand		200	300	400	100	

Hence, find the optimal solution.

Q7. (a) Consider:

$$S = \{(x,y) \in R^2 \mid xy \le 1, x \le 1, y \le 1, x \ge 0, y \ge 0\}.$$

Is S a convex set? Give reasons. Determine the convex hull of S and describe it using mathematical inequalities.

(b) Consider the following transportation problem:

	D_1	D_2	D_3	D_4	D_5	$a_i \downarrow$
S_1	40	50	30	10	70	20
S_2	100	80	75	65	20	20
S_3	30	60	45	50	40	50
$b_j \rightarrow$	15	25	20	10	20	

If $u_1 = -15$, $u_2 = 20$, $u_3 = 0$, $v_1 = 30$, $v_2 = 60$, $v_3 = 45$, $v_4 = 25$, $v_5 = 0$, then find the corresponding basic feasible solution of the problem. Is this solution optimal? Give reasons.

¤ ¤

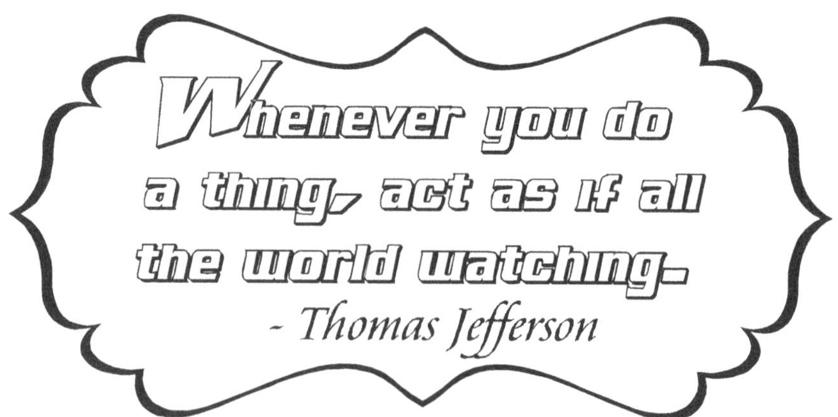

Linear Programming : MTE-12

December, 2017

Note: *Question no. 1 is compulsory. Answer any four questions from questions no. 2 to 7. Use of calculators is not allowed.*

Q1. Which of the following statements are true and which are false? Give a short proof or a counter-example in support of your answer.

(a) In an LPP, the number of variables in the primal problem are less than the number of constraints in the dual.

Ans. False.

The number of decision variables in the dual problem is equal to the number of constraints in the primal problems.

(b) If a constant is added to all the elements of a payoff matrix in a two-person zero-sum game, then the value of the game does not change.

Ans. True.

Value of the game is the maximum guaranteed game to player A (maximizing player) if both the players uses their best strategies.

(c) The set $S = \left\{(x, y) \middle| y^2 \geq 9x, x^2 + y^2 \leq 1\right\}$ is a convex set.

Ans. True.

(d) For each cell (i, j) in an optimal solution of a transportation problem, $\left(u_i + v_j - c_{ij}\right)x_{ij} = 0$.

Ans. True.

(e) For any two square matrices A and B, AB = BA.

Ans. False.

Let us take an example,

$$\text{Matrix} \rightarrow A \rightarrow \begin{bmatrix} a & b \\ c & d \end{bmatrix} B \rightarrow \begin{bmatrix} e & f \\ g & h \end{bmatrix}$$

then,

$$AB \rightarrow \begin{bmatrix} ae + bg & af + bh \\ ce + dg & cf + dh \end{bmatrix}, \text{ and}$$

$$BA = \begin{bmatrix} ea + cf & eb + fd \\ ga + ch & gb + hd \end{bmatrix}$$

$AB \neq BA$

Q2. (a) Obtain the dual of the following problem:

Maximize $Z = 5x_1 + 9x_2 + 8x_3$

subject to

$$2x_1 + 4x_2 - 8x_3 \leq 3$$
$$4x_1 - 2x_2 \leq 9$$
$$-8x_1 + 4x_2 + 3x_3 = 8$$

$x_1, x_2 \geq 0$ and x_3 is unrestricted in sign.

Ans. Same as Chapter-7, Q.No.-3 [Solved Practical Problem]

(b) A firm manufactures pills in two sizes, A and B. A contains 2 grams of aspirin, 5 grams of bicarbonate and 1 gram of codeine. B contains 1 gram of aspirin, 8 grams of bicarbonate and 6 grams of codeine. It requires at least 12 grams of aspirin, 74 grams of bicarbonate and 24 grams of codeine for providing immediate effect. It is required to determine the least number of pills a patient should take to get immediate relief. Formulate the problem as a standard LPP and solve it graphically.

Ans. let x and y be the no. of pills of size A and B, which gives immediate relief. Let the total no. of pills be z, Hence the objective function is – $\text{Min} z = x + y$.

Now,

Req. Product	A (x)	B (y)	Min. Req.
Aspirin	2	1	12
Bicarbonate	5	8	74
Codeine	1	6	12

$$2x + y \geq 12$$
$$5x + 8y \geq 74$$
$$x + 6y \geq 12$$
$$x, y \geq 0$$

Hence, the mathematical formulation of LPP Corresponding to given prob.

Max. $z = 3x + 4y$

$$2x + y \geq 12$$
$$5x + 8y \geq 74$$
$$x + 6y \geq 12$$
$$x, y \geq 0$$

To solve graphically. We consider the corresponding eqs. of straight lines, as,

$$2x+y=12 \text{ or } \frac{x}{6}+\frac{4}{12}=1$$

$$5x+8y=74 \text{ or } \frac{x}{14\cdot 8}+\frac{y}{9\cdot 25}=1$$

$$x+6y=12 \text{ or } \frac{x}{12}+\frac{y}{2}=1$$

$x=0$ and $y=0$

Drawing lines in 2 – D plane, then.

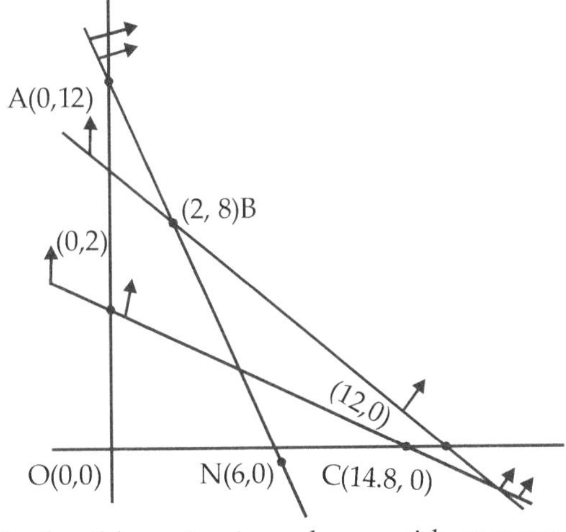

so, the feasible region is as shown with corner points A(0, 12), B (2, 8) C $(14\cdot 8,0)$

Point	Value of func.
A (0, 12)	$z=0+12=12$
B (2, 8)	$z=2+8=10$ (Min)
C $(14\cdot 8,0)$	$z=14\cdot 8+0=14\cdot 8$

Q3. (a) Use the two-phase method to find a basic feasible solution for the LPP:

Minimize $x_1-2x_2-3x_3$

subject to

$$-2x_1+3x_2+3x_3=2$$

$$2x_1+3x_2+4x_3=1$$

$$x_1, x_2, x_3 \geq 0.$$

Ans. Refer to Chapter-6, Q.No.-6 [Solved Practical Problem]

(b) A departmental head has four subordinates and four tasks are to be performed. The subordinates differ in efficiency and the tasks differ

in their intrinsic difficulty. Her estimate of the time each person would like to perform each task is given in the matrix form as follows:

Tasks	Workers			
	A	B	C	D
I	18	26	17	11
II	13	28	14	26
III	38	19	18	15
IV	19	26	24	10

How should the tasks be allocated, so as to minimise the total time taken?

Ans. Step 1 →

Identify the min. element in each row and subtract it from every element of that row, we get the reduced matrix

Men

Persons	1	2	3	4
A	7	15	6	0
B	0	15	1	13
C	23	4	3	0
D	9	16	14	0

Step 2 →

Identify the min. element in each column and subtract it from every element of that column.

Men

Persons	1	2	3	4
A	7	11	5	0
B	0	11	0	13
C	23	0	2	0
D	9	12	13	0

Step 3 →

Make the assignment for the reduced matrix obtain from steps 1 and 2:

Now proceed:

Opt. assignment is: A → G, B → E, C → F, D → H

The min. total time is

17 + 13 +19 + 10 or 59 man - hours

Q4. (a) Test for the convexity of the following sets:

(i) $S_1 = \{(x, y) | 3x^2 + 2y^2 \le 6\}$

Ans. Same as Chapter-2, Q.No.-8 [Solved Practical Problem]

(ii) $S_2 = \{(x, y) | x^2 + y^2 \ge 1, y \ge x, y \ge -x\}$

Ans. Same as Chapter-2, Q.No.-9 [Solved Practical Problem]

(b) Solve the following game graphically:

$$\text{Player A} \begin{matrix} \\ A_1 \\ A_2 \end{matrix} \overset{\text{Player B}}{\begin{matrix} B_1 & B_2 & B_3 \\ \end{matrix}} \begin{bmatrix} 12 & 8 & 6 \\ 5 & 9 & 14 \end{bmatrix}$$

Ans. Same as Chapter-15, Q.No.-1 [Solved Practical Problem]

Q5. (a) Solve the following cost minimizing transportation problem, starting with an initial basic feasible solution by matrix-minima method: availabilities

Destinations

		D_1	D_2	D_3	D_4	D_5	Availabilities
	O_1	5	8	8	6	3	800
Origins	O_2	4	7	7	6	6	500
	O_3	8	4	6	6	3	900
Requirements		400	400	200	400	800	

Ans. Same as Chapter-11, Q.No.-3 [Solved Practical Problem]

(b) For the game matrix

$$\begin{bmatrix} 3 & -2 & 4 \\ -1 & 4 & 2 \\ 3 & 2 & -3 \end{bmatrix},$$

Write the LPPs corresponding to the minimizing player and maximizing player.

Ans. Same as Chapter-13, Q.No.-3(a) [Solved Practical Problem]

Q6. (a) Determine whether the following set of vectors form a basis for E^3:

$$a = \begin{bmatrix} 0 \\ 1 \\ 2 \end{bmatrix}, b = \begin{bmatrix} 2 \\ 0 \\ 2 \end{bmatrix}, c = \begin{bmatrix} 0 \\ 2 \\ 3 \end{bmatrix}$$

Ans. Refer to Gullybaba.com "download section"

(b) Find all the basic solution of the system of equations

$$2x_1 + 3x_2 + 4x_3 = 4$$

$$x_1 + 2x_2 + 2x_3 = 2.$$

Identify the basic and non-basic variables in each of these solutions.

Ans. Refer to Gullybaba.com "download section"

Q7. (a) Write the LPP formulation of the following assignment problem:

$$\begin{array}{cc} & \textbf{Jobs} \\ & \begin{array}{ccc} \text{I} & \text{II} & \text{III} \end{array} \\ \begin{array}{r} A_1 \\ \text{Men } A_2 \\ A_3 \end{array} & \begin{bmatrix} 12 & 4 & 5 \\ 8 & 6 & 7 \\ 1 & 9 & 12 \end{bmatrix} \end{array}$$

Ans. Same as Chapter-12, Q.No.-1 [Solved Practical Problem]

(b) Using dominance solve the game whose payoff matrix is given by

$$\begin{bmatrix} 3 & 2 & 4 & 0 \\ 3 & 4 & 2 & 4 \\ 4 & 2 & 4 & 0 \\ 0 & 4 & 0 & 8 \end{bmatrix}$$

Ans. Same as Chapter-15, Q.No.-5 [Solved Practical Problem]

⌑⌑

Linear Programming : MTE-12

June, 2018

Note: *Question no. 1 is compulsory. Answer any four questions from questions no. 2 to 7. Use of calculators is not allowed.*

Q1. **Which of the following statements are True and which are False? Give a short proof or a counter-example in support of your answer.**

(a) There is no convex set with exactly three points.

(b) In a solution of a two-dimensional LPP, the objective function can assume same values at two distinct extreme points.

(c) For a 3 x 3 matrix A with $|A| = 3$, $|\text{Adj } A|$ is equal to 9.

(d) The pay-off matrix $\begin{bmatrix} 8 & 2 & 3 \\ 3 & 5 & 6 \\ 5 & 8 & 9 \end{bmatrix}$ has no saddle point.

(e) In a balanced transportation problem with 3 sources and 4 destinations, if the availability at the first source and the requirement at the first destination are equal, then the North-West corner method gives exactly 6 basic cells.

Q2. (a) In a game of matching coins with two players, suppose A wins one unit of value when there are two heads, wins nothing when there are 2 tails and loses 1/2 unit of the value when there is one head and one tail. Determine the pay-off matrix and optimal strategies for each player and the value of the game.

(b) A factory uses three different resources P, Q and R for the manufacture of two different products A and B. A total of 20 units of P, 12 units of Q and 16 units of R are available. 1 unit of product A requires 2 units of P, 2 units of Q and 4 units of R; whereas 1 unit of product B requires 4 units of P, 2 units of Q and 0 unit of R. One unit of product A when sold gives a profit of ₹200, and one unit of product B when sold gives a profit of ₹300. Formulate the linear programming problem. How many units of each product should be manufactured for maximizing the total profit? Solve it graphically.

Q3. **(a) Four salespersons are to be assigned to four territories. The returns (in thousands of ₹) obtained on assigning each salesperson to each territory is given in the following table:**

		Salespersons			
		I	II	III	IV
Territories	A	−1	−2	3	4
	B	2	−4	3	5
	C	4	3	−6	7
	D	3	2	5	7

Find an assignment that maximizes the returns. What is the maximal return?

(b) Solve the following LPP by the two-phase method and give your conclusions about the solution:

Maximize $z = 3x_1 + x_2$

subject to $2x_1 + x_2 \geq 4$

$x_2 \geq 2$

$x_1, x_2 \geq 0.$

Q4. (a) Obtain the dual for the following LPP:

Minimize $z = 3x_1 + 9x_2 + 8x_3$

subject to $2x_1 + 4x_2 - 8x_3 \geq 5$

$4x_1 - 2x_2 + 4x_3 \geq 9$

$-8x_1 + 3x_3 \leq 8$

$x_1, x_2, x_3 \geq 0.$

(b) Find the initial basic feasible solution using North-West corner method for the following transportation problem:

		Warehouse			
		W_1	W_2	W_3	Supply
	F_1	16	20	12	200
Factory	F_2	14	8	18	160
	F_3	26	24	16	90
Demand		180	120	150	

Also, find the optimal solution.

Q5. (a) Write the LPP form of the following transportation problem:

		Destinations				
		D_1	D_2	D_3	D_4	Supply
	O_1	5	11	2	6	40
Sources	O_2	4	9	7	1	30
	O_3	3	1	4	3	30
Demand		30	20	10	40	

(b) Solve the following game graphically:

$$A \overset{B}{\begin{bmatrix} 1 & -3 \\ 3 & 5 \\ -1 & 6 \\ 4 & 1 \end{bmatrix}}$$

Q6. (a) Formulate a suitable LPP of the game with respect to minimizing and maximizing p:

$$\text{Player A} \overset{\text{Player B}}{\begin{bmatrix} 5 & 0 & -10 \\ 10 & 6 & 2 \\ 20 & 15 & 10 \end{bmatrix}}$$

(b) Sketch the region $\{(x, y) \mid x^2 + y^2 \geq 1, y^2 \leq x\}$. Is the region convex? Justify your answer.

(c) Find all values of k for which the vectors $\begin{bmatrix} 1 \\ 0 \\ 1 \end{bmatrix}, \begin{bmatrix} 1 \\ -1 \\ 0 \end{bmatrix}$ and $\begin{bmatrix} k \\ -k \\ 2 \end{bmatrix}$ are linearly independent.

Q7. (a) Express $P\left(\frac{1}{2}, \frac{1}{4}\right)$ as a convex linear combination of A (0, 0), B (0, 1) and C (1, 0).

(b) Find all the basic solutions of the following system:

$4x_1 + 2x_2 + x_3 = 4$

$2x_1 + x_2 + 5x_3 = 5$

⌑⌑

Linear Programming : MTE-12

December, 2018

Note: *Question no. 1 is compulsory. Answer any four questions from questions no. 2 to 7. Use of calculators is not allowed.*

Q1. State which of the following statements are True and which are False. Give reasons for your answer with a short proof or a counter-example.

(a) The optimal solution for an LPP always lies on at least two vertices of the feasible region.

(b) In optimum simplex table, if $z_j - c_j = 0$ for at least one non-basic variable, then there will be no alternative solution.

(c) The right hand side constant of the constraint in a primal problem appears in the corresponding dual as a coefficient in the objective function.

(d) The transportation problem is balanced if the total demand and total supply are equal and the number of sources equals the number of destinations.

(e) The two players game with pay-off matrix $\begin{bmatrix} 1 & -2 & 4 \\ -1 & 4 & 2 \\ 2 & 2 & 6 \end{bmatrix}$ has no saddle point.

Q2. (a) Solve the following LPP graphically:

Maximize $z = 5x_1 + 3x_2$

subject to

$$x_1 + x_2 \le 6$$
$$2x_1 + 3x_2 \ge 6$$
$$0 \le x_1 \le 4$$
$$0 \le x_2 \le 3.$$

(b) Formulate the dual of the following LPP:

Maximize: $z = 10x_1 + 8x_2$

subject to

$x_1 + x_2 \geq 5$

$2x_1 - x_2 \geq 12$

$x_1 + 3x_2 \geq 4$

$x_1 \geq 0$ and x_2 is unrestricted.

Q3. (a) Use simplex method to solve the following LPP:

Maximize $z = 2x_1 - x_2 + x_3$

subject to the constraints

$3x_1 + x_2 + x_3 \leq 60$

$x_1 - x_2 + 2x_3 \leq 10$

$x_1 + x_2 - x_3 \leq 20$

$x_1, x_2, x_3 \geq 0.$

(b) Consider the following transportation problem:

	D_1	D_2	D_3	D_4	a_i
S_1	6	1	9	3	70
S_2	11	6	2	8	55
S_3	10	12	4	7	90
b_j	85	35	50	45	

Given $x_{13} = 50$, $x_{14} = 20$, $x_{21} = 55$, $x_{31} = 30$, $x_{32} = 35$ and $x_{34} = 25$. Check whether it is an optimal solution. If not, perform one iteration to obtain next basic feasible solution.

Q4. (a) Five persons are available to do five tasks. The cost for doing the tasks by each of the five persons is given below:

		Person				
		1	2	3	4	5
	1	23	29	27	20	28
	2	34	31	23	26	29
Task	3	29	26	27	25	29
	4	29	31	22	32	27
	5	24	27	25	28	27

Find the assignment that will minimize the total cost.

(b) Solve the following game by graphical method:

		Player B			
		B_1	B_2	B_3	B_4
Player A	A_1	3	1	1	−2
	A_2	2	0	4	2

Q5. (a) Use two-phase simplex method to solve the following LPP:

Maximize $z = 10x_1 + 20x_2$

subject to

$2x_1 + x_2 = 1$

$x_1 + 2x_2 = 5$

$x_1 \geq 0,\ x_2 \geq 0.$

(b) For the following pay-off matrix, write the equivalent linear programming problems for both the players.

Player B

		B_1	B_2	B_3
Player A	A_1	9	1	4
	A_2	0	6	3
	A_3	5	2	8

Q6. (a) Use dominance principle to solve the game whose pay-off matrix is given by;

Player B

		I	II	III	IV
Player A	I	2	− 2	4	1
	II	6	1	12	3
	III	− 3	2	0	6
	IV	2	− 3	7	1

(b) Let $S = \{(x, y): x - y \leq 4,\ x + y \geq -3,\ y \leq 8\}$. Find all the extreme points of S and represent (x, y) = (2, 1) as convex combination of the extreme points.

Q7. (a) Consider a plant which makes two types of automobile parts A and B. Each require 3 processes, machining, boring and polishing. The time required for one unit of each type on processes is given below:

Process	No. of hours		Maximum available hours
	A	B	
Machining	2	4	12
Boring	3	5	10
Polishing	3	2	8

The profit for one unit of type A is ₹30 and the profit for one unit of type B is ₹40. Formulate the problem as LPP to maximize the profit.

(b) Determine the initial basic feasible solution for the following transportation problem by North-West corner method.

$$\begin{array}{c c} & \begin{array}{cccc} D_1 & D_2 & D_3 & D_4 \end{array} \quad a_i \downarrow \\ \begin{array}{c} S_1 \\ S_2 \\ S_3 \end{array} & \begin{bmatrix} 23 & 17 & 25 & 14 \\ 15 & 10 & 18 & 24 \\ 16 & 20 & 8 & 13 \end{bmatrix} \begin{array}{c} 30 \\ 50 \\ 60 \end{array} \\ b_j \rightarrow & \begin{array}{cccc} 30 & 50 & 30 & 50 \end{array} \end{array}$$

Also, perform one complete iteration to find the next modified basic feasible solution.

⌑⌑

Linear Programming : MTE-12

June, 2019

Note: *Question no. 1 is compulsory. Answer any four questions from questions no. 2 to 7. Use of calculators is not allowed.*

Q1. State which of the following statements are True and which are False. Give reasons for your answer with a short proof or a counter-example.

(a) The set of all convex combinations of a finite number of points $X_1, X_2, \ldots X_n$ is not a convex set.

(b) If the pay-off matrix of a game is transferred, saddle point of the game if it exists, changes.

(c) If a negative value appears in the solution values (X_B) column of the simplex method, then the basic solution is optimum.

(d) In an assignment problem, if a constant is added to each element of the matrix, the optimal assignment does not change.

(e) In an LPP, every feasible solution is optimal.

Q2. (a) Use graphical method to solve the following LPP:

Maximize $z = 2x_1 + 3x_2$

subject to the constraints

$$x_1 + x_2 \leq 30$$
$$x_1 - x_2 \geq 0$$
$$x_2 \geq 12$$
$$x_1 \leq 20$$
$$x_1, x_2 \geq 0.$$

(b) Give the dual of the following LPP:

Maximize $z = 2x_1 + 3x_2 + x_3$

subject to the constraints

$$4x_1 + 3x_2 + x_3 = 6$$
$$x_1 + 2x_2 + 5x_3 = 4$$
$$x_1, x_2, x_3 \geq 0.$$

The dual must contain two variables and three constraints.

Q3. (a) Solve by simplex method the following LPP:

Maximize $z = -x_1 + 3x_2 - 2x_3$

subject to the constraints

$$3x_1 - x_2 + 2x_3 \le 7$$
$$-2x_1 + 4x_2 \le 12$$
$$-4x_1 + 3x_2 + 8x_3 \le 10$$
$$x_1, x_2, x_3 \ge 0$$

(b) There are five jobs to be assigned, one each to five machines and the associated cost matrix is as follows:

Machine

Job		1	2	3	4	5
	A	11	17	8	16	20
	B	9	7	12	6	15
Job	C	13	16	15	12	16
	D	21	24	17	28	26
	E	14	10	12	11	15

Find the assignment of machines to jobs that will minimize the total cost.

Q4. (a) Find the optimal solution of the following transportation problem:

	D_1	D_2	D_3	D_4	$a_i \downarrow$
O_1	1	2	1	4	30
O_2	3	3	2	1	50
O_3	4	2	5	9	20
$b_j \rightarrow$	20	40	30	10	100

(b) Solve the following game graphically:

Player B

		I	II	III	IV
Player A	I	1	3	− 3	7
	II	2	5	4	− 6

Q5. (a) Use dominance property to reduce the size of the following game and hence find the optimal strategies and the value of the game:

Player B

$$\text{Player A}\begin{bmatrix} 4 & 2 & 0 & 2 & 1 \\ 4 & 3 & 1 & 3 & 2 \\ 4 & 3 & 7 & -5 & 1 \\ 4 & 3 & 4 & -1 & 2 \\ 4 & 3 & 3 & -2 & 2 \end{bmatrix}$$

(b) For the transportation problem

		Market				Available
		A	B	C	D	
	X	14	9	18	6	11
Plant	Y	10	11	7	16	13
	Z	25	20	11	34	19
Requirements		6	10	12	15	

If $x_{14} = 11$, $x_{21} = 6$, $x_{22} = 3$, $x_{24} = 4$, $x_{32} = 7$ and $x_{33} = 12$, test whether this solution is optimal or not. If not, find the optimal solution.

Q6. (a) For the following pay-off matrix, transform the zero-sum game into an equivalent linear programming problem for both players:

		Player B		
		I	II	III
	I	−1	2	1
Player A	II	1	−2	2
	III	3	4	−3

(b) Check whether the following sets are convex or not:

(i) $S_1 = \{(x, y) \mid y - 3 \leq -x^2, x \geq 0, y \geq 0\}$

(ii) $S_2 = \{(x, y) \mid y - 3 \geq -x^2, x \geq 0, y \geq 0\}$

Q7. (a) A firm can produce three types of cloth, A, B and C. Three kinds of wool are required for it, red, green and blue. One unit of type A needs 2 units of red and 3 units of blue; one unit of B needs 3 units of red, 2 units of green and 2 units of blue, and one unit of C requires 5 units of green and 4 units of blue. The stock available is 8 units of red, 10 units of green and 15 units of blue. The income obtained is 3 per unit of A, ₹5 per unit of B and ₹4 per unit of C. Formulate the LPP to maximize the income from the finished cloth.

(b) Obtain all the basic solutions to the following system of linear equations:

$2x_1 + x_2 + x_3 = 6$

$x_1 + 2x_2 + x_3 = 3$

⌑⌑

Linear Programming : MTE-12

December, 2019

Note: *Question no. 1 is compulsory. Answer any four questions from questions no. 2 to 7. Use of calculators is not allowed.*

Q1. **State which of the following statements are true and which are false? Give reasons for your answer with a short proof or a counter example:**

(i) **In an LP model, replacing $\leq$ or $\geq$ z by = in the constraints can improve the Value of the objective function.**

(ii) **The dual of dud of an LPP is primal LPP.**

(iii) **Every feasible point in a bounded LP solution space can be determined from its feasible extreme points.**

(iv) **A balanced transportation problem may not have any feasible solution.**

(v) **In a two-person zero-sum game, if the optimal solution requires one player to use a pure strategy, the other player must do the same.**

Q2. **(a) A toy company manufactures two type of dolls; a basic version—doll A and a delux version—doll B. Each doll of type B takes twice as long to produce as one of type A and the company would have time to make a maximum 2000 dolls per day if it produces only type A. The supply of plastic is sufficient to produce 1500 dolls per day (both A and B combined). The type B version requires a fancy dress of which there are only 600 per day available. If the company makes profit of ₹3 and ₹5 per doll on doll A and doll B respectively; how many of each type of dolls should be produced per day in order to maximize profit?**

(b) **The pay-off matrix of a game is given below. Solve the game:**

		Player B				
		I	II	III	IV	V
Player A	1	–2	0	0	5	3
	2	3	2	1	2	2
	3	–4	–3	0	–2	6
	4	5	3	–4	2	–6

Q3. (a) Formulate the dual of the fallowing LPP:

Max.:

$$z' = 3x_1 - 2x_2$$

s. t.:

$$x_1 \le 4$$

$$x_2 \le 6$$

$$x_1 + x_2 = 5$$

$$-x_2 \le -1$$

Identify the nature of each of the dual variables.

(b) Find all the basic feasible solutions of the following system:

$$x_1 + 2x_2 + x_3 = 4$$

$$2x_1 + x_2 + 5x_3 = 5$$

Q4. (a) Solve the following. time-minimisation assignment problem:

Person

Job	1	2	3	4
I	18	26	17	11
II	13	28	14	26
III	38	19	18	15
IV	19	26	24	10

(b) Using dominance principles, solve the game whose pay-off matrix is:

Player B

Player A	I	II	III
I	–1	–2	8
II	7	5	–1
III	6	0	12

Q5. (a) A company has four plants P_1, P_2, P_3, P_4 from which it supplies to three markets M_1, M_2, M_3. Determine the optimal transportation schedule for the following data:

Plants

Market	P_1	P_2	P_3	P_4	Requirement
M_1	19	14	23	11	110
M_2	15	16	12	21	130
M_3	30	25	16	39	190
Availability	60	100	120	150	430

(b) Solve graphically the game whose pay-off matrix is:

		Player B			
		I	II	III	IV
Player A	I	1	3	−3	7
	II	2	5	4	−6

Q6. (a) Use two-phase method to solve the following LPP:

Min.:

$$z = 4x_1 + 3x_2$$

s. t.:

$$2x_1 + x_2 \geq 10$$
$$-3x_1 + 2x_2 \leq 6$$
$$x_1 + x_2 \geq 6$$
$$x_1, x_2 \geq 0$$

(b) Write the LPP model of the following Transportation problems:

		Destination				
		I	II	III	IV	Supply
Sources	I	5	7	6	4	70
	II	2	8	3	1	50
	III	1	7	4	5	90
Demand		50	40	50	70	

Q7. (a) Examine the convexity to the set:

$\{(x_1, x_2) \in R^2 : 4x_1 + 3x_2 \leq 6, x_1 + x_2 \geq 1, x_1, x_2 \geq 0\}$

(b) Solve the following linear programming problem by formulating its dual:

Min.:

$$z = 15x_1 + 10x_2$$

s.t.:

$$3x_1 + 5x_2 \geq 5$$
$$5x_1 + 2x_2 \geq 3$$
$$x_1, x_2 \geq 0$$

⌑⌑

Linear Programming : MTE-12

June, 2020

Note: *Question no. 1 is compulsory. Answer any four questions from questions no. 2 to 7. Use of calculators is not allowed.*

Q1. State which of the following statements are true and which are false? Give reasons for your answer with a short proof or a counter example:

(i) Every feasible point in a bounded LP solution space can be determined from its feasible extreme points.

(ii) Every two person zero-sum game can be represented by a pair of primal-dual linear programs.

(iii) If a constant value is added to every cost element C_{ij} in the transportation problem, the optimal values of the variables x_{ij} will change.

(iv) If the solution space of an LP model is unbounded, the objective value always will be unbounded.

(v) In a two-dimensional LP solution, the objective function can assume the same value of two distinct extreme points.

Q2. (a) Solve the following Assignment problem to minimize the total time:

		Tasks				
		I	II	III	IV	V
	A	8	26	17	11	9
	B	13	28	4	26	11
Machines	C	38	19	18	15	12
	D	19	26	24	10	30
	E	4	12	18	25	40

(b) Find the dual of the following LPP:

Maximize:

$$z = 4x_1 + x_2 + 7x_3$$

Subject to:

$$x_1 + x_2 + x_3 = 10$$

$5x_1 - x_2 + x_3 \geq 12$

$x_1 + 7x_2 - 3x_3 \leq 4$

$x_1, x_2, x_3 \geq 0.$

Your dual must contain one unrestricted variable.

Q3. (a) Determine the initial basic feasible solution of the transportation problem given in the following cost matrix

Demand

		I	II	III	IV	Availability
	A	8	2	7	6	50
Supply	B	7	5	2	3	60
	C	2	5	4	5	25
Requirement		60	40	20	15	135

Check its optimality and hence find the optimal solution.

(b) Solve the following game graphically:

Player B

		B_1	B_2
	I	2	7
Player A	II	3	5
	III	11	2

Q4. (a) Solve the following LPP by graphical method:

Max.:

$z = 5x_1 + 7x_2$

subject to:

$x_1 + x_2 \leq 4$

$3x_1 + 8x_2 \leq 24$

$10x_1 + 7x_2 \leq 35$

$x_1, x_2 \geq 0.$

Identify the optimal extreme point on the graph.

(b) Player A and Player B by a game in which each has three coins, a 5 P, a 10 P and a 20 P. Each player selects a coin without the knowledge of the other's choice. If the sum of the coins selected by players is an odd amount, A wins B's coin, if the sum is even B wins A's coin. Find the optimal strategy for each player using the principle of dominance and the value of the game

Q5. (a) Find all the basic solutions for the following equations:

$2x_1 + 6x_2 + 2x_3 + x_4 = 3$

$6x_1 + 4x_2 + 4x_3 + 6x_4 = 2$

$x_1, x_2, x_3, x_4 \geq 0$

Identify the basic feasible solutions.

(b) **Represent the following data of a 3 x 4 transportation problem in tabular form:**

$a_1 = 20, a_2 = 25, a_3 = 35$

$b_1 = 15, b_2 = 15, b_3 = 27, b_4 = 23$

$c_{11} = 7, c_{12} = 9, c_{13} = 4, c_{14} = 3$

$c_{21} = 4, c_{22} = 4, c_{23}\ 8, c_{24} = 8$

$c_{31} = 3, c_{32} = 5, c_{33} = 9, c_{34} = 6$

All symbols have their usual meanings. Also write the transportation, problem as LPP.

Q6. (a) **A hyperplane is given by the equation:**

$3x_1 + 2x_2 + 4x_3 + 7x_4 = 8.$

Find in which half spaces do the points (–6, 1, 7, 2) and (1, 2, –4, 1) lie.

(b) **Use simplex method to solve the following LPP:**

Max.:

$z = 2x_1 + 5x_2 + 7x_3$

Subject to:

$3x_1 + 2x_2 + 4x_3 \leq 100$

$x_1 + 4x_2 + 2x_3 \leq 100$

$x_1 + x_2 + 3x_3 \leq 100$

$x_1, x_2, x_3 \geq 0.$

Q7. (a) **Find the range of values of p and q which will make the entry (2, 2) a saddle point for the following game:**

		Player B		
		B_1	B_2	B_3
	A_1	2	4	5
Player A	A_2	10	7	q
	A_3	4	p	6

(b) **Solve the following LPP using the two-phase simplex method:**

Min.:

$$z = 3x_1 + 2x_2$$

Subject to:

$$2x_1 + x_2 \geq 2$$

$$3x_1 + 4x_2 \geq 12$$

$$x_1, x_2 \geq 0.$$

¤¤

Linear Programming : MTE-12

December, 2020

Note: *(i) Question no. 1 is compulsory. (ii) Answer any four questions from questions no. 2 to 7. (iii) Use of calculators is not allowed.*

Q1. Which of the following statements are *True* and which are *False*? Give a short proof or a counter-example in support of your answer:

(i) A two-dimensional solution space with two equality constraints can include infinity of feasible points only if the two lines coincide.

(ii) A balanced transportation problem may not have any feasible solution.

(iii) An unrestricted primal variable will have the effect of yielding an equality dual constraint.

(iv) The addition of a constant to all the elements of a payoff matrix in a two-person zero sum game can affect only the value of the game not the optimal mix of strategies.

(v) In a dual LPP, the number of variables in primal are more than the number of constraints in dual.

Q2. (a) A company has three operational departments (weaving, processing and packing) with capacity to produce three different types of clothes namely suitings, shirtings and woollens yielding the profit of ₹2, ₹4 and ₹3 per metre respectively. One metre suiting requires 3 minutes in weaving, 2 minutes in processing and 1 minute in packing. Similarly, one metre of shirting requires 4 minutes in weaving, 1 minute in processing and 3 minutes in packing while one meter woollen requires 3 minutes in each department. In a week, total runtime of each department is 60, 40 and 80 hours of weaving, processing and packing departments respectively are available. Formulate the LPP to find the product mix to maximize the profit.

(b) Obtain an initial basic feasible solution to the following transportation problem using (i) North-West Corner method, and (ii) Matrix-Minima method:

	Stores				
Warehouse	I	II	III	IV	Availability
A	7	3	5	5	34
B	5	5	7	6	15
C	8	6	6	5	12
D	6	1	6	4	19
Demand	21	25	17	17	80

Q3. (a) Express the point $P\left(\frac{1}{2}, \frac{1}{4}\right)$ as a convex linear combination of the points A (0, 0), B (0, 1) and C (1, 0).

(b) Consider a problem of assigning four clerks to four tasks. The time (hours) required to complete the tasks is given below:

Clerks \ Tasks	T_1	T_2	T_3	T_4
I	4	7	5	6
II	10	8	7	4
III	3	9	5	3
IV	6	6	4	2

Solve the assignment problem. Write alternative assignments also, if any.

Q4. (a) Using the principle of dominance, obtain the optimum strategies for both the players for the adjoining pay-off matrix:

Player A \ Player B	B_1	B_2	B_3
A_1	12	10	8
A_2	14	14	10
A_3	16	12	15

(b) Use graphical method to find the feasible solution of the following LP problem, if any:

Max.: $Z = 6x_1 - 4x_2$

s.t.:

$$2x_1 + 4x_2 \leq 4$$
$$4x_1 + 8x_2 \geq 16$$
$$x_1, x_2 \geq 0$$

Does it have optimal solution? Justify your answer.

Q5. (a) Formulate a suitable LPP of the game with respect to minimizing the maximizing players:

Player B

Player A	B_1	B_2	B_3
A_1	9	5	6
A_2	7	8	10
A_3	10	4	8

(b) Find all basic solutions of the following system:

$4x_1 + 2x_2 + x_3 = 4$

$2x_1 + x_2 + 5x_3 = 5$

Check which of them are basic feasible solutions.

Q6. (a) Write the LPP form of the following transportation problem:

	D_1	D_2	D_3	D_4	Capacity
R_1	5	7	13	10	700
R_2	8	6	14	13	400
R_3	12	10	9	11	800
Requirement	300	600	700	300	

(b) Solve the following game graphically:

Player B

Player A	B_1	B_2
A_1	1	−3
A_2	3	5
A_3	−1	6
A_4	4	1

Q7. (a) Solve by simplex method the following LPP:

Max.: $Z = 2x_1 + 4x_2 + x_3$

Subject to:

$x_1 + 2x_2 \le 4$

$2x_1 + x_2 \le 3$

$x_2 + 4x_3 \le 3$

$x_1, x_2, x_3 \ge 0$

(b) Write the dual of the following LPP:

Minimize: $Z = 3x_1 + 9x_2 + 8x_3$

Subject to:

$$x_1 + 4x_2 + 2x_3 = 5$$

$$3x_1 + x_2 + 2x_3 \geq 4$$

$$x_1, x_2, x_3 \geq 0$$

⌑ ⌑

Linear Programming : MTE-12

June, 2021

Note: *Question no. 1 is compulsory. Answer any four questions from questions no. 2 to 7. Use of calculators is not allowed.*

Q1. Which of the following statements are *True* and which are *False*? Give a short proof or a counter-example in support of your answer.

(a) Every feasible point in a bounded LP solution space can be determined from its feasible extreme points.

(b) The intersection of a finite number of convex sets need not be convex.

(c) The number of basic variables in a feasible solution of a balanced transportation problem with 'm' sources and 'n' destinations is mn.

(d) The optimal solution of a two-person zero-sum game always corresponds to a saddle point regardless of whether the players use pure or mixed strategies.

(e) In a dual LPP, the number of variables in primal are more than the number of constraints in dual.

Q2. (a) Solve the following LPP by graphical method:

Max $Z = x_1 + x_2 + 3$

Subject to

$$x_1 + 3x_2 \leq 9$$

$$2x_1 + x_2 \leq 8$$

$$3x_1 + 4x_2 \geq 12$$

$$x_1, x_2 \geq 0$$

(b) Write the dual of the following LPP:

Min $Z = x_1 + x_2 + 3x_3$

Subject to

$$3x_1 + 2x_2 + x_3 \leq 3$$

$$2x_1 + x_2 + 2x_3 = 2$$

$$x_1, x_2, x_3 \geq 0$$

Q3. (a) Consider the following transportation problem:

1	2	1	4	30
3	3	2	1	50
4	2	5	9	20
20	40	10	20	

(i) Is this transportation problem balanced? Give reasons for your answer.

(ii) Obtain a basic feasible solution to the above transportation problem by North-West Corner method.

(b) For the following matrix game, write down the equivalent LPPs, and solve the game.

$$A \overset{B}{\begin{bmatrix} -1 & 2 \\ 1 & 0 \end{bmatrix}}$$

Q4. (a) A company manufactures two models of rollers X and Y. When preparing the 2019 budget it was found that the limitations on capacity were represented by the following weekly production maxima:

Model	Foundry	Machine shop	Contribution per model
Model X	160	200	₹ 120
Model Y	240	150	₹ 90

In addition, the material required for Model X was in short supply and only sufficient for 140 units per week could be guaranteed for the year. Formulate the LPP.

(b) A company has 5 jobs to be processed by 5 mechanics. The following table gives the return in rupees when the ith job is assigned to the jth mechanic, (i, j = 1, 2, ... 5). How should the jobs be assigned to the mechanics so as to maximise the overall return?

		Jobs				
		1	2	3	4	5
Mechanics	1	22	28	30	18	30
	2	30	34	18	11	26
	3	31	17	23	20	27
	4	12	28	31	26	26
	5	19	23	30	25	29

Q5. (a) Is the set of vectors {(1, 2, 3), (3, 4, 1), (2, 3, 2)} linearly independent? Give reasons for your answer.

(b) Solve the following game:

$$A = \begin{bmatrix} 8 & 5 & 8 \\ 8 & 6 & 5 \\ 7 & 4 & 5 \\ 6 & 5 & 6 \end{bmatrix}$$

Q6. (a) A company has three plants and four warehouses. The supply and demand in units and the corresponding transportation costs are given below:

	Warehouse				
Plant	I	II	III	IV	Availability
A	7	(10) 10	(20) 14	8	30
B	7	11	(5) 12	(35) 16	40
C	(20) 5	(10) 8	15	9	30
Demand	20	20	25	35	80

(i) Is this solution degenerate? Give reason for your answer.

(ii) Check whether the given basic feasible solution is optimal. If not, modify the given solution and find an optimal solution.

(b) For the following Pay-off matrix, find the value of the game and the strategies of players A and B by using graphical method:

		Player B		
		B_1	B_2	B_3
Player A	A_1	6	2	7
	A_2	9	10	1

Q7. (a) Solve the following LPP using two-phase method:

Max. $Z = 3x_1 + 2x_2$

Subject to

$2x_1 + x_2 \leq 2$

$3x_1 + 4x_2 \geq 12$

$x_1, x_2 \leq 0$

(b) Sketch the region $\{(x, y) | x^2 + y^2 \geq 1, y2 \leq x\}$. Is the region convex? Justify your answer.

¤¤

Linear Programming : MTE-12

December, 2021

Note: *(i) Question no. 1 is compulsory. (ii) Answer any four questions from questions no. 2 to 7. (iii) Use of calculators is not allowed.*

Q1. Which of the following statements are True and which are False? Give a short proof or a counter-example in support of your answer :

(i) In a solution of a two-dimensional LPP, the objective function can assume same values at two distinct extreme points.

(ii) The right hand side constant of the constraint in a primal problem appears in the corresponding dual as a coefficient in the objective function.

(iii) An optimal solution in LPP does not necessarily involve all the constraints.

(iv) Every game matrix has a unique saddle point.

(v) A transportation problem with m rows and n columns is an LPP with m variables and n constraints.

Q2. (a) Formulate the dual of the following LPP :

Max. :

$Z = -3x_1 - 2x_2$

Subject to :

$x_1 + x_2 \geq 1$

$x_1 + x_2 \leq 7$

$x_1 + 2x_2 \leq 10$

$x_2 \leq 3$

and $x_1, x_2 \geq 0$.

(b) Let $S = \{(x, y) : x - y \leq 4, x + y \geq -3, y \leq 38\}$. Find all extreme points of S and represent $(x, y) = (2, 1)$ as convex combination of the extreme points.

Q3. (a) Solve the following game graphically :

Player B

$$\text{Player A} \begin{bmatrix} 2 & -3 \\ 3 & 5 \\ -2 & 6 \\ 4 & 1 \end{bmatrix}$$

(b) Solve the following LPP graphically :

Maximize :

$Z = 5x_1 + 8x_2$

Subject to :

$x_1 \leq 4$

$x_2 \geq 2$

$x_1 + x2 = 5$

$x_1 \geq 0, x_2 \geq 0.$

Q4. (a) Out of five contractors, four jobs are to be assigned to four contractors to minimize the cost. Which contractor of the five contractors will be unsuccessful in getting the job? The cost of each job with each contractor is given below :

Contractor \ Job	J_1	J_2	J_3	J_4
C_1	10	12	18	19
C_2	9	18	21	18
C_3	7	17	20	19
C_4	9	14	19	15
C_5	10	15	21	16

(b) Formulate a suitable LPP of the game with respect to minimization and maximization players :

Player B

$$\text{Player A} \begin{bmatrix} 3 & 1 & 1 \\ 2 & 0 & 4 \end{bmatrix}$$

Q5. (a) Find the initial basic feasible solution of the following transportation problem using matrix-minima method :

		Destination			
		D_1	D_2	D_3	Supply
	R_1	16	20	12	700
Resources	R_2	14	8	18	400
	R_3	26	24	16	800
Requirements		600	600	700	

And, hence find the optimal solution.

(b) Find all values of k for which the vectors $\begin{bmatrix} 0 \\ 1 \\ 1 \end{bmatrix}, \begin{bmatrix} -1 \\ 1 \\ 0 \end{bmatrix}$ and $\begin{bmatrix} -k \\ k \\ 2 \end{bmatrix}$ are linearly independent.

Q6. (a) Write the LPP formulation of the following assignment problem :

		Jobs		
		I	II	III
	A_1	10	2	3
Persons	A_2	6	4	5
	A_3	1	7	10

(b) Use the principle of dominance, to solve the following game :

Player B

$$\text{Player A} \begin{bmatrix} 8 & 10 & 9 & 14 \\ 10 & 11 & 8 & 12 \\ 13 & 12 & 14 & 13 \end{bmatrix}$$

Q7. (a) An airline agrees to arrange chartered planes for a group. The group needs at least 160 first class seats and at least 300 tourist class seats. The airline must use at least two of its model I planes which have 20 first class and 30 tourist class seats. The airline will also use some of its model II planes which have 20 first class and 60 tourist class seats. Each flight of model I costs ₹ 1 lakh and model II costs ₹ 1.5 lakh. Formulate the problem as LP model.

(b) Obtain all the basic solutions to the following system of linear equations :

$$2x_1 + x_2 + x_3 = 6$$

$$x_1 + 2x_2 + x_3 = 3.$$

¤¤

Linear Programming : MTE-12

June, 2022

Note: *Question no. 1 is compulsory. Answer any four questions from questions no. 2 to 7. Use of calculators is not allowed.*

Q1. State which of the following statements are True and which are False. Give a short proof or a counter-example in support of your answer.

(a) If the payoff matrix of a game is changed, saddle point of the game, if it exists, changes.

(b) In a transportation problem with 4 sources and 3 destinations, the number of basic variables in any basic feasible solution is 7.

(c) A subset of a linearly dependent set of vectors need not be linearly dependent.

(d) In a solution of a two-dimensional LPP, the objective function can assume same values at two distinct extreme points.

(e) In a solution of LPP, if $Z_j - C_j = 0$ for the basic variables, there exists an alternative solution.

Q2. (a) A company is making two products A and B. The cost of producing one unit of product A and B is ₹60 and ₹80, respectively. As per the agreement, the company has to supply at least 200 units of product B to its regular customers. One unit of product A requires one machine hour whereas product B has machine hours available abundantly within the company. Total machine hours available for product A are 400 hours. One unit of each product A and B requires one labour hour and total of 500 hours are available. Formulate the problem as an LP model so as to minimize the total cost.

(b) Use the principle of dominance to solve the following game :

$$\text{Player A}\ \begin{matrix} A_1 \\ A_2 \\ A_3 \end{matrix} \overset{\displaystyle\text{Player B}}{\overset{\begin{matrix} B_1 & B_2 & B_3 & B_4 \end{matrix}}{\begin{bmatrix} -5 & 3 & 1 & 20 \\ 5 & 5 & 4 & 6 \\ -4 & -2 & 0 & -5 \end{bmatrix}}}$$

Q3. (a) Formulate a suitable LPP of the following game with respect to minimization and maximization players :

Player B

$$\text{Player A}\begin{bmatrix} 1 & 2 & 1 \\ 2 & 1 & 0 \\ 3 & 4 & 4 \end{bmatrix}$$

(b) Is the set of vectors

{(1, 2, 3), (3, 4, 1), (2, 3, 2)} linearly independent ? Give reason.

Q4. (a) The following table provides the sales data of four salesmen in five sales territories :

Sales Territories

Salesmen		I	II	III	IV	V
	A	16	15	17	10	8
	B	16	16	20	15	12
	C	12	8	10	13	15
	D	18	16	17	12	10

Determine the optimal assignment of salesmen to territories, to maximize the total sale.

(b) Solve the following game graphically :

Player B

$$\text{Player A}\begin{bmatrix} 2 & 3 & -1 & 4 \\ -1 & 4 & 5 & 1 \end{bmatrix}$$

Q5. (a) Using North-West corner method, find the initial basic feasible solution of the following transportation problem :

Destination

		D_1	D_2	D_3	D_4	Capacity
Source	S_1	19	30	50	10	7
	S_2	70	30	40	60	9
	S_3	40	8	70	20	18
Demand		5	8	7	14	34

And, hence find the optimal solution.

(b) Formulate the dual of the following LPP :

$\text{Min } z = 3x_1 + 2x_2$

subject to

$x_1 - x_2 \leq 1$

$x_1 + x_2 \leq 7$

$x_1 + 2x_2 \geq 10$

$x_1, x_2 \geq 0$

Q6. (a) Solve the following LPP graphically :

$\text{Max } z = 60x_1 + 40x_2$

subject to

$x_1 + x_2 \leq 3000$

$x_2 \leq 1200$

$x_1 \geq 600$

$x_1 \geq x_2$

$x_1, x_2 \geq 0$

(b) Check whether the following sets are convex or not :

(i) $S_1 = \{(x, y) \mid y - 3 \leq -x^2, x \geq 0, y \geq 0\}$

(ii) $S_2 = \{(x, y) \mid y - 3 \geq -x^2, x \geq 0, y \geq 0\}$

Q7. (a) Use the two-phase simplex method to solve the following LPP :

$\text{Max } z = -3x_1 - 2x_2$

subject to

$x_1 + x_2 \geq 1$

$x_1 + 2x_2 \leq 7$

$x_1 + 2x_2 \geq 10$

$x_2 \leq 3$

$x_1, x_2 \geq 0$

(b) Obtain all the basic solutions to the following system of linear equations :

$y_1 + 2y_2 + y_3 = 6$

$y_1 + y_2 + 2y_3 = 3$

⌑⌑

Linear Programming : MTE-12

December, 2022

Note: *Question no. 1 is compulsory. Answer any four questions from questions no. 2 to 7. Use of calculators is not allowed.*

Q1. **State which of the following statements are *True* and which are *False*. Give a short proof or a counter-example in support of your answer.**

(a) **In a two-dimensional LPP solution, the objective function can assume the same value at two distinct extreme points.**

(b) **Both the primal and dual of an LPP can be infeasible.**

(c) **An unrestricted primal variable converts into an equality dual constraint.**

(d) **In a two-person zero-sum game, if the optimal solution requires one player to use a pure strategy, the other player must do the same.**

(e) **If 10 is added to each entry of a row in the cost matrix of an assignment problem, then the total cost of an optimal assignment for the changed cost matrix will also increase by 10.**

Q2. **(a) Solve the following linear programming problem using simplex method:**

$$\text{Maximize } z = 3x_1 + 5x_2 + 4x_3$$

$$\text{subject to } 2x_1 + 3x_2 \le 8$$

$$2x_1 + 5x_2 \le 10$$

$$3x_1 + 2x_2 + 4x_3 \le 15$$

$$x_1, x_2, x_3 \ge 0$$

(b) **Using the principle of dominance, reduce the size of the following game:**

$$\begin{bmatrix} -1 & -2 & 8 \\ 7 & 5 & -1 \\ 6 & 0 & 12 \end{bmatrix}$$

Hence, solve the game.

Q3. **(a) Find all the basic feasible solutions for the following set of equations:**

$2x_1 + 6x_2 + 2x_3 + x_4 = 3$

$6x_1 + 4x_2 + 4x_3 + 6x_4 = 2$

$x_1, x_2, x_3, x_4 \geq 0$

(b) Examine convexity of the following sets:

(i) $S_1 = \{(x_1, x_2) \in R^2 \mid 4x_1 + 3x_2 \leq 6, x_1 + x_2 \geq 1\}$.

(ii) $S_2 = \{(x, y) \in R^2 \mid x_2 + y^2 \geq 1\}$.

Q4. (a) Solve the following linear programming problem by graphical method:

Maximize $z = 5x_1 + 7x_2$

subject to $x_1 + x_2 \leq 4$

$3x_1 + 8x_2 \leq 24$

$10x_1 + 7x_2 \leq 35$

$x_1, x_2 \geq 0$

(b) Find the dual of the following LPP:

Minimize $z = x_1 + x_2 + x_3$

subject to $x_1 - 3x_2 + 4x_3 = 5$

$x_1 - 2x_2 \leq 3$

$2x_2 - x_3 \geq 4$

$x_1, x_2 \geq 0$ and x_3 is unrestricted in sign.

Q5. (a) Find the initial basic feasible solution of the following transportation problem using matrix-minima method:

	Destinations			Supply
	I	II	III	
Sources A	2	7	4	5
B	3	3	1	8
C	5	4	7	7
D	1	6	2	14
Demand	7	9	18	34

Also, find the optimal solution.

(b) Solve the following game graphically:

		Player B	
		B_1	B_2
Player A	A_1	2	7
	A_2	3	5
	A_3	11	2

Q6. (a) A firm manufactures two types of products A and B, and sells them at a profit of ₹2 on type A and ₹3 on type B. Each product is processed on two machines M_1 and M_2. Type A requires one minute of processing time on M_1 and two minutes on M_2; type B requires one minute on M_1 and one minute on M_2. The machine M_1 is available for not more than 6 hours 40 minutes, while machine M_2 is available for 10 hours during any working day. Formulate the problem as LPP.

(b) Solve the following assignment problem:

	A	B	C	D	E
I	2	9	2	7	1
II	6	8	7	6	1
III	4	6	5	3	1
IV	4	2	7	3	1
V	5	3	9	5	1

Q7. (a) The following table is obtained in the intermediate stage while solving an LPP by simplex method:

	C_j's	30	23	29	0	0	
B	C_B	x_1	x_2	x_3	S_1	S_2	RHS
S_1	0	0	2	$-\frac{9}{2}$	1	$-\frac{3}{2}$	$\frac{31}{2}$
x_1	30	1	$\frac{1}{2}$	$\frac{5}{4}$	0	$\frac{1}{4}$	$\frac{7}{4}$

Check whether an optimal solution of the LPP will exist or not.

(b) Write the LPP model of the following transportation problem:

5	7	6	4	70
2	8	3	1	50
1	7	4	5	90
50	40	50	70	

(c) Find the range of values of p and q which will render the entry (2, 2), a saddle point for the following game:

	Player B		
	2	4	5
Player A	10	7	q
	4	p	6

¤ ¤

NOTES

www.ingramcontent.com/pod-product-compliance
Ingram Content Group UK Ltd.
Pitfield, Milton Keynes, MK11 3LW, UK
UKHW021708190726
13853UKWH00001B/462